CROSSWAYS OF SEX

A STUDY IN EROTO-PATHOLOGY

BY

DR. JACOBUS X....

Author of "Untrodden Fields of Anthropology," "Genital Laws," etc., etc.

Fredonia Books
Amsterdam, The Netherlands

Crossways of Sex:
A Study in Eroto-Pathology

by
Dr. Jacobus X....

ISBN: 1-58963-737-2

Fredonia Books
Amsterdam, the Netherlands
http://www.fredoniabooks.com

In order to make original editions of historical works available to scholars at an economical price, this facsimile of the original edition is reproduced from the best available copy and has been digitally enhanced to improve legibility, but the text remains unaltered to retain historical authenticity.

CROSSWAYS OF SEX

PREFACE.

If ever a preface was useless it is in the present case. The author's past works speak more eloquently than any introductory panegyric could ever do. The writer of "Untrodden Fields of Anthropology;" "The Ethnology of the Sixth Sense·" "The Genital Laws;" "Medico-Legal Examination of the Abuses, Aberrations and Dementia of the Genital Sense" and "The Basis of Passional Psychology;" needs no introduction than the titles of these masterly books which form an encyclopædia of sexuality.

The main subject treated in "The Crossways of Sex," is one that has never been exhaustively and scientifically discussed before in English, and it will be seen that these plain words on pederasty will, to use a hackneyed phrase, supply a want long felt.

That humanity does frequently stray from the high road of normal procreation to wander blindly with halting step in the obscure, half-hidden tracks of weird carnality no one will gainsay. Therefore, it is logical that a great mind, such as that of the gifted author, should seize upon the subject, dissect it, and lay it bare *ad majoram scientiæ gloriam.*

In this pitiless and painstaking collection of authentic erotic errors and weaknesses will be found the most interesting, valuable and useful data, touching boldly, not only upon the outskirts of the forest and tangled undergrowth of sexual deviations, but also penetrating to the very depths of the abyss of mental maladies and wilful perversities of sex.

CONTENTS

PREFACE . . . . Page v

Genital Perversions.

CHAPTER I.

SEXUAL INVERSION.—GENERAL IDEAS.

Definition of Inversion of the Genital or Sexual Sense.—Antiquity and Universality of Sexual Inversion.—Inversion of the Genital Sense before Medical Science.—Serious Errors committed by Tardieu and his School.—Predecessors ef the Present School in the Disease of Inversion.—Ulrichs and the Uranists.—Present School of the Psychopathic Study of Inversion.—What is the Origin of Sexual Inversion?—Different Opinions of Doctors and Philosophers.—Classifications of Inversion.—Chevalier's Classification.—Laupts' Classification.—Importance of Laupts' Occasionally Inverted in the General Etiology of Inversion.—Different Types of Inverted Individuals according to Laupts.—Krafft Ebing's Classification.—Criticism upon Krafft Ebing's Classification.—Impossibility of giving a Classification of Inversion which will not meet with Criticism.—The General Law of Inversion. A. True Inversion, Morbid *through Sexual Perversion.* B. Artificial Inversion, the Vice of Inversion through Perversity.—Pederasts, Saphists and Uranists. What is the place of Sexual Inversion in the list of Anomalies of the Sexual Instinct?—Coexistence of Inversion with other Anomalies of the Sexual Instinct. Page . . . 1

General Perversion (*continued*).

CHAPTER II.

A. True Morbid Inversion through Sexual Perversion and its Divisions.

Division of Morbid Inversion through Sexual Perversion into two very distinct Categories.—Morbid Mental Inversion (or Artificial Inversion).—Its Classification into Groups by Chevalier.—General Physiognomy of Morbid Mental Inversion.—Observations of Cases of Morbid Mental Inversion.—Peculiar and Distinctive Characteristics of Morbid Mental Inversion.—The True Inversion of Degenerates or Uranism.—Uranism and its Different Degrees.—Division of True Inversion by Krafft Ebing into Acquired Homosexuality and Congenital Homosexuality.—Acquired Homosexuality.—First Degree. Simple Inversion of the Sexual Sense.—Observations.—*Lapin* at School.—*Loup de Mer* on Board Ship.—Second Degree. Eviratio et Defeminatio.—Unique Observation by Krafft Ebing.—The Disease of the Scythians.—The Mujerados of New Mexico.—Errors committed by Krafft Ebing.—Third degree. Transition to Paranoical Sexual Metamorphosis.—The Doctor changed into a Woman.—Fourth Degree. Paranoical Sexual Metamorphosis.—Krafft Ebing's and Esquinol's Observations.—Mixed Cases outside any Classification.—Dr. E. Laurent's Observation.—Latent Inversion.—The Sailor who practised Bestiality, was a latent Inverted and a Sadist 32

Genital Perversions (*continued*).

CHAPTER III.

Congenital Homosexuality and its Classification.

The Homosexual Sense as a Morbid and Congenital Phenomenon.—General and Distinctive Characteristics of Congenital Sexual Inversion.—Krafft Ebing's Classification generally accepted.—First Degree. Psychical Hermaphrodism.—Observations relating to Cases of Psychical Hermaphrodism.—Second degree. Homosexuals or Uranists.—Observations relating to Cases of Uranism.—Mixed Case. Uranist, Bestialist and Necrophilist.—Third Degree. Effemination and Viraginity.—Observation of Cases of Effemination and Viraginity.—The Effeminated Magistrate or the Dangers of an Amorous Correspondence.—Fourth Degree. Androgynia and Gynandria.—Dr. Legrain's Theories on the Inverted of this Group and Hermaphrodism.—Cases of Androgynia.—Count Sandor or a Gynander married to another Woman.—History of a Born-Inverted by Legrain.—Inferences and Lessons which he draws from it. . . 68

General Perversions (*continued*).

CHAPTER IV.

THE NATURE CAUSE AND TREATMENT OF SEXUAL INVERSION.

Returning Back! What is the reason of this Special Chapter?—Nature of Sexual Inversion.—Inversion is one in its Essence, and more than one in its Manifestations.—A man does not become Inverted, he is born Inverted: a man becomes a Pederast, he is not born a Pederast. The Causes of Sexual Inversion.—Different Opinions of Physicians who have treated of Inversions.—Krafft Ebing's Opinion, Moll's Opinion.—Heredity of Inverteds.—Occasional Causes favouring the Breaking-out of the Sexual Perversion.—Krafft Ebing's Theory on Atavism as a Cause of Sexual Inversion.—Masturbation, the Effect and not the Cause of Inversion.—Moll's Opinion on Heredity as a Cause of Sexual Inversion.—Inverted Daughters of a Pederast Father.—Theoretical Explanation of Sexual Inversion by Moll.—The Causes of Sexual Inversion according to Laupts.—Influence of Heredity upon Inversion according to Raffalovitch.—Theories of Dr. Legrain upon Inversion.—Explanation of the Phenomena of Sexual Inversion.—Duration of Inversion.—Treatment of this Aberration by Hypnotic Suggestion 132

Genital Perversions (*continued*).

CHAPTER V.

THE LIFE AND HABITS OF INVERTED INDIVIDUALS.

Necessity for this Special Chapter.—Physical Conformation of the Individual.—Development, Malformations and Working of the Genital Organs.—External Habitus, Tastes, Habits and Characteristics of Inverted Individuals.—General State of Mind of Inverteds and Uranists.—Social Relations of Uranists.—Marriage of Uranists.—Relation of Uranists among themselves.—The Uranists of Berlin.—Psychical Love of Uranists.—The Uranist is more jealous than the Woman!—Physical Love of Uranists.—The Death of an Inverted Individual.—The *Fellatores'* Evening Party.—The different Professions and the Number of Uranists. . . 177

CHAPTER VI.

BISEXUATEDS.—GYNÆCOMASTS.

General Considerations upon Bisexuateds.—Gynæcomasts and Hermaphrodites.—Gynæcomasts.—Heredity of Gynæcomastia.—Gynæcomasts are Degenerates.—Observations in Support of this Statement.—Accidental Gynæcomastia.—Structure of the Mammæ of Gynæcomasts.—The Gynæcomast J. . . .—Physical Condion of Gynæcomasts.—Genital Aptitude of Gynæcomasts.—Propensity of Gynæcomasts to Inversion.—Gynæcomasts are Weak-minded 202

Bisexuateds.

CHAPTER VII.

HERMAPHRODITES.

Hermaphrodites.—Hermaphrodism of the Human Fœtus.—Classification of Hermaphrodites.—A. True Hermaphrodism.—1. True Bilateral Hermaphrodism.—2. True Unilateral Hermaphrodism.—3. True Lateral or External Hermaphrodism.—Different Cases.—B. False or Pseudo-Hermaphrodism.—Internal Pseudo-Hermaphrodism, 1st, Masculine, 2nd, Feminine.—The Valet de Chambre Guiseppe Marzo.—External Pseudo-Hermaphrodism.—Alexina B . . . , the Boy-Governess.—Catherine Hohmann, Wife and Husband.—Rosine Gotlieb, Lover and Mistress.—Julie D . . . , the Inverted Hermaphrodite.—Ernestine G . . . , Man and Woman.—The Woman changed into a Man by Professor Perro's Bistoury.—Louise R . . . , the Woman Mechanician.—A Man-Prostitute.—Marie Marius, an Old Man's Sweetheart and a Male Nurse in a Religious House.—Madeleine Lefort, the Bearded Woman.—The Woman who refused to have her Clitoris cut.—The Priest in the Family Way.—The Tribade before the Parlement de Paris.—The Girl who was changed into a Boy by jumping over a Ditch.—Sexual Instincts of Hermaphrodites.—Sexual Satisfactions of Hermaphrodites.—Passive Pederast Hermaphrodite.—The Hermaphrodite Vicomtesse.—An Hermaphrodite Emperor.—The Debaucheries of Heliogabalus.—The Hymn to Venus and the Bloody Sacrifices.—The last Days and the Death of Heliogabalus.—Proofs that Heliogabalus was a Sadistic Hermaphrodite.—His Reign and his Life.—Artificial Hermaphrodism.—Infantilism and Effemination.—External Hermaphrodism of Young Pederasts.—A Little Jesus.—Henri de Blondin 216

Asexuateds.

CHAPTER VIII.

EUNUCHS AND SKOPTZYS.

Definition of Asexuateds.—Two Classes: A. Involuntary Asexuateds. B. Voluntary Asexuateds.—A. Involuntary Asexuateds or Eunuchs.—Causes of Eunuchism.—Castrati or Spadones.—Thlibias.—Lewd Employment of Spadones by the Roman Women.—Castration as a Punishment for Adulterers.—Employment of Castrated Women as Eunuchs.—Eunuchism predisposes to Inversion.—Genital Aptitude of Eunuchs.—Employment of Eunuchs for purposes of Masculine Prostitution.—The Castrati of the Sixtine Chapel.—Lasciviousness of Eunuchs.—An English Lady's Action against a Castratus. Eunuchs in the East and how they are employed.—Paul de Regla's opinion on Eunuchs from a Physical and Physiological Point of View.—B. Voluntary Asexuateds.—The Skoptzys.—Why do the Skoptzys castrate themselves?—Processes of the Operation of Castration.—Amputation and Bistournage.—Transfixion of the Different Cords.—Ligature of the Penis.—Places and Circumstances of Castration.—Material Proofs of the Operation.—Consequences of Castration.—Salacity of Skoptzys of the Little Seal.—Modification of the Organism in the Skoptzy.—Women Skoptzys.—How the Date of Castration may be known.—Two Men who Castrated themselves, one through Jealousy, the other through Love.—The Eunuch Priests of Cybele and their Infamous Habits. 263

Saphism.

CHAPTER IX.

Lesbians, Tribades, Fricarelles and Saphists.

Examination of Saphism in General.—Classification of the Inversion-Perversity given by Chevalier.—General Causes of Saphism.—Saphism through Lust.—Professional Saphism.—Saphism from Necessity and through Fear.—Origin of the Name of Saphism.—Women Tribades, Fricarelles, and Saphists properly so-called.—Injurious Influence of Modern Literaturo.—"Les Femmes Damnées," by Baudelaire.—Special Causes of Saphism.—Bashful or Occasional Saphists and Averred or Habitual Saphists of High-Life.—Brothels and Houses of Call for Lesbos.—Employment of the Lap-dog as a means of Saphism.—Saphism among Prostitutes.—The Brothels are Haunts of Tribadism.—Secret Alliances of Saphists.—Intermittent Tribades.—Saphism among Children.—Influence exerted by Men upon the Development of Saphism.—History of Two Alliances of Saphists.—Woman carried off by a Saphist.—The Pantomime of Saphism.—Tribadism in Nuns' Convents.—Special Hospitals, Prisons and Scholastic Establishments are Centres of Saphism.—Psychical Love of Saphists.—Undeniable Progress of Saphism.—Saphist Practices and accompanying Vulvary Deformations.—Local Lesions due to Clitoridian Manuelisation.—Clitoridian Deformations due to Lingual Friction and Suction.—Dangers of Saphism to the General Health.—Differentiation of the Signs of Saphism from Psysiological Clitoridian Symptoms.—Tribades and Fricarelles of the Court of France by Brantôme.—Do Lesbians make their Husbands Cuckolds?—The Noble Lady Fricarelle *Religieuse* 295

CHAPTER X.

Masculine Prostitution and Blackmail.

Various Definitions of Pederasty.—Sodomy and Anal Coition, by Raffalovich.—Acquired and Non-Morbid Pederasty.—Active and Passive Pederasts.—Moll's Opinion of Pederasts.—Pederasts and Inverteds, by Dimitri Stefanowski.—Various Causes of Pederasty.—I. Pederasty from Lust or from Taste.—The origin of Pederasty from Lust, by Krafft Ebing and Moll.—Pederasty from Taste belongs to all Classes of Society.—The Pederast Lord.—II. Professional Pederasty.—Profesional Pederasts, by Coffignon.—*Rivettes*, Little Jesuses, *Filles Galantes*, and *Pierreuses*.—The Aunts.—A *Bal Masqué* at the *Opera*.—The Portrait of the Duchess.—The Marriage of Pederasts.—Pederasts, by Canler.—Pederasty at the Brothel.—Masculine Prostitution in the Streets.—The Street-Walking of the little Jesus.—Pederast Prostitution and Blackmail.—Pederast Prostitution and Murder.—The Blackmail of Pederasty 336

CROSSWAYS OF SEX.

Genital Perversions.

CHAPTER I.

SEXUAL INVERSION.—GENERAL IDEAS.

Definition of Inversion of the Genital or Sexual Sense.—Antiquity and Universality of Sexual Inversion.—Inversion of the Genital Sensė before Medical Science.—Serious Errors committed by Tardieu and his School.—Predecessors of the Present School in the Disease of Inversion.—Ulrichs and the Uranists.—Present School of the Psycopathic Study of Inversion.—What is the Origin of Sexual Inversion? Different Opinions of Doctors and Philosophers.—Classifications of Inversion.—Chevalier's Classification.—Laupts' Classification.—Importance of Laupts' Occasionally Inverted in the General Etiology of Inversion.—Different Types of Inverted Individuals, according to Laupts.—Krafft Ebing's Classification.—Criticisms upon Krafft Ebing's Classification.—Impossibility of giving a Classification of Inversion which will not meet with Criticism.—The General Law of Inversion. A. *True Inversion, Morbid* through Sexual Perversion. B. *Artificial Inversion, the Vice of Inversion through Perversity.—Pederasts, Saphists and Uranists.—What is the place of Sexual Inversion in the list of Anomalies of the Sexual Instinct?—Coexistence of Inversion with other Anomalies of the Sexual Instinct.*

Definition of Inversion of the Genital Sense.

Together with Thoinot, we say that Inversion of the Genital or Sexual Sense is *the seeking for the sexual satisfaction in intercourse with individuals of the same sex, man with man, and woman with woman.*

This very wide definition does not concern itself with the manner, which is very variable, in which the satisfaction of the genital desire is accomplished. For the sake of brevity, instead of speaking of *the inversion of the genital sense,* we shall simply use the word *inversion.*

Certain authors employ the term *uni-sexual* love in opposition to normal love denominated hetero-sexual love. The term *inverted* (for short) appears to us sufficient.

Antiquity and Universality of Sexual Inversion.

This love is as old as the world itself. At all times there have been men who loved other men. These are the *pederasts,* a term under which they were generally designated in former times and which is inexact, for, properly speaking, it applies only to the category of men who love boys.

There have also been women who loved other women. These are the *Lesbians* or *Tribades.*

The Inversion of the Genital Sense before Medical Science.

In 1858, in his First Edition of his *Attentats aux Mœurs,* a work which was authority on the subject for a quarter of a century, Tardieu wrote as follows: "'Why can I not, cried Fodéré, avoid sullying my pen with the infamous wickedness of pederasts!' Like him, I have hesitated for a long while to bring into this study the repulsive picture of pederasty; but I cannot help recognizing the fact that it forms its indispensable complement, and is at the same time its least-known part. I have decided therefore not only not to pass over this sad subject in silence, but even to accord to it developments which no other author has yet given to it, either in France or in foreign countries."

These same words are also to be found in the 7th Edition of 1878, and naturally in the Edition published after the Master's death.

Thirty years later, Lacassagne speaking of Inversion, writes: "Owing to an assumption of ill-placed modesty, these questions have been only approached from the scientific point of view with a certain amount of timidity. The authors, even those who consider themselves the most emancipated, fearing to be suspected of pornography or scientific impropriety, launch out with the ardour of a preacher into various epithets on a vice which they stigmatize as an *abomination*, a *monstrosity*, an *infamy*, etc., etc., as if the truly extraordinary character of these facts, in all societies and at all periods of history, ought not to attract the attention of the psychologist.

Serious Errors committed by Tardieu and his School.

Tardieu had observed nearly 300 subjects in 90 cases where his knowledge as an expert had been appealed to. But neglecting the psychological side of this question, the only one which is really interesting, the author saw only the material side, the *anatomical* signs of anal coition. And again he has committed singular errors. At most he has but half-opened the door to the psychopathic study of this curious malady.

"It remains for us to say a word about those whose depraved tastes and inexplicable passion bear the expenses of this hideous profession. But of what use would it be to lift the veil behind which I have found only scandal and disgust? I might ask myself, as a physiologist and a doctor, what unknown causes could assist us to understand the aberration of pederasts; but I wish to spare those who will read me the painful and sterile surprise which must be caused them by an acquaintance with the characters and the social position of the adepts in Pederasty. I shall confine myself to pointing out the deplorable facilities which a large number of foreigners, who figure in the list of the victims of black mail, come to Paris to seek for.

. . . .

I do not pretend to make clear that which is incomprehensible and to penetrate into the causes of Pederasty. It is however allowable to ask oneself if there is anything else in this vice but a moral perversion, but one of the forms of *psychopathia sexualis*, the history of which has been traced by Kaan. Unbridled debauchery and wearied sensuality alone can explain habits of pederasty in the case of married men, of fathers of families, and reconcile these unnatural impulses with the taste for women."

A little further on however, Tardieu very gently pleads for extenuating circumstances: "There are cases in which it is difficult not to admit an absolute unhealthy perversion of the moral faculties in pederasts. To see the profound degradation, the revolting nastiness of individuals who are sought for and admitted near men apparently distinguished by education and fortune, we should be most frequently led to believe that their senses and reason are changed; but we can hardly doubt it, when we come to collect such facts as those which I have from a magistrate. One of these men descended from a high position to the lowest degree of depravity, entices to himself the sordid children of the streets, before whom he kneels, whose feet he kisses with passionate submission before he asks from them the most infamous enjoyments. Another one found a singular pleasure in having violent kicks administered to him from behind by a creature of the vilest kind. What an idea to inflict upon himself such horrors, if they are not to be imputed to the saddest and the most shameful form of insanity!"

But after thus half-opening the door, Tardieu shuts it again immediately, and thinks that he has buried the question by this erroneous and redundant declaration of principle: "however incomprehensible, however contrary to nature the acts of pederasty may appear, they should not escape the responsibility of the conscience, the just severity of the laws, and above all the contempt of all honourable people."

We see that, for Tardieu, the *inverted* are ignoble pederasts. His error is the more gross as a German physician, Caspar, Professor of Legal Medecine at Berlin, was the first to recognize the fact in 1852, that is six years before Tardieu, that all the followers of inverted love are not debauchees, deserving the contempt of all honourable people and amenable to the law, but that besides the vicious inverted, there are, as another German (Westphal) would prove thirty years later, the congenital inverted, sufferers who deserve the pity and the cares of Medical Science. Caspar wrote as follows:

"For the majority of those who are addicted to it (inverted love), it is *from birth*, and constitutes, so to say, a *moral hermaphrodism*. These men have an aversion for sexual intercourse with women, and their imagination is charmed at the sight of handsome young men, or at the sight of statues or pictures with which they love to surround their room.

"For others, on the contrary, this vice makes an inroad at a certain age, when they have grown weary of all natural pleasures, etc."

The Predecessors of the Present School of the Malady of Inversion.

Caspar has been followed in the path which he pointed out, and we regret to state that it is the Germans who have been the precursors of the present theories in which it is recognized that Inversion is *in the great majority of cases a mental disease.*

Ulrichs and the Uranists.

In 1868—69, a German magistrate, learned, highly educated and of distinguished appearance, displaying no signs of intellectual disorder, published a certain number of pamphlets all having reference to inversion. It so happened, says Chevalier, that he had specially favourable conditions for observation, being a moral hermaphrodite, thus he had no need to go beyond himself, and his self analysis is the more valuable as his observations served to plead his own cause. He maintained that the sexual life of the mind is not bound to the sex of the body, and that a large number of men, one out of every two hundred adults, by the fact of their natural constitution, feel themselves women in the presence of individuals of their own sex, and are impelled to the love of men exclusively, and that their feelings towards women amount to indifference or to an insurmountable repulsion. These men Ulrich calls "*Urnings*" in opposition to "*Dionings*" or normally constituted men.

In 1869. Dr. Fraenckel of Dessau, in appreciating the *mental condition* of *pederasts*, maintained that pederasty presupposes a disorder of the intellectual faculties, and that those who practise it are morose, suspicious, are possessed with ideas of persecution, have hallucinations and various disorders of the senses, and that some instances of heredity are also known. He adds that when the individual is absorbed by a single want, he ends in dementia and idiocy. The question remained so until 1870, and the public as well as the medical profession saw in the inversion of the genital sense only *vice* as the sole possible etiological reason.

Present Period of the Physiological Study of Inversion.

The period which has followed the preceding is that of the psychopathical study of inversion, in which inverted love is no longer considered solely as an infamous vice: this study shows us on the contrary, besides the vicious, *sufferers of different categories*, deserving of interest and often deserving of commiseration, whose defence ought to be undertaken by the physician against the over-just severity of the laws, which ought to take notice only of the guilty and not of sufferers from disease.

This period commences with Westphal, Professor of

Medecine at Berlin, whose treatise (*Die contrare sexual-empfindung, symptom eines nevropatischen, psychopatischen Zustand*) appeared in 1870 and established definitely the symptom of the *disease of inversion.*

The learned German Professor, with clearer sight and greater wisdom than Tardieu, evolved from the chaos of inverted love, hitherto studied only from the anatomo-clinical point of view of common pederasty, a clear and precise morbid type, *congenital inversion*, a state in which an individual is born with an irresistible genital inclination for his own sex and an invincible horror of normal intercourse, and finds himself naturally impelled to the pursuit of abnormal sexual satisfactions. Westphal published in his treatise two observations upon congenitally inverted individuals, referring, one to an *unmarried woman* aged 85, the other to a man aged 27, and traced by their aid the fundamental characteristies of the pathological type which he created: *congenital condition, clear conception of morbid disorder, hereditary defect, complete concomitance of other psychical disorders, etc.*

"The light was brought upon it, and the scientific phase was disclosed, succeeding to the phase of chaos.

"The medical movement inaugurated by Westphal has been followed up actively from 1870 to the present day, and has had a double effect. On the one hand, the type created by the eminent German neuropathologist has been more and more established, and has been set forth with all its characteristics; on the other hand, the shapeless block of anti-natural love has been deeply hollowed out, and an enlightened observation has been able to bring into relief, besides the Westphal type, other fresh elements, in such a manner that these facts which formerly *the single word, vice, defined, explained and completely included*, are now divided into clearly differentiated categories.

"The work of the Berlin Professor attracted the keen attention of the medical world, in Germany in the first place and then in foreign countries. The French physicians a little too much imbued with the narrow theories of Tardieu, followed the movement at last, beginning in 1882. Science now possesses a hundred cases which clearly show that degenerescence is the fundamental basis of the *disease* of inversion.

"We will not give the list of the numerous physicians whose observations have brought the question into its true light. We shall be satisfied with quoting those whose names are of authority in the matter and whose works we have consulted fruitfully in the composition of our work.

"In Germany, Westphal's best disciple was Krafft Ebing, Professor at Vienna, who surpassed his master and whose noble work, *Psychopathia Sexualis*, filled with facts, is a rich mine upon which all the physicians who have made a study of sexual inversion have drawn; and it may be said that this book, which has recently been translated into French, is pre-eminently the classical work on all the anomalies of the sexual instinct. After him, Dr. Moll of Berlin has published a very interesting book on inversion, full of references, to which we shall often have recourse, as well as to that of Krafft Ebing. Let us also make mention of Hammond.

"In Russia, the most complete work is that of Tarnowsky, Professor at the Imperial Academy at St. Petersburg, based upon a practise of 25 years as consulting physician. Tarnowsky endeavours (says Chevalier) to separate the different clinical varieties of the aberration, and he shows that far from arising from a single cause, degenerescence, it often results from very distinct cerebral affections.

"England holds an honourable rank with the work of Raffalovich (*Uranisme et Unisexualité*), translated into French and published in 1896 by Masson, Paris.

"It would be unjust not to mention the Italians, Lombroso and Mantegazza, who are two excellent compilers, particularly the former.

"In France, if subsequent to 1876, Legrand de Saulle, the eminent alienist, has occupied himself with the matter in an incidental manner, it is in reality Charcot and Magnan who have attacked it squarely with their important treatise, *Inversion du Sens genital et autres Perversions sexuelles*, which appeared in 1882. In the *Archives de Neurologie* they have proved "in an excellent way that the anomaly should not be considered as an instinctive monomania and morbid entity, but that it is only an episode of a deeper malady, one of the numerous singularities displayed by degenerate subjects. To show that the form of the obsessions does not in any way modify the basis itself of the affection, they offer some observations of different perversions, no less astonishing, such as the genital obsession for the nails of women's shoes, for a night-cap, or for white aprons. They ask in matters of morals for a rigorous report." (Chevalier.)

It is only just to recognize the fact that it is Magnan who has penetrated the farthest, through his deep researches into the mechanism and the genesis of sexual anomalies.

In his clinical instruction, in different publications, and by communications to the Academy of Medecine, the learned alienist has shown that inversion like many other sexual disorders, is often but an episodical syndrome of the hereditarily affected, and that in virtue of this it ranks with other no less curious psychical stigmata, such as Dipsomania, Kleptomania, etc., the principal characteristic of which, that is to say the possessing form, he has made very clear. In his classification of the anomalies of the sexual instinct, which we have studied in a previous chapter, he places the inverted among the anterior-cerebral-spinal.

To the two eminent Professors of Legal Medecine, Brouardel of Paris, and Lacassagne of Lyons, belongs the honour of having introduced the inversion symptom almost at the same time into official science and works of reference.

Brouardel, Tardieu's successor, after correcting the latter's too absolute ideas on the physical effets of pederasty, has made sexual perversions the subject of a series of lectures at the Faculty of Medecine. "He studies successively the innate, periodical, and acquired aberrations, and he establishes the fact that the inverse acts may affect one or the other of these forms. He shows besides the influence of certain arrested developments upon the genesic activity, fixes the rules of investigation and in the medico-legal question recommends the examination of the mental condition of the accused persons." (Chevalier.)

His pupil, Vibert, has popularized Brouardel's teaching in his works.

Lacassagne distinguishes the pederasty of morbid impulsions. He has taught that the anti-natural aberration arises from numerous causes, and, in certain cases, from a kind of moral hermaphrodism. In any way, it is necessary, in investigation, after searching for the physical signs of perverse acts, to proceed to the examination of the mental condition of the subject.

Magnan has followed the school of Garnier. Chevalier, the best pupil of Lacassagne, has published an excellent work on Sexual Inversion. We have quoted his theories on the laws of Sexual Instinct at the beginning of this Volume.

Thoinot finally closes the list with his lectures delivered at the Paris Faculty of Medecine on the *Attentats aux Mœurs et Perversions du Sens Génital*, published in a work which has recently appeared. Thoinot's work is eclectic. He offers few personal observations, but he has the great merit of summing up everything that has been written by the above-mentioned authors and of extracting their quintessence. With regard to Sexual Inversion, he belongs rather to the school of Krafft Ebing than to that of Lacassagne and Chevalier.

We have put under contribution to a large extent the authors mentioned above, for our aim, as we cannot repeat too often, is to elaborate a work which can be read by everybody and have the double characteristic of being both medical and philosophical.

Having said this let us approach the problem of how Sexual Inversion is produced.

What is the Origin of Sexual Perversion?

Different Opinions of Physicians and Philosophers.

At first, we find that there is no plausible reason for this sexual perversion. It appears incomprehensible. History bears record to its universality in every time and among every people. Physicians and philosophers have sought vainly for explanations, and these explanations are of the most varied character. Diderot subjects them to a searching analysis. Whence do these abominable tastes come? enquires Mlle de Lespinasse, and Borden answers: "Everywhere from a poverty of organization on the part of the young; from a corruption of the mind on the part of the old; from the attraction of beauty in Athens; from the scarcity of women in Rome, and from fear of the pox in Paris." And this analysis of Diderot is true in many points.

The German Schopenhauer finds a nebulous explanation. In his opinion, Nature, desirous of preserving the *integrity of the type*, impels those who are incapable of performing this work to a necessarily sterile love which, he thinks. has no great inconveniences for the human race.

Ulrichs, the Uranist, merely thinks that the inverted individual's mind is of a different sex to his body.

Mantegazza gives an anatomical explanation. In inverted individuals, through an error of Nature, the nerves intended for the genital parts spread into the intestine, so that the voluptuous excitation, which is generally provoked by the excitation, proceeds from the latter part. This definition is incomplete, for it only applies to the passive pederast who seeks for anal coition, and many inverted individuals hold this in horror.

Krafft Ebing believes that genital inversion might be explained by saying that it represents a special peculiarity of descent, but taking its origin by way of heredity. Atavism would be the morbid inclination for his own sex, an inclination acquired by the ancestor which becomes fixed as a morbid and congenital phenomenon in the descendant. This author appears to us to be right, and his opinion, which is maintained by Laupts, is confirmed by a personal observation which I give further on.

Binet explains the anomaly by an external circumstance, a fortuitous event which has occurred in infancy, and which led the patient to seek for persons of his own sex; it results, according to him, from an incident operating upon a predisposed subject.

Ribot thinks that the problem should find its explanation in the numerous elements of heredity, and in the complicated play of male and female influences which are face to face.

In Lacassagne's opinion the abnormal are retarded types. They have not marched in step with the others; they have remained stationary while all progressed around them; qualities slowly accumulated and fixed have not been so for them; they have no sooner risen than they have come down, "or rather, they find themselves still on the first steps of the ladder which the others have climbed; these are the retarded types."

Lombroso, on the contrary, maintains that the abnormal are atavic products. Chevalier's theory is based upon hermaphrodism: "the individual commences with the bisexuality of the embryo, continues with the undecided morphological and psychological sexuality of the 'youth', and ends with the strongly marked sexuality of the adult.... There is a period when there is an organic hermaphrodism, a plastic insexuality and double genital aptitudes. A struggle commences between the male element and female element face to face, and from the triumph of one or the other results, in the series, the separation of the sexes, and in the individual, a perfected sex; but this struggle, whatever may be the element which definitively prevails, involves an impregnation of the offspring and being by one or the other. Now, can we not suppose that this phase of sexual duality, the duration of which was so long in the rest of the species, but which has been rapidly recalled in the early times of fatal existence, must necessarily have left a trace of its passage, attenuated no doubt to the point of non-existence in the superior animal forms and in the adult individual, but still a trace?"

In Ledrain's opinion, "abnormal sexuality, whatever its appearance may be, is in short only a widely-extended disease of the instinct, whether that instinct seems to disappear, or adapts itself more to its object, that is to say becomes perverted, or is hypertrophied to some degree and obtains a mastery over the whole individual in his moral and intellectual sphere. This disease of the sexual appetite which is one of the two great forms of the instinct of conservation, is, to my idea, absolutely the counterpart of that which attacks the other of these forms, the *instinct of nutrition*, and which shows itself in those aberrations, anomalies and perversions of the appetite, so well-known under the names of Boulimia, Pica, Malacia and Coprophagia."

Ledrain is right. The causes of inversion are numerous, but it is an interesting fact to observe the diversity of medical opinions "*Tot medici, tot sententiæ.*" We shall meet with this same diversity in the Classification of Inversion.

Classifications of Inversion.

The different authors who have applied themselves the question of Inversion have a more or less different classification.

Krafft Ebing, Chevalier, Laupts, Raffalovitch, etc.; each of them has his own. It does not come within our limits to discuss the merits of each of these classifications. They have their good and their bad side. Among these classifications those of Krafft Ebing, Laupts and Chevalier seem to us to be the most rational, particularly that of Chevalier. We give it below in its schematic form which allows almost all the known and studied cases to be included in it.

Schematic Table of J. Chevalier's Classification.

I.

PERVERSITY.—PEDERASTY AND SAPHISM PROPERLY SO CALLED.

I. Artificial Acquired Inversion.	1. Pederasty of Saphism from Lust. 2. Professional Pederasty or Saphism. 3. Pederasty or Saphism from Necessity. 4. Pederasty or Saphism from Fear.	Sociological Factors. Medium.

II.

VARIATION OF SEXUAL TYPE.

II. Secondary Inversion.	1. Insexuality, more or less marked, resulting from a malformation of the Genital Organs together with reaction on the secondary sexual characteristics.	*a.* Acquired during Adolescence.	Feminism. Masculinsm.	Sociological and Individual Factors Isolated and Combined.
		b. Congenital (dating from the Fatal Existence.)	Hypospadias Exaggerated size of the Clitoris. Hermaphrodism.	

III.

MENTAL DISEASE.

2. Mental Disease with decided Lesions of the Nervous System.	Mania. Melancholia. Periodical Madness. Chronic Delirium. Hereditary Madness. Epilepsy. General Paralysis. Senile Dementia.	

IV.

PERVERSION.—INVERSION PROPERLY SO CALLED.

3. Instinctive Congenital Inversion.	Degenerescence.	Individual Factors. Heredity.

Although this schematic table is at the same time etiological and clinical and sums up clearly the different modalities of Sexual Inversion, we shall not however follow it in its outline of fact.

Laupts' Classification.

Laupts' classification is very original. He classes all the inverted in five categories, of which we give a succinct summary below in order that we may not enter on any lengthy details.

1. Inverted: born with apparent Physical Stigmata.		Man, inverted, born feminiformed.
		Woman, inverted, born masculiformed.
2. Inverted: born without Physical Stigmata. Cerebral.	Man	Cerebral, feminiphile, paidophile. Cerebral masculiphile.
	Woman	Cerebral Masculiphile. Cerebral Feminiphile.
3. Occasionally Inverted.	Man	Occasional feminiphil paidophile. Occasional masculiphile.
	Woman	Cerebral masculiphile. Cerebral feminiphile.
4. Indifferents.		Variety of occasionals or predisposed, perhaps also of inverted born malformed or cerebral.
5. Born inverted, disordered, degenerated.		Disordered, wanting in equilibrium, hereditary, alcoholic.

Laupts proposes this classification, not on account of its scientific rigour, but for the facility with which it allows, as he believes, the prognosis of the *pathological manifestation*.

We shall not follow this classification any more than that of Chevalier, but by reason of its importance, we shall analyze it in detail. We observe in the first place the important place given to the occasionally inverted; the author is logical, for this category is by far the most common; it alone in fact gives us the key to the development and to the important place which inversion holds in history.

Importance of Laupts' occasionally Inverted in the general Etiology of Inversion.

We shall give a very detailed treatment of all that concerns the occasionally inverted in the study of Inversion. Let us state here simply to confirm Laupts' opinion that these occasionally inverted individuals are always active when they arrive at the act, and if their tendency remains platonic, they are attracted by the feminines, the inverted born feminiformed. They seek for the man because they have no women, and only take them for want of anything better.

On the contrary, in the case of the inverted born deformed or malformed, it is the part of the opposite sex which tempts them; if they are men, they regret that they are not women, and indulge in the latters' part as far as they possibly can.

This, according to Laupts, is the main distinction, for between these two categories of inverted there exists a difference analogous to than observed by criminologists between murderers and delinquents.

The Italian School represented by Lombroso makes the criminal an hereditary, a blemished individual, forced to commit crimes by cerebral malformation innate or diseased. The French School, represented by Lacassagne, shows on the contrary that crime breaks out under the influence of social causes, poverty, hunger, disease, bad example, etc.

The French School, in our opinion, is right, and every man carries with him an innate instinct for destruction. The most honest man in the world may become a criminal under the influence of appropriate causes. This destructive tendency is restrained by the laws, by morality, by religion and by the development of the altruistic instincts. The child, the worthy Lafontaine has rightly said, is without pity. The adult becomes destructive under the influence of anger, poverty or drunkenness. Had he been born a millionnaire, says Laupts, Ravachol would not have blown up houses, and Caserio would not have assassinated Carnot.

We have been present, in Senegal, in Tonquin and during the campaign of 1870—71, at veritable acts of ferocious cruelty, committed without any plausible reason by men who were kind and gentle in the ordinary course of life. And this occurs among all races, just as much in the case of the white European as in that of the black African and of the yellow Asiatic.

It is certain that there are in existence *born destructors*, men who shed blood for the pleasure of doing so. But these are deformed and their centre of destruction is much more powerful than is the case with normal individuals, and their case is exceptional. They reproduce ancestral forms of humanity, or they are the produce of a criminal line, or again they display a malformation of their centre of destruction, a hypertrophy of the instinct which impels them to break and destroy, an evil, primitive instinct, but necessary to our ancestors. This instinct slumbers at the bottom of every man's heart, and it is enough to put a game-bag on the back of a worthy citizen, and a gun in his hand, to make of him a savage sportsman, whose feelings are unmoved at the most revolting spectacles and who massacres poor birds and unfortunate rabbits with delight.

It is the same with inversion. "Every man has within his heart a hog which slumbers," says Alfred de Musset; and again the proverb says, "Opportunity makes the thief."

It is not therefore surprising to find among the *occasionally inverted*, persons in whom the inversion has only been an accident, developed in favourable surroundings, under the influence of an exaggerated continence, and sometimes also under a contagious impulse comparable to one of those epidemics of suicide or religious mania which occur at all times and all epochs. Self-restraint and modesty disappear very quickly. It will be enough for those of our readers who have been boarders in a large school to recall to mind the scenes of impropriety between boys, the *lapins* and the *chasseurs*, under which terms are designated the children who serve as a butt to the sexual pleasure of the others.

The private soldier quartered in the Colonies, where the woman is repugnant to the white man like the female of New Caledonia, or diseased like the Annamite Congaï, inevitably becomes a masturbator or an occasionally inverted. It is the same with the sailor. As for the convict, he offers an admirable ground for the growth of inversion.

In Europe there are the "swells," those who want to be different to the rest. They begin through curiosity; they try inversion to see what it is like; the majority are disgusted with it, but a considerable number after finding at first that it is funny, acquire a taste for it. Here in fact are two very suggestive anecdotes, clearly showing us this state of mind which is not so uncommon as is believed.

"A very celebrated painter, a most honourable man from every point of view, said to me one day: 'Who is there who has not wanted to try inversion once at least, and through mere curiosity?' And his words had a tone of regret."

"An officer belonging to a foreign Navy stated in my presence with simple-minded cynicism that inversion had been his ordinary habit in certain colonies. On my expressing my surprise: 'What can one do?' he replied, 'when one arrives at Saigon, one looks for an Annamite woman. In those countries it is difficult for a stranger to distinguish a man from a woman in the street: they dress in the same way and resemble one another exactly: one doesn't know the sex of the creature one is following and so commit inversion almost by the necessity of things." (Laupts.)

This language, here ascribed to a foreign officer, how frequently have we heard it uttered by Naval officers, by officers in the Marines, and by civil functionaries of every rank in Cochin-China and Tonkin! And those who thus expressed themselves were gifted, intelligent men who made use of Chinese boys or Annamite naïs, generally for want of European women or through disgust at the indigenous Congaïs. There was also the fear of syphilis which is terrible throughout the whole of the Extreme East and rages with a virulence almost unknown in Europe at the present day. At one period, syphilis alone supplied half the patients under treatment in the Hospitals of Saigon, Mytho, Vinh-Long, etc.

And then the Annamite Congaïs had a special talent in the art of buccal coition. The naïs were quite as expert as they: some indeed declared that their play was softer. This is an opinion which I heard seriously maintained by an occasionally inverted individual. He had begun with having himself polluted labially, gone on to active anal coition, and finally ended with passive coition, the sensations of which, he declared were much more voluptuous than those of active coition!

There is no need therefore to explain the frequency of occasional inversion by admitting hereditary causes or congenital malformations.

Different Types of Inverted Individuals, according to Laupts.

We continue our study by giving, from Laupts, the description of the different types of the inverted from his classification.

1. *Inverted-born with apparent physical stigmata.*

A . . ., from the most tender age, has displayed in his general structure striking resemblances to persons of the opposite sex to his own. Born a man, he has the development of the hips and pelvis, the prominence of the buttocks and the delicate beardless skin of a woman. He has had, at a period of his fatal existence, a double devolution, which while allowing the organs of one of the two sexualities to remain, has permitted the development of certain characteristics of the other. When he attains the age of puberty, he is inverted, and that in a very specialized manner: in an abnormal union, he takes the part of the other sex: if he has been born a man, he will be the woman of the combination. In this case then there is a phenomenon analogous to that of hermaphrodism. This born-inverted, deformed, feminiformed (if it is a man), masculiformed (if it is a woman), is a pure and simple monstrosity.

2. *Occasionally-Inverted.*

With this one we are acquainted. B . . . has been born a man, and has always been a man in his character and habits. He has made use and even abuse of women in Europe. The lottery of existence has brought him to Africa or China, or perhaps he has gone round the world in a sailing-ship. He has great sexual wants. Finding himself amid surroundings from which woman is banished, if he comes across a feminiformed born-inverted, or an occasionally inverted more perverted than himself, he gives a free rein to his instinct and indulges in condemnable acts. Later, when he returns to normal surroundings, he may recover himself and become again a hetero-sexual.

He may also, if he remains long enough amid contaminated surroundings, grow completely perverted and seek later on for the same pleasures with a woman as with a man and become a sodomist as he is no longer able to be a pederast. I shall give some convincing instances of this.

3. *Inverted-born cerebral.*

C . . . has not any physical stigmata. There is nothing apparently to distinguish him from a normal man, were it not for a singular taste which attracts him to those of his own sex. For members of the opposite sex he has only a feeling of coldness and almost of repulsion. He has been born a complete man and has all the attributes of the latter, but from his earliest youth, man has had a seductive influence over him and in the man it is the genital organ which attracts him. C . . . is an inverted-born cerebral: in his case the blemish is of a *purely nervous nature, and is not* accompanied by any visible physical characteristic. (Laupts.)

But the feature in the man which this inverted individual will admire is resemblance with the female form, and it is for this reason that Laupts names him feminiphile or paidophile cerebral. He will run after beardless youths and boys of 15 years of age. If C . . . meets A . . ., C . . . will take the part of the man and A . . . that of the woman. It is while he is a boarder at a College that this type of inverted, seduced by a companion of the types of A . . . or B . . ., contracts his vice. Later on, when he is with women, he may be cured if he is submitted to a female influence.

But the cerebral masculiphile inverted-born loves those, on the contrary, who are more masculine than himself. He takes the passive part in intercourse with B . . . or C . . . and in this he closely approaches to A . . . the feminiformed inverted-born with physical stigmata. How is the singularity of this type to be explained? Laupts gives a very ingenious explanation. "It seems to me natural to admit as follows. The children of an occasionally-inverted individual, born after the occasional act, or after numerous and overmastering acts which have grown into habits, ought to display this predisposition. And if the tendencies to inversion, strong not only in one but in a series of paternal ancestors, are still further confirmed and consolidated by analogous dispositions on the side of the maternal ancestors, may not, must not the product display all the symptoms of an affection susceptible of coinciding with a normal physical structure, of even being at birth a mere simple predisposition, for it is a question of a nervous psychological heredity—or of an atavism—and not of an error of nature. of a visible physical deformation, of a fault of construction of the orgasm, let us say of an apparent monstrosity, as in the case of the inverted-born?"

4. *Inverted-born indifferent.*

Laupts defines them as follows:

"Besides the congenital and incurable malformation, there is the simple accident on the appearance of which the external conditions have such an influence that I have come across absolutely *indifferent* subjects, sometimes androphiles, sometimes gamophiles, according to circumstances. Two subjects have declared to me that when they are placed amid male surroundings, they felt a love, as pure as it is keen for males with a feminine shape, a love which rapidly disappeared when they were brought into surroundings in which women were to be found, and then they quickly fell in love with one of the latter.

"If search were made in the Colleges, numerous instances of this latter case would undoubtedly be found."

Laupts' last type is the born-inverted and is only a symptom of a deep or generalized degenerescence.

In this category we see inverteds figuring whose aberration is due to very different causes. Those whom Laupts denominates born inverteds, are classed by Chevalier some among the pederasts, the perverted, and others among the inverted sufferers from dementia affected with secondary inversion owing to diseases such as Insanity and Paralysis.

Krafft Ebing's Classification.

Krafft Ebing's classification deserves to be analyzed in its turn, for it cannot be denied that he is one of the authors of the present day who has expatiated most judiciously upon the matter. He divides sexual inversion into *acquired homosexuality* and *congenital homosexuality.*

Acquired homosexuality allows of the four following degrees.

1st Degree: Simple Inversion of the Genital Sense.

This is met with when a person of the same sex produces an aphrodisiac effect upon another individual and the latter feels in consequence a sexual feeling for the former. But the character and feelings remain conformable to the sex of which the patient is a member; the individual is always conscious of his active part, if he is a man, of her passive part, if she is a woman; he looks upon his inclination as an aberration and seeks eventually for a remedy.

2nd Degree: Eviratio et defeminatio.

This is the preceding case, only without revolt of the conscience, and with aggravation of the progressive transformation of the ideas, tastes and feelings in conformity with the characteristics of the new sex which the patient ends by attributing to himself by the fact that he has been attracted by an individual of his own sex. He only has a taste then for the part of his new sex, that is to say that he becomes *passive* if he is normally a man, and *active* if normally a woman.

Krafft Ebing includes in this category the well-known disease of the Scythians characterized by a psychical transformation of the sexual personality through popular customs and usages, having for its object among other things the suppression, through atrophy, of the genital organs. The same singularity is met with among the Pueblo Indians who bring up for their pleasures what they call *mujerados*, men whose feminine tastes and aptitudes they gradually develop through emasculating them by very complicated practices.

3rd Degree: Transition towards the Metamorphosis sexualis paranoica.

Here we enter upon the region of Insanity. Krafft Ebing quotes a single instance in which a veritable Uranist created for himself by auto-suggestion a series of genital hallucinations, giving to the patient gradually the idea of a complete metamorphosis of his person.

4th Degree: Complete paranoic sexual Metamorphosis.

This fourth and last degree is relative to those maniacs who, at first, by the fact of genital hallucinations, believe themselves completely transformed into individuals of the opposite sex, of whom they have not only the mental state, but also the material feelings.

Against this classification the objection may be brought, according to Laupts, that these two latter degrees form but a single one.

Let us now look at Congenital Homosexualily.

Here we re-enter the veritable domain of Inversion; it is a native condition characterized by sexual frigidity, extending sometimes to horror of the opposite sex, while inclinations, sentiments and feelings exist, provoked by members of the same sex. According to Krafft Ebing this is coincident with a very marked and developed physical sexual type. In this case there exists congenitally a singular metamorphosis of the patients by virtue of which the external genital attributes are no longer in conformity with the actual psychical aptitudes: a masculine physique is coincident with feminine psychical aptitudes, and *vice versa.*

Krafft Ebing admits four degrees in this congenital hermaphrodism.

1st Degree: Psycho-Sexual Hermaphrodism.

This is the case of those patients who, while having predominant homosexual inclinations, still however have traces of heterosexual sensations. Disgust for the opposite sex is not pronounced, and we see patients such as these, who in reality are very numerous, voluptarily keeping up alternative or simultaneous connections with men and women. It is therefore an absolute hermaphrodism. When it is well defined, the patients having and instinctive desire for both sexes, they are in reality neutrals. (Laupts.)

2nd Degree: Homosexuality properly so called, or Uranism.

Here there is no longer any bilateral instinctive desire, or apparent hermaphrodism. The inclination is clearly marked for members of the same sex as that of the patient, with the same sentiments and with the same varieties and intensities of sentiment as a normal creature ought to feel for the opposite sex. But he does not lay aside his personality, and preserves in his attitude the part inherent in his physical sex; the individual remains a man, and consequently active if he is masculine: she remains a woman, and consequently passive if she is feminine. The hetero-sexual evolution remains limited to the acts of the genital life alone, that is to say that as regards the other acts of life, the patients remain confined within the attributes of their natural sex.

3rd Degree: Effemination and Viraginity.

In this degree, homosexuality is conditioned by an innate sentiment of the transformation of the personality. The man seeks for the contact of the man because he feels himself a woman, and *vice versa.* The genital life is no longer alone in question. Therefore, in his attitude and in his manners the patient takes the part opposite to that of the sex of which he bears the external attributes; the individual becomes passive if he is masculine, and active if she is feminine. This is the veritable inversion. The homosexual sentiments are in reality normal and heterosexual, since the patients have inverted their sex. The aberration is no longer the same as in the preceding case where we saw a man, *believing himself to be a man*, seeking after the contact of another man; here on the contrary, we see a man *believing himself to be a woman*, seeking quite naturally for the approaches of another man.

4th Degree: Androgynia and Gynandria.

Here the patient's transformation does not any longer appear to be confined within psychical limits: the conformation of the body is modified and draws nearer to that which corresponds to the psychical, that is to say abnormal sex. In other terms, the woman seems to gradually become a man, physically and morally; if I may be allowed the expression, she is an abortive man. And it is the same with the man.

Criticisms upon Krafft Ebing's Classification.

Krafft Ebing's classification, scientific though it may be and resting upon a wealth of unpublished and very interesting observations to which we shall often have recourse, does not escape criticism.

Legrain justly finds fault with Krafft Ebing "for endeavouring to show that sexual inversion is nothing but a wholly psychical anomaly which has no connection with the physical conformation. This, in my opinion, is holding too cheaply and without adequate reason those physical anomalies which he justly points out in the gynandres and androgynes of his fourth degree. It appears to me on the contrary that physical and moral malformations are of the same nature, that they have the same value, that they must be regarded from the same plane, and that bodily hetero-morphism casts a vivid light upon sexual inversion. Without deriving one from the other, they are both on the other hand dependent upon one and the same morbid processus.

"It is not correct, moreover, to assert that there is no real transition in the inverted to hermaphrodism, that is to say to the bisexuality of the creature or, what comes to the same, to its sexual neutrality." (Ledrain. *op. cit.*)

The author quotes a very complete case of hermaphrodism in which the subject displayed physically numerous masculine and feminine indications, so that it was impossible to determine exactly his sex. As regards the psychical point of view, it was impossible to establish his preferences. He appeared rather to be indifferent and neutral, and inclined, according to his wants, which were rare, and according to his opportunities, to the part of the woman as much as to the part of the man. It is natural therefore, adopting the theories of Legrain, to regard the physical anomalies of androgynes and gynandres as transitions towards complete hermaphrodism. This hermaphrodism also exists from the psychical point of view. Krafft Ebing's 1st and 4th degrees may therefore be brought together and even coalesced. The Uranists properly so called (2nd degree) and the patients of the 3rd degree (viraginity and effemination) are therefore the clearly marked transition between the normal condition and psycho-psychical hermaphrodism, the extreme degree of degenerescence which is characterized by complete sexual neutrality and consequently by sterility.

Besides this, the genital organs do not constitute the

exclusive qualification of sex. The latter is characterized quite as much by the external habitus and by the cerebral conformation as by the genital organs which in short are but the instruments at the service of the sexual function.

Chevalier has laid down as his first law of sexual attraction that *it is the anatomical constitution of the individual which forms the sex, and that is the organ which forms the function.* Legrain and Laupts are totally opposed to him, and in their opinion the organ is absolutely dependent upon the function and it is impossible to separate one from the other.

"Krafft Ebing," says Legrain, "thinks that he ought not to attach any importance to the malformation known by the names of *epispadias* and *hypospadias*, owing to the fact that in the cases which he has observed, the sex was very clearly differentiated in spite of the malformation. But I do not at all share his opinion on this differentiation of sex, seeing that the patients in question were undoubtedly Uranists, which clearly proves that their sex was very uncertain. Males or females from the genital point of view, they were females or males from the psychical point of view. What therefore was their true sex? Nothing shows more clearly in my opinion, that it is impossible, in the determination of sex, to dissociate the signs belonging to the physical and the moral."

Impossibility of giving a Classification of Inversion which will not meet with Criticism.

We have just seen Chevalier, Laupts and Krafft Ebing, all of them giving a different classification more or less open to criticism. Moll has not attempted to establish a classification of his own. In his explanation of the matter he employs that of Krafft Ebing while bringing forward those cases in which that classification is defective.

Raffalovich proposes a very ingenious but very complicated classification in which he takes the opposite side to Chevalier. He does not in fact concern himself with the genital organ but bases his whole classification on the psychical inclination, boldly placing the *cerebral* side of the sexual instinct before the anatomical. This is going too far, and Chevalier's opinion which rectifies the tendencies to excess in those of Chevalier and Raffalovich, appears to us to be more correct.

We shall not stay to give Raffalovich's classification here, as we are by no means a supporter of it: it would serve only to complicate our work without any appreciable advantage.

But we may clearly conclude from what has gone before that *it is almost impossible to give a classification which will not meet with criticism.* We shall not therefore attempt to give one which perhaps would be still more open to criticism than the preceding.

Nevertheless, as a guide is requisite in order that we may not lose ourselves in the tangled maze of Inversion, we shall sometimes make use of Chevalier's and sometimes of Krafft Ebing's in our exposition of facts. We shall also give prominence to the works of Moll, Laupts, Ledrain and Raffalovich.

We can therefore extract the quintessence of all these authors for the requirements of our work which is above all things eclectic, as we stated in our Preface.

The General Law of Inversion.

From the preceding classifications we are able to lay down the general law of inversion.

Inverted individuals are in fact divided into two clearly distinct groups which have no point of contact but in their sexual habits.

The first group includes all the subjects who are not responsible for the abnormal sexual act which they perform. They often have knowledge of the unlawful act and of the social fault which they commit, but *conscious or not,* they are irresponsible, for they are diseased and invincibly impelled by a *morbid inclination* against which they struggle in vain. This may be called Group A, true morbid inversion through sexual perversion.

In the second group, we include pederasts and sodomists *responsible for their perverted act*, which they perform through *vice and perversity*.

We give to this group B the name of *artificial inversion*, or *inversion through vice and perversity*.

We owe this separation into two very distinct groups to Krafft Ebing. In his opinion, *perversion* is every manifestation of the sexual instinct which does not agree with the end assigned by nature, that is to say which does not conduce to reproduction. Krafft Ebing moreover calls attention, says Moll, to the necessity of establishing a rigorous separation between *perversion* and *perversity*. We speak of perversion when the sexual instinct is a perverse instinct, without taking account of the motive which has occasioned the action, which may be a perverse inclination or any other motive, a criminal intention for instance. It is greatly to Krafft Ebing's merit that he has so clearly separated these two conceptions. Perversion is an inclination independent of the will and for which no one can be held responsible, at least in the eyes of an impartial judge; on the other hand the perversity which shows itself in the action must often be laid to the account of the individual. It may be seen how the confusion between these two terms has made it difficult to appreciate sexual inversion, owing to the idea expressed by Chevalier that in acquired sexual perversion, the perversion depends upon the will of the individual. There is nothing more untrue than this assertion, as we have just shown.

Pederasts, Saphists and Uranists.

The subjects of the second group are usually designated by the term of pederasts. Although Moll asserts that only those subjects ought to be thus designated *qui membrum in anum immittunt*, we hold to Tardieu's definition. In our opinion, pederasts are depraved men who seek for boys and young men, and that independently of the sexual act committed. The name of Sodomy characterizes anal coition performed upon a man or a woman.

The *Tribade* or *Saphist* is the depraved woman who tries to corrupt a young girl.

As for the subjects of the first group, we adopt the generic name of Uranists applied to them by Krafft Ebing, Moll, Raffalovich and so many other authors, by reason of its brevity and it will be applied generally to all male persons who display homo-sexual tendencies. The fuller term of *inverted* is applied to the generality of persons of both sexes who have unisexual tendencies.

What is the place of Inversion in the list of Anomalies of the Sexual Instinct?

As regards the place of Inversion in the list of anomalies of the sexual instinct, it cannot be established with any exactitude. It would in fact be illusory to attempt to do so. As we have already remarked, the causes of the diseases of the instinct of reproduction are as numerous as those of the diseases of the instinct of nutrition.

Between a surfeited debauchee who mounts a man in order to learn the sensation, and the poor — who does the same to his pal because he has not a copper to give to a woman, there is the same difference as there is between the epicure with a surfeited palate who sprinkles his steak with Cayenne pepper and the poor devil who eats a bit of bread because he has nothing else to put in his mouth. And those men who indulge in abnormal sexual acts are strangely different from the born-inverted who believes himself to be a woman, and whose tastes, inclinations and external habits are those of a woman. The latter, as a degree of an inveterate disease may be compared to a patient affected with pica who eats unmentionable things.

The reader will now understand why we have made of sexual inversion a peculiar class entered under the general title of Genital Perversions.

Coexistence of Inversion with other Anomalies of the Sexual Instinct.

The anomalies of the sexual instinct, proceeding from

a common basis of mental degeneracy, are all linked together. Now there are inverted subjects who are at the same time affected with another sexual anomaly. And it was therefore more logical to study the other anomalies first, and as we made our way, we have met with inverted Sadists, Masochists, Exhibitionists, Fetishists and even practisers of bestiality. The study of these different anomalies of the sexual instincts contributes largely to that of Inversion and even renders the task more easy. In our personal observations we shall see fresh cases of this superposition (may we call it?), of several anomalies of the sexual instinct.

We are now well equipped to commence the study of the inverted subjects of Group A.

Genital Perversions. *(Continued.)*

CHAPTER II.

A. True Morbid Inversion through Sexual Perversion and its Divisions.

*Division of Morbid Inversion through Sexual Perversion into two very distinct Categories.—Morbid Mental Inversion (or Artificial Inversion).—Its Classification into Groups by Chevalier.—General Psysiognomy of Morbid Mental Inversion.—Observations of Cases of Morbid Mental Inversion.—Peculiar and Distinctive Characteristics of Morbid Mental Inversion.—The True Inversion of Degenerates or Uranism.—Uranism and its Different Degrees.—Division of True Inversion by Krafft Ebing into acquired Homosexuality and congenital Homosexuality.—Acquired Homosexuality.—First Degree. Simple Inversion of the Sexual Sense.—Observations.—*Lapin *at School,* Loup de Mer *on Board Ship.—Second Degree. Eviratio et Defeminatio.—Unique Observation by Krafft Ebing.—The Disease of the Scythians.—The Mujerados of New Mexico.—Errors committed by Krafft Ebing.—Third Degrec. Transition to Paranoical Sexual Metamorphosis.—The Doctor changed into a Woman.—Fourth Degree. Paranoical Sexual Metamorphosis.—Krafft Ebing's and Esquinol's Observations.—Mixed Cases outside any Classification.—Dr. E. Laurent's Observation.—Latent Inversion.—The Sailor who practised Bestiality, was a latent Inverted and a Sadist.*

Division of True Morbid Inversion into two very Distinct Categories.

True morbid Inversion forming the inverted of Group A, includes two very distinct categories. In the first, Inversion appears *accidentally* and *intermittently* in the course of various mental diseases. It is a simple episode, says Thoinot, which has no interest. We have seen, however, that Chevalier has made of it a secondary branch of inversion which, according to that author, includes the vitiation of the sexual type and the mental diseases of different natures. Let us reserve for a later period the study of inversion through vitiation of the sexual type, which in our opinion ought to form a special group and ought not to be confounded with the mental diseases.

The second group includes the Uranists in whom the perversion is permanent. These are the *true inverted.*

Morbid Mental Inversion.

It has a very clear etiology. It is connected with the course of certain nervous or mental diseases, with a definite type, with described or suspected anatomical lesions of the nervous centres: disorders of nutrition, of vascularity, modification of the cerebral substance, alteration of the structure of the nervous elements; atrophies, scleroses, degenerescences, etc., such as *Mania, Melancholia, Periodical Madness, Chronic Delirium, Hereditary Madness, Epilepsy, General Paralysis, Senile Dementia,* affections which are congenital or acquired.

Classification into Groups by Chevalier.

Chevalier is the author who has treated the subject of morbid mental inversion in the most successful manner. Without lingering upon the subject too long, it seems to us advantageous not to pass over this form of inversion in silence. "The error of the sexual instinct is originally central; it is due to a well-defined cerebral disorder: it comes from above."

All the alienist doctors have remarked the number, the frequency and the importance of sexual psychopathias in lunatics. All the forms of sexual aberrations and perversions are met with in lunatics, but sexual inversion holds a preponderant place; so that in enumerating the forms of lunacy in which it has been pointed out, it would be possible to review the whole of mental pathology.

Chevalier proposes the following methodical classification:

Two Greater Series.

1st. The series of lunacies properly so-called or *psychoses*. These affections are unaccompanied by any fixed and determined lesion of the nervous centres. This series is subdivided into two groups, according as the mental disorder is or is not complicated with degenerescence.

The first group includes Mania, Melancholia, periodical Madness, chronic delirium with progessive symptomatic evolution. Up to the day when the disease breaks forth, the brain has been free from all lesion, the intelligence has performed its functions in a normal way; from being sane of mind, the subject has become a madman.

The second group includes the different degrees of degenerative lunacy or *hereditary lunacy*, either want of balance and mental debility, imbecility and idiocy. A vicious working of the intelligence is preexistent to the explosion of lunacy, when, as is not invariably the case, the explosion occurs.

2nd. The series of *mixed conditions* which are connected at the same time with ordinary pathology and psychiatria. They include: 1st, mental alienation connected with a general morbid condition, with a greater neurosis and with epilepsy. 2nd, mental alienation connected with a cerebral affection with constant lesions, caused either A, by *general progessive paralysis* (diffuse interstitial encephalitis), or B, by *senile dementia.* (Chevalier, *op. cit.*)

General Physiognomy of Morbid Mental Inversion.

It may be rapidly summarized as follows:

In the first place, the sexual inversion appearing at a given period of some form of lunacy is never but a symptom of a pathological condition to be decided upon.

In the second place, inversion is always *acquired*, and it is of little moment whether the morbid form on which it depends be acquired like mania, or congenital like idiocy.

In the third place, the inverse impulsion is of short duration, fugitive and transitory: it is intimately connected with the attacks of the principal malady, appearing and disappearing with it, and reappearing with it in the same way from time to time at certain epochs. In the periods of remission the genital function is performed in a normal and regular way; the subject can marry, become a good husband and father of a family and give no grounds for his disease to be suspected.

"There are therefore intermittent periods, and the inversion comes in attacks."

Lastly, the inversion is never accompanied by parallel and remarkable modification of the secondary sexual psychical characteristics, as is the case in the innate form. In this connection the man remains a man and the woman a woman. "Moreover, even during the attack, there is no inversion for the other sex. but a simple momentary indifference. It may therefore be said that the inversion is void of feeling."

We shall not follow Chevalier in the detailed study of the inversion syndrome in the different mental diseases. He quotes a good number of observations, some hitherto unpublished, others borrowed from various authors. We shall be satisfied with quoting three of them, which will be enough, we think, to edify the reader upon Chevalier's theories.

Observations on Cases of Morbid Mental Inversion.

The first is borrowed from Krafft Ebing.

M. X . . ., aged 80, of good social position, sprung from a family suffering from defects, of a cynical disposition, has always had great sexual requirements. According to his own confession, he preferred, when he was still a young man, masturbation to coition. He had mistresses and had a child by one of them, married for love when he was 48, and again had six children; during the period of his wedded life he never gave his wife any cause for complaint. I have only been able to obtain incomplete details regarding his family. It is however an established fact that his brother was suspected of homosexual love and that one of his nephews went mad in consequence of excessive masturbation. For some years past, the patient's character, which was strange and subject to violent outbursts of passion, grew more and more eccentric. He became mistrustful and the slightest opposition to his desires put him into a state which might bring on fits of passion during which he would even lift his hand against his wife.

For a year past evident symptoms of *dementia senilis incipiens* have been noticed in him. His memory has grown feeble; he makes mistakes about past occurrences and at times is unable to collect himself. For the past fourteen months, absolute outbursts of love have been observed in this old man for certain of his male domestics, particularly for a gardener's boy. Though he is habitually peremptory and distant towards his subordinates, he overwhelms this favourite with kindnesses and gifts, and orders both his family and his servants to show the greatest deference to this boy. He waits, in an absolute state of rut, for the times of meeting him. He sends his family away from home in order that he may remain with his favourite alone and without restraint; he shuts himself up alone with him for whole hours and, when the doors are opened, the old man is found lying exhausted upon his bed. Besides this lover, the old man also has periodically intercourse with other male domestics. *Hoc constat amatos eum ad se trahere, ab iis oscula concupiscere, genitalia sua tangi itaque masturbationem mutuam fieri.* These manias produce an absolute demoralization in him. He no longer has any consciousness of the perversity of his sexual acts, so that his worthy family are in great distress and have no other resource than to put him under restraint and to place him in a lunatic asylum. No erotic excitation can be observed in him for the other sex, although he still shares a bedroom in common with his wife. As regards this unhappy man's perverted sexuality and the utter weakening of his moral sense, it is to be remarked as a curious fact, that he puts questions to his servants regarding his daughter-in-law to know if she has a lover.

Senile dementia is here the principal cause of the inversion, but it is worthy of note that the subject was sprung from a family suffering from hereditary defects, and that he always had great sexual requirements: he was moreover an avowed masturbator. I could quote an almost analogous case observed in the course of my medical practice, but one observation of this kind is enough.

The second observation relates to an act of pederasty committed on a child aged 16 months by an idiot. It is due to an Italian physician. "On April 8th, 1884, at 10 o'clock in the morning, a certain V... entered into conversation in the street with Madame X... who was holding in her lap a child aged 16 months. V... took the child away from her under the pretext that he wanted to take it for a walk. He went away with it for a distance of half a kilomètre, and when he came back declared that the child had fallen out of his arms and, in the fall, had hurt its arms. This part of the body was torn and blood was flowing from it. At the spot where the accident had taken place, traces of sperm were found. V... confessed his abominable crime, but during his examination his attitude was so strange that an enquiry was ordered into his mental condition. He gave the prison-warders the impression that he was an imbecile."

"V... aged 45, a journeyman mason, physically and morally blemished, is dolichomicrocephalous; he has a narrow and contracted face, an asymmetrical figure and ears, and a low and retreating forehead. The genital parts are normal. V... gives evidence generally of a very slight cutaneous sensibility; he is an imbecile and has no conception of anything. He lives from day to day without disturbing himself about anything, lives for himself and does nothing of his own initiative. He has neither desires nor affection; *he has never performed coition*. It is impossible to obtain from him other details regarding his *vita sexualis*. Intellectual and moral idiocy is proved by his microcephaly: the crime should be attributed to a sexual instinct, ungovernable and perverse. He is confined in a lunatic asylum."

(Vigilio. *Il Manicomio*. V^e^ année. No. 3.)

The third observation relates to a case of sexual inversion as syndrome of a general paralysis. I take the observation from one of my colleagues.

"M. G... de M..., a man of remarkable literary talents, very intelligent, robust and apparently possessing a well-balanced mind, was in the habit, according to the common expression, of burning the candle at both ends. His health beginning to fail, he made a voyage round the Mediterranean in a yacht, visiting more especially the coasts of Algeria and Tunis. Upon his return he wrote a book in which he speaks several times of African pederasts, and quotes some curious facts. I have it from the lips of one of his friends, that he made a personal study of their manners and customs. One fine day, the public was astonished to hear that the brilliant writer had been taken to a lunatic asylum where he died two years after of general paralysis."

From the perusal of these three observations and especially of the more numerous ones by Chevalier, Tarnowsky and Krafft Ebing, we may gather the peculiar and distinctive characteristics of this modality of sexual inversion.

Peculiar and Distinctive Characteristics of Morbid Mental Inversion.

Its characteristics are the following:

1st. The perversion proceeds by crises, in an unexpected and sudden manner; it breaks forth one fine day without being expected and disappears in the same way without leaving any trace of its passage, and nothing which could give ground for supposing that it has shown itself or that it will reappear. It is essentially *transitory*.

2nd. The inversion is clearly impulsive and almost always incoercible. The abnormal sexual act is produced in some (lunatics, maniacs, idiots, sufferers from dementia) in an almost automatic manner, executed almost as soon as it is conceived, without deliberation, without any intervention of the subject's will, who yields to a kind of suggestion of which he has no consciousness. Others, certain epileptics and periodics yield to "hypertrophied tendencies," of which they are more or less conscious, but which they are powerless to subdue. Chevalier gives to these different cases the name of delirious or sub-delirious inversion.

3rd. The inversion is similar to itself at each fresh reappearance in the uniformity of the acts which it suggests.

4th. There is an absence of any other characteristic either physical, or correlative psychical. "To sum up, it is difficult not to recognize the mark of a pathological condition in these facts; it is a question of a delirious condition, obscuring the consciousness, annihilating the will and involving irresponsibility." (Chevalier, *op. cit.*)

It may therefore be said that morbid mental inversion is a false inversion, in opposition to the veritable morbid inversion, in one word to Uranism.

The True Inversion of Degenerates or Uranism.

This constitutes the second category, thus called on account of its frequency and on account of the physiological and psychological interest which it presents.

It is more frequently designated by the name of Uranism.

It may be found among all degenerates of every order, from the top to the bottom of the scale of degenerescence.

In what follows we shall only concern ourselves with the inversion of the *superior degenerate*, an inversion which displays itself with *peculiar distinctive* characteristics which make of it a veritable morbid type. This inversion was first discovered by Westphal, on which account some authors are in the habit of denominating it *inversion of the Westphal type.*

It is named Uranism, a term invented by Ulrich, one of the pioneers of inversion, as we have already seen.

Uranism and its Different Degrees.

We shall study the Uranism of the man conjointly with that of the woman. It does not appear to us to be advantageous to give a separate description of it, although at first sight this would seem to be more convenient.

It appears to us, on the other hand, indispensable to follow a classification allowing us to group together the similar cases and to deduce our conclusions from them. Of all the classifications that of Krafft Ebing is the most logical, for this author has made the greatest researches into Uranism. This takes nothing from the value of Dr. Legrain's criticisms, but we shall make use of the classification of the learned Viennese and we shall parallel our personal observations with his. We shall only meet with a difficulting in making our selection.

Division of True Inversion into Acquired Homosexuality and Congenital Homosexuality.

These are the two great divisions established by Krafft Ebing, each of them allowing of four different degrees, as we have seen above in analyzing this author's classification. Let us accept them and view them in succession.

Following the order established by the learned Viennese who proceeds from the simple to the complex, we find in the first place as the first stage of homosexuality, what he names the simple inversion of the sexual sense.

Acquired Homosexuality.

First Degree. Simple Inversion of the Sexual Sense.

This degree is reached, Krafft Ebing says, when a person of the same sex produces an aphrodisiac effect on an individual, and the latter experiences a sexual feeling for the other, but the character and the kind of the feeling remains conformed to the individual's sex. He feels himself to be in an active part, he looks upon his inclination for his own sex as an aberration and seeks eventually for a remedy.

Of the four observations of this case given by Krafft Ebing we only give the first, for this is the one which appears to him completely suitable for showing by a striking instance the persistence of the normal sexual feelings at the beginning of the neurosis.

I am a public official: I was born, as far as I know, of a family exempt from defects: my father died suddenly, my mother is still alive; she is somewhat nervous. One of my sisters for some years past has been excessively religious.

As for myself, I am tall and I have every virile characteristic in my speech, my gait and my bearing. I have had no complaints, except the measles; but, since I was 13 years old, I have suffered from what are called nervous headaches.

My sexual life commenced at the age of 13, by my making the acquaintance of a boy slightly older than myself; it was our common pleasure to tickle our genital parts. At the age of 14, I had my first ejaculation. Led into onanism by two of my school-fellows, I practised it sometimes with them and sometimes in solitude, but always representing in my imagination creatures of the female sex. My *libido sexualis* was very great, and it is the same to-day. Later on, I tried to enter into relations with a maidservant, pretty, tall and with large *mammæ; id solum assecutus sum, ut me præsente superiorem corporis sui partem enudaret mihique concederet os mammasque osculari, dum ipsa penem meum valde erectum in manum suam recepit cumque trivit. Quamquam violentissime coitum rogavi hoc solum concessit ut genitalia ejus tangerem.*

When I became a student at the University, I visited a brothel, and I succeeded in coition without any effort.

But an incident occurred which caused an evolution in me. One evening I was accompanying a friend who was returning home and, as I was rather drunk, I caught hold of his *genitalia* in joke. He did not make much resistance; I then went upstairs with him to his room. We masturbated one another, and we afterwards frequently practised this mutual masturbation; there was also *immissio penis in os* with ejaculation. It is a strange thing that I was not at all fond of this companion, but passionately attached to another whose approach never produced in me the sexual excitation, and, in my ideas, I never placed his person in connection with sexual facts. My visits to the brothel, where I was a welcome client, grew rarer and rarer; I found a compensation at my friend's and I no longer desired any sexual relations with women.

We never practised pederasty; we did not even utter the word. From the commencement of this *liaison* with my friend, I again began to masturbate myself to a still greater extent; naturally the idea of the woman was relegated more and more to the second rank; I only thought of vigorous young men with large members. I especially preferred beardless youths from 16 to 25 years of age, but it was necessary that they should be good-looking and clean. I was particularly excited by young men in corduroy trousers; masons principally produced this impression upon me.

Persons of my own rank did not excite me at all; but, at the sight of a son of the people, vigorous and energetic; I had a very pronounced sexual excitation. Touching his trousers, unfastening them, taking hold of his penis, appeared to me the greatest of pleasures.

My sensibility to feminine charms is somewhat blunted, but, in my sexual intercourse with the woman, especially when she has fine breasts, I always have my powers without having any need to create exciting scenes in my imagination. I have never attempted to seduce to my vile desires a young workman or any member of his class, and I will never do so; but I have often felt a wish for it. Sometimes I fix the image of one of these youths in my mind and masturbate myself at home.

Observations.

Krafft Ebing's first degree of inversion is in our opinion nothing else but the *occasionally* inverted of Laupts and in support of it we give the following observation.

It relates to a naval officer, the transmission of whose disease to his descendants I have related above.

"Lapin" at School, "Loup de Mer" on Board Ship.

X... was a companion of mine at school where he was preparing himself for the examination of the *Ecole Navale*, which he entered when he was 14. He was a handsome dark youth, above the average height, with a bright complexion and glorious dark eyes. He was very salacious, and had masturbated himself, he said, when he was only 8 years old. He had his first ejaculation when he was 12. His genital organs were very developed, especially his penis, which was very long, almost without any prepuce, and entered very easily into erection.

X... often proposed to his companions parties for mutual pollution, and if his pal desired it was in the habit of "drawing his feather," while he masturbated himself. His salacity however was not confined to the man, for once at the *Ecole Navale* he disguised himself on a leave-out day as an apprentice in order that he might go round the sailors' brothels.

Sent as a young midshipman to Cochin China, and

having but little to do on the *lorcha* which he commanded, he bought at first a little Annamite girl aged 14 and warranted to be a virgin. I do not know if she had the whites or if her vulva was two narrow, it happened however in the first days of this ill-assorted union that X... caught his first clap. Furious at this, he sent the girl away and then indulged almost exclusively in coition with *nats* and *boys*. This was the more easy for him as he was detached upon native affairs to inspect the boundaries of Cochin China and Cambodia, under the orders of the principal inspector of Mytho, who was one of the greatest pederasts I have ever known.

From the "drawing of feathers," X... passed to active anal coition, and then one fine day wishing to try for himself what he made others undergo, he proceeded to lend himself to passive coition with a Chinese boy for whom he had a great affection. He came at length to coition with two men, one in front generally a small, slim and beardless *nai*, and another behind, a vigorous native. It was a case of saying with the Colonel of Turcos: "Which of the three was the lewdest?" He carried his lewd behaviour to the length of finding out and inventing positions in which four men could satisfy themselves sexually. He confided all these details to me in a visit which I paid him at his small command at Tan-Lo.

Returning to France in 1870, he nobly did his duty in one of the provincial armies in which as Naval Lieutenant he commanded a company in a battalion of Marine Fusiliers.

While he was still comparatively young he was promoted to the command of a frigate, and distinguished himself in the Tonkin Expedition in 188.. I have stated that he was married and extremely fond of his wife and children. Unfortunately for him his normal love left him when he was on board ship and in the foreign countries to which he was brought in the course of his life as a sailor. He always declared to me that on board ship he never sought for intercourse with a cabin-boy or apprentice as it would have been easy for him to do, for catamites are not lacking on our ships of war. I may say the same *en passant* of all foreign ships of war as well.

Each time he landed, his first care was to search (like Diogenes) for a man, and he would take the first one that he came across, playing indifferently the active or the passive part according to the virile qualities of his companion.

He was fully aware of the objectionable nature of his conduct and had for a long time made vain efforts to resist his passion. He only succeeded during the too short sojourns which he made in France in the bosom of his family.

Played an evil turn by one of his enemies who had been able to discover the secret of his vice, and aware that he was in the bad books of one of the chiefs in the Ministry of Marine with whom he had formerly copulated in one of his voyages, he retired as soon as he was entitled to do so, in full maturity of body and mind. He was very brave under fire, gifted with considerable coolness, and passed for an accomplished *loup de mer.*

Second Degree. Eviratio et Defeminatio.

This is the same as the preceding case, as we have already remarked, but without revolt of the conscience and with aggravation of the progressive transformation of ideas, tastes and feelings in conformity with the characteristics of the new sex which the patient finally attributes to himself through the fact that he has been attracted by an individual of his own sex. He has then no taste except for the part of his new sex, that is to say he becomes passive if he is normally a man and active if he is normally a woman.

Krafft quotes only one observation which is absolutely conclusive and which furnishes a classical instance of a sexual inversion acquired in this way and then become permanent. We will give a summary of it.

Sch..., aged 30, a physician, imparted to me one

day his biography and the history of his disease, requesting information and advice from me regarding certain anomalies of his *sexual life*.

The issue of healthy parents, I was a weakly child, but I throve well owing to the care which was taken of me, and I made rapid progress at school.

When I was 11 years old, I was led into masturbation by a companion with whom I was playing: I indulged in these practices with passion. Up to the age of 15, I had no difficulty in learning. In proportion as the pollutions became more frequent, my power for work and study grew less. I was no longer able to follow my school lessons with the same facility. When the Professor called me up to his desk I was uncomfortable; I felt oppressed and embarrassed. Alarmed at seeing my faculties decaying and recognizing the fact that the great losses of sperm were the cause of it, I gave up onanism; pollutions however were frequent, so that I ejaculated two or three times in a night.

In despair, I consulted several physicians one after the other. None of them could do anything.

As I grew weaker and weaker, enfeebled by the seminal losses, and as the genital instinct tormented me more and more violently, I went to the brothel. But I was unable to satisfy myself there; for, though the sight of a naked woman gave me pleasure, no orgasm or erection was produced, and even manustupration on the part of the puella could not bring about erection.

One evening, when I was at the theatre, I had for my neighbour an elderly gentleman. He paid court to me. I laughed heartily at this sportive old man, and took his jests in good part. *Exopinato genitalia mea prehendit*, *quo facto statim penis meus se erexit.* I was alarmed and asked him to explain what he wanted of me. He declared that he was in love with me. As in my clinical studies I had heard hermaphrodites spoken of, I believed that I had one before me, *curiosus factus genitalia ejus videre volui*. The old man joyfully consented and came with me to a water-closet.

Sicuti penem maximum ejus erectum adspexi, per territus effugi.

The other followed me about and made strange proposals to me which I did not understand and which I rejected. He would not leave me alone, and I was instructed in the mysteries of homosexual love and felt how greatly my sensuality became excited by it; but I resisted such a shameful passion (according to my ideas at that time) and I remained exempt from it for three years following this incident. During this time I made several attempts but in vain to have connection with girls. My efforts to cure my impotence by medical art did not meet with any more success.

One day when I was tormented anew by the *libido sexualis*, I remembered my conversation with the old gentleman and his telling me that the homosexuals met one another on the promenade.

It was not without a long struggle with myself and a beating at my heart that I went to the spot indicated; I made acquaintance with a fair gentleman and allowed him to seduce me. The first step was taken. This kind of sexual love was adequate for me, and what I loved the most was to be in the arms of a vigorous man.

The satisfaction consisted in mutual manustupration, and occasionally in *osculum ad penem alterius*. I had just reached the age of 23. The mere fact of sitting beside my colleagues in the lecture hall or on the patients' beds in the hospital, excited me so violently that I could hardly follow the Professor's lecture. In the same year I formed a veritable love-attachment with a merchant aged 34. We lived together as husband and wife. X... wished to play the part of the man and became more and more fond of it. I allowed him to do so, but he had to let me play the part of the man from time to time. In course of time I grew tired of him, I became unfaithful and he became jealous. There were terrible scenes, temporary reconciliations and finally a definitive rupture; (the merchant was afterwards seized with mental alienation and ended his days by suicide.)

I made numerous acquaintances, being fond of the commonest people. I preferred those who were bearded, tall, middle-aged, and capable of playing the active part well.

Later on, I fell in love with a public official, 40 years of age, and remained faithful to him for a year. We lived together like a loving couple. I was the woman and as such was petted by my lover. One day I was transferred to a small town. We were in despair. *Per totam noctem postremam nos vicissim osculati et amplexati sumus.*

At T... I was very unhappy, in spite of several "sisters" whom I met there. In order to appease the grossly sexual inclination which unceasingly demanded satisfaction, I made choice of some troopers. These men did everything for money; but they remained cold and I had no pleasure with them. I succeeded in getting transferred again to the capital. I had a fresh love affair, but there were many scenes of jealousy, for my lover liked to frequent the society of "sisters," he was absurdly vain and coquettish. There was a rupture between us.

I was intensely unhappy and in consequence was very content to be able to quit the capital again by having myself transferred to a small garrison town. At C... I was solitary and inconsolable. I gave my lesson to two privates in the infantry, but the result was as unsatisfactory as before. When shall I meet with the true love again?

I am a little above the ordinary height and physically well developed; I have a somewhat worn-out appearance, and for that reason, when I want to make a conquest, I am obliged to have recourse to the artifices of the toilette. My bearing, gestures and voice are manly. Physically, I feel as young as a youth of 20. I am fond of the theatre and the arts in general. At the theatre my attention is attracted principally by the actresses whose every movement and the very folds of whose dresses I remark and criticize.

In the company of men I am timid and embarrassed;

in the society of people of my own kind, I am exceedingly lively and full of wit; I can be as wheedling as a cat if the man is sympathetic to me. When I am loveless, I fall into a very deep melancholy, which vanishes away before the consolations offered me by a handsome man. As for the rest, I am very flighty and have no kind of ambition. My rank in the Army has no interest for me. Manly occupations are not agreeable to me. What I like to do best is to read novels, go to the theatre, etc. I am sensitive, gentle, easily affected and as easily offended, and nervous. A sudden noise makes my whole body tremble, and I am then forced to restrain myself from crying out.

This is evidently a case of acquired sexual inversion, for the feeling and the genital inclination were at first directed towards the woman. Through masturbation Sch . . . became neurasthenic. As a partial phenomenon of the neurasthenic neurosis, a diminution was produced of the power of the centre of erection and thus of a relative impotence. The feeling for the other sex cooled at the same time as the *libido sexualis* continued to exist. The acquired inversion must be morbid, for the first touch by a person of the same sex already constitutes an adequate charm for the centre of erection of the individual in question. The perversion of the sexual feelings become pronounced. At the commencement, Sch . . . stills retains the part of the man during the sexual act; in the course of these practices, these sexual feelings and inclinations are transformed, as is the rule in the case of the congenital Uranist.

This eviration causes a desire for the passive part and later on for (passive) pederasty. The eviration extends also to the character of the individual which becomes feminine. Sch . . . prefers the company of real women; he has a growing taste for feminine occupations; he even has recourse to paint and to the artifices of the toilette to restore his faded "charms," and in order to be able to make "conquests." (Krafft Ebing.)

The Disease of the Scythians.

In the Caucasus (*vide* Moulyet, Moreau, Esquirol, Morel, Luys and Azam) individuals exist who lose the attributes of virility before they reach old age: their beard falls off, their genital organs become atrophied, their sexual appetites disappear, the voice grows weak, the body loses its force and energy, and at length they come to such a condition that they assume the feminine costume and devote themselves to the ordinary occupations of women. Herodotus and Hippocrates have spoken of this disease. According to Herodotus it was a disease inflicted on the Scythians by Venus for having pillaged the temple of Ascalon. Hippocrates says that these impotent Scythians were called *anandres* and he attributes this condition to their habits of riding carried to excess. According to Allemand, the disease results from seminal emissions produced by riding.

The Mujerados of New Mexico.

Hammond (American Journal of Neurology and Psychiatry, August 1882) states that in New Mexico, among the Pueblo Indians who are descended from the Aztecs, individuals exist who are called *mujerados*, that is to say men who have the attributes of the female sex. They have a protuberant abdomen, well developed breasts, flabby limbs of rounded shape, a shrill, weak voice, a smooth pubis, and sunken genital organs. This author describes the cases of two who had remained *mujerados*, one for seven and the other for ten years: both of them were dressed as women and had a completely feminine appearance both in their clothes and without them. Hammond asserts in every Pueblo tribe there exists a *mujerado* who is a very important personage in the religious ceremonies which are performed in spring-time with the greatest secrecy. To form a *mujerado* a very strong man is selected who is submitted to masturbation several times a day and is made to ride on horseback without a saddle almost continually. This causes a very lively excitation of the genital organs which is accompanied by seminal losses; the nutrition of these organs is diminished, they grow smaller and weaker, the desires disappear and impotence is created. Changes in the character are then seen to appear, and a desire to dress as a woman and to engage in feminine occupations, as among the Scythians. Courage and a manly attitude no longer exist. The wife and the children, for those who have them, cease to be under their authority.

The *mujerado* is held in great honour although the men do not keep company with them, and they are only admitted into the society of women. The only difference which exists between these *mujerados* and the *anandres* of the Scythians is that, in the case of the latter, it is only a question of a state produced accidentally by excessive horse-riding, while in the case of the Indians it is a state created intentionally for a religious object. In the two cases the process is the same: masturbation and excessive riding. The masturbation brings on a state of abnormal excitability of the genital organs which prepares them for the involuntary emissions following upon the excessive riding.

Error committed by Krafft Ebing.

We do not very well see how Krafft Ebing can draw from these facts any arguments in favour of his second degree of acquired inversion.

The only observation which he quotes relates to *mentally* diseased individual, an aberrant having woman's tastes, it is true, but possessing a complete sexual organ. He becomes a passive pederast, but, although he does not say so, anal coition must produce erection and ejaculation in him. It is an unanswerable proof of the moral upon the physical.

The Scythian subjects and the *mujerados* are on the contrary *artificial eunuchs*, as we may say. The cruel steel of the castrator has not cut their parts, but a special treatment has atrophied them. In fact, in the two cases quoted by Hammond, the penis and testicles are atrophied, the hair of the beard has fallen off, the voice has lost its full tone and its masculine accent, and the physical force and energy have enormously decreased.

These are all the characteristics of the *acquired* eunuch, castrated after virility, and we refer the reader to the First Volume, in which we have spoken of eunuchs.

These unhappy creatures who are men no longer assume feminine tastes and habits, as we have observed. We have even quoted, from Larrey, a case in which a valiant and courageous soldier, having had his testicles carried away by a bursting shell, a robust and virile man with a black beard, became hairless and puny without courage and without energy.

But there is precisely the influence *of the physical upon the moral*, of the organ-instrument upon the sexual sense, its habitual motive power. This has absolutely nothing in common with the second degree of acquired homosexuality of Krafft Ebing. It is the same thing, if it is not quite the contrary.

Third Degree. Transition towards Paranoical Sexual Metamorphosis.

"We arrive at a second degree of development in the cases where the physical sensations are transformed also in the sense of a *transmutatio sexus*." (Krafft Ebing.)

Krafft Ebing rears the structure of his Third Degree upon a single case, a veritable autobiography, written by the patient himself who, being a doctor, was in a good position to analyze his feelings. This observation which is very interesting and very detailed, occupies no less than 20 pages (in small print) of the Psychopathia of the learned Viennese. On account of its length, we shall only give the most prominent parts of it.

The Doctor changed into a Woman.

The subject, weak and unhealthy from birth, was descended from a family in which psychical and nervous diseases were frequent. In childhood he was calm and docile, he had a lively imagination and feminine tastes.

In his youth he had an extreme pleasure in dressing up as a woman. His manners were those of a little girl and brought upon him the ridicule of his companions. He endured with difficulty his cloth trousers in contact with his genital parts. From the age of 12, when he remained seated for a long time and worked at night, a tickling and burning sensation came over him and a trembling passing from his penis to his *os sacrum*. About the same time he had a very pronounced feeling that he would prefer to be a woman. "I know full well that at that period I should not have feared the knife of the castrator in order that I might attain my object (to be a woman)."

He began to delight in women's society.

At the age of 17, he fell into the society of some dissolute young men, and did as they did. He practised onanism somewhat often; and during this act he figured to himself that he was a man divided in two. "I cannot describe to you my feelings, I believe that they were virile, but mixed with feminine sensations. I remember it is true, that I was tenderly attached to a very handsome friend with black curls and a girl's face, but I believe that I only wished that both of us were girls.

When I was a student at the University, I succeeded once in performing coition: *hoc modo sensi, me libentius sub puella concuisse, et penem meum cum cunno mutatum maluisse*. The girl, to her great astonishment, had to treat me as a girl, which she willingly did; she treated me as though I had had to fill her part. She was still rather simple-minded and did not laugh at me for that.

When I was a student, I was wild at times, but I was fully aware that I assumed that wild air to mask and disguise my real character; I drank, I fought, but I could not however attend the dancing lesson, as I was afraid of betraying myself. I had intimate friendships, but they were without any mental reservation; and what caused me the greatest pleasure was where a friend disguised himself as a woman, or when I could examine the ladies' toilettes at a ball; I had a thorough knowledge of myself, and I began more and more to feel myself a woman.

On account of this unhappy situation I made two attempts at suicide; on one occasion I remained sleepless for a fortnight for no cause; I then had many hallucinations of the sight and hearing at the same time, and I used to speak with the dead as well as the living as an ordinary daily occurrence.

The subject took great pleasure in the society of women and could not endure any gross conversation in their presence. They on their part treated him as a woman disguised as a soldier. The first time on which he put on his uniform as army surgeon, he would have much preferred to don a woman's dress and veil.

Riding a horse in the ordinary way fatigued him greatly, for his genital parts transmitted feminine sensations to him. He was compelled to marry owing to family matters and in the interests of his medical profession. But he loved his fiancée as a woman loves her sweetheart. "From my wedding-night, I felt that I should only perform my marital duties like a woman endowed with a masculine conformation: *sub feminâ locum meum esse visum est.* Nevertheless he had several children. In coition, the position of the man on the woman was repugnant to him, and it was difficult for him to conform to it. He would have preferred the other part.

He was attacked with gout and became neurasthenic and anæmic. Then he grew arthritic.

While he was having a warm bath, he felt entirely changed and almost dead. "With a final effort I jumped out of the bath, but feeling a woman with the desires of a woman." One evening, being almost poisoned with a strong dose of haschisch, he had a very strange attack of delirium, produced by the drug. "All at once, I saw myself a woman from my feet up to my chest; I felt, as I did before in the bath, that my genital parts had receded into the interior of my body, that my pelvis had enlarged, and my breasts bulged out on my chest; an indescribable feeling of pleasure took possession of me.

"But how can I depict my terror when, the next morning, I wake up feeling myself altogether transformed into a woman, and on perceiving when I was walking or standing upright that I had a vulva and woman's breasts."

After this attack, the subject because an absolute woman in character, and "the idea which possessed me that I was a woman endured and became so strong that to-day I only carry the mask of a man, as for the rest I feel myself a woman from every point of view and in every part; for the moment I have even lost the memory of former days."

We pass over in silence the mournful complaints of the unhappy inverted who analyzes very conscientiously all his feminine sensations, tastes and habits in his daily existence, so that we may concern ourselves with his genital aptitudes alone.

"Perfumes generally have an incredible influence upon the female organism; thus for example I am soothed by the smell of the rose or the violet; other perfumes give me a feeling of nausea; ylang-ylang causes me such a sexual excitation that I am unable to contain myself. Contact with a woman appears to me to be homogenous. Coition with a woman is not possible for me unless she is slightly older than myself with a harder skin, and in any case it is an *amor lesbicus*. However I feel myself to be always passive.

"One of the friends of my youth has felt like a girl ever since his childhood; but he has an affection for the masculine sex; in the case of his sister it was the opposite; but when the uterus demanded its rights in any case and she saw herself to be a loving woman in spite of her masculine character, she solved the difficulty by committing suicide.

"I give herewith the principal changes which I have

observed in myself since my effemination has become complete:

"1. The constant feeling of being a woman from head to foot.

"2. The constant feeling of having feminine genital parts.

"3. The periodicity of the molimen every four weeks.

"4. The feminine lubricity which periodically shows itself, but without my having a preference for any man.

"5. Passive feminine sensation during coition.

"6. Then a sensation of the part.

"7. Feminine sensation in the presence of pictures representing coition.

"8. Feeling of similarity at the sight of women and of feminine interest in them.

"9. Feminine interest at the sight of gentlemen.

"10. It is the same at the sight of children.

"11. Changed humour,—a greater patience.

"12. Lastly, resignation to my lot, resignation which, it is true, I only own to positive religion; without that I should have already committed suicide a long time ago."

Epicrisis. The patient, with numerous hereditary defects, is originally abnormal from the psycho-sexual point of view, for during the sexual act he has a characteristic feminine sensation. This abnormal sensation remained purely a psychical anomaly until three years ago, an anomaly based upon serious neurasthenia, and powerfully accentuated by physical sensation in the sense of a *transmutatio sexualis*, sensations suggested to his consciousness by obsession. The patient, to his great alarm, then feels himself physically a woman, he believes that he experiences a complete metamorphosis of his former thoughts, feelings and aspirations, and even of his *vita sexualis* in the sense of an eviration. His "ego" however is capable of retaining its empire over these morbid processus of the mind and body, and of saving him from *paranoia*. This is a remarkable example of sensations and of obsessing ideas based upon nervous defects, a case of great value for arriving at the study of how psycho-sexual transformation can be accomplished." (Krafft Ebing. *op. cit.*)

Fourth Degree. Paranoical Sexual Transformation.

Here the transformation is complete. The patient believes himself to be really of the opposite sex, and he has not only the mental condition but also the material sensations of that sex.

For reality the 3rd and 4th degrees form only one, that of the third degree being a case of the 4th degree not having completed its evolution. If it had not been given by a medical man who wrote the history of his life, and if it had been the case of an ordinary patient, in whom the sexual metamorphosis would not have been recognized until the final stage, the 3rd degree would not even have had the single observation given by Krafft Ebing upon which to found its existence.

We give a summary of the following case observed in the Illenon Asylum: "a manifest instance of lasting and maniacal inversion of the sexual consciousness," as Krafft Ebing declares.

N..., 23 years of age, a pianist, was received into the Illenon Asylum towards the end of the month of October, 1865. He was born of a tuberculous family. The patient when a child was weak and of limited intelligence, but had an exclusive talent for music. He was always of an abnormal character, taciturn, reserved, unsociable and with uncouth manners.

From his 15th year, he indulged in masturbation, and a few years later he became neurasthenic and hypochondriacal. He then fell in love with an actress but began to be affected with the mania of persecution which necessitated his entering the hospital. At his entrance he still displayed the typical image of persecution together with symptoms of sexual neurasthenia which later on became general: but his monomania of persecution was in no way founded on this nervous basis.

Between the years 1866—68, the mania of persecution was relegated more and more to the second rank and was replaced to a great degree by erotic ideas. The somatico-physical basis was a violent and continual excitation of the sexual sphere. The patient became enamoured of every lady whom he saw; he heard voices which encouraged him to approach them; he demanded imperiously that they should agree to marriage, and declared that if a wife was not procured for him he would die of consumption. Thanks to his continual practice of masturbation, the signs of an approaching eviration showed themselves already in 1869. He said that if a wife were given to him, he would only love her "platonically." The patient becomes more and more eccentric, he only lives in a sphere of erotic ideas, sees prostitution going on everywhere in the Asylum, and hears voices here and there which accuse him of having an indecent attitude before women. He therefore avoids the society of ladies, and consents to play before them only on condition that he has two men as witnesses.

Commencing from the month of August 1872, the signs of eviration become more and more numerous. He behaves with great affectation and declares that he could not live among men who drink and smoke. He thinks and feels just like a woman. He must be treated henceforth as a woman, and be placed in the women's side of the building. He asks for jams and little cakes. Seized with tenesmus and spasm of the bladder he asks to be taken away to a lying-in hospital, and to be treated as a patient who is pregnant. The morbid magnetism of the men who attend to him has a hurtful action upon him.

At transitory moments, he still feels himself a man, but he argues in a very significant manner for his inverted, morbid sexual sense; he wants satisfaction by masturbation, marriage without coition. Marriage is an institution of pleasure: the girl whom he marries must be an onanist.

Beginning from the month of December 1872, the

consciousness of his personality is definitively transformed into a feminine consciousness. He has always been a woman, but, when he was between one and three years old, a quack, a French charlatan grafted masculine genital parts upon him and prevented the development of his breasts by rubbing and preparing his thorax.

He demands energetically to be confined in the women's section, to be protected against the men who wish to prostitute him and to be dressed as a woman. Eventually he would be disposed to occupy himself in a children's doll shop, in cutting out patterns, or in working for a milliner. From the moment of the *transformatio sexus*, a new era begins for him. In his recollections he looks upon his former individuality as that of a cousin of his.

For the moment, he speaks of himself in the third person; he declares that he is the Comtesse V..., the Empress Eugénie's dearest friend, asks for perfumes, corsets, etc. He takes the other men in the Asylum for women, tries to plait his hair, asks for an Oriental cosmetie for epilation, in order that there may be no doubt about his sex as a woman. He likes to make apologies for onanism, for "he was an onanist ever since the age of 15, and has never sought for satisfactions of another kind." Occasionally neurasthenic uneasiness, olfactory hallucinations and ideas of persecution are still to be observed in him. All the facts of his life which passed up to December 1892, revert to the personality of his cousin.

The patient cannot be dissuaded from his fixed idea that he is the Comtesse V... He declares that he has been examined by the midwife who established the fact of his feminine sex. Not being able to obtain feminine garments, he remains all the day in bed, pretends to be modest and unwell, arranges his hair in plaits and pulls out the hair of his beard.

He died in 1894. His cranium was normal, the frontal lobe was atrophied, the brain anæmiated. The genital parts were very large, the testicles small and flaccid. (Krafft Ebing.)

Mixed Cases outside all Classifications.

We have followed Krafft Ebing's classification for the necessary setting-forth of facts, without hiding from ourselves that like all classifications whatever they may be, it was unable to include or rather to unite the whole number of cases which may appear. Every classification of groups and species founded upon objective characteristics which have no organic basis necessarily entails something conventional and artificial.

Observation by Dr. E. Laurent.

Chevalier quotes the following observation which he borrows from Dr. Laurent and which we reproduce in our turn:

C..., detained in the Prison de la Santé; forty years of age; born in Paris. Slightly epileptic; mother violent; aunt a lunatic; cousin a lunatic. Has had convulsions in infancy; began to walk and talk very late; has never learnt to read.

Was a cow-boy. Haughty, mischievous, violent, unmanageable. Was engaged as cabin-boy. Has had nervous attacks.

Height: 1 m. 69. A wild-looking face, seeming as if he were 50 years of age. Tremblings of the hands and limbs preventing sleep. Alcoholic excesses. Constant cephalalgy. Shooting pains between the shoulders.

At times, nocturnal incontinence of urine. Cutaneous anæsthesia. Genital organs normal. No perception of consequence. Incoordination of ideas. Difficulty of speech. Four times condemned for rabbit stealing. Habits of onanism since childhood.

Where he was 13 years old, as he was wandering about without any home and starving in the streets of Paris, he was met by a stranger who under pretext of taking him into his service, took him home and abused him. He remained this man's lover for ten years.

Later became a pederast by inclination, paid for favours instead of being paid. Then ceased to work:

lived by robbery and prostitution; grew celebrated in the world of pederasty: lived maritally with several individuals, with the Arab "Bec de Gaz" and then with a waiter at a café calling himself Loupat!

In prison he appeared repugnant, old, used-up and blear-eyed. His passion continues; he implores and begs for the caresses of his fellow-prisoners. Assumes a soft voice, copies women's manners, seeks for provocating attitudes. Loves virile, well-made men.

During his sojourn in the Infirmary, commits numerous eccentricities, drinks his urine, strikes with a probe a fellow-patient who refused his caresses and called him a whore. A short time after his release was arrested for brawling in a low tavern. (Dr. E. Laurent. *Les Habitués des Prisons de Paris.* Lyon, Storck. 1890.)

Latent Inversion.

This example appears to me typical as escaping a classification which is merely schematic, clinical or based upon the psychological symptoms.

As regards Chevalier, the subject is an hereditary who becomes a pederast by profession, then a pederast by inclination and finds at length the Eden of his dreams.

Krafft Ebing would probably place him, with Chevalier, in the group of pederasts.

Laupts would see in him an occasionally inverted.

None of these appears to us to be an exact method of classifying him, and it cannot at all be said that the subject is a pederast. No doubt he began for money's sake to satisfy a man's wants. Be it so! But in what manner did he perform his office? Was he the fellator, or did his master make him undergo that treatment? In anal coition, was he active or passive? These are questions which remain without any answer, and the observation of the subject being incomplete, the basis is wanting.

Let us remark his heredity. His relatives were epileptics or lunatics. He was therefore a degenerate in the full acceptation of the terms, very probably slightly idiotic as he was unable to learn to read. His character was cunning below the surface.

What was his childhood? All that we know is that he acquired at an early period the habit of onanism in which he must have indulged while watching his cows.

Did he, while quite a boy, have sexual relations with other young rogues of his own age? Did he masturbate himself with them in common? This is very probable, but we know nothing about it. He must however have committed some misdeed since he was engaged as a cabin-boy. Certainly on board ship he must have contracted habits of inversion with the sailors. Cabin-boys indulge freely in this in sight of the immensity of the ocean, and many sailors avail themselves of their services, if not for anal coition, at all events for being masturbated. He was dismissed from the navy, perhaps on account of his anti-physical habits.

At Paris he found an inverted, followed and began to practise with him probably the whole scale of anti-sexual habits. But it is exceedingly probable that he knew it before and had no repugnance to lending himself to it. In any case, the field was admirably prepared and the seed of the evil weed germinated in a rich soil.

He was not therefore a pederast but an inverted. But I shall not place him among the *occasionally inverted* of Laupts, nor among the *acquired inverted* of Krafft Ebing. I shall form a special category for him and I shall say that he was a *latent inverted.*

I can quote another case of this kind, a personal observation relating to a marine infantryman, formerly a goat-herd.

The Sailor who practised Bestiality, was a Latent Inverted and a Sadist.

Joseph E..., 24 years of age, cook to a Captain in New Caledonia, was surprised by his superior officer while in the act of amusing himself with a hired native of the New Hebrides, belonging to a colonist who lived near the Captain. The latter agreed to bring him before the Council of War on the complaint of the aforesaid neighbour.

Physical Examination. A vigorous subject, 1 m. 68 in height. Broad shoulders, back arched, high-coloured complexion, brown skin, very dark eyes and hair. Few hairs on his body except on the pubis which is well furnished. Short moustache on his lip. Genital parts very developed. Penis long and thick; when it is not in erection the gland is half shown. When in erection, the prepuce which is short comes together behind the crown of the gland which is very developed and of a diameter superior to that of the body of the penis. Testicles very large. The subject however has a soft and feminine voice, corresponding to the quasi-smoothness of his face.

When interrogated, Joseph E... declares that his mother suffered from epilepsy; that his father drank a great deal; and that one of his brothers had been certified as unfit for military service by the Board of Examination as an imbecile and weak-minded. He himself tried to be certified as unfit for the same reason, but was passed for the service on account of his drawing a number which relegated him to the navy.

He was born in a village of the Cevennes above Lodève (Hérault), and herded goats together with his brother the imbecile, who was a year older, until he was 15 years old. He used to pollute himself with his brother, and even went so far as to practise anal coition with him, and when his brother left him made use of the she-goats in order to satisfy himself. He practised anal and not vulvary coition upon them, and derived much pleasure from it. He also amused himself with his dog, masturbated it and endeavoured in vain to make the animal cover him. "He used to mount me very well when I had well masturbated him, but he got off again directly without doing anything." (*sic*) His master dismissed him for half-killing the he-goat which disturbed him when he was mounting the she-goats. (*sic*)

He then became a farm-servant and afterwards a waiter in a brothel at Montpellier. He had relations with the women of the house, but did not much care for it, and preferred anal coition with old debauchees who ask in these houses to have connection with a man and a woman at the same time: it was indifferent whether he played the active or the passive part at the wish of the client. With women he preferred the anus to the vulva and always in the first place asked for the former, and found a large number to whom this gave pleasure. (*sic*)

He then enlisted as a soldier in the 10th Regiment at Toulon and had sexual relations with old soldiers who had returned from Tonquin and Cochin China. He wanted to go out to one of these two colonies where the men have hair like women and are *very nice* (*sic*). He was employed in the canteen by favour of the adjutant who had culpable relations with him. There he learnt how to cook, but was dismissed by the head of the canteen who caught him masturbating himself with another lad. No fuss however was made about the matter as the head of the canteen did not wish to have any trouble with the Colonel who was somewhat of a martinet.

He sailed from Brest for Noumea in the sailing-transport Navarin, which took 145 days in the voyage, and while on board was employed by the purser to wait on the second-class passengers. During the voyage he had plenty of amusement with the sailors and apprentices whom he managed to bring at night into the passengers' dining-saloon where he slept, in order to keep watch over the sideboard where the absinthe and liqueurs were kept.

At Noumea he was employed in the company's kitchen, and then as cook to Captain P. . . . who, it appeared, was fond of well-made youths. He cynically declared that the Captain would not dare to bring him before the Council of War, as he was no better than himself, and that if he did, he would tell everything.

And in fact he was only sent off by the Captain

to a post in the New Hebrides, from which he came back to me four months after with a terrible attack of fever. He was well cared for in the Hospital by my orders and gratefully accepted the small presents of fruit, tobacco, etc. There was a complete absence of moral sense in him, as it is easy to see. The subject gave me most valuable details about the sensations of active as well as passive pederasty, and these details find their place in the chapter relating to pederasty.

This is not all yet. In addition to his complete blemishes of inversion Joseph E... possesses that of Sadism also. He confessed to me, in fact, one evening where I had made him drink a little more than usual the day before he returned to France (he was there under observation at the Infirmary as a convalescent to be sent home, having left the Hospital two days previously) that he had always liked hurting animals. Having made his dog have connection with a bitch belonging to another blackguard like himself, while the two animals were stuck together (*sic*) he had closely tied up his dog's jaws with a strap going twice round its muzzle and neck; then while his accomplice held the animal by its ears, he had quickly passed a small piece of twine tightly drawn round the root of the dog's penis and tied it in a strong knot. After playing this cruel trick, he was much amused at seeing the contorsions of the two unhappy animals, which were not able to separate. At length, after considerable efforts, the dog (the ligature at the base of its penis preventing the return of the blood from the veins and consequently also preventing the diminution of the size of the penial bone) got away by turning the bitch's — completely inside out, which hung outside all covered with blood like a piece of the bowels.

When I asked him if he had ever had an idea of committing similar acts of cruelty upon men, he coolly replied: "Yes; but I was too much afraid of being caught and hung. Ah! for instance, if I had gone to Tonkin. I should have done what I was told at Toulon the sergeant did. It seems that when the Tirailleurs caught a Chinaman on a reconnoitring expedition, they used to abuse the man before they killed him. For my part I should have asked him to do so to me, and just when he was enjoying it I should have cut off his —." (We have already quoted the case of this sergeant in the chapter on Sadism.)

When Joseph, in his capacity as cook used to kill a fowl or a rabbit, he had terrible erections. "When it was a male, I used to cut off his testicles and used to go and masturbate myself in a corner of the garden while I ate them." All this was told to me with the greatest coolness and related as if it were a matter of no consequence. *In vino veritas.*

The subject had never been attacked with epilepsy like his mother, but he has had attacks during which he displayed a bad disposition and was very irritable. In the regiment he had the reputation of being a troublesome fellow and was feared on account of his physical strength.

In the case of this man the blemish was of a nervous nature, his physical organisation was very robust and his sexual capacity very great.

The picture, as may be observed is complete. Joseph E... was at the same time an onanist, an inverted, an active and passive pederast, a Sadist with animals and also guilty of bestiality. He was not a Sadist with men owing to lack of courage. His case is identical with that of the sergeant with which we are already acquainted.

In what category from the point of view of inversion ought we to place him? He was not an innate inverted, nor an acquired, the perversion being already developed *before* the subject had coition with woman. Homosexual at first, he then became heterosexual, afterwards reverting to his original inclinations. It is therefore a mixed case and I shall classify him among the *latent inverted*, the same as E. Laurent's subject.

I have hesitated for a long time to relate such aberrations as these, but I am inspired with the declaration of principles which I made in the Preface to another Volume: *let knowledge prevail.*

Genital Perversions. *(Continued.)*

CHAPTER III.

Congenital Homosexuality and its Classification.

The Homosexual Sense as a Morbid and Congenital Phenomenon.—General and Distinctive Characteristics of Congenital Sexual Inversion.—Krafft Ebing's Classification generally accepted.—First Degree. Psychical Hermaphrodism.—Observations relating to Cases of Psychical Hermaphrodism.—Second Degree. Homosexuals or Uranists.—Observations relating to Cases of Uranism.—Mixed Case.—Uranist, Bestialist and Necrophilist.—Third Degree. Effemination and Viraginity.—Observations of Cases of Effemination and Viraginity.—The effeminated Magistrate or the Dangers of an Amorous Correspondence.—Fourth Degree. Androgynia and Gynandria.—Dr. Legrain's theories on the inverted of this Group and Hermaphrodism.—Cases of Androgynia.—Count of Sandor, or a Gynander married to another woman.—History of a born-inverted by Legrain.—Inferences and Lessons which he draws from it.

In our study of congenital homosexuality, we shall continue to follow Krafft Ebing's classification, making use of his most interesting observations, and following them up by personal observations which cannot be included in any of the divisions proposed by Krafft

Ebing, thus affording a fresh proof of the artificial character of any classification.

General and Distinctive Characteristics of Congenital Sexual Inversion.

Westphal leaves it undecided whether sexual inversion is a symptom of a neuropathic or of a psychopathic condition, or whether it constitutes an isolated phenomenon. He holds fast to the opinion that the condition is congenital.

From the cases published up to 1877, I have designated this peculiar sexual feeling as a functional sign of degenerescence, and as a partial manifestation of a neuro-psycho-pathological state, in most cases hereditary. This supposition has been confirmed by the analysis of cases which have occurred subsequently. We may give the following points as symptoms of this neuro-psycho-pathological taint.

1. The sexual life of individuals thus organized manifests itself, as a rule, abnormally early, and thereafter with abnormal power. Not unfrequently yet other perverse manifestations are displayed besides the abnormal method of sexual satisfaction, which in itself is conditioned by the peculiar sexual feeling.

2. The psychical love of these individuals is often romantic and exalted; just in the same way as their genital instinct is manifested in their consciousness, with a strange, and even possessing force.

3. By the side of the functional signs of degenerescence attending sexual inversion are found other functional, and in many cases anatomical, evidences of degenerescence.

4. Neuroses (hysteria, neurasthenia, epileptoid states, etc.) co-exist. The existence of temporary or permanent neurasthenia may almost always be proved. As a rule, this is constitutional, having its root in congenital conditions. It is awakened and maintained by masturbation or enforced abstinence.

In male individuals, owing to these practices or to congenital disposition, there is finally *neurasthenia sexualis*, which manifests itself essentially in irritable weakness of the centre of ejaculation. Thus it is explained that, in most of the cases, simply embracing or kissing, or even the mere sight of the loved person, provoke ejaculation. This is frequently accompanied by an abnormally powerful feeling of lustful pleasure, which may be so intense as to suggest a feeling of magnetic currents passing through the body.

5. In the majority of cases, psychical anomalies (brilliant talents for the fair arts, especially for music, poetry, etc.) by the side of weakness of the intellectual powers are present, which may even go as far as pronounced conditions of mental degenerescence, (dementia, moral insanity).

In many Uranists, either temporarily or permanently, insanity of a degenerative character (pathological emotional states, periodical insanity, paranoia, etc.) makes its appearance.

6. In almost all cases where an examination of the physical and mental peculiarities of the ancestors and near relatives has been possible, neuroses, psychoses, degenerative signs, etc., have been found in the families.

The depth of congenital sexual inversion is shown by the fact that the erotic dreams of the male Uranist have only men for their object, and those of the homosexual woman only female individuals.

Krafft Ebing's Classification.

We have seen that Krafft Ebing has divided Homosexuality into four degrees.

1st Degree. Psychical Homosexuality.

2nd Degree. Homosexuality properly so called or Uranism.

3rd Degree. Effemination and Viraginity,

4th Degree. Androgynia and Gynandria.

First Degree. Psychical Homosexuality.

This degree of Inversion is characterized by the fact that, besides a sentiment and a pronounced sexual inclination for individuals of their own sex, there is also an inclination for their own sex, but that the latter is much more feeble than the former and is only manifested episodically, while the homosexual feeling holds the chief rank, and is manifested from the point of view of its duration, its continuity and its intensity as the dominant instinct of the sexual life.

These sexual feelings for the other sex may be consolidated and strengthened by the power of the will, by self-discipline, by moral treatment, by hypnotism, by the improvement of the physical constitution, by the cure of neuroses (neurasthenia), and above all by *abstention from masturbation.*

But if the subject gives way completely to the influence of homosexual feelings, he may there arrive at exclusive and permanent inversion.

On the other hand the æsthetic and ethical taste for persons of the other sex may favour the development of heterosexual feelings.

It is thus possible for the individual, according to the predominance of favourable or unfavourable influences to experience sometimes a heterosexual feeling and sometimes a homosexual feeling.

Krafft Ebing is of opinion that these *blemished hermaphrodites* are not very uncommon, and he believes that as in social life it attracts little or no attention at all, this important group from the practical point of view has hitherto escaped scientific investigation.

He believes that many cases of coldness of the husband or the wife for their partner are probably due to this anomaly. Sexual intercourse with the other sex is possible, although not frequent, and there is no horror of the opposite sex.

"In the state of the first degree, the satisfaction of the homosexual inclination is obtained by passive and mutual onanism, *coitus inter femora.*"

Observations relating to Cases of Psychical Hermaphrodism.

Of Krafft Ebing's six observations we give only

the two most striking, and those in a summary on account of their great development.

Psychical Hermaphrodism in a Lady. Madame M . . ., 44 years of age, is a living example of the fact that in a person of either the male or the female sex, sexual tendencies to inversion may subsist together with a normal sexual life.

This lady's father was very musical, gifted with great artistic talent, led a loose life, was a great admirer of the other sex and uncommonly handsome. He died from dementia in a lunatic asylum, after having had several attacks of apoplexy. Her father's brother was neuropathic; he was a fantastical person, at all times affected with sexual hyperæsthesia. Athough he was married and the father of several married sons, he wanted to carry off Madame M . . . his niece, who was eighteen years old and with whom he was desperately in love. Her father's father was very eccentric; a remarkable artist; he at first studied theology, but, owing to a pressing vocation for the dramatic art, he became an actor and a singer. He committed excesses *in Baccho et Venere;* was extravagant and fond of luxury; he died at the age of 49 of cerebral apoplexy. Her mother's parents died of pulmonary tuberculosis.

Madame M . . .'s eleven brothers and sisters were some of them consumptive and others nervous, all more or less blemished. She had four children, several of them of a very delicate and neuropathic constitution. When she was ten years old, having an idea that her mother did not love her, she one day steeped some matches in coffee and drank the decoction in order to became very ill and by this means to excite her mother's affection.

Puberty began without difficulty at the age of 11. Since that period the menses were regular. Sexuality manifested itself before that time, and, according to the patient's own statements, its promptings have been abnormally intense all her life. The first feelings and promptings were decidedly homosexual. She conceived a passionate but platonic love for a young lady; she wrote verses and sonnets to her, and was perfectly happy if she could admire the "entrancing charms" of her goddess in the bath, or steal a glimpse of her neck, shoulders and breasts while she was dressing. While a young girl, she had actually been in love with Madonnas of Raphael and Guido Reni. For hours together she would run after pretty girls and ladies in the streets, whatever was the weather, admiring their beauty, losing no opportunity to please them, offering them bouquets, etc. The patient declared to me that, until the age of 19, she had absolutely no idea of the difference between the sexes; for she had been brought up as in a cloister by a very prudish aunt, who was an old maid. As a result of this ignorance, the patient became the victim of a man who was passionately in love with her and who induced her to have coition with him. She became the wife of this man, bore one child and lived an "eccentric" sexual life with him. She felt perfectly sattsfied with married intercourse. A few years afterwards she became a widow. Since then, women have again become the object of her affection, primarily, as the patient thinks, from fear of the results of sexual intercourse with men.

When she was 27, she contracted a second marriage with a weakly husband, for whom she had no affection. The patient was three times confined and fulfilled her maternal duties. Her physical health failed, and in the latter years of this married life she had an increasing aversion for her husband, partly due to a sense of his disease, though, at the same time, there was constantly present an intense desire for sexual indulgence.

Three years after the death of her second husband, the patient discovered the fact that her nine-year-old daughter, by her first husband, was given to masturbation, and that she was failing in physical health. The patient referred to the Encyclopedia upon this vice, and could not overcome the impulse to indulge in this practise becoming, in consequence, an onanist.

She is unable to bring herself to give the details of this period of her life. She declares that she was terribly excited sexually and had to send her two daughters away from home to save them from "terrible consequences;" but the two boys she was able to keep with her.

The patient became neurasthenic *ex masturbatione* (spinal irritation, feeling of pressure in head, weariness, lack of mental control, etc.), and at times had dysthymia and painful *tædium vita.* Her sexual feeling would be directed at one time to women, at another to men. She was able to restrain herself, and suffered much from abstinence, especially because, on account of her neurasthenic troubles, she sought to obtain relief in masturbation, though only in case of great necessity. At the present time, though 44 years old and menstruating regularly, she suffers intensely from a passion for a young man whose presence she cannot avoid on account of the exigencies of occupation.

The patient displays nothing remarkable in external appearance. She is gracefully formed, but the muscular system is not strongly developed. The pelvis is, in all respects, that of a female, but the arms and legs are decidedly large and of masculine form. Ladies' shoes do not fit her, but, being unwilling to excite attention, she forces her feet into women's shoes, and they are, therefore, much deformed. The genital parts are developed in a perfectly normal manner and display no other abnormal feature than a *descensus uteri*, with hypertrophy of the vaginal portion. On thorough examination it is seen that the patient is essentially homosexual and that the desire for the other sex is but episodical and sensual. It is true that at the present time she suffers intensely from her sexual inclination for this young man of her acquaintance, but she considers that it is a more refined and elevated pleasure for her to imprint a kiss on the fair round cheek of a young girl. This pleasure is one that she often enjoys, because, she is much beloved as the "dear aunt" by all the "sweet creatures," for she voluntarily does for them the most chivalrous favours, always feeling herself at such times to be a man.

Sexual Inversion with Satisfaction in Hetero-Sexual Intercourse.

M. Z..., aged 36, an independent gentleman, consulted me on account of an anomaly of his sexual feelings, which had become a matter of anxiety to him in connection with an intended marriage. The patient's father was neuropathic, and suffered from nightmare and night-terrors. His grandfather was also neuropathic, and his father's brother an idiot. The patient's mother and her family were healthy and normal mentally. There were three sisters and one brother, the latter being subject to moral insanity. The three sisters are healthy and leading happy married lives.

As a child, the patient was weak, nervous and suffered from night-terrors like his father; but he never had any severe illness except coxitis, as a result of which he limps slightly. Sexual impulses were manifested early. When he was 8 years old, without any teaching, he began to masturbate himself, and from the age of 14 he ejaculated sperm. Mentally he was well endowed, and his principal interest was in art and literature. He was always weak muscularly, and took no interest in boyish sports or later in manly occupations. He felt a certain interest for female *toilettes*, ornaments and occupations. From the age of puberty, the patient noticed in himself an inexplicable inclination for male persons. Youths of the lower classes were especially attractive to him. Men on horseback excited his interest particularly.

Impetu libidinoso saepc affectus est et ad tales homines aversos se premere. Quodsi in turba populi, si occasio fuerit bene successit, voluptate erat perfusus; ab vigesimo secundo anno interdum talis occasionibus semen ejaculavit. Ab hoc tempore idem factum est si quis, qui ipsi placuit, manum ad femora poscurat. Ab hinc metuit ne viris manum adferret. Maximc periculosus sibi homines plcbeios fuscis et adstrictis bracis indutos esse putat. Summum gaudium ei esset si viros tales amplecti et ad se trahere sibi concessum esset; sed patriae mores hoc fieri vetant. Pæderastia ei displacet; magnam voluptatem genitalium virorum adspectus ei affert. Virorum occurentium genitalia adspici semper coactus est.

At the age of 28, the patient was already neurasthenic, probably as a result of excessive masturbation. In order to cure himself of his habit of masturbation and to satisfy his *libido nimia*, he decided to pay a visit to a brothel. He first attempted sexual satisfaction with a woman when he was 21 years of age, after over-indulgence in wine. The beauty of the female form, and female nudity in general, made scarcely any impression upon him. But he was able to perform coition with pleasure and henceforward frequented the brothel regularly, "for purposes of health," as he said.

From this time he took great pleasure in hearing men tell stories of their sexual relations with the other sex. Ideas of flagellation would also come to him while in a brothel, but the retention of such fancies was not essential for the performance of coition. He considers sexual intercourse with prostitutes only as a remedy against the desire for masturbation and men—a kind of safety-value to prevent him from compromising himself with some man.

The patient now desires to marry, but fears that he may have no love for and, consequently, be impotent in intercourse with a decent woman. Hence his scruples and need of medical advice.

The patient is very intelligent and, in all respects of masculine appearance. In dress or manner he displays nothing that would attract attention. His gait and voice are perfectly manly, and so are his skeleton and pelvis. His genital parts are normally developed. The normal growth of hair for a male is abundant. The patient's relatives and friends have no suspicion of his sexual anomalies. In his inverted sexual fancies. he has never felt himself in the rôle of a woman toward a man. For some years he has been entirely free from neurasthenic troubles.

Second Degree. Homosexuals or Uranists.

The patients of this degree have *congenitally* an exclusive sexual feeling and inclination for persons of the same sex; but, contrary to the group which follows, the anomaly of the individuals is confined to the sexual life only. The latter is, in their case, exactly similar to that of normal heterosexual love; but, as it is contrary to the natural sentiment, it becomes a caricature, the more so as these individuals are generally affected with sexual hyperæsthesia and consequently, their love for their own sex is an ardent and ecstatic affection.

The individual, as we have already said, loves the individuals of his own sex with the same feelings and the same varieties and intensities of feeling as a normal creature ought to experience for the opposite sex. But it does not deprive him of his personality, he retains in his attitude the part inherent to his physical sex: he remains a man and consequently active, if a male; she remains a woman and consequently passive, if a female. The heterosexual inversion remains invited to the acts of the genital life alone, that is to say that as regards the other acts of life, the patients remain confined to the attributes of their natural sex.

According to Krafft Ebing there are intermediate cases, forming a transition towards the 3rd group, in the sense that the person imagines, desires or dreams of the sexual part which would correspond to his homosexual feelings, and that he displays incompletely inclinations for the occupations and tendencies of taste which are not conformable to the sex which the individual represents. For certain cases an impression is given that these phenomena have been artificially produced by the influence of education, in others that they represent deeper degenerescencies produced, within the limits of the degree in question by a perverse sexual activity; these latter cases display phenomena of progressive degenerescence analogous to those which we have observed in acquired sexual inversions.

Krafft Ebing offers eight observations of patients of this degree. We shall borrow only the most interesting from him and we shall add thereto four personal observations.

Observations relating to Cases of Uranism.

I am now 40 years old, of a very healthy family,[1] and have always been considered a model of physical and mental strength and energy. I am of a good constitution, but have only a moderate beard, and, with the exception of hair on the *axillæ* and on the *mons veneris*, my body is hairless. A short time after my birth, my penis was already extraordinarily large; at the present time, it measures *in statu erectionis* 24 centimetres in length, and 11 in circumference. I am a skilful rider, athlete and swimmer, and have taken part in two campaigns as an army surgeon. I never experienced any taste for female attire and vocation. Up to the age of puberty, I was shy toward the female sex, and I am so still in the presence of women with whom I have only recently become acquainted.

I have always had an antipathy for dancing. In my eighth year an inclination for my own sex made its appearance. All at once I felt a pleasure in regarding my brother's genital parts. *Fratrem meum juniorem impuli ut alter alterius genitalibus luderet, quibus factis penis meus se erexit.* Later, in bathing with the schoolchildren, the boys excited a lively interest in me, the girls none at all. I had so little interest in them that, as late as my fifteenth year, I believed that they also had a penis. For company with boys like myself, we amused ourselves *vicissim genitalibus nostris ludere.* At the age of eleven and a half, was given a very strict tutor, and after that coul

[1] Later it became known that a near relative died insane, and further, that eight of his brothers and sisters had died of acute or chronic hydrocephalus at ages ranging from one to fifteen.

steal away to my friends but seldom. I learned very easily, but I could not agree with my tutor, and one day when he made it too hard for me, I became furious and struck at him with a knife; I would willingly have killed him, had he not seized my arm. In my thirteenth year, I left my father's house for a similar reason, and wandered about the neighbouring country for six weeks.

I now entered the Gymnasium. At that time I was already sexually developed, and amused myself while bathing with my comrades in the way above mentioned, and later by *imitatio coitus inter femora.* I was then 13 years old. I took absolutely no pleasure with girls. Violent erections caused me to play with my genital parts; and the idea occurred to me of *penem in os recipere,* which I succeeded in doing by bending over. This induced ejaculation. I thus learned masturbation. I was much frightened and looked upon myself as a criminal, and revealed the fact to a fellow pupil aged 16. He enlightened me about it, reassured me and entered into a love-bond with me. We were happy and satisfied ourselves with mutual onanism. Besides this, I also masturbated myself. At the end of two years this union was broken off, but, to this day, when we happen to meet—my friend is a high official—the old fire breaks out afresh.

The time that I passed with my friend H.... was a very happy one, the return of which I would gladly buy with my heart's blood. Life was there a pleasure to me, learning was mere play, and I had a keen enjoyment for everything that was beautiful.

During this time, a physician, a friend of my father's, seduced me by caressing me and practising onanism upon me on the occasion of a visit, and by explaining the sexual act to me. He made me promise never to practise manustupration, since it was injurious to health. He then practised mutual onanism with me, and explained to me that this was the only way in which he could perform the sexual function. He had a horror of women, and therefore had lived unhappily with his wife, then deceased. He gave me a pressing invitation to visit him as often as possible. The physician was a man of fine presence, and the father of two sons aged 14 and 15 respectively, with whom in the following year I entered into love relations similar to those I had with my friend H...

I was ashamed of my unfaithfulness to him, but continued my relations with the physician. He practised mutual onanism with me, showed me our spermatozoa under the microscope, and pornographic works and pictures, which however did not please me, for I had no interest except for male forms. On the occasion of later visits, he asked me to accord him a favour which he had never yet enjoyed, and which he very much desired. Since I loved him, I acquiesced in everything. *Instrumentis anum dilatavit, me paedicavit, dum simul penem meum trivit ita ut eodem tempore dolore et voluptate affectus sim.* After this discovery, I went immediately to my friend H..., believing that this beloved man would give me a still greater pleasure. *Alter alterum paedicavit*, but we were both deceived and did not repeat it; for in the passive part I only felt pain, and in the active I had no pleasure, while mutual onanism gave us both the greatest enjoyment. I allowed myself to be operated upon several times again by the physician, but only from gratitude. Up to the age of 15, I practised passive or mutual onanism with friends.

I had grown tall; all kinds of advances were made to me by women and girls, but I fled from them as Joseph did from Potiphar's wife. At fifteen I came up to the capital. I had but rare opportunities for the satisfaction of my sexual inclinations. On the other hand, I revelled in the sight of pictures and statues of men, aud could not help kissing warmly the beloved statues. The vine-leaves which covered the genital parts were my principal annoyance.

When I was 17, I went to the University. There again I lived two years with H...

When I was seventeen and a half, which in a state

of mild intoxication, I was urged to practise coition with a woman. I forced myself to do so, but as soon as the act was performed I fled from the house, overcome with disgust. Just as after my first active manustupration, I felt as if I had committed a crime. On the occasion of a fresh attempt, while in a sober condition, *puella nuda pulcherrima operante erectio non cvenit;* though the mere sight of a boy or the touch of a man's hand on my thigh, would always throw my penis into a state of violent erection. A short time before, my friend H... had a similar experience. We racked our brains in vain to discover the reason for this. Now I let women alone, and found enjoyment with friends in passive and mutual onanism, among others with the two sons of the physician, who, after my departure, had abused them both by making them commit *pædicatio.*

When I was 19 years old, I made the acquaintance of two genuine Uranists:—

A..., aged 56, of effeminate appearance, beardless, of small endowment mentally, with a very strong sexual instinct which had shown itself abnormally early, had indulged in uranist love since he was six years old. He visited the capital once a month. I was obliged to sleep with him. He was insatiable in mutual onanism, and made me take part in active and passive *pædicatio*, which was an unpleasant part of the bargain for me.

B..., a merchant, of masculine appearance, was as passionate as I was. He knew how to give such a charm to his manipulations on my body that I had to serve him passively in pederasty. He was the only one with whom I ever had any pleasure in passive pederasty. He confessed to me that when he but knew that I was near, he had the most painful erections, and that when I could not serve him, he was compelled to satisfy himself by masturbation.

In spite of these love-affairs, I was clinical assistant in hospital, and was considered to be very zealous and capable in my profession. I naturally searched through the whole range of medical literature for an explanation of my sexual peculiarity. I found it everywhere stigmatized as a crime deserving of punishment, while for my own part I could only regard it as a simple and natural satisfaction of my sexual desires. I was aware that this peculiarity was congenital with me; but, feeling myself to be in antagonism with the whole world, often nigh to insanity and suicide, I sought again and again to satisfy my immense sexual appetite with women. The result was always the same,—either absence of any erection at all, or, when I succeeded in performing the act, disgust and horror of its repetition.

As an army surgeon, I suffered greatly from the sight and touch of thousands of naked male forms. Fortunately, I contracted a love-bond with a lieutenant who shared my sentiments, and I again passed a time of extreme delight.

For love of him I consented to *pædicatio*, for which he greatly longed. We loved one another until his death, which occurred in the battle of Sedan. Since then I have never agreed to active or passive *pædicatio*, although I had many love-affairs, and was a person much sought after.

When I was 23, I set up as a country doctor, and was sought after and esteemed in my profession. During that period, I satisfied myself with boys of fourteen. I interested myself in political affairs and made the clergy my enemies. One of my lovers betrayed me and the clergy denounced me: I was compelled to flee. The legal investigation resulted in my favour. I was able to return, but I was greatly shaken, and when the war broke out in 1870, I went as a soldier, hoping to meet my death. I returned, however, with many distinctions, calm and matured, and I found my only pleasure in earnest professional work. I hoped that the extinction of my excessive genital appetite was near at hand, exhausted as I was by the great hardships of the campaign.

Scarcely had I recovered when the old unbounded

desire returned, and led to fresh unbridled satisfactions. I often examined my conscience, and reproached myself for my inclination which, though reprehensible in the eyes of the world, did not seem so to me.

For a year, by means of the greatest exercise of my will, I abstained; then I went to the capital to force myself to cohabit with a woman. I, who at the sight of the dirtiest stable-lad was seized with the most violent erections, felt scarcely any emotion in the presence of the most beautiful woman. I returned home quite overcome and obtained a young man-servant for my service and at the same time for my sexual satisfaction.

The solitude of a country doctor's life and the longing for children, drove me to marriage; besides, I wanted to make an end of gossip, and I hoped finally to triumph over my fatal inclination.

I knew a young girl full of kindness and affection, of whose love for me I felt convinced. Through the esteem and adoration in which I held my wife, I was able to fulfil my conjugal duties. What facilitated my task was the boyish appearance of my wife. I called her my Raphaël, I stimulated my imagination to summon up images of boys and thus induce erection. My imagination failed after a minute, and with it my erection. I was unable to sleep with my wife. During the last two years, coition has become constantly harder to perform, and we have given it up. My wife is acquainted with my mental condition. Her goodness of heart and her love for me may have induced her to attach no importance to it.

My sexual inclination for my own sex has always remained the same, and unfortunately often compels me to be untrue to my wife.

To this day, the sight of a youth of 16 puts me into a state of violent sexual excitation with troublesome erections, so that I relieve myself by manustupration of the youth or by onanism on myself.

The sufferings I endure are indescribable. *Faute de mieux, uxor mea penem tirit, sed quod mulieris manus magno opere post dimidiam horam adsequitur, pueri manus post nonnulla momenta adsequitur.* And thus I pass my miserable life, a slave of the law and of my duty to my wife!

I have never had any desire for active or passive pederasty. When I have practised or suffered it, it was only from gratitude or desire to please.

The physician to whom I owe the preceding autobiography assures me that he, up to this time, has had sexual intercourse with at least six hundred Uranists. There are many of them still alive and occupying high and respected positions. Only about 10 % of them came later to love women. Another portion did not avoid women, but had more inclination for their own sex; the remainder were exclusively and lastingly Uranists.

The physician asserted that among the six hundred he never found any abnormal conformations of the genital parts, but that he has often been able to remark certain approaches to the female form, as well as incomplete growth of hair, more delicate complexion and higher voice. Development of the mamma was not unfrequent; *affirmat ab 13—15 anno lac in mammis suis habuisse quod amicus H... eruxit.* Only about 10 % of these men showed any taste for feminine occupations. All his friends were affected with an abnormally precocious and strong sexual inclination. The large majority of them felt themselves as the man in their relations with one another, and satisfied themselves by mutual onanism or by manustupration on or by the lover. The greater number were inclined to active pederasty, but very often the fear of the Law or æsthetic feeling against the anus were reasons for the non-performance of the act. Those feeling themselves towards the others as women were few, and the inclination to passive pederasty was very uncommon. (Krafft Ebing.)

We attach great importance to these indications of

the learned Viennese relative to the tastes and resemblances to the female form, for we find part of them in the personal observation which we shall give of a patient whose case lies between the 1st and 2nd group and enters on the domain of pederasty, as we shall see.

I shall complete the study of this group with a personal observation, which is almost an autobiography. The subject is one of my old College companions, a surgeon in the navy, like myself. His observation presents this remarkable feature that it is connected with that of the superior officer of whom we have spoken above. The pair amused themselves together at College and continued their relations afterwards both in France and in the Colonies. But while the one displays a case of intermediate psychical hermaphrodism, the other is a veritable Uranist clearly characterized, with tendencies to Necrophily and Bestiality.

As I have frequently come across these two men since, and kept up a friendship which dates back to our youth, I have been the recipient of very curious confessions and confidences. I am not betraying their confidences, for the initials which I have given are not their own, and it is impossible for anyone, apart from a few intimate friends who shared their tastes, to recognize them.

Mixed Case. Uranist, Bestialist and Necrophilist.

G. . . ., a doctor of medecine, committed suicide when he was 41 years of age. He was born of a tainted family. His father, an English engineer, who came to France at the time of the construction of the first railways, was an intelligent man but of a very eccentric character. He committed suicide when he was 41 years of age, just as his son did at the same age. The subject's mother was Southern by race, and hysterical; her father was an epileptic, and one of her uncles, her father's brother, was a man of very loose character and an alcoholist like his father. A great-uncle on the mother's side was an hermaphrodite.

G.... was very nervous from his childhood and had fits of violent anger. The death of his father, who hung himself like the good Englishman he was, had deeply affected him. He was a quiet child, thoughtful, cold, of lively intelligence, but fantastical, sometimes working incessantly, at others idle as a drone. In his youthful days he took no part in boys' games. He amused himself in preference with feminine occupations and took great delight in dressing his eldest sister's hair.

When he was 14 years old he was sent to a boarding-school. There, he practised mutual onanism, reciprocal labial pollution and anal coition upon those of his fellow-pupils who were willing to allow themselves to be operated upon; but he would never (at least while he was at the school) allow another boy to perform anal coition upon him. It was he who found out the bitch Soumise and performed vaginal coition upon her. He, together with L..., became implicated in an affair of pollution in common with four children, and they were both expelled from the school where they had corrupted a large number of the scholars.

G.... entered the Medical School at Montpellier as a student at the age of 18, and there proceeded to study as a medical student for the Naval branch of the profession at T.... There he again met with L.... and the latter in his confession relates the history of their orgies in common.

What attracted G.... to medical studies was an inclination for men, especially for their genital parts. He had always felt a disgust for women, and it was only the penis of the male which had any attraction for him. He felt an indescribable pleasure in dissecting a man's parts, while he was never able to make up his mind to wield the scalpel upon a woman's corpse. He had quitted the Medical School at Montpellier owing to the corpses of men not being sufficient there, while at T.... the bodies of convicts, sailors and soldiers who died in the Hospital were very numerous.

It was there that I met him again, having myself quitted Paris in order to enter the Naval branch of the Medical Service. Y... had grown into a handsome youth, tall (1 m. 79 c.), a veritable type of the Anglo-Saxon, with red hair, strongly developed muscles, square-built and astonishingly like his father, but, curious to say, with the brown eyes of his mother. There were but few hairs upon his body, the conformation of which was normal. The expression of his face was manly. He wore long and very bushy whiskers. His voice was deep and his genital parts were normally developed. He had the phlegmatic look of an Englishman, but when he grew animated he became as impetuous as a Southerner. In anal coition with a man who pleased him, he almost had crises of epilepsy and gave vent to the cries of a wild beast; he became brutal at the moment of ejaculation and being very strong in his arms, he used to squeeze his partner's sides with such vigour as almost to stop his breathing.

He and L... lived together in a poor little furnished apartment in the sailors' quarter. Both of them, disguised as merchant seamen, used to prowl by night round the Chapeau Rouge quarter (a haunt of prostitutes and filled with sailors' brothels), seeking for some apprentice or young sailor in liquor, whom they would make completely drunk in order to bring him into their lodging, which was converted into a brothel for the occasion. Y... declared that in the case of a man who was dead drunk, anal coition was an easy matter with a little precaution on account of the relaxation of the anal sphincter permitting the introduction of a medium-sized penis, and leaving no physical sign of its passage except by a slight feeling of heaviness and discomfort in the fundament. The man pederated in spite of himself not being aware of the nature of the act committed, could not thus have any suspicions.

Y... besides this had fancies of extraordinary perversity. He introduced into his apartment male genital organs which he had abstracted from the amphitheatre of the Medical School; these he dissected together with L... to whom he acted as Professor. There in the evening after dinner during their excursions in the Chapeau Rouge quarter, they would enter one of the cheap brothels, go upstairs into a woman's room and, while L.. was engaged with the woman, Y... would stuff into the bed testicles, penes and scrotums etc., smeared with red like blood, as though they had been cut off quite recently.

Terrible scenes would occur when an unfortunate client came to sleep with the woman and found such objects as these in the bed. Several unfortunate women were nearly beaten to death by angry clients. Complaints were made by the Police to the Naval Authorities who were obliged to have a watch set on the corpses in the amphitheatre. Y... however was able on one occasion to cut off the whole of the enormous organ of an Arab who died in the convict-prison; he injected an antiseptic liquid into it and sent it by post in a sweetmeat box as a present to the mistress of a Professor of the School of whom he believed he had reason to complain. This occasioned a terrible scandal.

It was owing to his hatred of women that Y... played such jokes as these. He declared that there ought not to be any prostitutes or women of light character, and that we ought only to have relations with women for the sake of the procreation of the species.

He was of uncommon salacity, able to have connection five or six times in a night without fatigue, but the most beautiful woman left him cold and produced no erection in him. When he had intercourse with a woman, in default of a man, he always sodomized her. He would hardly agree to labial pollution from one, and he declared that he was unable to obtain ejaculation without shutting his eyes and picturing to himself that a handsome boy was operating upon him.

He was subject to gloomy moods and thought of

suicide. "I shall die," he would say, "by hanging like my father, and it will be a woman who will cause my death." He did not think what truth there was in this, for in Cochin China, having allowed a prostitute who had refused anal coition and was infected with buccal mucous sores to "draw his feather," he contracted one of those intense attacks of syphilis of which the Annamite race has the privilege—if privilege it be. My poor friend, who for once had relinquished his usual habit, had no chance. He lost half his prepuce and a considerable portion of his gland through a phagedonic chancre. In spite of most careful treatment, the disease followed its course, and tormented by a very serious tertiary syphilis, beset and distracted by ideas of suicide, Y... hung himself like his father when he was 41 years of age.

Death had never had any terrors for him. He had made a passionate study of everything concerning the various means which men have invented to quit this world. He was a necrophile and was fond of following funerals; where he saw a patient he pictured him to himself naked lying on the slabs in the amphitheatre. But it was the man which attracted him and when he was cutting a subject's genital parts, he had terrible erections, and sometimes ejaculated. He confessed to me at Guiana that he made an arrangement with the attendant in the amphitheatre, of whom we have spoken in Chapter II to violate the corpse of a young negro who had died from a sabre-cut received in a conflict with some soldiers and who was still warm.

Third Degree. Effemination and Viraginity. The characteristics of the third degree are in a general way the same as those of the second degree, but with a more pronounced distaste if possible for the heterosexual act and a still more marked inability to accomplish that act. But here, as Thoinot says, "the anomaly is not confined to the sexual sphere alone: *the whole psychical personality and individuality are inverted.*"

Between this and the preceding group there are many intermediate cases which serve as a transition and which are characterized by the degree of influence of the sexual inclination on the psychical personality, especially on the inclinations and the feelings as a whole. In the most advanced cases of this group, men feel themselves to be women in the presence of men, and women feel themselves to be men in the presence of women. And so in his attitude and manners, the patient assumes the character contrary to the sex of which he bears the external attributes; he becomes passive if he is a male and active if a female. This anomaly in the development of the feelings and character often shows itself from childhood. The little boy likes to pass his time in the society of little girls, and takes part in their games and occupations. As he grows older, he delights in women's society and takes no pleasure in sport and manly games.

The counterpart of this is displayed in the little girl who is an Uranist. She is absolutely a little boy spoilt, and loves the society of little boys, shares in their games and tastes, has a hatred of feminine occupations, neglects her toilette and inclines rather to the sciences than to the arts. She occasionally goes so far as to smoke and drink like a man, and she is disconsolate because she is a woman.

A man's soul beneath a woman's breast is betrayed by her Amazonian inclination for manly sports, as well as by acts of courage and and manly feelings. The female Uranist likes to cut her hair short and to dress like a man, and the height of pleasure to her would be to occasionally show herself dressed as a woman. Her ideal is to be found among the female personages of history or among her contemporaries who signalized themselves by their courage and energy. (Krafft Ebing.)

As for the sexual inclinations and feelings of those Uranists whose whole psychical being is equally affected, they are in reality normal and hetero-sexual, since the sex of the patients is inverted. The aberration is no longer the same as in the preceding case in which we saw a man knowing himself to be a man seeking for contact with another man; here, on the contrary, we see a man, believing himself to be a woman seeking *quite naturally* intercourse with another man. They therefore feel the same jealousy which is to be met with in normal sexual life, when their love is menaced with rivalry; this jealousy, according to Krafft Ebing, is often incommensurable with the object, it being granted that the inverted in the majority of cases are sexually hyperæsthetical.

When the inversion is completely developed, hetero-sexual love is impossible for them and an attempt meets with failure owing to the impossibility of erection. Krafft Ebing has pointed out only two subjects, cases of transition between the second and third groups, who were able at times to perform hetero-sexual coition by having recourse to efforts of their imagination and figuring to themselves that the woman they held in their arms was a man. "But this act which was inadequate for them was a great sacrifice and gave them no enjoyment."

Observations of Cases of Effemination and Viraginity.

Krafft Ebing quotes ten different cases, but we shall give only two of them, one for each sex, and we shall add to them a third, a personal observation which enters into considerable detail.

Mlle Z...., aged 31, an artist, comes for consultation on account of neurasthenic symptoms. She is noticeable for her coarse masculine features, for her deep voice, short hair, manly style of dress, masculine gait, and self-consciousness. In other respects she is perfectly feminine, with well-developed mammæ and a female pelvis, and without any indication of beard.

Examination with regard to sexual inversion gives a positive result:—

The patient states that even when a little girl she

preferred to play with boys, and particularly at "soldiers," "merchants," and "robbers." She was very wild and unrestrained in these games with boys, but never had any proclivity for dolls or female employment, of which she learned only the most ordinary things—knitting and sewing.

At school she made good progress, being especially interested in mathematics and chemistry. She displayed at a very early age an inclination for the fine arts and considerable talent. Her highest ambition was to become a great artist. In her dreams of the future she never thought of marriage. As an artist she was interested in handsome forms, but it was only female forms that really attracted her; she saw male forms "in the distance." She could not endure "women's trumpery fashions," and only manly dress pleased her. The ordinary society of girls was repugnant to her, because their conversation turned only upon dress, ornaments and love affairs with men, etc., which seemed to her insipid and tiresome. On the other hand she had had ever since her childhood enthusiastic friendships with certain girls; at the age of ten she was deeply in love with a girl companion and wrote her name everywhere.

Since then she had numerous female friends, upon whom she lavished passionate kisses. She pleased the girls, as a rule, on account of her boyish manners. She addressed poems to her female friends and could have done anything out of love for them. It was very remarkable to her that she felt embarrassed in the presence of girls, especially when they were her friends. She could not undress before them. The more she loved a friend, the more modest she was before her.

At the present time she has such a relation. She kisses and embraces her Laura, walks up and down before her windows, and suffers all the pangs of jealousy, especially when she sees her conversing with men. Her only wish is to live always with this female friend.

The patient states, however, that twice in her life

men have made an impression upon her. She thinks that if she had been really wooed, there would have been a marriage; for she is very fond of family life and children. If a gentleman wished to possess her, it would be necessary for him to win her; she herself would prefer to win a female friend. She thinks that woman is more beautiful and more ideal than man. On the rare occassions when she has erotic dreams, the subject has always been a female. She has never dreamed of men. She does not think that she could now love a man; for men are false, and she herself is nervous and anæmic.

She considers herself a woman in all respects, but regrets that she is not a man. Even at the age of four, her greatest pleasure was to put on boys' clothes. She decidedly had a masculine character and so she had never wept in all her life. Her greatest passion was for riding, gymnastics, fencing and driving. She suffered much because no one about her understood her. It seemed silly to her to talk about feminine matters. Many of her acquaintances thought that she ought to have been born a man.

The patient says that she has never had a sensual temperament. In embracing female friends, she had often felt a curious sensation of pleasure. Embracing and kissing were her only manifestations of friendship.

The patient states that she comes of a nervous father and an insane mother, who, as a young girl, had fallen in love with her own brother and had tried to persuade him to go away with her to America. The patient's brother is a very strange. eccentric man.

The patient displays no external degenerative signs; the skull is normal. She says her menses began when she was 14 years old, and that they have been regular but always painful. (Krafft Ebing.)

Autobiography. In what follows, you will find the description, as well as the mental and sexual disposition of a Uranist, who, in spite of his masculine form, feels just like a woman, and whose senses are only excited by men.

I am 34 years of age; a merchant, with a fair income; somewhat above the average height, slim, weak of muscle, with full beard, and quite an ordinary face, and, at first sight, in no wise different to other men. On the other hand, my gait is feminine, particularly when I am walking fast, and slightly mincing; the movements are awkward and displeasing, indicative of a want of manly feeling. My voice is neither feminine nor shrill, but rather a baritone.

Such is my external appearance.

I do not smoke or drink; I can neither whistle, ride, do gymnastic feats, fence, nor shoot. I have no interest in horses or dogs, and I have never had a gun or sword in my hand. In inner feelings and sexual desires, I am completely a woman. Without any thorough instruction—I passed only five years at the Lycée—I am nevertheless intelligent, like to read well-written, improving books, and have good judgment; but I always allow myself to be carried away by the feelings of the moment, and I am easily influenced by any one who knows my weakness and how to make use of it. I am always forming resolutions without ever finding the energy to carry them out. Like a woman, I am capricious and nervous, often irritated without reason, and sometimes disagreeable to persons whose appearance does not please me, and I am then arrogant, unjust, and often shamefully insulting.

In all my actions and gestures I am superficial, often frivolous, and I have no deep moral feeling. I have little consideration for my parents, brothers and sisters. I am not egotistical, but, on occasion, I am self-sacrificing. I cannot withstand tears, and can—like a woman—be won by amiability and entreaty.

In my earliest years I avoided playing at soldiers, gymnastics, or the rough games of my male companions. I always kept company with little girls, with whom I had more in sympathy than with boys: I was timid, bashful and often blushed. When I was no more than 12 or 13 years old, the close-fitting uniform of a soldier gave me the most peculiar feeling;

and during the next few years, while my companions were always talking about girls, and even engaged in love affairs, I could, for hours at a time, run after a well-built man with well-developed hips, and feast my eyes on the sight.

Without reflecting much on these impressions, so different from the feelings of my companions, I began to masturbate myself, always thinking during the act of men built like heroes and well proportioned. This lasted until my 17th year, when I learned from a companion constituted like myself a true explanation of my condition. Since that time I have been with girls eight or ten times; but, in order to have an erection it was always necessary for me to think of a handsome man of my acquaintance; and I am convinced that to-day, even with the help of imagination, I should be unable to have intercourse with a girl.

Shortly after this discovery, I preferred to associate with vigorous Uranists of full age; for at this time I had neither means nor opportunity to associate with real men. Since then, however, my taste has completely changed, and men, real men, between 25 and 35 years of age, with vigorous and supple forms, are the only ones that excite my senses to the highest degree and charm me as if I were a woman. Circumstances have permitted me, during these years to make about a dozen male acquaintances who would serve my ends for a present of 1 or 2 florins a visit. When I find myself alone in a room with a handsome youth, my great pleasure above all is *membrum ejus vel maxime si magnum et crassum est, manibus capere et apprehendere et premere, turgentes natis femoraque tangere et totum corpus manibus contrectare et, si conseditur, os faciem atque totum corpus, immovero nates, ardentibus osculis obligere. Quodsi membrum magnum purumque est, dominusque ejus mihi placet, ardente libidine mentulam ejus in os meum receptam complures horas sugere possum, neque autem delector, si semen in os meum ejaculatur, cum maxima eorum qui* „Uranist" *nominantur pars hac re non modo delectatur, sed etiam semen nonnunquam devorat.*

I feel, however, the most intense delight when I find a real man *qui membrum meum in os recipit et erectionem in ore suo concedit.*

Improbable as it may appear, I can always find, if I give a little money, smart young fellows who allow this to be done. They learn the thing generally while in military service, for Uranists well know that among soldiers a little money is thought much of; and when they are once trained, circumstances often compel them to continue it, in spite of their passion for the other sex.

Uranists, with some exceptions, make no impression upon me, because everything feminine is repugnant to me in the highest degree. There are, however, some individuals among them who can charm me as much as a real man, and with whom I love still the more to have intercourse because they respond to my burning caresses with equal ardour. When I find myself in company with one of these individuals, I throw all restraint from my excited feelings, and give my animal passions free rein: *osculor, premo, amplector eum, linguam meam in os ejus immitto; ore cupiditate tremente ejus labrum superius sugo, faciem meam ad ejus nates adpono et odore voluptari et natibus emanente voluptate obstupescor.* Real men, in close fitting uniform make the deepest impression on me; and if I have an opportunity to embrace and kiss such a ravishing fellow, ejaculation takes place at once—a weakness which I attribute to my frequent masturbation. For I often masturbated myself in my earlier years, almost every time I saw a man pleasing to me, whose image I kept before me during the act. In this my taste is by no means hard to please,—like that of a servant girl who finds her ideal in a lusty dragoon. A handsome face is in fact a pleasant adjunct, but by no means indispensable to the excitation of my sensual desire; the principal condition is and remains that he should be *vir inferiore corporis parte robusta et bene formosâ, turgidis femoribus durisque natibus,* while the upper part of the body may be slim. Corpulence disgusts me. A sensual mouth with fine teeth keenly excites and stimulates me. If this individual has in addition *membrum pulchrum magnum et aequaliter formatum*, all my requirements—even the most far-reaching—are satisfied.

When I was younger, with men that pleased me and excited my passions intensely, ejaculation took place from five to eight times in a night; even now it takes place from four to six times, for I am excessively lustful and sensual, so that even the clanking of a hussar's sword may cause me emotion. At the same time I have a very lively imagination, and spend most of my leisure hours in thinking of handsome men with strong limbs; and I should be delighted to look on while a powerful fellow *magnâ mentulâ praeditus me praesente puellam futuat; mihi persuasum est, fore ut hoc aspectu sensus mei vehementissima perturbatione afficiantur et dum futuit corpus adolescentis pulchri tangam et si liceat ascendam in eum dum cum puella concumbit atque idem cum eo faciam et membrum meum in ejus anum immittam.* The carrying-out of these cynical ideas—with which my mind is often filled—is hindered only by my limited means, otherwise I should have realized them long ago.

Soldiers have the greatest charm for me, but I have a weakness also for butchers, cabmen, draymen, and circus-riders, provided that they are supple and well-built. Uranists are hateful to me for intimate intercourse, and I have for most of them an unjustifiable aversion which I cannot explain. With a single exception, I have never had intimate relations with any Uranist. On the other hand, the most affectionate and enduring ties bind me to many normal men, in whose society I delight, but with whom I have never had any sexual relations, and who have no idea of my condition.

Conversations on political and economic matters, like any other serious subject, are hateful to me, though I talk with considerable sense and peculiar pleasure about the theatre. At operas I see myself on the stage, feel myself applauded by the public, and would prefer to sing as a passive heroine, or in the dramatic rôle of a woman.

The most interesting subject of conversation, however, for me and those like me, is always men; for us this is an inexhaustible theme. Their most secret charms are there minutely explained, *mentulae aestimantur, quanta sint magnitudine, quanta crassitudine; de forma earum et rigiditate conferimus, alter ab altero cognoscit cujus semen celerius, cujus tardius ejaculatur.* I may add that of my four brothers one allowed himself to be led into Uranist acts, without being one himself; and all four are passionate adorers of the female sex and unceasingly indulge in sexual excesses. The genital parts of the men in our family are, without exception, unusually developed.

In conclusion, I repeat the words with which I began these lines. I could not choose my expressions, because my object has been to afford material for the study of the Uranist's existence, and the absolute truth was essential. Pray excuse them, on this account, the cynicism of these lines.

In October 1890, the writer of the foregoing lines presented himself to me. His appearance in general corresponded with the description he has given of himself. His genital parts are large, with an abundant growth of hair. His parents had been healthy from the nervous point of view; one brother had blown out his brains on account of nervous trouble; three others were intensely nervous. The patient came to me in a state of the greatest despair. He could no longer endure the life he was leading, for he has been reduced to intercourse with venal individuals, and cannot abstain owing to his excessive predisposition to sensuality. Also, he could not understand how he could be made to love women and enjoy the noblest joys of life, for, ever since his 13th year, he had had inclinations for men.

He felt in all respects like a woman and aspires to be won by men who are not Uranists. When he is in company with an Uranist, it is as if two women were together. He would prefer being sexless to leading an existence such as his any longer. Would not castration assist him?

An attempt at hypnosis with the highly excited patient induced only a very slight degree of lethargy. (Krafft Ebing.)

Taylor had to examine a woman called Eliza Edwards, aged 24. The examination revealed the fact that she was of the male sex. Eliza had worn woman's dress our since she was 14 years old; she had also come out on the stage as an actress; she wore her hair long and had a parting in the middle like a woman. The conformation of her face was somewhat feminine; as for the rest of her body she was altogether masculine. She had carefully pulled out the hairs of her beard. The genital parts were virile, vigorous and well developed, and were fixed up with a bandage to the upper part of her belly. An examination of the anus gave indications of the practise of passive sodomy. (Taylor. Medical Jurisprudence, 1873.)

We bring to a close at length the portion which treats upon the third group, with a personal observation, which I consider interesting, on a case of complete effemination with a tendency to physical hermaphrodism.

The Effeminated Magistrate, or the Dangers of an Amorous Correspondence.

This last observation came under my own notice. I consider it to be very suggestive, as it is a fine instance of physical and moral effemination.

In 188.., I was employed in Army Surgical duties in New Caledonia. I was then, for some months, detached for duty to the Isle de Nou, in the Penitentiary Service, as surgeon to the Company of Marine Infantry which was quartered on that island, the principal centre of transportation. I therefore had one foot in the den of the Penitentiary.

The head of the Judicial Department in New Caledonia

was a M. C . . ., a native of Bordeaux, who had been for a long time in the Colonial Magistracy. He was about forty years of age. He was a man above the average height, dark-skinned, with long curling hair and large dark eyes which were soft and expressive. He had the suspicion of a moustache on his upper lip. His feet and hands were remarkably small, and he had largely developed thighs and hips. Looked at from behind he gave from the soles of his feet the idea of a woman dressed in man's clothes. He had a mincing gait when walking just like some women.

In his social relations he was a very amiable man, with a fine and cultivated mind, well acquainted with all branches of literature and with a thorough knowledge of all the Latin authors, especially of Virgil, Ovid, Martial, Suetonius, Petronius, etc. His conversation was very interesting and instructive. He delighted in women's society, would willingly talk to them of fashions and other trifles and gave them judicious advice about their dress. But though he was a bachelor, he was never seen paying court to any woman or girl, and he was never known to have a mistress.

Although there were disagreeable rumours current about him in connection with pederasty, he was esteemed by his colleagues of the Privy Council, and particulary by the Military Commandant, Colonel B . . . He was held in high regard by the Governor of the Colony, L . . ., on account of the good advice he gave regarding local politics. Very clever, very persuasive, of a pliant and conciliatory character, he enjoyed everybody's confidence to some extent. As regards his physical habitus, he was sober and had no taste for alcohol, a few mouthfuls of good wine causing him to become slightly intoxicated. He was as greedy as a cat and adored all kinds of sweetmeats. His character was absolutely feminine and very timid. He could not endure the sight of a drawn sword or cutlass and the report of a gun made him jump and cry out like a woman.

When in the course of the duties of his office he had to conduct an enquiry into a case of murder, he was completely overcome by it beforehand and almost ill, but he declared that the sight of the naked corpse of the murdered man caused him a kind of horrible yet delightful sensation. He would never be present however when a man condemned to death was guillotined. Nevertheless he carried out with firmness his duties as Procureur de la République; but at times he was strangely indulgent to some of the prisoners, particularly to some of the freed convicts who, after their liberation, became amenable to Civil Law.

I had gained his sympathy and I may say his friendship during our voyage together from France to New Caledonia. He had almost continually a terrible headache, such as I have only observed in certain nervous women, and by my assiduous care I was able to relieve it. He was very grateful to me for this.

At Noumea, I often went to see him and sometimes dined with him. He almost always turned the conversation upon Cochin China and the pederastic habits of the *naïs* and *boys.* He also asked of me details regarding the negroes of Senegal, their genital aptitude and the large size of their virile member. I had heard it stated that there was a story about him and a Sergeant of Marine Infantry at Bourbon some years before, that he had been obliged to leave the Colony under plea of ill health. and that, had it not been for the protection of a powerful personage, he might have had to suffer for it. He did not confess his inclinations to me, which however I strongly suspected, until one day he consulted me for some slight ailment of his anus, which he accounted for to me by some ridiculous story.

I subjected him to a close medical examination, and he displayed all the signs of the most inveterate passive pederasty. His genital organs were under the average size. His penis was small and short; in a state of erection it was no larger than a 12 bore cartridge ($6^1/_2$ centimetres in length by 2 in diameter), and had a very pronounced phimosis. It was impossible to uncover it owing to the shortness of the frænum. The scrotum enclosed two testicles, that on the right was small, hardly the size of a large nut, that on the left, as large as a hen's egg, was tumefied and congested. I diagnosed a tertiary syphilitic orchitis of a selerotic form, but the patient would never confess that he had had syphilis. The pubis was covered with abundant black hair, distinctly confined to the triangular space of the pubis, just as it is in women; there were no hairs upon the body. His thighs and calves were large and his hips were excessively developed, but his arms were weak and showed little muscular development. His breasts were prominent and were of the size of an apple. Underneath the fatty panicle, the presence of a glandular body could be detected. Slight general obesity.

The so-called slight ailment was due to an excess of anal coition by a penis of too voluminous a size. After pressing M. C.... with questions he at length confessed to me his mental disease.

From his very earliest childhood, he had felt his to be a feminine mind: passing his time with little girls and playing with dolls with them, he was so pretty with his long curly hair that he was always taken for a girl, and this gave him great pleasure. He had a great taste and disposition for the manual work and occupations of women, used to play at being mistress of the house with his little companions and had a great desire to learn to sew and to do woman's work with one of his cousins about his own age. He wept bitterly when he was obliged to discard his child's dress and to put on trousers when he was four years old.

As soon as he was capable of reflecting and concerning himself about the difference between the sexes, he had a strong desire to be a girl, as long as he remained among them. He was the only boy in a family of six children, and his five sisters, a troop of little girls, were always under the paternal roof. But at a later period when he went to school as a boarder after the death of his mother, he soon found out that he was a man by seeing the genital parts of his companions when they were bathing.

During the holidays, he was always very intimate with his sisters' girl-friends, talked with them as a person of their own sex and got them to teach him crochet and lace work. During one of his holidays, he disguised himself as a girl in one of his sister's dresses, an act which caused him great pleasure. All his life, he had a taste for fine white linen and never went to bed except in a woman's chemise. He took exaggerated care of his hâir and hands.

Sexual inclinations. When he was over 13 and nearly 14 years of age, he attained puberty. The development of his genital glands was disagreeable to him and he tried to prevent their increasing in size by compressing them, but the pain caused him to renounce these attempts. To this he attributed the degenerescence of his left testicle. Since the age of 15, he had nocturnal erections followed by pollutions. *He has never masturbated himself.* On account of his very pronounced phimosis, any touching of his penis when in erection was painful to him and procured him no voluptuous feeling, as it would a normal man. Though he is fond of women's society, has never had the idea of sexual intercourse with them. When he was a law-student, he was sometimes taken to a brothel by his companions. But "the sight of all this flesh exposed as it were in a market, of these naked bosoms and thighs disgusted me deeply. The very idea of wallowing on a woman's belly chilled my virility. The smell and above all the sight of the genital parts of women when having their menses occasioned me nausea. In short, I am still a virgin as regards women, having never been able to make up my mind to copulate with them.

"With regard to men, during the whole time that I was a boarder at College, I kept up the most tender friendships with my companions. I felt happy when I was able to render a service to a little friend. There were several whom I adored, particularly a handsome red-haired boy, with white skin, three years older than myself, who was preparing for the *École Polytechnique.*

His genital organs were greatly developed. We used to write one another love-letters. I really idolized him and would have sacrificed my life for him. I understand feminine devotion in all its grandeur. He was the first to have intercourse with me: he came one night into my bed and lying down behind me on his *me præsente superiorem corporis sui partem enudaret mihique concederet os mammasque osculari, dum ipsa* me. This caused me rather acute pain (in spite of the precautions he took) and at the same time an intensely voluptuous sensation, so that I entered on erection and ejaculated almost at the same time as he did. Up to that time, when we met together, generally in the lavatories of the dormitory, I had been satisfied with *immissio penis in os* with ejaculation.

"Some time afterwards, I learnt from another schoolfellow, that my friend had gone to a brothel and that he had intercourse with women. A terrible scene of jealousy took place between us, and I should have killed him if I had had strength to do so; I threatened to stab him to the heart with a dagger and to kill myself afterwards. I should have done so, had I had the means within my reach. But the little friend who had revealed to me the traitor's infidelity was so pretty, so gentle and so coaxing, that he made me forget the ungrateful wretch. Having begun to amuse myself with him, I soon loved him with a frantic passion. Without this diversion, I believe that I should have committed suicide. He had a smaller penis by half than that of my first lover, and so its intromission only caused me pleasure. He wanted me to do the same to him, but I did not care for that, as its introduction alone almost always made me ejaculate."

I abbreviate the account of M. C...'s adventures which he gave me at length on several occasions. His taste for passive pederasty increased as he grew older. Practising in a large country Circuit, he often met companions who shared his tastes in the sense that they were active *and he was always passive*.

He saw clearly that as a young magistrate in France his vice would be found out. He contrived therefore to be transferred into the Colonial Magistracy, in the first place to India, then to the Antilles and Bourbon, and finally to New Caledonia. In the three first colonies he had had dealings principally with sailors and marines, and had found no difficulty in meeting with what he wanted. Men of the inferior races, such as negroes, Indians or Chinese, left him cold on account of the smoothness of their face. He had all his lifetime liked tall, strong men with large moustaches, with their skin well covered with hair and, above all, with large genital parts.

After his adventure at Bourbon with a sergeant of Marines who had let out his secret in the canteen when he was drunk, he had no more to do with soldiers and selected his lovers in preference from among the liberated convicts under his jurisdiction with whom the duties of his office had brought him into contact. There were some of them of whom he believed himself sure and whom he never saw except without the walls of the town, in a little country-house on the shore of the roadstead.

It was fated that his confidence should cost him dear. The registrar of the 1st Council of War, who had formerly been a sergeant of Marines, was acquainted with the story of M. L. . . . 's adventure at Bourbon. This man having committed certain improprieties had to be dismissed from his employment. He had gained a knowledge of M. C. . . . 's pederastic relations from the liberated convicts who were still under military jurisdiction, and, by some means or other, he obtained possession of some letters from him clearly establishing the nature of these relations.

He blackmailed the unfortunate magistrate, obtained money to indemnify the complainants and compelled him to intercede with the Military Authorities that he might be retained in his employment.

But the registrar wrote articles in the local Opposition paper against the Governor. The latter discovered at length who was the author of these attacks, and took advantage of Colonel B . . ., the Military Commandant departing for France (the Colonel being an opponent of his, who had known and viewed with favour the registrar's attacks on the Governor), to obtain from the *interim* Lt. Colonel the dismissal of the registrar and amateur journalist who had again committed some impropriety.

Inde iræ. The registrar was dismissed and lost his right to a pension, whereupon he founded a weekly paper called the *Lanterne de Nouméa*, issued in a lithographed form, and after an attack upon the Governor, commenced a violent campaign against the unfortunate Head of the Judicial Department, who did not loose his purse-strings quickly enough. He published a very virulent article against him which ended thus: "Yes, Mr. C . . ., the Procureur de la Republique, is a pederast. We shall prove it by the publication of his amatory correspondence which we shall begin next week in the following number!"

M. C . . ., when enjoined by the Governor to put a stop to the scandal raised by the registrar immediately by using all his power as a magistrate insulted in the performance of his duties, could do nothing but groan and utter lamentations, and resolutely refused to take any action against the registrar. He became ill with grief and went into the Marine Hospital, suffering from nervous crises like a woman; he would neither eat nor drink, and wept night and day continually.

It was necessary to send him back to France by the next steamer in order that he might recover his health. As soon as he had landed on his native soil, he sent in his resignation of his post as magistrate and shut himself up, I was informed, in a Convent of Trappists.

Such was the history of this unhappy magistrate, the unfortunate victim of his abnormal sexual conformation, who had done nothing but good and who possessed numerous friends. On the bridge of the steamer which carried him back to France, there were only three of us who came to grasp him by the hand in token of our sympathy for him in his sad adventure. The cowardice of man knows no limits! *Væ Victis!*

Fourth Degree. Androgynia and Gynandria.

Instances in this group are uncommon. I have never observed a single case of it. It is an aggravation of the symptoms of the preceding group. "Not only," says Krafft Ebing, "are the character and all the sensations of the sexual sense coexistent, but also through the conformation of the skeleton, the features, voice, etc. In one word, the individual approaches the opposite sex anatomically, and in more than a psychical and psycho-sexual manner. This anthropological form of the cerebral anomaly apparently represents a very high degree of degeneration; but that this variety is based on an entirely different ground than the teratological manifestation of hermaphrodism, in an anatomical sense, is clearly shown by the fact that thus far, in the domain of sexual inversion, no transitions to hermaphroditic malformation of the genital parts have been observed. The genital parts of these persons always prove to be fully differentiated sexually, though not infrequently there are present anatomical signs of degenerescence (epispadiasis, etc.), in the sense of arrests of development in organs that are otherwise well differentiated from the sexual point of view."

Dr. Legrain's Theories upon the Inverted of this Group and Hermaphrodism.

The preceding opinion of Krafft Ebing regarding the purely psychical evolution of the inverted of this group is strongly opposed by Dr. Legrain, and not without reason. Let us compare the two.

"As for Krafft Ebing, we do not observe any true transition towards hermaphrodism. Androgynia and gynandria are according to him deviations based upon conditions quite different to the teratological phenomena of hermaphrodism, viewed in the anatomical sense.

"It appears to me to be difficult to follow the author in his conclusion, and I cannot explain to myself this restriction. The theory which would show in androgynia and gynandria processûs tending to the perfect realization of anatomical hermaphrodism appears to me on the other hand to be of a nature to simplify to a singular degree the theoretical explanation of sexual inversions, as I hope to establish farther on. As for Krafft Ebing, the confusion is not possible, seeing that hitherto in the sphere of sexual inversion, tendencies to hermaphroditic malformations of the genital parts have never been met with.

"Relying upon this fact which is not absolutely exact, he endeavours to show that sexual inversion is but a perfectly psychical anomaly which has nothing to do with the physical conformation. This is to hold in light estimation and without adequate reason, says Ledrain, those physical anomalies which Krafft Ebing justly points out among gynandres and androgynes of his 4th degree.

"It seems to me, on the contrary that in this case physical and moral malformations are of the same nature, that they have the same value, that they must be regarded from the same point of view, and that bodily hetero-morphism throws a vivid light upon sexual inversion, without however causing one to be derived from the other both of them originating from one and the same morbid processus.

"Moreover it is incorrect to maintain that there is any real transition in the inverted to hermaphrodism, that is to say to the bisexuality of the creature, or, to sexual neutrality which amounts to the same thing. In fact, I remember perfectly well having observed the case of a patient which was very striking from this point of view. Physically he displayed numerous signs both of the male and female sex, *so that it was impossible to determine his sex with any exactness.* The height, the voice, the breasts, the hips and the thighs were those of a woman, which did not prevent the pilous system being that of a man. From the genital point of view, he had a well-developed penis, but beneath that there was the opening of a vulva with a vaginal infundibulum. The testicles were wanting. He had been declared a girl at his birth and had been regarded as such until he was 20 years old, at which time he was looked upon as a man and his dress was altered. He had served alternately as mistress to an old man and as lover to a maid-servant. From the psychical point of view, it was impossible to decide what his preferences were. He appeared on the whole to be indifferent and neutral, inclined according to his wants, *which however were rare*, and according to opportunity, to the woman's part as much as to that of the man.

"Is it therefore not natural to look upon the physical anomalies of androgynes and gynandres as transitions to the state of complete hermaphrodism? And, moreover, does not hermaphrodism exist from the psychical point of view? Krafft Ebing makes no difficulty in admitting this. Why endeavour then to establish an impassable barrier between it and physical hermaphrodism? Are the physical and moral states more separable here than they are in any other condition? It appears only logical to me to bring the 1st and 4th degrees together and even to blend them. The Uranists properly so called (the 2nd degree) and the patients of the 3rd degree (viraginity, effemination) are then the clearly marked transition between the normal state and psycho-physical hermaphrodism, *the extreme degree of degenerescence which is characterized by complete sexual neutrality and consequently by sterility*.

"And besides, does sex find its exclusive qualification in the conformation of the external genital organs? If they are an important element in determining it, they are not the only one, and sex is characterized quite as much by the external habitus and by the cerebral conformation as by the genital organs which, in fact, are but the *instruments* at the disposal of a complex function, the anatomical substratum of which, of an equally complex nature, is partly hidden from view.

"Krafft Ebing does not think that importance ought to be attached to the malformations known under the names of *epispadiasis* and *hypospadiasis* owing to the fact that in the cases which he has observed, sex was very clearly differentiated in spite of the malformation. But I do not share his opinion at all regarding this differentiation of sex, seeing that the patients were beyond any doubt Uranists, which clearly proves that their sex was very uncertain. Males or females from the genital point of view, they were females or males from the psychical point of view. What therefore was their real sex? There is nothing, in my opinion, which shows more clearly that, in determining the sex, it is impossible to dissociate the physical from the moral signs." (Dr. Legrain. *op. cit.*)

We are completely in accord with the view of the learned alienist. We shall have, however, to quote it again when we come to speak of a case which he quotes in great detail; a case which cludes any classification.

Let us now quote, from Krafft Ebing's work, the only two cases which he gives of the inverted of this degree. We shall offer a summary of them, so as to abridge their length.

Androgynia.

"M. v. H . . ., single, aged 30, was born of a neuropathic mother. It is stated that no nervous or mental diseases have occurred in the patient's family, and that his only brother is perfectly normal from the intellectual and physical point of view. The patient is said to have had a retarded physical development, and was therefore sent several times to take a course of sea baths and to stay at climatic resorts. From his childhood he was of a neuropathic constitution and, according to the evidence of a relative, he was unlike other boys. At a very early period his aversion to boys' amusements and his preference for feminine occupations were a subject of remark. He detested all boyish games and gymnastic exercises, while playing with dolls, and feminine diversions were particularly pleasing to him. After that the patient developed well physically, and had no serious illnesses; but, from the intellectual point of view, his individuality remained abnormal, incapable of taking a serious view of life, and decidedly feminine in his thoughts and feelings.

In his seventeenth year pollutions took place, became more and more frequent, and finally occurred during the day; they weakened the patient and caused numerous nervous troubles. Symptoms of *neurasthenia spinalis* made their appearance and have lasted up to the last few years, but they have become weaker with the decrease in the number of pollutions. Onanism is denied, but is very probable. An indolent effeminate, dreamy habit of thought has become more and more noticeable ever since puberty. All efforts to induce the patient to take up an earnest pursuit in life were vain. His intellectual faculties, though really in a healthy state, were never equal to the motive of an independent character, and the higher ideals of life. He remained dependent, an overgrown child; and nothing more clearly indicated his abnormal conformation than his absolute incapability of taking care of money, and his own confession that he had no ability to spend money in a reasonable way. As soon as he had any money he wasted it on trinkets, toilette articles, and other kinds of rubbish.

With these indications of a psychically defective conformation, the patient had a perverse sexual feeling; he felt himself as a woman before men, and felt indifference, if not actual disinclination for females.

He declares that when he was 22 he performed coition, but he soon became disgusted at it, because his neurasthenic symptoms increased after each coition, and because it gave him no satisfaction and he had fear of infection. Concerning his abnormal sexual condition, he is not perfectly clear; he is conscious of an inclination for the male sex, but he only confesses it in a shame-faced way, declaring that he has delightful friendships with certain men which are unaccompanied by sexual desires. He denied having had sexual intercourse with men, but his blushing and embarrassed air, and, still more, an incident at N . . ., where the patient, some time before, provoked a scandal by attempting to have sexual intercourse with youths, gave him the lie.

His external appearance also, his *habitus*, form, gestures, manner and dress attract attention, and decidedly recall the feminine form and characteristics. The patient is above the average height, but the thorax and pelvis are decidedly of feminine shape. The body is rich in fat, the skin well cared for, delicate and soft. This impression of a woman in male attire is further increased by there being no beard on the face, which is shaven, with the exception of a small moustache; by the mincing gait, the shy, effeminate manner, the feminine features, the swimming neuropathic expression of the eyes, the traces of powder and paint on the face, the dandy cut of his clothing, with the bosom-like protuberance of the waistcoat, the fringed cravat knotted like a woman's, and the hair parted in the middle and brought down close to the temples.

An examination of his body permitted me to observe the undoubtedly feminine conformation of his body. The external genital parts are, it is true, well developed, but the left testicle has remained in the inguinal canal; there is but little hair on the *Mons Veneris*, which is abnormally rich in fat and prominent. The voice is high and without manly characteristics.

V... de H...'s occupations and thoughts also have very pronounced feminine characteristics. He has a boudoir and a well-supplied toilet-table, before which he spends hours at a time, occupied in all kinds of artifices for beautifying himself; he abhors hunting, practise with arms, and such-like masculine pursuits; he calls himself an *æsthete*, speaks in preference of his paintings and attempts at poetry, interests himself in feminine occupations which—such as embroidery—he engages in; he says that his highest pleasure would be to pass his life in a circle of ladies and gentlemen with artistic tastes and an æsthetic education, spending his time in conversation, music and discussing æsthetic questions, etc. His talk turns in preference upon feminine matters,--fashions, needlework, cookery, and household affairs.

The patient is in good health, but anæmic. He is of neuropathic constitution and displays symptoms of neurasthenia, which are maintained by a bad manner of life, lying abed, living indoors and effeminacy.

Gynandria.

Count Sandor, a Gynander married to a woman.

There are few cases more curious than the story of Count Sandor, published by Krafft Ebing. I give the most characteristic passages.

On November 4th, 1889, the father-in-law of a certain Count V. Sandor complained that the latter had obtained from him 800 florins, under the pretext that he required this sum as a deposit to enable him to become Secretary to a public company. It was also ascertained that Sandor had forged bills, that the nuptial ceremony when he married his wife in the spring of 1889, was fictitious, and, more than this, that the pretended Count Sandor was no man at all, but a woman in male attire, whose real name was the Comtesse Sarolta (Charlotte) de V...

Sandor was arrested and put upon his trial for swindling and falsification of public documents. At the first hearing, Sandor confessed that she was born on December 6th, 1866, that she was a female, a Catholic and single, and gained her livelihood as an author, under the name of Count Sandor V...

From the autobiography of this man-woman I have gleaned the following remarkable facts which have been independently confirmed.

S... comes of a ancient, noble and highly-respected family in Hungary, a family which is peculiarly eccentric and has hysterical and lunatic members in the maternal branch. Her mother was nervous and a lunatic. On the father's side, two near relatives had committed suicide; her father himself was eccentric and extravagant. He had her brought up as a boy, made her ride on horseback, drive, and hunt, admired her manly energy, and called her Sandor.

Sarolta Sandor remained under her father's influence till her twelfth year; she was then sent to her grandmother's who placed her in a girl's school.

At thirteen she had a love affair with an English girl, to whom she represented herself as a boy and ran away with her.

Saralto then returned to her mother who however could do nothing with her, and was obliged to allow Sarolta to again become Sandor, wear boy's clothes, and, at least once a year, to fall in love with persons of her own sex. At the same time, Sarolta received a careful education, made long journeys with her father—always dressed of course as a young gentlemen. She used to frequent *cafés*, even those of doubtful repute, and indeed boasted that she had one day in a brothel *in utroque genu puellas sedisse*. Sarolta was often intoxicated, had a passion for manly sports, and was a very skilful fencer. She felt herself particularly drawn to actresses, or others of similar position, and, if possible, toward those who were not very young. She declares that she never had any affection for a young man, and that she has felt, from year to year, an increasing aversion to individuals of the male sex. "I preferred to go with ugly, ill-favoured men into the society of ladies, so that none of them could eclipse me. If I noticed that one of my companions awakened the ladies' sympathies, I grew jealous. Among the ladies, I preferred those who were witty to those who had physical beauty. I could not endure them if they were fat or much inclined toward men. It delighted me if the passion of a lady were disclosed under a poetic veil. All immodesty in a woman inspired me with disgust. I had an indescribable aversion for female attire,—indeed for everything feminine—but only in as far as it concerns myself; for, on the other hand, I was all enthusiasm for the fair sex."

For about ten years, Sarolta has always lived apart from her family and in the guise of a man. She had had many *liaisons* with ladies, travelled with them, spent much money and contracted many debts.

At the same time, she devoted herself to literary work and became a valued collaborator on two of the principal newspapers in the capital.

Her passion for ladies was very changeable. She had no constancy in love.

Only once did one of her *liaisons* last for three years. Some years ago Sarolta made the acquaintance of Mdlle. Emma E..., at the Château de G.... She fell in love with this lady, made a marriage contract with her, and they lived together for three years, as husband and wife, in the capital.

A new love affair which was fatal to her, decided her to sever her "matrimonial bonds" with E... The latter would not leave Sarolta. It was only at great material sacrifices that Sarolta purchased her freedom. E... it is said, still gives herself out as a divorced wife and considers herself as Comtesse V... Sarolta must have been able to inspire other women with passion, and this is shown by the fact that, before her "marriage" with E..., when she had grown tired of a Mdlle. D..., after having spent thousands of florins upon her, the latter threatened to blow out her brains, if she did not remain faithful to her.

It was in the summer of 1887, while she was staying at a watering-place, that Sarolta made the acquaintance of the family of a very distinguished official. Immediately she fell in love with the daughter, Marie, and her love was returned. The young girl's mother and cousin tried in vain to break off this affair. During the winter, the two lovers corresponded. In April, 1888, Count Sandor paid her a visit, and in May, 1889, he attained the height of his wishes: Marie, who meanwhile had given up her situation as governess, was married by a false Hungarian priest to her adored Sandor in a chapel improvised out of an arbour; a friend of Sandor acted as witness.

The pair lived happily together, and, had not the charge been brought against him by his father-in-law, this false marriage would probably have lasted still longer. It is remarkable that during the long period during which Sandor was engaged, she succeeded in deceiving the bride's family completely with regard to her true sex.

Sandor was a passionate smoker, and in all respects her tastes and ideas were masculine. Her letters and even her legal documents reached her under the name of Count Sandor; she frequently spoke of having to go through her period of military training. From remarks of the father-in-law, it seems that Sandor—(and this was acknowledged later on)—knew how to imitate a scrotum with a glove or handkerchief stuffed into one of the trouser pockets. The father-in-law also, on one occasion noticed on his future son-in-law something like a member in a state of erection, (probably a priapus). She also give him to understand that she was always obliged to wear a suspensory bandage when riding. The fact is, Sandor wore a bandage round the body, probably to hold up the priapus.

Though Sandor often had herself shaved *pro formâ*, the servants in the hotel where she lived were convinced that she was a woman, because the chamber-maid found traces of menstrual blood on her linen (which Sandor however explained as being hæmorrhoidal); the same chamber-maid declared that she had convinced herself *de visu* that Sandor was a woman by looking through the key-hole.

We must suppose that Mdlle. Marie's family were for a long time in error as to the true sex of her pseudo-bridegroom.

Nothing is more characteristic of the simplicity and innocence of this unfortunate girl than the following passage in a letter written by Marie to Sandor on August 26th, 1889:

"I don't love other people's children, but a little baby by my Sandi, a sweet little doll,—ah, my Sandi, what happiness!"

As for Sandor's mental individuality, a large number of letters give us the requisite information. The handwriting has a character of firmness and assurance. The letters are genuinely masculine. The same peculiarities show themselves everywhere in their contents,—wild, unbridled passion; hate and resistance to all that opposes the heart thirsting for love; poetical love which is not marred by one ignoble blot; enthusiasm for the beautiful and noble, taste for the sciences and fine arts.

Her writings denote a rich acquaintance with the literature of all languages; there are quotations from the poets and prose-writers of every country. Persons competent to judge declare that Sandor's productions in poetry and prose are not without value.

The letters and writing concerning her relations with Marie are very remarkable from a psychological point of view. Sandor speaks of the happiness there was for her when by Marie's side, and expresses boundless longing to see her adored one, were it only for a moment. After so much shame she only wishes to exchange her cell for the grave. The bitterest thing was to feel that Marie now would hate her too. She had shed scalding tears over her lost happiness, tears enough to drown herself in. Whole pages are devoted to the glorification of this love and to reminiscences of the time of their first love and first acquaintance.

Sardon is 153 centimètres in height, her osseous structure is delicate; she is thin, but surprisingly muscular on the breast and upper part to the thighs. Her gait in female attire is awkward. Her movements are vigorous, not unpleasing, though they have a somewhat masculine stiffness, and are wanting in grace. She greets one with a firm grasp of the hand. Her whole attitude has a resolute, energetic air, and denotes a certain confidence in her own powers. Her glance is intelligent; her mien somewhat sombre. Her feet and hands are remarkably small, like a child's. The extensor surfaces of the extremities are well covered with hair, while there is no trace of beard or down discernible, in spite of her experiments with the razor. The upper part of the body does not in any way correspond with that of a woman. The waist is wanting. The pelvis is so thin and so little prominent, that a line drawn from the axilla to the corresponding knee is straight,—not curved inward at the waist, or outward by the pelvis. The skull is slightly oxycephalous, and in all its measurements falls below the average of the female skull by about a centimètre.

The circumference of the skull is 52 centimètres. The upper jaw projects beyond the lower jaw by 0.5 of a centimètre. The position of the teeth is not fully normal; the right upper canine has never developed. The mouth is remarkably small. The ears are prominent; the lobes are not separated from but are joined to the skin of the cheeks. The palate is hard, narrow and arched; the voice rough and deep. The breasts are fairly developed, but without secretion. *Mons veneris* covered with thick dark hair. The genital parts are altogether feminine, without any traces of hermaphrodism, but their stage of development is that of a girl of ten years old. The *labia majora* are almost completely touching; the *labia minora* are shaped like a cock's comb and project under the *labia majora*. The clitoris is small and very sensitive. The *frenulum* is tender; *perineum* very narrow; *introitus vaginae* narrow: mucous membrane normal. The hymen is wanting (probably congenitally), likewise the *carunculae myrtiformes*. The *vagina* is so narrow that the introduction of a *membrum virile* would be impossible: it is also very sensitive. It is evident that coition has not taken place. The uterus is felt through the rectum, about the size of a walnut, immovable and retroflected.

The pelvis generally narrowed (dwarf pelvis) and of decidedly masculine type. On account of the narrowness of the pelvis, the thighs are not convergent as in a woman, but their position is quite straight.

The medical report showed that in Sarolta there was a morbid congenital inversion of the sexual feeling, which showed itself even anthropologically in anomalies in the development of the body, depending upon considerable hereditary taint; further, that the acts of which she was accused were explained by the patient's morbid and irresistible sexuality.

Sandor's characteristic remark— "God put love into my heart: if he created me so and not otherwise, is it my fault, or is it the incomprehensible way of Providence?" is in this connection, quite justified.

The Court declared her not guilty. "The Countess in male attire," as she was called in the newspapers, returned home and figured again as Count Sandor. Her only grief is that her happy love with her ardently loved Marie is now lost.

A married woman, in Brandon, (Wisconsin), whose case is reported by Dr. Kiernan (*Medical Standard*, 1888, Nov. and Dec.) was more fortunate. She eloped with a young girl in 1883; married her in church and lived with her as her husband undisturbed.

A case reported by Spitzka, (*Chicago Medical Review*, Aug. 20th 1881), supplies an intresting historical example of androgynia. It relates to Lord Cornbury, Governor of New York, who lived in the reign of Queen Anne. He was apparently affected with *moral insanity*, and was an unbridled libertine: in spite of his high position, he could not keep himself from going about the streets in female attire, using all the arts and wiles of a prostitute.

In a picture of him, that has been preserved, his narrow brow, asymmetrical face, feminine features, and sensual mouth at once attract attention. It is certain that he never actually regarded himself as a woman. (Krafft Ebing.)

We have already said, that, in order to facilitate our study, we should adopt Krafft Ebing's classification, without however losing sight of the fact that it is incomplete and defective. It has been of service to us for the exposition and grouping of cases, but we must not go beyond that. We give below *in extenso* the history of a born inverted which we find in Legrain. He deduces from it, as will be seen, some logical conclusions which confirm his criticisms, already set forth above, upon Krafft Ebing's classification.

History of a Born Inverted, by Legrain.

His history, which I shall often leave him to narrate in his own words, is as follows:

B.... owns a high position. He is 28 years of age. He received a careful training and superior education, by which he has largely profited. Very learned, with a good knowledge of literature, intelligent and even witty, he shows all the appearance of a really distinguished man, had not the unhappy sexual perversions from which he suffers, ruined his future for ever. After briefly pointing out that he belongs to a family of neuropaths; that, on his father's side, he had a drunken uncle whose son died a lunatic; that, on his mother's side, one uncle was a lunatic, another committed suicide in a fit of insanity, and that a cousin german was a drunkard, I shall confirm my account, over long already, to the details relating to his sexual life alone.

He began to indulge in masturbation when he was 13 years old at the Lycée, at first in solitude. But shortly afterwards he eagerly sought for every opportunity of indulging in caresses on his companions; not on all, but on those in particular whose physiognomy pleased him. Thus he attained the age of 17 without dreaming of any other erotic pleasures than those to which he was addicted, but without any desire for either active or passive pederasty; besides, he had no wish for or idea of the woman.

He then went through his first year's course of law. But gradually he grew less and less assiduous at the courts, and passed his time in lounging about the streets of Paris, merely for the purpose of meeting with young fellows of his own age, elegantly dressed and physically agreeable. He did not seek as yet to enter into relations with them. He only noted their appearance in his mind and, when he returned home, masturbated himself in solitude calling up their picture before him. It seemed to him then as though he were exchanging caresses with them.

About that period, he began to read Petronius, Martial, Suetonius, etc., and borrowed from these authors the beginning of a vague desire for passive pederasty.

In 1886 he went through his time of voluntary military service. He found himself placed amid surroundings in which his ignorance about woman was a subject of raillery, and, thus in a way constrained, he had to cohabit with a woman of about 30. He had the greatest wish to run away, but, held back by his own self-respect, he accomplished the sexual act, possessed by this idea alone that if he did not succeed in ejaculating, his comrades would know it and would laugh at him. The same thing occurred again three or four times. These meetings were an absolute torture to him.

In 1887 he returned to civil life and resumed his legal studies, but his attendance at the Courts grew less and less regular. Almost all his time was taken up in searching for young men of seductive appearance.

At this time, his antiphysical desires, which had hitherto appeared to him to be *perhaps* contrary to reason, began to appear quite natural. Thenceforth he desired to find a friend, of his own age or younger than himself, with whom he could keep up a carnal and intellectual intercourse. He dreamed of his friend as being fair, beardless, elegant, and learned. He did not hide from himself that what he was looking for was not easy to find, but he said to himself that he had still many years before him, and that in a city of two millions of inhabitants, it was merely a matter of time and patience. However, he said to himself that this revived love of the Greeks was only the appanage of youth, and that after he was 26 or 28 years old, he would no longer have any chance of realizing it.

Towards the end of this period (188—9) he felt anew desires for passive pederasty, which were aroused in him at the sight of certain individuals of various ages (from 20 to 30), but always of elegant carriage. These desires did not possess him like those which had youths for their object. However, in April 1889, he met a young man in the Bois de Vincennes who in one of the walks indulged in exhibitions before him. He followed him, saying to himself that perhaps he was at length about to find the sensation which he was seeking. The individual, as a matter of fact, led him into a thicket and our patient yielded himself to him playing the passive part. After several unsuccessful efforts, he found himself, as he expressed it, *hurt* and chilled because the individual could not even attain to an erection. He left him and returned home.

In July 1889, he took his degree in Law. While he was waiting to select a profession, it was decided that he should spend two years in studying for a solicitor. He pretended to agree to the arrangement, fully resolved that he would do no work; the laborious life which he would have to lead not lending itself to the carrying out of his daily pursuits. And so, for four years subsequent to this period, he played the following comedy: He left home in the morning at 9 o'clock, nominally to go to his studies, and returned in the evening at 6.30, after having passed the whole day in scrutinizing the young fellows that he met in the course of his walks. "The slightest physical defect," he said, "put an absolute stop to the matter as far as I was concerned, and when by chance I met with a young man who pleased me in every way, and who appeared to pay some attention to me, I refrained from giving evidence of my desires, for the unisexual love of which I dreamed must be absolutely reciprocal."

During this time, the days passed away without bringing him any new sensations. Without the knowledge of his relatives, he had for some time decided to write plays, and without hiding from himself the enormous difficulties which beginners meet with in getting a play accepted, he reckoned that the three years which he would be supposed to be spending in his solicitor's office, would be time enough to enable him to get his first play produced. And, in fact, whenever he was free from his besetting erotic ideas, he spent his time in drawing up plots and in writing pieces which he himself offered to managers with a few words of vague recommendation, and which were declined by one after another.

The few adventures which he had between 1890 and 1893 were as follows: In January 1890, in the Musée du Louvre, he met a young man about 18 years of age who, by his provocative attitude, induced him to accost him, although he detected at once that he was a professional. "I had decided on principle," he says, "never to have anything to do with professionals, as for my own part, when the question of money enters in, love cannot exist." However, at the sight of this young man, although he only partly realized his physical ideal, he forgot his principles and decided to go with him. "For at last," he adds, "it was really necessary to do something." He allowed the young man to perform buccal coition upon him in one of the dressing rooms of the Pont-Royal baths. He found no pleasure in it and thought the scene extremely ridiculous.

The years 1890 and 1891 passed away without his finding what he was looking for. He began to be anxious and to fear that he would not realize his dream. In 1892, he began to boast in the presence of some of his companions of his anti-natural disposition. Only he flattered himself at having realized his ideal, that is to say having relations with a young man of about 18, of good family, elegant and of irreproachable physique.

In April 1892, he met a young man who provoked him by his gestures to accost him. They made an appointment to meet that evening at an hotel, where they slept together. He felt nothing, and did not even have an erection. But it must be said that the young man was of an inferior station, was not well dressed, and only came with him for the money which he hoped to obtain. These ideas did not leave him as long as he was in bed, and contact with his companion was disagreeable to him. His proposals of coition seemed absolutely grotesque to him; he only agreed to allow himself to be onanized *without feeling any satisfaction*.

He consoled himself for his want of success by indulging daily in onanism at home. He summoned up the likeness of the young man who had struck him the most during his walks, and masturbated himself without however having any wish to proceed to ejaculation. He merely depicts to himself *that he is desired* by the individuals of whom he thinks *just as he desires them.* On every occasion when he goes as far as ejaculation, it is his will which betrays him.

In September 1892, during his period of military training, he had himself onanized by a young soldier, but always *without pleasure* and finding this operation ridiculous from beginning to end.

In October, he was accosted in a urinal by a young exhibitionist of elegant appearance. He had a moment of hope; he had perhaps found his ideal. He went out of the urinal saying to himself that if the young man "*wanted him*, he would follow and speak to him." This is, in fact, what happened; but after a few words he again saw that he had to do with a professional. He followed him, nevertheless, but without any enthusiasm, underwent buccal onanism without any pleasure, settled his bill and went away grieved at his *shattered illusion*.

In February, 1893, he was accosted by a young man with whom he got into a cab. He did so with the greatest pleasure, for the youth's face and dress corresponded entirely with his dream. It was another illusion. He was seized by the testicles and compelled to empty his purse.

During the summer of 1893, he went almost every day to the Bois de Vincennes. Very often vagrants would come and make proposals to him which he always declined, for these individuals, *who were ill-dressed and often dirty*, did not inspire him with any desire. At this time, however, his desire for passive pederasty returned to him with greater force than ever, and one day he followed one of these vagrants who proposed to play the active part with him.

"I followed him," he says, "*without any erotic desire*, led simply *by a purely cerebral curiosity* and wishing to know what that act was of which I was always thinking and with which I was not yet acquainted." It turned out badly for him. He was seized by five or six confederates, ill-treated and duly robbed.

At the end of the year 1893, he had an inexpressible feeling of depression. Everything failed him at once. In the place of the unisexual love of which he had dreamed, he had only found unnumbered deceptions and four or five grotesque adventures. He was nearing his 26th year, and now it was all over and he felt that he would never find what he was looking for. On the other hand the period fixed by his forged agreement was drawing near, and his family were already surprised to find that the piece was not being rehearsed. He would be compelled to confess all his false statements, to inform them that no piece of his had been accepted, and that for the past four years he had been roaming about the streets in quest of sensations which it was impossible for him to avow. This prospect terrified him.

To escape from these thoughts, he had recourse more than ever to his habits of masturbation and even adopted new ones. It was at this period that he began to introduce into his anus balls previously coated with vaseline. When the ball had entered, he expelled it again by defecation, doing this several times in succession. At the same time he called to mind the appearance of one of the individuals who had struck him most in the course of his walks, and imagined to himself that the same individual was playing the active part upon him. He meanwhile masturbated himself with his right hand, and he thus had at the same time both an active and a passive pleasure.

At this same period (1893) he acquired a habit of

writing inscriptions in the public water-closets. The inscription was always the same. It is absolutely pornographic, and my respect for the reader prevents me from reproducing it here. It always recalls the dominant idea of passive pederasty with handsome men wearing polished boots. He was in a state of erection during the time he was writing, and masturbated himself for a few moments without proceeding to ejaculation; he then went away to another water-closet.

At length, in 1893, he acquired something which greatly modified his erotic habits: he bought a pair of varnished boots. But to understand what follows, we must retrace our steps a little way.

Varnished boots at all times had had a peculiar fascination for him. It was the detail of dress which had the greatest importance in his eyes. In course of time this anomaly increased, and in 1893 he used to take up his position in front of shops where varnished boots were exposed for sale. But it was the sight above everything of varnished boots which pleased him. The desire of possessing them became an obsession. He resisted it for a long time, considering this desire "absolutely insensate and grotesque." In the end he could no longer restrain it and purchased them. From this time forth every time that he onanized himself, that is to say every day, he placed the boots on two chairs in front of the window, so that they might appear as shining as possible, and then masturbated himself generally without going so far as ejaculation. During this, he did not summon up any seductive images, but kept his eyes obstinately fixed upon the shining parts of the boots, without thinking in any way.

He occupied his days as follows: Almost every morning, from 9 to 11 o'clock, he masturbated himself without ejaculation before the boots, as we have said. Several times he tried something else. He would put on a pair of rose-silk drawers, over which he drew the boots, and opened the glass-door of his wardrobe halfway, so as to be able to see himself both in front and behind in another glass hung over the chimneypiece.

Than stretching apart his legs, he introduced balls into his anus with his left hand, while he onanized himself with his right. He thus procured for himself an intense feeling of pleasure, but inferior however to that he obtained before the boots placed in the full light.

During the day he went to the Bois de Vinçennes, hoping to meet, if not the ideal youth with whom he wished to "associate his life," at least with an adventure, with an erotic sensation "which would not be ridiculous," but all his hopes were vain. Instead of adventures he only met with vagrants whom he avoided. "These individuals," he says, "did not inspire me with any desire, but at that time I felt *such a want to be desired* that their proposals caused me a certain amount of pleasure, although I could only attribute them to their wanting to get some money out of me."

In June 1894, he had his last adventure, followed by a conclusion which he was far from anticipating. He met in the Bois de Vincennes, with a bicyclist about 18 years of age, whose appearance "gave him that electric shock" for which he was looking. I leave him to describe the scene. "After taking a few steps, he stopped to urinate by the side of a clump of bushes. This act occasioned me a lively feeling of hope. Is it an invitation to follow him? I said to myself. And I followed him. He turned round several times, and each time I applied my hand sharply to my genital organs. On reaching the Joinville road, I sat down on a bench, saying to myself that it was now for him to come and seat himself close to me, *if he really desired me.* But he merely sat down on the grass, in front of me, on the opposite side of the road. I got up in my turn, extremely sad at this fresh illusion and saying to myself that I must renounce not only unisexual love affairs but even any kind of adventure such as I had wished for. I then saw the bicyclist returning to meet me, with his eyes fixed upon me. This sight made all my hopes suddenly revive in me. I felt absolutely persuaded that he desired me. At length, as he passed by me, he cast his eyes upon my varnished boots. Then I restrained myself no longer. Throwing myself against a tree, I indulged in an exhibition and in a commencement of masturbation which was followed by ejaculation." But then a park-keeper came up, and brutally cut short the romance which had just begun, by arresting him.

Inferences and Lessons drawn from this Case.

Dr. Legrain establishes very easily the fact of the morbidity of this unfortunate man, and shows that, according to the story, he had opportunity to attend to himself and leisure to moralize. But in spite of all his attempts to recover himself, his opinion is that he remains and always will remain an inverted.

Legrain then shows very clearly and rightly the striking characteristics of this case, and draws from it the numerous lessons of which it allows. We give a summing-up of his development.

B.... displays very numerous sexual anomalies and perversions. Although his antiphysical tendencies dominate the scene with the persistent search for a creature of the same sex who would realize his ideal, he shows himself episodically under other aspects. In the first place as onanist, and not voluntarily carrying the act as far as ejaculation. At College, he was accustomed to practise solitary and reciprocal onanism. He became a pederast, but only a passive one, dissociating this material act from what he cultivated with ardour under the name of unisexual love. Then he sought after special pleasures by the introduction of foreign bodies into the anus, and later on he became a fetishist of the varnished boot. And lastly he became a pornograph in the public lavatories.

In Magnan's classification he would appear simultaneously as *pure psychic, or anterior celebral spinal, or posterior* celebral. Each of these aspects may be considered as a clinical anomaly susceptible of a separate description and of a special physiological interpretation.

And yet it is here that the observation shows attempts at sub-division to be useless; the psychological analysis reveals a *narrow bond between all these anomalies*, which are not in juxtaposition nor coexistent, but perfectly combined, and guided by a *common dominant*. We ought not to view him by the accidents of his imaginative fancy under such varied figures. Everything depends upon and gravitates round this passion, this need for the unisexual which, grasped more and more by the analysis, supplies us with a key to all the rest.

We shall not follow Dr. Legrain further in this absolutely conclusive analysis. It would be necessary to quote the half of his work from which we have already borrowed enough. We shall rest content with quoting the position which Legrain attributes to B....'s case in Krafft Ebing's classification, which will justify the estimate which we have given above of the relative character of this classification.

According to Legrain, B.... is not a hermaphrodite, but he certainly has androgynical attributes; his aspect and physical conformation give him a feminine look, but it is a singular thing that his tastes and occupations are masculine. His psychical personality therefore takes after both sexes.

We thus come back to psychical hermaphrodism which, as is seen, cannot be separated from androgynia and, consequently, in my opinion, from genital hermaphrodism. But here the psychical hermaphrodism no longer has the same characteristics as those of Krafft Ebing's 1st degree. Our patient is cerebrally constituted like a bisexual: feminine tendencies from the psycho-sexual point of viex, masculine tendencies from the pure, intellectual point of view.

But he also belongs to the 2nd degree, the category of Uranists, while belonging to the 4th degree, and partially also to the first. In fact he has a very marked inclination for the same sex, and his type of youth is a man endowed with masculine attributes, whom he seeks that he may love and be loved by him at the same time. In that he therefore has clearly feminine tendencies; he thus casts off his own sex and becomes effeminate, and he falls into the 3rd degree.

B.... therefore is in every way excedingly complex, belonging at the same time to all the four degrees of Krafft Ebing.

He is a Uranist, an effeminate; in reality, he is a veritable hermaphrodite whose feminine characteristics prevail over the others, Can it be said then that the categories admitted by Krafft Ebing are illusory? Such is not my opinion, but my case proves only that there are no clear limits between the different degrees of sexual inversion which may become deeply entangled. It also proves that the patients belonging to the different degrees suffer from one and the same complaint, very unequally developed in different cases. This complaint consists, in my opinion, in the persistence of a congentital hermaphrodism, not ultimately differentiated, and it is consequently to the conception of hermaphrodison that everything must be referred.

There is a point upon which Legrain insists particularly in the ease of his patient, because it is not common among the inverted, and that is the essentially psychical character of his anomaly. He perfectly dissociates the psychical from the physical element of love. Carnal love, even with the adored youth, is only a very secondary episode to which he attaches no importance and which he subordinates to intellectual love. He is disgusted at the carnal approaches of men "*whom he does not like,*" because they do not previously realize his *ideal. Never*, (and he is very positive upon this point), during his cohabitation with men whom he has only approached in moments of the deepest despair, has he felt the slightest sensation of pleasure. Before anything else, it is an intellectual intercourse which he desires. It is the pleasure of friendship increased a hundredfold by love. Perhaps, if he had met with his ideal he would have made a distinct choice, either for the passive part or for the active part, and he might iu consequence have become an absolute Uranist or an absolute effeminate. It is possible; but while waiting for it, he remained neuter and confined himself to the pure worship of what he calls *anti-physical love*; a love which is above all love and the antiphysical qualificative of which only means that it is the opposite to natural love, that is to say between individuals of opposite sexes.

It is from this point of view that our patient is truly original. (Legrain, *op. cit.*)

We are the more disposed to accord the first place to the theories on sexual inversion of Legrain, another who, in our opinion, is up to the present time the most correct of all his contemporaries, as the case of our magistrate at Noumea tends to confirm them.

In the case of our magistrate, let us put on one side the male genital apparatus, and all the rest of his body is feminine. Let us allow, at the most, a hypospadias excessively developed as far as the prostate, with a vaginal infundibulum, and we then have an absolute hermaphrodite, who has nothing of the male but a small atrophied and degenerate male apparatus, while all the rest of the physical and psychical individual is absolutely and entirely feminine.

Inversion has only been known for the past twenty years. When the observations of the inverteds of all categories and of the more or less complete hermaphrodites are counted by thousands, we shall then see the full series of all these malformations and degenerescencies, from the true procreative male to the impotent hermaphrodite who is neuter, incapable of procreation and a degraded being. *Natura non facit saltum.*

We might introduce here the history of our born-inverted, but as it is connected with clearly defined cases of pederasty, we prefer to conclude it in the Chapter on Pederasty, which allows us to analyze it in the same detailed manner as Legrain has in the preceding case.

Genital Perversions. *(Continued).*

CHAPTER IV.

The Nature, Cause and Treatment of Sexual Inversion.

Returning Back! What is the reason of this Special Chapter?—Nature of Sexual Inversion.—Inversion is one in its Essence, and more than one in its Manifestations.—A Man does not become Inverted, he is born Inverted; a Man becomes a Pederast, he is not born a Pederast.—The Causes of Sexual Inversion.—Different Opinions of Physicans who have treated of Inversions.—Krafft Ebing's Opinion, Moll's Opinion.—Heredity of Inverteds.—Occasional favouring the Breaking-out of the Sexual Perversion.—Krafft Ebing's Theory on Atavism as a Cause of Sexual Inversion.—Masturbation, the Effect and not the Cause of Inversion.—Moll's Opinion on Heredity as a Cause of Sexual Inversion.— Inverted Daughters of a Pederast Father.—Theoretical Explanation of Sexual Inversion by Moll.—The Causes of Sexual Inversion according to Laupts.—Influence of Heredity upon Inversion according to Raffalovitch.—Theories of Dr. Legrain upon Inversion.—Explanation of the Phenomena of Sexual Inversion.—Duration of Inversion.—Treatment of this Aberration by Hypnotic Suggestion.

Returning Back! What is the Reason of this Special Chapter?

In the Chapter upon the general ideas of Inversion we have touched upon the causes of Sexual Inversion in a few words and rapidly summed up in two pages the opinion of the principal physicians who have concerned themselves with it.

We have now to take up the question again *ab ovo* and to give it all the developments which befit it. The observations contained in the preceding chapters give us the solution of many facts which are still the subjects of much controversy. The reader therefore will not be surprised at our devoting a whole chapter to this Study.

Nature of Sexual Inversion.

The very decided separation of Inversion as a vice through perversity from Morbid Inversion through perversion is a thoroughly ascertained fact. In Morbid Inversion through perversion, Krafft Ebing one of the first, and all the authors who have followed him in his path, (with but few exceptions), have together with him admitted its division into two very distinct groups:

A. Acquired Homo-Sexuality.

B. Congenital Homo-Sexuality.

The latter group would be that of the true inverted or Uranist. We have followed in each of these groups, A. and B., Krafft Ebing's classification into four degrees, for the facility of setting forth the facts, but with certain reserves. It appears to us, in fact, to be demonstrated by the attentive examination of the numerous preceding observations that if Uranism (not always to say inversion), is in the majority of cases congenital (we may say, with Thoinot, in the great majority), Krafft Ebing has not brought out with sufficient clearness the close bonds which unite the acquired homosexuals to the congenital homosexuals.

Thoinot justly makes the remark that *acquired inversion* would be rather a retarded inversion, and it seems to him more appropriate to designate it by this name.

"The inversion, in fact, is latent in the tainted individual until the day when, under the influence of a variable orginal cause, it comes to light, and henceforward the sexual life of the degenerate individual is diverted into its true path; he deviates from the normal path, in which he has only been straying, to enter upon the inverted path which is his very own." (Thoinot, *op. cit.*)

And in support of his statement, Thoinot quotes three observations from Krafft Ebing. In the first of these, inversion was developed because the subject, when slightly intoxicated, seized hold of a friend's genital parts by way of a joke. In the second, as a bath-attendant was rubbing the subject, the latter was very excited sexually, for the sight of the attendant's penis in a state of erection attracted the patient. He would not forbear from squeezing himself against and kissing the attendant and from getting himself masturbated by him, which the latter did willingly. From this time forth, this kind of sexual satisfaction was the only one which suited him. Woman became wholly indifferent to him, and he ran after men only.

The third observation is that of the hysterical Ilma S...., wildly in love at first with a man, The latter abandoned her, and she then disguised herself as a man; having then given up this life of disguise, she was brought one day to the Hospital for a hystero-epileptic crisis, and then showed the most decided inclination for her own sex. The patient became troublesome through her running after the female nurses and her companions in hospital, and confessed her now decided taste for her own sex and her aversion for men.

Moll, for his part, quotes an observation quite as conclusive:

"Here is an instance which well shows what is to be understood by an occasional cause in a predisposed individual. It refers to an individual who, up to that time perfectly normal from the sexual point of view, in the sense that he had only had intercourse with women, went to Paris and there made the acquaintance of a person who asked him to accompany her home. He agreed to this proposal and, being very excited, wished to pass the night with her. The young person undressed herself, when, to his stupefaction, he discovered that she whom he had followed was a man dressed as a woman. Under normal conditions, the mere idea of intercourse with a man would have been sufficient for him to reject all physical contact. But here such was not the case; the man allowed himself to be masturbated by the other, and from that time forth, became a prey to the most decided sexual inversion." (Moll, *op. cit.*)

Inversion is One in its Essence and more than One in its Manifestations.

From these four observations and from a large number of others hitherto unpublished, we shall draw the clear conclusion that inversion like light, is one in its essence: it is more than one in its manifestations. It is a degree of intensity. Between the psychical hermaphrodite, the inverted who sees a man now and again, and the androgyne, there is a distance similar to that between a farthing rushlight and a Jablokoff electric light. Or if a more medical comparison is desired, between simple bronchitis or catarrh, and phthisis of the worst type. This is clear. The seed of the poisonous plant falls: if it falls into fertile soil and the season is favourable, it grows: if the soil is poor, and the season unfavourable, it must wait for fine weather, rain and sunshine. The germ, though retarded, shoots forth and often becomes a finer plant. Lastly, if the seed falls on a barren rock, it withers away and produces nothing. A number of youths pollute themselves in educational establishments. How many of them are there who, when they have left school and are able to have women keep up their intercourse with men? But a very small number. Who are they, on the other hand, who have more or less horror of woman and continue to seek for men? Those who have acted as "*lapins*" at school, who have provoked their companions to the act, have masturbated them, have "drawn their feathers," and have felt an intense pleasure in the act, often without *asking for reciprocity!* These are the true inverteds. The others allow it to be done, find it amusing and make use of "*lapins*" for want of women, but when once they have left the barriers of school behind and women are known, think of the acts they have committed with disgust. The reader will certainly be of our opinion and will admit the truth of the following proposition.

A Man does not become Inverted; he is born Inverted: a Man becomes a Pederast, but he is not born a Pederast.

The first part of this proposition appears to us to be now sufficiently demonstrated. As for the second, it will equally be so after the study of Pederasty. It is through confounding two orders of facts which are so different that the old school of Tardieu was for so long a time entangled in the morasses of error, and veiled its ignorance under the fine and pompous phrases of Prudhomme.

Causes of Sexual Inversion. Different Opinions of Physicians who have treated of Inversion.

Let us now proceed to search for the causes of sexual inversion. Here we shall find among the different physicians who have treated of inversion, considerable divergencies and frequently contradictions of opinion upon the causes of this curious malady. We will first reproduce the theories of Krafft Ebing.

Krafft Ebing's Opinion:

Westphal, says Krafft Ebing, does not touch upon the question of knowing if sexual inversion is the symptom of a neuropathic condition, or whether it constitutes an isolated phenomenon. He firmly maintains that the condition is congenital.

Relying upon the cases which I have published up to 1877, I have designated this peculiar sexual feeling as a functional sign of degenerescence, and as a partial manifestation of a neuro-psycho-pathological state, having heredity as its cause in the majority of cases. This supposition has been confirmed by the analysis of cases which have occurred since. The following points may be given as symptoms of this neuro-psycho-pathological state:

1st. The sexual life of individuals thus organized regularly manifests itself long before the normal period and long after it in a very violent manner. Not unfrequently it displays still other perverse manifestations, besides this abnormal direction impressed upon it by the peculiar sexual feeling.

2nd. The psychical love of these individuals is romantic and exalted in the same way as their sexual instinct is manifested in their consciousness with a strange and even compelling force.

3rd. By the side of the functional signs of degenerescence attending sexual inversion are found other functional, and in many cases anatomical evidences of degenerescence.

4th. Neuroses, (hysteria, neurasthenia, epileptoid states, etc.), coexist. Almost always the existence of temporary or permanent neurasthenia may be proved. As a rule, this neurasthenia is constitutional, that is to say, it is produced by congenital causes. It is awakened and maintained by masturbation or forced abstinence.

In male individuals, *neurasthenia sexualis* is developed on this morbid or congenitally predisposed ground. It then manifests itself especially by the irritative weakness of the centre of ejaculation. Thus the fact is explained that, in the majority of affected individuals, a simple embrace or kiss given to the beloved person, sometimes even the mere sight of the latter, induce ejaculation. Frequently the ejaculation is then accompanied by an abnormally strong sensation of pleasure, which may be so intense as to suggest a feeling of an electric shock through the body.

5th. In the majority of cases, there exist psychical anomalies (brilliant talents for the fine arts, especially for music, poetry, etc.), at the same time a weakness of the intellectual faculties (eccentric disposition), and even very pronounced conditions of psychical degenerescence, (dementia, moral insanity).

In many Uranists, insanity of degenerative character (pathological emotional states, perodical insanity, paranoia, etc.) makes its appearance either temporarily or permanently.

6th. In almost all cases where I was allowed to investigate the physical and mental condition of the ancestors and near relations, I have found neuroses, psychoses, degenerative signs, etc.

Congenital sexual inversion is very deep and well rooted, as has been already shown by the fact that the erotic dreams of male Uranists have only men for their subject, and those of the female homo-sexual, only women.

Westphal's observation, that the consciousness of one congenitally defective in sexual desires toward the other sex and in his inclination towards his own sex is painfully felt by the affected individual, is only true in a certain number of cases. Many individuals do not even have any consciousness of the morbid nature of their condition. The majority of Uranists are happy in their perverse sexual feelings and in the tendency of their instinct; they are only rendered unhappy by the idea that the Law and Society have raised obstacles against the satisfaction of their inclination for their own sex.

The study of sexual inversion clearly shows the anomalies of the cerebral organization of individuals affected with this perversion. Gley (*Revue Philosophique*, January, 1884), believes that he is able to give the answer to this enigma by supposing that these individuals have a female brain and male genital glands, and that in their case, it is the morbid cerebral life which determines the sexual life contrary to the normal condition in which the genital organs determine the sexual functions of the brain.

One of my patients offered me an interesting theory which might be admitted in explanation of original congenital inversion. He started with the actual bisexuality such as is shown anatomically in every fœtus up to a certain age.

We ought, he said, to take into consideration the fact that to the originally hermaphroditic character of the congenital parts, there probably corresponds an originally hermaphroditic character with latent germs of all the secondary traits of sex, such as the hair, the beard, the devolopement of the *mammae*, etc. The hypothesis of a latent hermaphrodism of the secondary traits of sex subsisting in each individual during his whole life is justified by the phenomena of partial regression of a sexual type in the other, even after the complete development of the body, phenomena which can be fully established in the case of *castrati*, *mujerados*, and, at the time of the menopause, in woman.

The celebral part of the sexual apparatus, the male or female psychological centre, represents one of the most important secondary traits of sex; it is even equal in value to the other half of the sexual apparatus. When there is a perfectly normal development of the individual, the hermaphroditic genital organs of the fœtus, that is to say the glands of the germs and organs of copulation, form at first organs which bear the pronounced character of a single sex; next, the secondary traits of the sexual character—physical and psychical—undergo the same transition of the hermaphroditic conformation to the monosexual comformation (in any case while they are in the latent condition; or during the fœtal life, simultaneously with the organs of generation; or, later when they are on the point of emerging from their latent condition.) Thirdly, during this transition, the secondary traits of the sexual character follow the evolution effected on one of the two sexes by the genital organs, to render possible the harmonious performance of the functions of the sexual life.

This uniform evolution of all the traits of the sexual character occurs regularly, through a special disposition in the process of development. The origin and maintenance of this disposition are sufficiently explained by their absolute necessity.

But, in abnormal conditions, (hereditary degenerescence, etc.) this harmony of development may be thrown out of order in different ways. Not only may the evolution of the sexual organs from the hermaphroditic state to the monosexual state be wanting, but the same fact may even occur also with regard to the secondary traits of the sexual character, to physical traits and even to the pyschical traits. Lastly, the harmony of the development of the sexual apparatus may be so disordered that one part may follow the evolution towards one sex and the other towards the opposite sex.

Four principal types of hermaphrodism are therefore possible, (there are secondary types, like men with *mammae*, women with a beard, etc); 1st, purely physical hermaphrodism of the genital parts together with psychical monosexuality; 2nd, purely psychical hermaphrodism, together with monosexual genital parts: 3rd, perfect hermaphrodism physical and mental, with all the sexual apparatus bisexually constituted; 4th, crossed hermaphrodism, in which the psychical part and the physical part are monosexual, but each in an opposite sense to the other.

On taking a closer view, the first physical form of heramphrodism may be considered as crossed, for the genital glands correspond to one sex and the external genital parts to an opposite sex.

The second and the fourth form of hermaphrodism are nothing else, at bottom, than congenital sexual inversion. (1)

(1) Frank Lyston, (*Philadelphia Medical and Surgical Reporter*, Sept. 1888), and Kierman (*Medical Standard*, Nov. 1888), attempt to explain in a similar manner a part of the cases of congenital sexual *Paranoia* by placing them in a subordinate category of hermaphrodism. Kiernan, to complete his explanation, supposes that, in tainted individuals regressions to the primitive forms of hermaphrodism of the animal series are more easily produced. "The original bisexuality of the ancestors of the race, shown in the rudimentary female organs of the male, could not fail to occasion functional, if not organic, reversions, when mental or physical manifestations were interfered with by disease or congenital defect. It seems certain that a femininely functionating brain can occupy

The third form appears to be very rare. Nevertheless, the canonical law of the Church concerns itself with it; for it requires an oath from the hermaphrodite before his marriage as to the way in which he will behave. (See Philip, *Kirchenrecht*, p. 633 of the 7th Edition.)

By the monosexual psychical genital apparatus in a monsexual body belonging to the opposite sex, we must not understand " a female soul in a male brain," or *vice versâ*, a way of looking at it which would be in plain contradiction to all scientific ideas. Nor must we imagine that a female brain can exist in a male body, as this would contradict all the anatomical facts; but it must be admitted that a female psycho-sexual centre can exist in a male brain and *vice versâ*.

This psycho-sexual centre (the existence of which it is necessary to assume, were it only in order to explain the physiological phenomena), cannot be anything else than a point of concentration and interlacing of the conductory nerves which make their way to the motive and sensitive apparatus of the genital organs, but which, on the other hand, lead also to the visual, olfactory and other centres, bearing those manifestations of consciousness which, altogether, make up the idea of a "male" or "female" being.

How could we represent this psychical genital apparatus in the state of primitive hermaphrodism which we have supposed above? There also we ought to admit that the future conductory paths were already traced, although very slightly, or prepared by the grouping of elements.

These hermaphroditic "latent paths" are contrived in order to bind the organs of copulation (which are themselves still in the hermaphroditic state), to the future seat of the elements of representation of the two sexes. When the whole organism is devel-

a male body and *vice versâ*. Males may be born with female external genitals and *vice versâ*. The lowest animals are bisexual, and the various types of hermaphrodism are more or less complete reversions to the original type." (*Op. cit.* p. 9. Author's note.)

oped in a normal manner, half of these paths must develop later on in order to become capable of performing their functions while the other half must remain in a latent state; and, in this case, all depends probably on the condition of the interlacing point which we have assumed, as an intercalated subcortical centre.

This very complicated hypothesis does not necessarily contradict the fact that the fœtal brain is not of the structure. This absence of structure is only admitted owing to the insufficiency of our means of actual investigation. But, on the other hand, this hypothesis rests in its turn on a very doubtful supposition: it admits an already existing localization for representations which do not yet exist, in other terms: a kind of differentiation of the parts of the brain which are in connection with future representations. We are no great distance from that theory of "innate representation" which has fallen into such disrepute. But we are also in the presence of the general problem of all the instincts, a problem which always impels us to similar hypotheses.

Perhaps a path will now be opened to us by which we shall be able to take a step towards the solution of these problems of psychical heredity. With the help of the far more extended modern knowledge of the facts of generation in all the series of organisms and also of the knowledge of the connexity of these facts which biology is beginning to give us, we shall be able to take a much deeper view of the nature of physical and psychical heredity.

We are now acquainted with the process of generation, that is to say the transformation of individuals in its most simple manifestation. It shows us the divisions of two sister cellules which qualitatively are identical with the mother cell.

Going further, we see the detachment in the process of budding of a part quantitatively reduced, but indentical in quality with the whole.

The original phenomenon of all generation is not therefore a reproduction, but a continuation If then, in proportion as the types become larger and more complicated the germs of organism appear, in comparison with the mother-organism, not only quanitatively diminished but also qualitatively simplified, morphologically and physiologically, the conviction that generation is a continuation and not a reproduction leads us to the general supposition of a latent but interrupted continuation of the life of the parents in their descendants. For, in the infinitely little, there is room for all, and it is as wrong to imagine that the reduction of size progressing to infinity, a deduction which is but in comparison with the size of the human being who observes it, somewhere reaches a limit insuperable for the differentiation of matter, as it would be erroneous to suppose that the illimitable greatness of universal space somewhere reaches a limit in which it can be filled with individualized formations. What appears to require explanation is rather the fact that it is not all the qualities of the parents, either morphological in size, or physiological with the way of the movements of the particles, which are spontaneously manifested in the development of the germ. This fact, I say, stands more in need of explanation than the hypothesis of an hereditary differentiation of the substance of the brain which has fixed relations with the representations which have not been perceived by the individual, an hypothesis without which the instincts remain inexplicable.

(Krafft Ebing.)

Moll's Opinion.

Moll sees in inversion above all a malformation, an innate anomaly, which render the inverted almost always a diseased individual. This author must be placed in the same rank as Krafft Ebing, for the works of these two foreign *savants* have principally contributed to the real knowledge of all the facts of sexual psychopathy.

He has treated at length upon the etiology of sexual inversion in three chapters. Without giving *in extenso* all the theories which he enunciates, we shall give the most striking passages, summing up the rest as well as we can.

He first begins by giving Caspar's opinion, dividing the patients into two groups; one, in which the inclination for the same sex was congenital, and the others in which it was acquired owing to abuse of coition with woman, and abuse producing a kind of disgust. He recalls the fact that Tarnowsky accepts in a general way Caspar's division, but at the same time includes in the second group the cases of sexual inversion due to bad bringing-up, to evil example and to certain mental diseases.

Moll then passes on to the examination of Krafft Ebing's theories distinguishing acquired from congenital sexual inversion.

He believes, says Moll, that certain causes which we enumerate further on, principally sexual abuse and onanism, may later on produce sexual inversion in a normal individual. The time when these causes may intervene with the greatest efficacy, is when the genital organs are developing, an opinion also shared by Tarnowsky. Unlike acquired sexual inversion, genital inversion is infected with perversion from the beginning, without any inclination for women having previously existed.

However, the majority of cases of sexual inversion, considered as acquired, do not appear to me very convincing, Krafft Ebing's conscientious classification contains but a very few cases of acquired perversion, and I am convinced that even these are not free from all objection, in the sense that the sexual perversion precedes the hetero-sexual inclination.

Moll quotes three observations from Krafft Ebing on simple acquired sexual inversion, which in his opinion are cases of psycho-sexual hermaphrodism. It is true that all the difference is explained by the fact that Krafft Ebing takes a more restricted view of psycho-sexual hermaphrodism than Moll.

It appears however to the latter that an insufficient voluptuous sensation during the sexual act ought, in a great number of cases, to be attributed directly to sexual inversion.

"I am well acquainted will some men who, with no well marked inclination for women, had no voluptuous sensations during coition, in spite of their having erection and ejaculation; en the other hand, this sensation was most intense when they performed a sexual act with a man for whom they had a psycho-sexual hermaphroditic inclination."

Heredity of Inverteds.

All writers are agreed iu saying that the etiological causes are the same for congenital inversion and for acquired inversion.

What is certain, says Moll, is that in all cases of sexual inversion where it is a question of acquired perversion or of congenital inversion the heredity is found to be very tainted. Krafft Ebing, Rabon, Charcot, Magnan, Blumenstock, Kowolewsky, Bourneville, Raoul, Gley, Tarnowsky and a great number of other authors are agreed upon this point.

Besides the well-known nervous and mental diseases, other causes must also be mentioned, such as alcoholism, suicide, consanguineous marriages. "I know several cases of consanguineous marriages in which the father of an Uranist child was a free-liver, celebrated for his successes among women." Krafft Ebing says that he knows of cases where sexual inversion existed to a very slight degree among the ancestors. Tarnowsky again points out syphilis as a cause, an opinion with which Moll does not agree. He considers on the other hand, that a particular part in nervous heredity ought to be attributed to atavism, for if the father and mother are healthy, a nervous or psychical affection will be found to exist in the grand-parents.

"It is therefore certain, says Moll, that a large number of Uranists are descended from families possessing a neuropathic heredity."

Occasional Causes favouring the Breaking out of the Sexual Perversion.

We have said that the predisposition to sexual

inversion was almost always congenital. We must however, admit the existence of occasional causes which favour the breaking out of the sexual perversion, just as in acquired inversion. Even in the cases where sexual inversion can be followed from childhood, we are only able to find a morbid predisposition, in such wise that it is impossible to deny that the breaking out of this perversion may not sometimes be produced by an external cause. In the case of a child, this cause may be purely accidental touching of the genital organs by a man; and the morbid affection there develops through a fatal association between the remembrance of this touch and the mental representation of the man.

It is impossible therefore to draw a rigorous line between the congenital cases properly so called, and those in which the sexual perversion is manifested on the occasion of an accidental cause.

Hammond tells the story of an individual affected with sexual inversion under the form of pederasty, a passion to which he was led by having, when a child, seen two dogs coupling together. The young boy thought that it was done through the anus. In order to imitate the act in question, he introduced a pencil into his rectum and felt simultaneously with the pain another sensation which was very agreeable.

Ought we to say that, in the case of this boy who later on became a passive pederast, the sexual perversion was declared in consequence of the scene at which he was present? We do not think so, for how can that pleasurable sensation be explained which he experienced on introducing the pencil into his rectum and which caused him to repeat the same experience? It is certain that any other occasional cause would have been sufficient to produce in this individual who had never felt any inclination for women, the sexual inversion and the tendency to passive pederasty. A child, or a man in a normal condition might introduce a pencil into the rectum every day without a sexual perversion declaring itself in him.

"What appears to me to be possible is that in the case of a predisposition to sexual inversion, the occasional causes may play a certain part in the way in which the genital instinct will be satisfied. But, on the other hand, it must be said that here again, as we have already seen, a predisposition exists for such and such a sexual act, passive pederasty for example. Otherwise it is impossible for me to explain how it is that individuals exist who, from the beginning, are only satisfied with passive pederasty." (Moll.)

In support of Moll, let us quote our case of the Uranist magistrate who, all his life long, was never anything but a pederast.

"If we admit the part played by occasional causes, still we must not confound those which lead to the realization of an act of perversion with those which produce the breaking out of an inclination to perversion. When a man who for a long time has been a prey to sexual inversion finds an opportunity of satisfying this inclination with another man, this meeting must not however, be considered as the occasional cause which has led the breaking out of this inclination. That is an error which is frequently committed." And here Moll relates the story which we have mentioned above, of an individual who went to bed with a man, under the belief that he was doing so with a woman, and became inverted.

Krafft Ebing's Opinion on Atavism as a Cause of Sexual Inversion.

By the side of Moll's opinion upon heredity as a principal cause of inversion, let us mention that of Krafft Ebing which finds its natural place here.

An explanation of congenital inversion may perhaps be found in the fact that it represents a peculiarity bred in descendants, but arising in ancestry. Atavism might be the morbid inclination for the same sex, an inclination acquired by the ancestor which becomes fixed as a morbid and congenital phenomenon in the descendant. This hypothesis is, in fact, tenable, since, according to the experience of acquired physical and moral attributes, not only the good qualities, but also and above all the defects, are transmitted by heredity. Since individuals affected with inversion not unfrequently beget children—at least they are not absolutely impotent (women never are)—a transmission to descendants is possible.

This supposition is decidedly favoured by Observation 124, in which the daughter of an inverted individual when she was 8 years old practised mutual onanism, a sexual act which, considering her age, gives reason for the presumption of sexual inversion. No less significant is the communication made to me by a young man, aged 20, classed in the 3rd group.

He knew positively that his father, who had died some years before, was also subject to sexual inversion. He declared that he knew many men with whom his father had maintained "relations." Whether in the case of the father, it was an acquired or a congenital inversion, and to what group he belonged, could not be ascertained.

The foregoing hypothesis seems the more plausible, when it is considered that the first three degrees of congenital inversion correspond exactly with the degrees of development which are discoverable in the genesis of acquired inversion.

One therefore feels inclined to designate the different degrees of congenital inversion as various degrees of sexual anomalies acquired or developed in another way in the ancestor, and transmitted by procreation to the descendant. Here too the law of progressive heredity must be taken into consideration.

Others, for want of anything better, have recourse to onanism for the same numerous reasons which, frequently, cause coition to be rejected by non-Uranists. In the case of Uranists endowed with an originally irritable nervous system, or who have been injured by onanism (irritable weakness of the centre of ejaculation) mere embraces or caresses with or without touching the genital parts are sufficient to produce ejaculation, and procure thereby a sexual satisfaction. In less excitable individuals, the sexual act consists in manustupration performed by the loved person, or in mutual onanism, or in a counterfeit coition *inter femora.* In Uranists morally perverse and potent *quoad erectionem*, the sexual impulsion is satisfied by pederasty—an act however which is repugnant to individuals who are not morally defective, much in the same way as it is to heterosexual men. It is a noteworthy fact that Uranists state that the sexual act with persons of the same sex, which is adequate for them, gives them a feeling of great satisfaction and accession of strength, while satisfaction by solitary onanism or by enforced coition with a woman, affects them unfavourably, making them miserable and increasing their neurasthenic symptoms. The way in which female Uranists satisfy themselves is but little known. In one of my personal observations the girl masturbated herself, feeling herself to be taking the part of a man, and imagining herself to have to do with a loved woman. In another case, the act consisted in practising onanism on the person loved and fondling her genital parts. (Krafft Ebing.)

Masturbation, the Effect and not the Cause of Inversion.

Moll is agreed with Krafft Ebing in rejecting masturbation as a cause of inversion.

Tarnowsky is of the same opinion as Collignon that mutual masturbation in boarding-schools and prisons plays a considerable part. Theoretically, in fact, it may be granted that the repeated excitation produced by mutual onanism may lead to sexual inversion. But when we observe the existence of sexual inversion in an individual who has previously practised mutual masturbation with boys, we must not from that lightly conclude that masturbation has led to sexual inversion in the case of this individual; most frequently inversion existed in him before that time. It must also be said that mutual masturbation is so rife in certain circles, that if later on a Uranist springs from them, this is not a sufficient reason for establishing between masturbation and Uranism a relation of cause and effect.

I absolutely reject the opinion of Moreau according to which masturbation would be the cause of the inversion of the sexual inclination. This is an absolutely false conception which confuses cause and effect. If a large number of Uranists masturbate themselves, this is for want of being able to satisfy their genital instinct in another way. If I do not consider masturbation as the cause of Uranism, I admit however that under certain conditions, it may favour the development of sexual inversion. The fact that at the beginning of his sexual evolution, the Uranist, while masturbating himself, thinks only of men aggravates the sexual inversion in the sense that the sexual desires become more and more associated in his case with the idea of men. Therefore it happens that masturbation practised under these conditions, ends in impotence towards women and drives the individual to a greater degree towards men.

Krafft Ebing and J. Caspar insist on the unhealthy influence of masturbation upon individuals affected with sexual inversion or displaying a morbid predisposition to this disease. They admit that masturbation destroys the æsthetic inclination, pure and ideal, which the man feels for the woman. (Moll.)

Moll's Opinion on Heredity as a Cause of Sexual Inversion.

Moll considers in the first place the rigorous distinction which Krafft Ebing draws between acquired and congenital homo-sexuality does not appear to him to be indispensable to confirm the theory of heredity as a principal factor in inversion.

I think that the morbid inclination for individuals of the same sex was perhaps acquired by an ancestor, and has then been transmitted to the descendants in whom it is found in the congenital state. Sexual inversion being met with in individuals who are far from being impotent, Krafft Ebing's theory deserves to be taken into consideration. It is naturally based upon the ideas of Darwin who, as far as I know, does not in any of his works speak of sexual inversion or of kindred phenomena. Krafft Ebing's hypothesis is none the less in accord with Darwin's theories. "I know, says Darwin, of authentic cases of propensity to theft and lying, even in families of very high position. Theft is a somewhat rare crime among the classes which are in easy circumstances, we cannot, therefore, look upon this tendency in two or three members of the same family as a simple coincidence." *It is certain that we could argue in the same way regarding sexual inversion.*

Certain observations may serve as proofs in support of Krafft Ebing's theory. This author, for instance, relates the history of a young man affected with sexual inversion, who maintained that his father was a Uranist like himself. Another patient said to Krafft Ebing that his father had a very pronounced taste for handsome and well-made male servants.

Monsieur N. N.... who has been mentioned in the preface, wrote to me as follows: "I have taken up in my late father's library a large number of books. My father was in the habit of making notes on the margin of the pages, and these—I was greatly struck by the fact—referred almost always to passages where there was a question of sexual inversion. My father had five children in a short time; he was not therefore impotent and I do not pretend to maintain that he was affected with sexual inversion. But I strongly suspect one of my near relatives of having been affected with that malady, and that, I think, is the reason for my father interesting himself so much in this question.

The cases reported by Lucas ([1]) present a very peculiar interest: there is a question of heredity in pederasty.

([1]) *Traité physiologique et philosophique d'hérédité naturelle.* Paris, 1850.

A cook, a very skilful man in his profession, had a passion for his wife which was carried to frenzy, and at the same time an inclination for pederasty. His natural son, who lived at a distance from his father and did not know him, displayed the same passion for the two sexes.

Lastly let us say that the disease of the Scythians was, according to Herodotus, reputed to be hereditary.

Other proofs in support of the theory of the part played by heredity in sexual inversion, are supplied by the existence of this malady in blood relatives, or by its simultaneous development in two brothers. I knew two brothers, both affected with sexual inversion; another similar case has been communicated to me by a credible individual.

Two other Uranists each have a brother displaying a complete sexual anæsthesia. Sometimes, we also find, in the sisters of these patients, a singular coldness and indifference to men's attentions. In one of Krafft Ebing's cases, the patient's sister did not feel any inclination for men, and was, on the contrary, in love with some of her female friends.

Cases also are known of other morbid sexual perversions existing in several members of the same family. The Sadist whose history I communicated to Krafft Ebing and which was published by him, had a brother who displayed very clearly the same sadistic tendencies. While the one liked to beat a woman until she cried out with pain, the other had a passion for ejaculating on a woman's face, and he felt a keen feeling of satisfaction when this act made her weep. Krafft Ebing also has a case of hereditary transmission of sadistic tendencies. The patient in question was seized with genital excitation when he saw fowls being killed; his father had a singular passion for violently squeezing the hands of young women or young girls with cords.

Ribot, who attributes such a great importance to heredity, lays stress upon the hereditary transmission of sexual anomalies and quotes a large number of instances, among others that of Pope Alexander VI. [1] and his children.

After this study relating to the influence of heredity, it remains for me to say a few words upon an opposite theory, that of Schopenhauer. For this author, Uranism, like every other phenomenon of Nature, has a determinate aim. This opinion was, rightly, contested in a volume devoted to the critical study of Schopenhauer's works. The existence of homo-sexual love at all periods is, in Schopenhauer's opinion, the proof that this phenomenon springs from human nature. He then quotes Aristotle's opinion that men, when they have passed the age of fifty, can only procreate weakly children and, on this account, give up reproduction.

In order to assist the preservation of the species and to prevent the procreation of miserable individuals, the hetero-sexual inclination is transformed at this age, according to Schopenhauer, into the homo-sexual inclination. In this theory, the first premise, that men of fifty can no longer produce vigorous children, is wholly wrong. But the error consists principally in the hypothesis of the constant appearance of homo-sexual tendencies in old men. We have seen in fact, that these tendencies, when they exist in old men, date from childhood. Then, when they appear towards the age of fifty or later, their existence, far from being normal, ought to be rather considered as the sign of the commencement of a celebral affection.

The starting-point of the theory lately enunciated by Gyurkovechky is as wrong as that of Schopenhauer's hypothesis. Gyurkovechky admits that, in normal physiological conditions, taste disappears with the advance of age. The man then becomes less fastidious and he can have intercourse with persons whom he would not have wished to approach before. This lower-

(1) This Pope was named Roderigo Borgia and was descended, on his mother's side from the celebrated family of Borgia, whose name he afterwards assumed. Both as Cardinal and Pope, Alexander was celebrated for his life of debauchery: the best known of his children are Cæsar and Lucrezia Borgia.

ing, this physiological disappearance of taste, makes ready the ground, in this author's opinion, in which sexual inversion can gradually develop. In this group Gyukovechky places the individuals who, after leading a normal existence for many years become late in life pederasts and exhibitionists.

To the instances given by Moll we can add the two following. The first is that of Krafft Ebing's 112th observation. The subject was seduced by a doctor who was the father of two sons, aged respectively 14 and 15, with whom in the following year he formed a love-attachment. The second observation came under our own notice.

Inverted Daughters of a Pederast Father.

X...., a officer of high rank in the French navy, whom I had known as a midshipman in Cochin China in 186.. had become occasionally inverted. (Vide Chapter VIII.) Being in command of a *lorcha* (guard-boat) at the entrance to Soi-rap, and having no distractions, the young officer had fallen into the practice of vice with men, at first by simple labial pollution and afterwards by active anal coition. Entering the colonial service, he remained for several years consecutively in Cochin China, where he continued to indulge in this vice, and did not return to France until the beginning of 1870, on his promotion to Lieutenant. He served brilliantly in the war in a battalion of marine Fusiliers, forming a part of one of the provincial armies.

He married, immediately after the war, a woman of very rigid principles, regarding whom scandal, always ready to carp at wives whose husbands are absent, could find no evil to report. In the intervals between his long periods of service abroad, X.... had four children by his wife, but all daughters. The two eldest; now 26 and 23 years old respectively, are born celebral inverteds, but it is a curious thing that the the eldest, who is a desperate Saphist, is a cerebral feminiphil. She has been expelled from two educational establishments into which she introduced this vice. The younger one, on the contrary, is a cerebral masculiphil and attacks all the maid-servants in the house, especially those who are man-like and whose general *habitus* resembles that of a man. She has no repugnance to marriage, if she found a man who pleased her. The eldest, on the other hand, has an instinctive repugnance to men. The mere idea of sleeping in the same bed with a man is horrible to her. The two youngest (15 and 18 years of age) are normal, particularly the one aged 18. It is only as a doctor and an old friend of the family that I have been able to obtain these confidences.

It will be noticed that the inversion decreases in proportion as the father discarded his occasional morbid habit. Obviously we cannot draw from this single observation an absolute conclusion, but it serves nevertheless to confirm in a singular manner the facts of this kind given by Moll and Krafft Ebing.

Theoretical Explanation of Sexual Inversion by Moll.

Following upon all these considerations, I wish to set forth in a very general way how I explain theoretically sexual inversion. The defect of the greater part of the theories is that they do not grasp the fact of the analogy which exists between the sexual instinct and the other functions.

To understand the homo-sexual inclination, the genital instinct must be considered not as a phenomenon apart among the other functions, but rather as a psychical function. In any case, the morbid modifications of the genital instinct will appear less incomprehensible to us, if we admit that almost all the other psychical or physical functions may be susceptible of similar modifications. If, in the species, the anomalies strike us so strongly, it is that, in the majority of individuals possessing the attributes of the masculine sex, there exists a sexual inclination for the woman. But we must not allow ourselves to be led into error by the frequency and the regularity with which this phenomenon is observed. From the teleological point of view, that is to say from the point of view of the reproduction of the species, we ought to consider as natural the inclination which the normal man feels for the woman; it does not remain less true that, in certain pathological conditions, the organs do not fulfil the purpose which is assigned to them. The teeth are intended to masticate the food and yet there are men who have no teeth, or very few. The function of the liver is to secrete the bile which is diverted into the intestine, but in certain affections of the liver or of the biliary ducts, the bile is not secreted and does not reach the intestine.

The object of hunger is to recall to the organism the fact that it requires food. Pathological conditions are however to be found in which the feeling of hunger is absent, although the stomach remains normal. It is the same with the absence of the sexual inclination for the woman in the case of a man possessing normal genital organs. As we have said, it is hardly possible for us to establish a relation between the genital organs of the man and his inclination for the woman except from the teleological point of view. Otherwise, it is not clear for what reason the man should feel impelled to intercourse with the woman, since the ejaculation of sperm can be obtained in another way. It would rather be astonishing if the genital instinct did not display the same morbid anomalies as the other functions of the body and mind. Neither its peculiar importance nor its social character should make us look upon the sexual instinct as a solitary phenomenon.

If the phenomena of sexual inversion appear striking to us, it is because from the social point of view few psychical disorders play such an important part as the aberrations of the sexual instinct. This instinct, in all civilized countries remains hidden as it were behind a veil. The species of mystery which surrounds it is the cause of the peculiar impression produced upon us by the anomalies in question, when they come to the light of day. There is a further and special explanation of this in the fact that the sexual instinct is a psychical function which requires the cooperation of another individual and thus acquires a peculiar social importance. But from the physiological point of view, the anomalies of the genital instinct do not in any way differ from the anomalies of the function of nutrition. If, from the social point of view, great importance is not attributed to these latter anomalies, it is because the regular accomplishment of the function does not require, in this case the cooperation of another indivividual.

After all these considerations, it is unnecessary to enter into a detailed theoretical study of certain other manifestations, although sexual inversion, according to Westphal, does not remain strictly limited to the genital sphere. The phenomena of effemination are likewise very important. I shall merely say that effemination may be looked at in two ways: either the psychical functions of an individual become modified owing to a homosexual inclination, or the effemination is congenital in the same way as the sexual inversion itself. If we consider the effemination as secondary, we shall find a certain analogy, in this hypothesis, with what happens subsequent to castration; in the latter case, in consequence of a local mutilation, the genital sense becomes extinct and the phenomena of effemination, woman's voice, etc., appear a certain time after the operation. (Moll.)

The reader will pardon the long quotations which we have thought it right to make from Krafft Ebing and especially from Moll. But these authors (the latter especially) have the merit of putting forth their theories and opinions in a clear and striking form.

We do not however limit ourselves to these two authors and we shall now proceed to consider the opinions of the authors of the New French School which has taken the place of the old pedagogic conception of Tardieu and his allies.

Causes of Sexual Inversion according to Laupts.

Laupts has studied in detail the story of a born-inverted and the case of Oscar Wilde. In order that this work may not reach an excessive development, we see ourselves obliged, to our great regret, to pass over in silence the critical examination of it which this author makes and we confine ourselves to giving merely his opinion upon the causes of sexual inversion.

Lauphts places himself distinctly on Lacassagne's side in the face of the German School of Moll and Krafft Ebing. He is of opinion that these latter have gone too far in finding that inversion is, in the majority of cases, a mental disease.

A great number of oral and written confessions, collected in the course of enquiries which I have made in collaboration with my excellent and eminent master, Professor Lacassagne; numerous commnnications which I have had upon this subject from well-known physicians; and lastly a certain number of very confidential documents which I have in my possession, have led me to think that it was time for a reaction in the contrary direction, and that putting oneself into a position as scientific perhaps in appearance but undoubtedly more fruitful in results, it is of moment to study the remedy by the side of the disease, to cure it, and for that purpose to know that between the different cases there exist not only differences of *intensity*, but also differences of *nature*, that one case depends upon pathology, while an analogous one is a pure accident, an occasional manifestation, arising from external, transitory circumstances, without any deep roots in the organism, capable of passing away with the disappearance of the same causes which gave birth to it.

The first observation, which has been made by every author and is confirmed by the slightest study, is the following, that, in every abnormal association between two men, the parts whether the union be platonic or not—are very distinct. One is *strong*, active, the protector; he fulfils the function and office of the male: the other is *weak*, passive, the protected; he is the woman.

A point which it is necessary to observe in the first place, is that, in the weaker one, not only are the mind, the feelings, the soul (whatever meaning may be attached to this word) feminine, but the body also is feminine. In the majority of cases this individual *is* and *has been* feminine in his physical *habitus*; not only does his character, deceitful, coquettish and vain, betray the woman, but the development of his hips, pelvis and buttocks, the prominence of his breasts, the liquid look of his eyes, the whiteness and delicacy of his skin, the slimness of his limbs, enable one to declare that there exists in him not an acquired, but an innate error in his formation. His is a feminine soul placed in a body feminine in its characteristics—save one; he is a born-inverted, a true type, really existing and easily recognizable by his external form. You will often come across him in the street, in the railway-carriage, or at a restaurant. If you have any doubt about it, make friends with him, induce him to give you his confidence and his confessions; you will then soon gain information as to his acts or his tendencies, as the case may be. It is not then a question of a creature hard to be recognized and still hypothetical, as some authors suppose: *the born-inverted exists.* Look for him and you will find him, if not frequently at least without any difficulty.

There is a very opposite and essentially different type: a man morally, he is also a man physically; with normal antecedents and normal conduct in the past, he has only been inverted since the time when, in an abnormal combination of circumstances (surrounded, I mean to say, only by individuals of his own sex) he was unable to give satisfaction to the most important of his instincts, that which insures the perpetuation of the species. Scorning to indulge in solitary debauchery, urged by his wants, more powerful perhaps in him than in others, he has felt himself invincibly attracted by those who offered him the charm, the grace and the delicacy of the other sex, and quasi-normal satisfaction. He has been the male, the strong one, of the partnership. He has lived in this way, until fresh circumstances have taken him out of his bad surroundings and placed him again in healthy and normal conditions, under the influence of which, with an appropriate treatment and a legitimate affection, he will again become what he has never ceased to be at bottom. This is an *occasionally inverted* individual.

But, it will be said, must not a man be mad, or at least degenerate, to come to such ignominy as this? To this I shall reply that many do not go so far as the act: their will resists the final fall and perhaps comes forth victorious, but sometimes, let us observe, at the price of other deviations: some individuals, ignorant of the nature of the feeling which animates them, give it the name of comradeship, true friendship, or fondness, an inclination to which they do not imagine that it could be sacrificed. That the attraction exists, is evident, for a crowd of adult subjects placed in the midst of anti-normal, agyorical conditions, the instinct is powerful and imperative. The case is not exceptional in the human species any more than it has devolved upon it exclusively; it occurs in all collections of males with differences in the case of men; those which separate the ignorant, often preserved from ultimately falling by their want of knowledge and of powers of observation, from the intelligent who understand, are often dismayed, and either resist or do not resist, as the case may be. The more genitally inclined the subject, the greater is the privation, the less the force of resistance, and the more frequent the excitations and inducements of the born-inverteds, instinctively impelled towards the more masculine individuals.

Let us add to this the rapid disappearance of the feelings of propriety and ideas of morality, the frequency of opportunities among all the individuals crowded together, the contagion of evil, *a law of the most corrupt, corrupting the less corrupt* in a community; and we shall find the explanation of those epidemics which break out in schools, in prisons, in barracks, among troops on a campaign, afforded by the presence of some born-inverteds, or of normal men with a feminine form.

We shall find in that the explanation of those partnerships in which there is almost always found a feminine (born-inverted), and a masculine (occasionally inverted), for though it is unnecessary to assert that this kind of partnership is always the same, it is nevertheless shown in the great majority of cases. Let us quote, as we go along, the instances supplied by the *tale of a born-inverted*, a true story, and which I have already published in the *Archives d'Anthropologie* of Dr. Laccassagne. ([1]) We see there a *born-inverted* of an extremely clear type; an occasionally-inverted who succumbed on contact with the former, and finally, a perverted individual whose continuous debanchery made him wish to find less commonplace excitations than those to which he was accustomed.

Between the two extreme types which we have just discussed there is placed—and very unfortunately for the convenience of study and description—a third, more frequent perhaps and more complex. It is that of the normal man *without physical malformations*, whose sole anomaly consists in the attraction which he feels for those of his own sex, and the coldness and sometimes repulsion which he evinces for those of the opposite sex. He was born a man, but when he was quite young, man seduced him and not woman. He has a predisposition and habit which will render him inverted.

Curious as this individual may be, his case can be explained: ought not the children of an occasionally-inverted, born after the act has taken place, or after these occasional practices have become habits, to display this predisposition? And if the tendencies to inversion which were strong not only in one but in a whole series of paternal ancestors, are again strengthened and consolidated by *similar* dispositions upon the

([1]) This tale will be published in the Chapter of this volume relating to the modes of enjoyment of Inverteds and Pederasts.

maternal side, ought not the descendant to display all the symptoms of an affection capable of coinciding with a normal physical structure, of even being at birth only a simple predisposition, for it is a question of a psychological nervous heredity—or atavism—and not of an error of nature, of a visible physical malformation, of a faulty construction of the organism, (shall we say?) of an externally apparent monstrosity, as in the case of the born-inverted? (Laupts. *op. cit.*)

We see that Laupts is of the same opinion as ourselves, that the principal factor is heredity, atavism, and that the different hereditary causes do not appear to him to deserve to be taken into serious consideration. Our opinion completely coincides with his. We could not give a better comparison of inversion than by comparing it with a virulent disease like syphilis. There are born syphilitics, in whom the disease appears with all its symptoms from birth. There are syphilitics, in whom the disease is attenuated, going back to a grandfather or to a father who has attended to himself; and with careful regimen and no excesses of any kind, the disease may remain latent and the subject may not feel it in any way. But if the patient commits excesses of alcohol or coition, if he passes his nights in a gaming-house or in a brothel, the tertiary symptoms of syphilis make their appearance. They do not arise from alcohol, nor from abuse of coition with a healthy woman, nor is it the Queen of Spades who has given them syphilis. They have acted but as accessory causes. The argument is the same with regard to inversion.

Let us remark that Laupts forms a very natural transition between the old school of Tardieu which saw in the inverted only infamous pederasts, and the German school, Moll and Krafft Ebing, which sees in them nothing but sufferers from dementia or degeneracy. The truth, as is always the case, is to be found halfway between the two. There are no diseases, there are only sufferers.

The learned English physician, Marc André Raffalovich, a pupil of Lacassagne, has written a very interesting book on Uranism and Unisexuality. His theories are very remarkable, for he treats these questions from a higher point of view than the majority of physicians, and principally from the philosophical point of view.

Influence of Heredity upon Inversion, according to Raffalovich.

Up to the present time I have concerned myself but little about heredity. I do not find that the details which are given as regarding the ancestors, the brothers and the sisters of Uranists facilitate our acquaintance with, or our knowledge of their Uranism. I think, on the other hand, that I rendered the fact clear that the weakness, neurosis, or alcoholism of the parents explains rather the want of courage and want of initiative of certain unisexuals, than their unisexuality. The unisexuals who have no pleasure in life, who have no courage, who believe themselves to be the bastards of nature, have a more tainted heredity than the unisexuals who accept their instinct and do not rebel against nature. Hereditary neuroses rather contradicts unisexuality than explains it.

Those who will not or cannot admit the possibility of Uranism being an almost primordial instinct, and who cannot conscientiously find all Uranists to be degenerates or of the lowest physiological value, must certainly fall back upon heredity. It draws all the embarrassed writers out of their dead-lock in the following way: the normal hetero-sexual acquires habits of inversion and a taste for men. Heredity transforms this acquired taste into a congenital taste under the adverse influence of the physical or psychical disease of the ancestors, of their neurasthenias, their alcoholism, or of any other tiresome or vexatious thing which may happen to the parents. It may be thus made use of for Uranism, to blame the parents and to commiserate the children. It will end in finding all this to be illusory and ephemeral from these points of view. It is illogical, because a man is not degenerate, to hunt out or to invent if necessary, vicious or degenerate parents for him.

It seems that all heredities lead to Uranism, just as Uranism leads to all heredities and all transmissions. History shows us uncontested Uranists who were without any doubt fathers of hetero-sexuals. The contrary too is not uncommon. Henri IV. was the father of the Uranist Vendôme who, in his turn, was grandfather of the unisexual Vendôme "who took Barcelona and the pox on the wrong side," and of his brother the Prior who was also unisexual. The two Condé's were unisexual; the father, whom Henri IV. married to Mdlle de Montmorency because he knew that he was a woman-hater; and the son, the conqueror of Rocroi.

Dr. Legrain's Theories on Inversion.

Dr. Legrain begins by studying sexual inversion from the theoretical and anthropological point of view. He endeavours to show the independence of the sexual evolution and of the genital instinct, starting from this principal datum that every created being is hermaphroditic. "There are therefore in the evolutionary order beings who are born and remain clearly hermaphroditic: that is a principal point to lay down. The sexual differentiation of superior beings is only the fact of an evolution. What is the reason of it? Is it intended to favour a special selection? I do not know. In any case it is a fact. But it still holds good that in order to reproduce, the accoupling of the two opposite sexes, the intimate *reconjunction* of the two elements which primordially were but one (hermaphrodism) will be indispensable. Without this reconstitution into a single being, no reproductiou is possible."

From the following argument, the author draws this conclusion.

"The true differentiation of sex is therefore not contemporary with the development and working of the genital apparatus: on the contrary, it is preexistent, but remains latent. And as a final proof of this I would take the history itself of Uranists whose organs, perfectly differentiated and properly formed, arouse only homo-sexual desires in the brain at the time of puberty. We know, on the other hand, that the practice of onanism has no influence upon the development of Uranism. It is proper to add however, that, under normal circumstances, the instinct finds at its disposition at the time of which I speak a large psycho-sexual organism, the two elements of which are perfectly enclosed and harmonized.

"Sex therefore does not have the genital apparatus for its exclusive or principal emblem. How then, and at what period do the hetero-sexual inclinations develop? By what power is a normal being clearly differentiated from the genital point of view at the time of puberty naturally attracted towards the other sex? What part belongs to the natural predisposition, to education, to the habits, etc., in the psychical differentiation which we have seen to be sometimes the reverse of the genital differentiation? Such are the points which I must shortly examine."

These points are thus decided by the author:

1. The period of conception is the period of sexual differentation.

2. It is merely by virtue of physiological and essentially material properties falling under the empire of the senses, that *an affinity exists between opposite sexes.* And these properties are inherent to each sex properly differentiated: but, in order that they may be clearly perceived, it is necessary that this differentiation should be as complete as possible and that the antagonist sex should itself be properly differentiated, if not, the affinity ceases or is perturbed and we fall into the anomaly.

3. At puberty it remains for the individual to find his definitive psychical sexual form. For the whole of his data, he has only those which are supplied him by his education and the customs of his surroundings. These data should nourish, and make fruitful or destroy

the native sexual disposition more or less clearly differentiated. It is here that we observe the very important part played by education especially for those who are *sexually undecided*, and, it must also be said, that the responsibility of the social state in the production of certain sexual monstrosities is not unimportant.

How the charge that Legrain justly brings against the social conditions to which we are absolute prisoners, is that they introduce a deep disorder into the regular and normal evolution of the sexes, that they develop numerous degenerescences and that they warp many views. "The least evil which springs from them is that they destroy in the child's mind the idea of parallelism which ought to exist between the genital appetites and the sexual appetites, that they force the development of the one to the detriment of the other, that they allow both the one and the other to free themselves from their reciprocal influence, and finally that they draw, according to circumstances, the one to contemplative love, and the other to auto-frequentation or homosexuality. In a similar occurrence the individual is by birth as completely differentiated as possible from the sexual point of view, matters settle down of themselves in the natural order after some hesitation and indecision, but, for the few which differentiation apportions to the category of undecideds, social exigencies and combinations allow the irregular appetites to develop without any remedy, appetites which it would have been easy to correct and to direct into a normal path by means of appropriate surroundings."

Explanation of the Phenomena of Sexual Inversion.

Supplied with the preceding data, we can now enter upon the distinctly pathological field and endeavour to explain the phenomena of sexual inversion. This explanation, in my opinion, entirely gravitates round the conception of primordial hermaphrodism and the more or less complete sexual differentiation which springs from it in the natural order of things.

But a fresh idea is joined to it. All the patients with whom we have occupied ourselves are primordially deteriorated and degenerate creatures; their evolution consequently is irregular. The observations point this out very clearly; we always find in them an hereditary predisposition and the patients are clearly placed amid decadent family surroundings. Our case forms no exception to the rule.

Now, two things characterize the states of degenerescence: firstly, from the anatomo-physiological point of view, the irregularity of development ending in psycho-physical monstrosities;—secondly, from the anthropological point of view, a fatal tendency to the disappearance of the species passing through stages recalling, without however being confounded with them, the stages of ancestral evolution, a phenomenon which has been able to qualify the degenerative conditions of *regressives*. We shall see these two points of view realized in the case of our inverteds.

Let us turn back to the four degrees adopted by Krafft Ebing, which are in fact the best symptomatic subdivision of inversions. These are, it will be remembered:

1. Psychical Hermaphrodism.
2. Uranism.
3. Effemination and Viraginity.
4. Androgynia and Gynandria.

One common feature unites the four, hermaphrodism, which they do not altogether assume but exist as varieties. Moreover, they are not strictly limited to their divisions and a number of transitions exists between them just as certain clinical cases, as I have shown, enter indifferently into several of these forms.

Psychical hermaphrodism is the result of a sexual differentiation which was nil at the period of the membryonnary evolution. The appetence is equal for the two sexes, which comes to the same thing as saying that the patients when born have masculine and feminine potentialities. Are these aptitudes really equal? Very rarely so, and if we refer to the observations, it is manifest that there always exists a somewhat more marked tendency towards one sex, whether there is a preponderating hetero-sexuality, which brings us near to the normal condition and forms the transition between the physiological ground and the morbid ground, or whether there is a preponderating homosexuality, which brings us little by little to Uranism.

The cases of the first degree differ therefore from the normal condition in that the homosexual tendencies, instead of being concealed by heterosexual tendencies and always stifled, assume enough importance to demand satisfaction and become an obsession to the patients. It is in this category that we must include the majority of those individuals, of whom I have spoken above, individuals of undecided sexuality, half-differentiated, who form the frontier zone between the normal state and degenerescence, and for whom a faulty education is a source of danger.

Is there then no categorical differentiation here? Why? Can it be said that the bilateral influences would be exactly in equilibrium? Evidently not: for we should easily arrive at the idea that perfect psychical hermaphrodism must be the rule in normal individuals, whereas it is, under a certain limit, a pathological case. In reality, at the time of conception the bilateral influences are clearly shown as being always equivalent, but the sexual evolution, from which a clear differentiation must ultimately be derived, has been arrested *ab ovo*. This is one of those phenomena of arrested development such as are commonly observed in degenerates. The sexual evolution has been nil or has been barely delineated and the individual is born *bisexual*. But this bisexuation is but the first term of more serious conditions in which this bisexuation will be seen to be simply equivalent to an asexuation, either by the concomitant disappearance of all reproductive instinct, or by an equivalent aberration of this instinct, the result of which will be to destroy its useful effects. This conception explains why I have usually employed together two terms which are hardly equal, the expressions hermaphrodites and neuters (I might say asexuated), hermaphrodites in reality being, whatever their appearance may be, neuters from the functional reproductive point of view, and in process of becoming complete neuters, physically and morally, from the point of view of reproduction.

But during this time, our psycho-sexual hermaphrodites have become clearly differentiated from the genital point of view. This is again one of the phenomena of the absence of equilibrium so commonly marked in the evolution of degenerates. While they are bisexuated as to their instinctive tendencies, they are unisexuated from the genital point of view. This clearly proves, in parenthesis, on the one hand the independence of the instinct and organ from the physiological point of view; and on the other hand the little importance of the genital organs in the differentiation of sex.

Thus our first degree is characterized by an anomaly of the development of the sexual instinctivity coincident with a regular organic evolution. A reservation must again be made with regard to this regular evolution, for it is not uncommon to meet with more or less attenuated signs in patients of bisexuality besides the genital organs, which brings us, by a gradual transition, towards another degree, (Krafft Ebing's 4th degree), which precisely draws its characteristics from the co-existence in the same subject of psychical and physical signs of bisexuality.

Here the double semeiology is evident, and complete hermaphrodism tends to be established. Sufferers from epispadiasis and hypospadiasis, cryptorchides, etc., are the malformed individuals who belong to this group. Making a step further, we reach true hermaphrodism, which Krafft Ebing does not admit, but which forms so naturally the last term of the series that, for my part, I do not hesitate to form its natural conclusion. What are, as we go on, these androgynes and gynandres from the psychical point of view? They are, either the exact inversion of psychical hermaphrodites, that is to say they are psychically monosexuated and consequently normal;—or they are physically hermaphrodites and morally so also; or, as in my opinion is more important, they are really neuter, asexuated and null and void as to the sexual appetite. This was the case with that hermaphrodite whose case I have briefly related above.

Thus in proportion as we descend the scale of the degradations which apply, in a more or less parallel way, to the psycho-genital sexual organization, and as we see the hermaphrodite, the original double creature reconstituted, but now on a morbid ground, we see the sexual instinct becoming extinct, or, what comes to the same thing, destroying the function of reproduction as a prelude to the disappearance of the instinct itself.

The evolutionary disorders of gynandres and androgynes are explained by the same mechanism as those of psycho-sexual hermaphrodites. In these cases there is no anatomical differentiation any more than there is any psychical sexual differentiation. While, in normal cases, differentiation is the fruit of an arrested development of the organs of the opposite sex, here the development is continued more or less regularly in all the cellular parts from which the genital organs of the two sexes emanate. The individual finds himself at birth in possession of a group of useless organs just as other degenerates are in possession of a sixth toe or of supplementary teeth.

Who does not now perceive with the greatest ease in Krafft Ebing's two intermediary groups, very marked transitions between the two extremes, transitions which can be explained by always starting from the idea of a congenital hermaphrodism?

What are the Uranists, (2nd degree)? They are creatures *genitally* formed according to a determinate sex, and psychically formed according to another sex. The man eagerly seeks for intercourse with men, and the woman with women; consequently, if the man, in his contact with men, experiences feelings which the man ought normally to feel in presence of women; if the contact with men produces in him the venereal orgasm, it is because he is in reality a woman, whose external organs are not properly differentiated. If he appears in the act of coition in the part of the male, that is to say the active part, it is because in this circumstance he acts by the aid of purely medullary reflexes which are connected with the conformation of the external genital organs. No mistake must therefore be made regarding the true sex (anthropologically and physiologically speaking) of this Uranist whom we are regarding and who is entered as a male; he is a woman. He is the counterpart of those badly differentiated individuals whom we have seen on the frontier zone: if, in the case of these latter who are differentiated as males, the male psycho-sexual aptitudes could be represented by 8, the psycho-sexual feminine attributes would be represented by 2. In the case of the Uranist, the proportion is reversed.

Now, possessing indubitable psychical and physical signs of bisexuality, our Uranist is not only an inverted, but although differentiated in his inversion, he is bisexuated and consequently an hermaphrodite by the same title as the others, and this is the point at which I wished to arrive.

What I have just said of the Uranist male naturally applies also to the Uranist female.

Thus, an embryo, almost completely differentiated from the sexual point of view, is arrested in its ulterior embryo-fœtal evolution, not from the sexual point of view, the physical attributes proper to the sex are reduced to a minimum so that they disappear behind the hypertrophical development of the physical attributes of the opposite sex. It is thus that, sexually feminine, he happens at birth to display externally all the masculine attributes. This is how Uranism is constituted.

It is proper to recall the fact that the Uranists who retain in their genital intercourse the part which corresponds to their external sex (the active part for the male Uranist, the passive part for the female Uranist), are extremely rare. Among the majority of those who are displayed as such, the anomaly is, in fact, much more a genital matter than a sexual matter. The Uranist then has the sex of which his external genital organs are the evidence, but it is perverted rather than inverted in the accoupling. If he seeks solely for intercourse with the same sex, it is because he is endowed with a particular sensibility by virtue of which the homosexual contact produces the venereal orgasm. It is upon this point of detail only that he is inverted; he is a man or a woman, having in his medullary axis certain reserves of the woman or the man. As we see, the question of sex in this case remains altogether foreign to the constitution of the anomaly.

All that I have just said about Uranism applies, finally, very easily to effemination and viraginity. Inversion is a more accomplished fact than in the preceding case, and the explanation which I proposed for the latter, becomes still more acceptable for this. Here, in fact, psycho-genital hermaphrodism is imposed; the antagonism is still strong between the sexual instinctivity and the instrumentation which it finds at its service. And further, in the accoupling the patient plays the part contrary to that which is ordered him by his genital organization: he becomes passive if a female.

Here again it is a question of a patient who, at the embryonic period, is almost completely differentiated from the sexual point of view, but whose ulterior evolution has been completely disordered, in the sense that the almost parallel development of the physical sexual attributes, male and female, has made of him a genital hybrid, save that in this simultaneous double development, the genital marks of the other sex are a little more advanced, which allows a legal sex to be given to their possessor, different in reality to his true sex.

The disorder however in this case is less serious, in spite of appearances, than in the case of the Uranist, who is deficient in all the physical sexual attributes which correspond to his true psychical sex. Comparatively, the two cases may be interpreted in this way: the effeminated individual and the virago have everything belonging to the opposite sex, except the genital organs; the Uranist has only the sexual tendencies of the opposite sex, without having their material realization. Both of them are moreover, at different degrees, on the road of true psycho-sexual hermaphrodism, in which we have seen the bisexual aptitudes counterbalancing themselves almost exactly.

Thus then the inverted, to whatever degree they belong, are so many varieties of hermaphrodites, and all proceed from a fault in the normal differentiation of original hermaphrodism.

But they are not only hermaphrodites. This congenital deformity is also accompanied by sexual *neutrality*. I have already pointed this out, but I ought to insist upon it again. In fact, for the hermaphrodites of the 1st and 4th degree, the anomaly is accompanied by an equal inclination for either sex; the sex is therefore indifferent, it is neuter, although some still retain, temporarily, the power of reproduction. As for the Uranists, the effeminated and the viragos, their neutrality springs from their fatally unproductive intercourse with members of the same sex. They still retain the aptitude for reproduction, it is true, but this aptitude is destroyed, since it is necessarily unutilized for want of normal sexual appetence.

Lastly the inverted are not only *hermaphrodites* and *neuters*, but they also deserve the qualification of *frigid*. The term frigidity ought to be taken in its widest sense and extended to every creature in whom the sexual appetence has disappeared. Frigid is not a synonym for impotent, and is not applied to the genital action itself. Frigidity is to the sexual impulsion what impotence is to copulation. Now, the inverted not being normally differentiated but being naturally deprived of one of the most imperious feelings of requirement of the species, the requirement of reproduction, are fatally frigid at the place of the sex called to play the part of supernumerary in the reproductory act. They are struck with *anorexia sexualis.*

If we look at it closely, in fact, the inverted individual no longer has a genital appetence, and the satisfactions which he seeks for are of a purely medullary order. We must not judge after appearances and see in the burlesque attempts at accoupling among the inverted, the accomplishment of a sexual requirement, but merely a seeking for sensations of a special order which have nothing to do with the *sexual instinct.*

In fact the sexual instinct has disappeared; from which follows this conclusion that in the inverted, the hermaphrodite, the bisexual, this objective *bisexuation* is only the token of a subjective *asexuation.* The sex is only the aptitude for reproduction under normal and regular conditions. As soon as this aptitude disappears, the creature is asexuated. And this deduction, which is very important from the anthropological point of view is the latest conclusion of the psycho-physiological study of the inverted. (Dr. Legrain. *op. cit.*)

And if the author now asks us which is the author among all those who have been quoted in this chapter whose theories on the explanation of the phenomena of inversion appear to us to be most plausible, we shall decidedly answer, "Dr. Legrain."

Treatment of Inversion by Hypnotic Suggestion.

Kraft Ebing in Austria, and Laupts in France have devoted their particular attention to the treatment of inversion by hypnotic suggestion. These two physicians are agreed in saying that the prognosis of acquired sexual inversion is more favourable than that of innate inversion. "In the former, the occurrence of effemination—the mental inversion of the individual, in the sense of perverse sexual feeling—is the limit beyond which there is no hope of benefit from therapy. In the congenital cases, the various categories enumerated in this book represent so many stages of psycho-sexual taint, and cure is possible only in the category of hermaphrodites, and only probable in the states of more serious degenerescence." (Krafft Ebing.)

The Viennese physician gives a dozen very interesting observations, in which he has obtained, if not a complete cure, at least a considerable amelioration.

Laupts, for his part, has studied in great detail (Chapter V.), the diagnosis, the prognosis, and the treatment of inverteds. He gives the individual and general prophylaxia of it. We cannot follow this author into a subject which lies beyond our scope, and we shall advise every inverted individual who reads these lines to procure for himself Laupts' work and to endeavour to cure himself by it.

"Each man is the worker-out of his own destiny," has said some great moralist or other.

Duration and Prognosis of Uranism.

As a general rule it may be said that Uranism *is born with a patient and dies with him.* (Thoinot.)

As long as the Uranist retains his genital vigour, he is in the service of his inversion. I will go even further. When, in the case of a hetero-sexual, old age comes and chills the genital organs which become flaccid and withered, when ejaculation at first and then even erection no longer take place, when the old man is more unhappy than the youth who has not yet reached puberty and cannot even satisfy himself with the phantom of pleasure obtained by the rubbing of his feeble member in a vagina, then he gives up love. Some become devout, for "when the devil was old, the devil a saint would be." Others when they are obliged to turn off the tap of love, turn on that of the barrel.

The old Uranist, on the contrary, is able to continue his habits. If he is a *fellator*, and has money, he can surround himself with vigorous, well-equipped man-servants and pollute them labially. If he has not much money, he seeks to seduce the little boys of the neighbourhood. And as much may be said for the pederast, who for his part is not contented with labial pollution and asks for anal coition in which he is only passive.

Nothing then can stop the Uranist or the Pederast from following their tastes, and like the gambler who can play cards an hour before his death, the inverted individual can indulge himself, whatever may be his age. Moll quotes the case of an old man, aged 68, who had sexual intercourse every week, and another, aged 82, who retained his habits of sexual inversion to his very last moments, and who, in Uranist circles, was known as the "grandmother."

Genital Perversions. *(Continued.)*

CHAPTER V.

THE LIFE AND HABITS OF INVERTED INDIVIDUALS.

Necessity for this Special Chapter.—Physical Conformation of the Individual.—Development, Malformations and Working of the Genital Organs.—External Habitus, Tastes, Habits and Characteristics of Inverted Individuals.—General State of Mind of Inverteds and Uranists.—Social Relations of Uranists.—Marriage of Uranists.—Relations of Uranists among themselves.—The Uranists of Berlin.—Psychical Love of Uranists.—The Uranist is more Jealous than the Woman!—Physical Love of Uranists.—The Death of an Inverted Individual.—The Fellatores' *Evening Party.—The different Professions and the Number of Uranists.*

Necessity for this Special Chapter.

Our study of Inversion requires, for its completion, a special Chapter upon the manners and customs of inverted individuals. It will be the summing-up, in addition, of what is to be found in the preceding Chapters.

We shall examine the following points in succession.

1. The Physical Conformation of the Individual.

2. The Development and Malformations of his Genital Organs, and the Working of the said Organs.

3. The External Habitus, Tastes, Habits and Characteristics.
4. The Psychical Love.
5. The Physical Love.
6. The Different Professions.
7. The Number of Inverted Individuals.

It is therefore a veritable Social Study which we shall take in hand. We shall give to it only that development which is strictly necessary.

Physical Conformation of the Individual.

This, it will be understood, is exceedingly variable, according to the group and class of the subject. Between the acquired inverted forming part of the first degree of acquired homosexuality, and the effeminated individual of the third degree of innate homosexuality, there is a complete abyss. The former is quasi-normal, who resembles any other normal man, and like him is manly, potent, with a deep voice and full beard, and differs from him only in one special point, the mental deviation which impels him towards his own sex.

The latter is a quasi-hermaphrodite, who has the genital organs only of his own sex. Except in this point, the effeminated individual is a quasi-woman. In an inverse manner, the virago who has only a woman's genital organ, and that often malformed, is otherwise a man and her physical conformation sensibly approaches to that of one.

Development, Malformations and Working of the Genital Organs.

The same differentiation is reproduced with regard to the genital organs. They vary according to the class of the individual. The acquired homo-sexuals, simple inverteds, or hermaphrodites, and innate homo-sexuals have normal virile organs often above the average. I will say even that more than often men of these categories are very potent both in the size of their organs and in their aptitude for coition. Thus in an observation given by Krafft Ebing we find he describes an individual whose penis was 24 centimetres in length by 11 in circumference.

The occasionally inverted naval officer, whose transmission of inversion to two of his children I have already mentioned, had a short but very thick penis with testicles much above the average, and his virile powers enabled him to indulge in coition every day in such an enervating climate as that of Cochin-China.

On the other hand, innate inverted androgynes and effeminated, whose physical habitus approaches that of the hermaphrodite, have ill-developed genital organs and a very feeble aptitude for coition. Observe the genital apparatus of the magistrate, whose case we have previously noticed his penis when in a state of erection was no larger than a sporting artridge, with small testicles. This explains the reason of Moll's saying that: "in certain Uranists, the virile member only attains the size of that of a small boy. In some cases the penis has been found to be exceedingly long, but in the majority of cases no anomaly is to be found on this point."

This also explains Tardieu's remark that he is unable to discover the reason for the following anomaly. He finds that in pederasts: "the dimensions of the penis are either very slender or very voluminous: inferiority of size is the very general rule, excessive size the very rare exception, but in every case the dimensions are excessive either in one sense or the other." In Tardieu's view all inverteds were pederasts in act.

With regard to the genital organs of Uranists, Moll remarks: "The erections of Uranists are, generally speaking, good and vigorous, and, in the state of erection, their virile member displays the same direction as that of healthy individuals. It may easily be understood that in the case of those who have made an abuse of masturbation, erection may sometimes be altogether wanting, just as it is in the case of those men who have made an abuse of normal coition with women. A physician who communicated to Krafft Ebing a detailed account of his own disease, stated to him that he had relations with more than 600 Uranists without ever finding in them any malformation with regard to their genital organs.

"As far as I am aware, the hair on the genital parts is well developed in the case of Uranists. On the other hand, some among them have very little hair on the body while they have a strong beard. Others have a very thin beard. I am acquainted with one, verging upon 30, who has hardly any hairs upon his chin: however in his family, the members of which do not appear to be suspected of sexual perversion, the beard is generally very slight.

"It is also said that Uranists display a considerable development of the mammary glands. In one of his observations, Krafft Ebing relates the history of a Uranist who declared that, when he was between 13 and 15 years of age, he had milk in his breasts which one of his friends drank. In certain Uranists, I have noticed, on a level with the mammary region, an accumulation of adipose tissue, which gave to the breasts the rounded appearance of a woman's; but I have never observed any very typical development of the glands. Sometimes a very small foot, like that of a woman, is to be remarked.

"Some of them wear their hair very long and curling, have painted eyebrows, powder themselves and deck themselves out with women's ornaments: others are satisfied with wearing women's *under-garments*, long silk stockings, women's boots and corsets.

"The home of many of them resembles a fast woman's boudoir. Engravings and statues are to seen there, representing the fine types of male Greek beauty, (Apollo, Antinous, the Indian Bacchus, etc.). They have a strong taste and remarkable skill in feminine occupations, crochet, lace, woolwork, and sewing. On the other hand they detest physical exercise and the normal occupations of a man.

"They swing about as they walk, twisting their hips like an hetaira flaunting herself on the pavement.

"This effemination may also extend to the character,

and inverteds are to be found who resemble women in their vanity, their love of gossip and of talking about dress for hours at a time, and in their inability to keep a secret.

"The handwriting of Uranists sometimes resembles that of women and I have been able to establish this undeniably in two cases.

"The voice and the language of Uranists play a very important part. It is well known that a woman's voice has a different sound and a different tonality to that of a man, and is termed a falsetto voice. Now this kind of voice is sometimes very marked in Uranists. When they assume this voice for speaking, they do so without any difficulty; and even when they are in society, they find it hard to talk in an ordinary manner, so easy and natural does the falsetto voice come to them.

"Among the properties which distinguish the woman from the man is that of modesty. Now it is interesting to note that, according to certain writers, modesty is far more developed in the Uranist than it is in the normal man. There are some Uranists who confess that during their childhood and even during their state of puberty, they were distinguished among their companions for their modesty. According to Tarnowsky, the modesty of Uranists, while they are still children, manifests itself in an abnormal manner. This feeling is especially shown in the presence of a strange man, and children with a Uranist predisposition feel more embarrassment in undressing before a man than before a woman." (Moll. *op. cit.*)

General State of Mind of Inverteds and Uranists.

Many inverteds and especially many Uranists are *fully conscious of their anomaly*, and Westphal declares that this consciousness renders them unhappy. Many of them have suicidal ideas and put an end to their life. It is enough to read over again the preceding observations and particularly that of the physician P....

I will add an extract from Krafft Ebing's observation, no. 144.

I even believe that under other social conditions, I should be capable of great and noble affection and self-sacrifice. My ideas are in no way exclusively carnal or morbidly sensual. How often, at the sight of a handsome young man, a deep and romantic feeling seizes me, and I utter, like a prayer that fine line of Heine:

> "Thou art like a flower, so sweet, so fair, so pure, etc."

And once, when I was compelled to separate from a young man whom I esteemed and appreciated, although he did not know of my love for him, those fine lines of Scheffel recurred to my mind, the last couplet of which, *mutatis mutandis*, especially found an echo in my soul:

> "Lowering like the heavens, frowns the world on me,
> Yet, blessed or cursed be the fate I meet,
> With trusting heart I think, dear friend, of thee!
> God keep thee dear, it would have been too sweet!
> God keep thee dear, such happiness was not to be."

I have never independently revealed my love to a young man; I have never spoiled or injured any one morally; but I have, now and then, made the way easy for many. Then I shrink from no trouble, and make all the sacrifices I can.

When I have an opportunity of having a loved friend near me, to educate, protect and help, when my love, remaining unknown, finds a return, (not, be it understood, by a sexual affection) then the disgusting images of my imagination are dissipated. Then my love grows almost platonic; it becomes ennobled, to fall back again into the mire when this seemly satisfaction is removed.

Otherwise I am, without flattering myself, not one of the worst of men. Brighter mentally than the average, I take interest in all that moves humanity. I am kind-hearted, gentle and easily moved to pity; I would not hurt an animal, and much less a human being; on the contrary, I do good and kindly actions wherever I can.

While I have nothing to reproach myself with in my own conscience, and reject with all my power the world's opinion of us, I suffer very much. It is true that I have never hurt anybody and that I believe my love, in its noble manifestations, to be as elevated a sentiment as that of any normal man; but, with the unhappy lot which ignorance and intolerance impose upon us, I suffer very keenly; to such an extent that I am tired of life.

No pen, no tongue can describe all the misery, all the unhappy situations, the constant fear that our anomaly will be discovered and that we shall be placed under the ban of society. The mere idea of discovery and of loss of position and of being repudiated by everybody is more painful than can be believed. Then all the good that one had done would be forgotten; strong in his feeling of high morality, every man of normal disposition would be moved to scorn, even though he himself had been most frivolous in his own love. I know of more than one normal individual whose frivolity in love always seems hard for me to understand.

And yet, what matters our unhappiness? We may, cursing mankind, end our unhappy days. In truth, I often long for the calm of a lunatic asylum. Let my life end when it must, the sooner the better; I am ready.

To pass to another question. I too believe like others who have written to you, that our nervousness is but the result of our unhappy and infinitely miserable life among our fellow creatures.

And yet another remark. At the end of your work, you speak of the suppression of that article of the Code which relates to our acts. Certainly, the human race would not perish through that suppression. In Italy, as far as I know, there is no paragraph of that kind, and yet Italy is a civilized country.[1] And I, who am obliged to undermine my life with onanism, could not be touched by that law, none of whose articles I have broken hitherto. And yet I suffer from that cursed contempt which weighs upon us. But how can the opinion of society become modified, as long as an article of the Code confirms it in its false morality. The law ought in any case to correspond with the conscience of the people, not with the popular conscience which is erroneous, but with the opinions of the best and deepest thinkers of the nation; it ought not to be ruled by the desires and prejudices of a superstitious and obscure populace.

Clear-thinking minds ought not to persevere any longer in antiquated ideas upon this subject.

Social Relations of Uranists.

Moll has given a lengthy description of the social relations of Uranists with men and with women. We will give a rapid summary of it.' A large number of these individuals feel no repugnance for the society of women; it is to be remarked that they well know how to get themselves appreciated by women whose tastes they possess themselves and know how to analyze with great skill. They are in fact generally very expert in questions of female dress.

"On the other hand, there are Uranists who carefully avoid all female society, and for this cause pass as being model young men. With their tastes, in fact, there is no difficulty for a man to retain his chastity with women." (Moll.)

Marriage of Uranists.

"Let us add, too that there are many Uranists who are married. Some of them are psychical hermaphrodites who have relations sometimes with their wife and sometimes with a man; others only have intercourse with men. I know a couple in Berlin; the husband is a declared Uranist, and the wife takes her revenge, without troubling herself much about it, by having relations with men. Besides, these marriages are not always unhappy, for a moral and strong tie often binds husband and wife together; sometimes even they are not barren." (Moll.)

A last category of inverteds is that of those who, in order to conceal their real condition, willingly affect the society of girls, and try to have a reputation for being successful with the fair sex.

Relations of Uranists among themselves.

We find in Krafft Ebing's 115th observation, some interesting information regarding the relations of inverteds among themselves. The subject of this observation is a German physician, prosecuted for having been caught in the very act by a rural policeman at the moment when he was "having his feather drawn" by a tramp, on the high road. A long and numerous correspondence with Uranists was seized at his house, by which it was clearly established that for some years he had continuous Uranist relations with persons belonging to all classes of society. It may therefore be said that this worthy Prussian was an absolute master of pederasty, both physically and morally.

With reference to the degree in which many inverteds feel themselves as women, or which is not the case with all, two persons in Vienna are instances. Both these individuals have feminine nick-names; one is a hair-dresser who styles himself "French Laura," the other is a retired butcher who is named "Fanny, the female pork-butcher." Both of them never miss an opportunity, during the Carnival, of showing themselves disguised as women. At Hamburg there is a person whom many people take for a woman, because he always goes about the house in feminine attire, and on the rare occasions when he goes out, always does so in a similar dress. This individual wished to stand as godmother at a christening, and thereby occasioned much scandal.

Since I have not seen, in any of the works on sexual inversion which I have come across, anything concerning the intercourse of pederasts among themselves, I wish to give you, in conclusion, some information upon this subject.

As soon as two inverteds become acquainted, they exchange communications regarding the incidents of their past life, their loves and their conquests; unless such conversation is impossible owing to the great social distance separating one Uranist from the other. It is only rarely that they abstain from such conversation upon making a new acquaintance. Among themselves they are designated as "aunts"; in Vienna as "sisters." Two very masculine-looking Viennese prostitutes, whose acquaintance I happened to make, and who had relations of sexual inversion together, told me that for the corresponding condition in women, the name "uncle" was used. Since I became conscious of my abnormal condition, I have entered into relations with more than a thousand individuals, with sentiments conformable to mine. In almost every large town there is a place of meeting for them, a so-called promenade. In small towns there are relatively few "aunts," though in a small town of 2300 inhabitants I found eight, and in one of 7000, eighteen of whom I was absolutely sure,—to say nothing of those whom I suspected. In my native city of 30,000 inhabitants, I knew personally about 120 "aunts." The majority of them have the power, and for my own part I possess it in the highest degree, of judging at the first glance whether an individual has our tendencies or not, or, to employ the "aunts'" slang, whether he is "reasonable" or "unreasonable." My friends were often astonished at the extraordinary certainty of my judgment. I recognized at the first glance as "aunts," persons who, to all appearance, were organized in a perfectly masculine way. On the other hand, I am able to behave in such a perfectly masculine way, that in circles where I have been introduced by friends, doubts are at first expressed as to the genuineness of my character. When I am in a mischievous mood I can behave exactly like a woman. The majority of "aunts," myself included, do not look upon their anomaly as a misfortune; they would rather regret if the conditions were altered. As, in my opinion and that of other "aunts," the congenital state cannot be altered, we have only one hope: which is to see the articles of the (German) Code one day modified, so that only rape, or instigation to acts of indecency in public shall be punishable. (Krafft Ebing. *op. cit.*)

The Uranists of Berlin.

Strangers often raise a chorus of protest against the immorality of the great Babylon, under which title they designate our fair Paris. In the Chapter on Pederasty we shall treat on the question of those strangers who come to Paris to play their little games. For the present it is sufficient to give an account, according to Moll, of the usual habits of the Berlin Uranists.

In Berlin the Uranists make choice in preference of public places wherein to meet. I know five of these places in Berlin, some of the best known and most frequented restaurants and cafés in the Friedrichstadt. Sometimes, when they have compromised themselves by speaking in their falsetto voice or by calling one another by women's names, they change their café. But generally their conduct in the cafés leaves nothing to be desired, especially when it is remembered what happened only a short time ago. There is now no reason to fear a repetition of the disgraceful conduct of certain individuals which a few years ago gave rise to a notorious case in which a restaurant-keeper and his clients were implicated. No one who is not initiated would recognize the Uranists among the ordinary clients, but, when once informed, it will be easy for him to observe their manners, their way of speaking, and the glances which they give from one table to another.

Uranists often form little parties consisting of from 3 to 12 persons, who are on terms of intimate friendship among themselves. But, as may be supposed, this habit is not general, for a large number of them have no sympathy with one another outside their sexual relations. In their meetings they often celebrate in serious fashion their official "espousals."

Uranists again love to have private meetings where they feel no embarrassment; sometimes they even give balls. But what they prefer above all are "little teas," to which a dozen persons are generally invited. It is in meetings of this kind that the feminine character of Uranists is shown with the greatest clearness. The facts which I am about to relate will appear incredible, but I have them from Uranists in whom I can place confidence. In the first place, at these parties, as is already indicated by the name, nothing but tea is drunk, and this purely feminine habit gives some evidence of the Uranists peculiar character. Round the table were seated men with a Hamburg cap on their head, some of them even in an apron: one was knitting, another sewing, another doing crochet-work and so on. The conversation in no way resembles that of men, and no one talks politics, science, etc., it is mere gossip about their love-affairs, their jealousies, etc. At these parties, Uranists permit themselves a certain absence of reserve and sometimes go so far as to touch one another, without however overstepping the bounds of what is allowable.

As we have just said, Uranists also give large balls, at which sometimes a hundred people are present. The female element is but sparely represented: the women who are present at these balls are generally *tribades:* on the other hand, the majority of the men are dressed as women, Bohemian girls, Spanish dancers, Chinese, etc. The ball dress is a subject of the deepest care to the Uranist, for each one wishes to eclipse the other. Thus, a Uranist, after taking advice as to what dress he should wear at a ball, said: "You will see that my dress will create excitement." At these balls the men dance together and their movements can then be seen revealing quite a feminine grace.

Uranists are very fond of these balls, as one of them told me, because they grow tired of always playing a part in order that they may not betray themselves. There—at all events--they are free and able to give a loose rein to their inclinations. In Uranist circles the differences in the social scale are very clearly defined. A Uranist will never look upon one of his companions as being superior to himself, but he will always look down upon a Uranist whose social position is inferior to his own. A few Uranists declared to me that no anti-Semite feeling existed among Uranists, and another told me that he had frequently had relations with men of noble rank without meeting with what is called the pride of nobility. The same individual however looked upon the poorer Uranists as inferior to himself, and spoke of them, artisans for instance, with evident scorn. But, on the other hand, the social distinctions sometimes disappear completely, or for a certain time, under the influence of their passion. In this way, we sometimes see a Uranist, occupying a high position, attracted through a peculiar perversion towards a Uranist who belongs to the lower classes. (Moll. *op. cit.*)

Physical Love of Uranists.

The reader is aware that the Uranists' love applies to his own sex and that there are different degrees in this aberration according to the category in which the inverted is classed.

The love of an inverted towards a person of his own sex is as passionate and as strong as that of a hetero-sexual for one of the opposite sex. This love for his adored one renders the Uranist capable of the greatest sacrifices, and its power and intensity is in every way comparable to that of the woman for the man. Just as the love of the woman is more powerful and more disinterested than that of the man, so the Uranist's love, according to Ulrichs, is in this respect superior to that which can be felt by a normal man.

"Sometimes the Uranist's love goes as far as the sacrifice of his own self. The unhappy creature is unable to resist the desires and requirements of the persons he loves, and he often becomes a mere instrument in the latter's hands; just as in love between man and woman, one of the two is often reduced to the part of a slave. This feeling of submission and slavery is to be found in the Uranist, and he takes a pleasure in it." (Moll. *op. cit.*)

The fancies, the caprices and the tastes of inverted love are absolutely the same as those of normal love. One loves a fair, handsome youth without any beard, another a delicate young fellow with dark complexion, a third likes little men, while others care only for fine, strong men with large moustaches, But it should be observed that the inverted's love applies to grown men or to stalwart young fellows from 18 to 20 years of age. Love for a child who has hardly reached the age of puberty is very rare among Uranists, and Krafft correctly remarks that *the man who seeks for the child,* for the little boy, is a licentious individual, a *vicious inverted*, and not a Uranist.

It will naturally be understood that Uranists feel little inclination for one another, for in the eyes of a Uranist, another Uranist is only a woman like himself. Generally they have a weakness for soldiers, particularly for the cavalry, whose uniform is better made and smarter than that of the infantry. The young sergeants in the light cavalry are often the objects of solicitation on the part of inverteds who sometimes occupy high positions socially. Many scandals are hushed up, but they exist all the same, and only a few months ago, the newspapers related how a rich Jewish financier was slapped on the face in the middle of the street by a Sergeant in the Cuirassiers to whom he had made indecent proposals in a urinal near the Bourse.

This love of the inverted for the normal, vigorous man is the bond which unites pederasty to inversion, and is the principal cause of the male prostitution which has spread to such a serious extent of late years.

The common characteristic of inverted love is its violence and its passionate exaltation. The Uranist who *loves like a woman*, as we have remarked, writes impassioned letters, which he often signs in a woman's name; in his confessions he is able to depict his love with features of the greatest ardour. Tardieu quotes a document entitled "*My Confession*," which was produced in a trial for blackmailing in 1845.

"*1st Love.* The first one that I loved, oh! how can I explain how much I loved him. How can I tell of the delicious thrill that ran through me when I heard his voice, the happiness I felt when I met his gaze, and the tender care I took to bring a smile to his lips. And yet, I must admit, this was the first creature who made my heart flutter every day, who filled my dreams with ever-laughing pictures, who opened out to me a new life, and since then I felt no happiness which did not come to me through him, I had no feelings which were not for him, and no duties which I would not sacrifice for him. Every word of his thrilled through me like a tender melody; his look, whether smiling or in repose, reflected itself in sweet joys at the bottom of my heart, and I felt that the pleasure of angels must be like this.

"And thus, by his side, I felt all the feelings of life wane away. What to me were now the prejudices imposed by laws or by custom! What were the pleasures of society, or the triumphs of self-love! How many a time did I flee from my childhood's friends in order to remain by him! Oh! what on earth would I not have done for him! What would I not have asked of heaven, and what rival affection would come nigh my soul!

"*2nd Love.* And yet, must I say it? . . . Three years of this first intoxication had scarcely ended before another feeling forced its way into my heart. No power could withstand the interest inspired in me by a being who held over me no power of the past, but his frank look awoke within me a thousand charming hopes. He had great blue eyes, from which I loved to draw forth all their tenderness; and when his head was resting on my shoulder, and his lips breathed forth my name in sweet friendship's first accord, I said to myself: By him too shall I have the happiness of being loved.

"*3rd Love.* How long after that there came to me a fair youth, with pale complexion and dark eyes, I cannot truly tell you. . . . However, since my pen would pledge itself to truth, and my heart would reveal all its secrets here, I will confess that this fresh passion was no mere attractive episode, such as often passes in the life of men, like a falling star which shoots across the sky without disturbing its harmony. My young lover came and took his part of love within my soul; and to keep him there, I lavished upon him my most secret caresses. I loved to follow the first development of his feelings, to keep to myself alone the first efforts of his sensibility. I could not resist the fresh experience he imparted to me; I became mad.

"*4th Love.* Oh! could I but envelope in mystery what remains for me to tell, could I but hide within my soul this last weakness of nature, I would stop at this mystic number of my first loves. But, alas! Destiny is great and cannot be explained; and in spite of myself I had to end by adoring a child who fell, I believe, from the ethereal vault. Fair as the Cherubim who hold up the veil on the Virgin's brow, his little mouth had one of those smiles which must have made Eve fall, if 'twas thus the devil ensnared her; in his eyes there was a pleasure of innocence which made one hope for all and forgive all. Amiable and kindly, yielding to your caprices, anticipating your wishes, he covered you with sweet looks and charming caresses; to see him was to love him . . . . and that is why I loved him.

"And yet, if you would understand, if you would know how I love them all, how they love me, how we live together, lift the curtain which casts a shadow on this picture . . . . it is one of those incomprehensible mysteries which Nature alone reveals."

Terrible Jealousy of Uranists.

The Uranist tastes all the joys of happy love, but he

is also a prey to the tortures and despair of unhappy love, and he has fits of terrible jealousy which may lead him into crime. We will give two instances of this.

The first is taken from Garnier. A congenital inverted who also had a fetish in the workman's blouse, met one day in the Champs Elysées the ideal type of his imagination, the man that he could *no longer do without:* he attached himself to him and both of them entered upon homosexual relations. Our inverted was desperately in love.

"I became, he says, extremely jealous. Having observed that he went with women, I felt broken-hearted. I should have liked to kill the woman who had taken him away from me and thus *possessed herself of my life.* My torments were so violent that I had jaundice and fell ill." Repulsed by his friend, he took a criminal resolution. "I determined to spoil that pretty face which I had loved so much, and which he was yielding to others. The day on which I ran after him with a razor to cut his face, to disfigure him rather than to kill him, I had taken two glasses of absinthe in order to keep up my courage." (Garnier. *op. cit.*)

The inverted of the female sex is quite as terrible in her passion and jealousy. Krafft Ebing relates a tragical occurrence at Memphis (U. S. A.) in 1892. Two young girls, Alice and Freda, had contracted a tribadic love-bond; the families intervened and separated the two lovers, and Freda was affianced to a young man. Being unable to possess her friend and not wishing her to belong to another, Alice killed Freda in the middle of the street at Memphis by cutting her with a razor.

Moll, on his part, quotes several instances of the jealousy of Uranists. "I have to relate a scene of jealousy described to me by the Uranist, A . . . , who has already been mentioned. A . . . , who had for some time maintained intimate relations with B . . ., went to see him one day after hearing that he (B . . .) had received a visit from another Uranist, C . . . , and that he had accepted the presents which the latter had offered him. When he came in, A . . . demanded of B . . . in a very excited manner if it was true that he had accepted a present from C . . . , but B . . . denied it. Then A . . ., drawing a knife from his pocket, said: 'You have done well not to accept any presents, otherwise I should have stabbed you with the knife which I have brought here for that purpose.' A . . ., who is of a very impressionable nature, told me that one day his jealousy would drive him to murder.

"The following scene shows how far the jealousy of Uranists can go. A certain individual named D . . . had sexual relations with one E . . . When D . . . accompanies E . . . to his door, and when the latter does not wish D . . . to go upstairs, D . . . becomes suspicious and supposes that E . . . is expecting another man: he then stays all the night watching E . . .'s house to see if any one comes out. On the other hand, when D . . . wishes to go away for a time, he has to take every precaution not to arouse E . . .'s suspicions. If D . . . talks for a short time with a man, E . . . is convinced that the man is a Uranist, who has come to take away his friend: he becomes jealous and makes him promise not to see the same man again.

"Another Uranist F . . ., who had relations with G . . ., looks at men on purpose. G . . . is very jealous and frequently beats him for this, but F . . . declares that he is pleased at receiving blows from G . . . because they show him G . . .'s love.

"Apart from their passionate love, the jealousy of Uranists is explained by the nervous disposition of these individuals. The idea that the man they love is deceiving them may become for the Uranist a veritable idea of persecution which, becoming more and more rooted in him, deprives him of appetite and sleep, and destroys his capacity for work. I know a case in which jealousy so altered the character of a Uranist that his family were apprehensive of the breaking out of a mental disease." (Moll. *op. cit.*)

Tarnowsky has remarked that, in the case of Uranists who cherish an unrequited love for a normal man, jealousy is felt especially towards the women whom they look upon as their rivals. I have had opportunities of observing the justice of this remark.

But if a fierce jealousy is one of the features of the psychical love of Uranists, they have not the qualities of fidelity and constancy. With rare exceptions, Uranists are very fickle in their love, and their attachments do not last long. They love passionately, but these fatal love-affairs, like fires of straw, are extinguished as quickly as they blaze forth. Regarded in this light, Uranists resemble certain ladies of light character, who dote on men of a certain type, but who change their lover as often as they do their dress.

The Physical Love of Inverteds.

Owing to the intimate relationship between Inversion and Pederasty, we shall investigate the question of the physical love of Uranists at the same time as that of Pederasts, for many sexual practices are common to them both.

Let us merely state the fact that in the immense majority of cases, the inverted individual is an onanist who pollutes himself while thinking of a man, for lack of having one with whom to have intercourse. There are however *very rare* cases in which this pollution is sufficient for the Uranist who never has had and never will have sexual intercourse with a man.

The Professions of Inverteds.

We have stated that inverteds are met with in all classes of society. According to Moll and Mantegazza, a larger proportion is to be found among the upper classes. Moll is acquainted with a large number who belong to very different professions; among them were lawyers, doctors, theologians, philologists, merchants, officers, writers, labourers, gardeners and artisans.

Certain professions supply a greater number of inverteds than others, without however it being possible to establish any trustworthy statistics. Among these professions may be mentioned, in the first degree, that of actors, then writers, florists, upholsterers, painters, decorators, cooks, hairdressers and ladies' tailors. Hartmann, the German, has observed that among spiritualists and doctors in particular, a large number of inverteds are to be found.

The Number of Inverteds.

Moll is of opinion that it is impossible to know exactly the number of Uranists, or what proportion they bear to the population as a whole. According to information which he has gathered from different sources, there would be in Berlin nearly "4000 men whose favours can be bought, but I believe that this number is exaggerated. What I am able to state is that for my own part I have seen in Berlin 300 or 400 Uranists and I have heard 100 to 200 others talked about. Accordingly, there would be approximately in Berlin at least 500 Uranists; but it is very probable that this number is below the true figure. In any case, it is impossible for me to say if there are in Berlin 3000 or 10.000 Uranists or even more, which however does not appear to me to be demonstrated." (Moll.)

This approximate calculation which has been made for Berlin, could be made with equal inexactitude for Paris, London, or Vienna. It may readily be conceived that, unless there is some scandal or particular fact (such as syphilitic disease in the anus or throat), which obliges them to consult a physician and to make confessions to him which are always painful, Uranists do not make any boast of their taint. Many children display symptoms of sexual inversion which remain latent after puberty, owing to fear of public opinion, or religion, or through want of opportunity, etc. These latter, who are the most numerous, form the *acquired* inverteds, and are only retarded or latent, and their inclination is only developed by an occasional cause.

The calculation of Ulrichs, the protagonist of inverteds, that there is on an average in Germany *one* Uranist in every 500 men, must be treated as a fanciful opinion. According to our belief, there are many more. The inverted, who are rare in the country, in the villages and small towns, increase in the large centres, and become legion in the great capitals. Berlin has no reason to envy Paris. As for London, in spite of the rigour of a barbarous law which dates from the time of King Alfred, there are perhaps more inverteds there than in Paris. But like practical people, the sons of modest Albion come to Paris to play their little games, which does not prevent them from clamouring against French immorality. Oh! Shocking!

We will conclude the Chapter on inverteds with the account of the death of an inverted by Jean Richepin, and the Fellatores Party by Dr. Luiz.

An Emperor.—The Death of an Inverted.

On Feb. 13th, 1876, at half past seven o'clock in the morning, the woman in charge of the water-closets in the Passage Jouffroy was engaged in opening her establishment when she saw a woman come in enveloped in a large waterproof.

This early visit surprised her a little, the more so as the visitor had a mysterious air, with her head almost covered with her hood and her face hidden under a thick woollen veil. This untimely arrival could not even plead the extenuating circumstance that she was greatly pressed, for she walked with a leisurely tread and with no display of feverish haste.

However, her air of decision seemed to show that if she had not to satisfy a want, she had at least a duty to fulfil. The closet-keeper thought that she saw before her some Englishwoman of punctual and regular habits who did not wish to begin her day with a weight upon her conscience. Then the mercantile spirit and the thirst for gain make us overlook much. She opened the door to her unexpected client and indulged the pleasing thought that such a queer windfall would mean a good tip for the whole day.

At the end of five minutes, she began to say to herself that the Englishwoman was very conscientious.

At the end of ten minutes she commenced to walk up and down, as restless as a mother, in front of the closed door, behind which she could hear no sound.

At the end of a quarter of an hour, she grew alarmed. Twenty minutes! She no longer doubted but that something extraordinary was taking place.

In dismay, she ran to look for the watchman who was taking an early nip at a wine-shop in the Rue Batelière. As they made their way back, she related to him the strange adventure, and informed him of her suspicions.

"I assure you," she said, "that she is some sentimental Englishwoman who has fainted there."

They knocked at the window. There was no answer! "It's not natural," said the grizzled old soldier, with a profound air. They broke in the door which was fastened with a bolt inside.

"It's a man," cried the watchman. "What nonsense were you telling me about an Englishwoman?"

"My word!" was the attendant's reply, "she was an Englishwoman but a little while ago. The proof of it is that she had a waterproof and no hips. How the devil has she changed into a man?"

It was a man, beyond all doubt, and what is more a young man. The face was absolutely smooth and painted and powdered like a prostitute's. The eyebrows were pencilled, the lips reddened, and the fair hair powdered with gold. A pair of earrings sparkled in his ears. The fingers were covered with rings, and there were bracelets round the wrists. On his bare bosom shone a ruby hanging from a pearl necklace.

The dress, the waterproof and the rest of the feminine apparel were lying on the floor.

The young man was dead. A long silver pin was fixed in his left breast at the heart.

The corpse was sitting on the filthy seat.

At the end of the pin, near the head which was formed of a diamond, was fastened a piece of rose-coloured paper.

It was a letter, and ran as follows:

"I am eighteen years old, and my passions are extraordinary. I was born to be an Emperor at the period of the decadence of Rome. But the present time is not good for those who possess such fancies as mine. That is why I am going away. As I could not live like the Emperor Heliogabalus, I wished at least to die like him in a privy." (Jean Richepin. *Les Morts Bizarres.* Paris, Maurice Dreyfus.)

The Fellatores' Party. Preparations for the Entertainment.

As soon as the little Club in the Champs Elysées had decided upon giving a grand fellatorian party, Titine was chosen to be General Manager.

Then all the Parisian celebrities of a certain class danced attendance at the little fellow's five o'clock teas.

There were second-rate sportsmen who called their horses by the names of their male favourites; old debauchees, painted like actresses, whose lips were a testimony to their sucking propensities: young fellows with a pale complexion and indolent walk, enervated by their sodomitical promises; and fine ladies, the Old Guard of Cythera's battalions, female *souteneurs* who had young men for their darlings, whom they kept for purposes of the vilest debauchery and the most degrading luxury.

The party promised to be an extraordinary one. Titine impressed in his service not only his own friends, but also amateurs in the vice, and artistes to lend more brilliancy to the spectacle.

The programme was drawn up: there was to be a promenade in which everybody must appear in fancy dress, a free competition with money prizes for the winners, a supper and a general conflagration of hearts. Titine performed his duties as General Manager with peculiar zeal, He received the little boys who were to be provided for the pleasure of the guests, submitted them to a rigorous examination, overlooking no defect, and placed them in the hands of old members of the Club, with whom they could stay until the day of the party, and who would watch over their chastity. The conditions required were Strength, Elegance and Variety.

These requirements were too great. The boldest drew back before the necessity of a preliminary training.

. . . .

The Party reaches its Height.

A ringing of bells gave notice to those present that the party had begun. The reception rooms were filled.

The lighting, Bock's masterpiece, was a great success.

In the corners were lamps in the shape of *phalli*, in the centre, hanging from the ceiling, were clusters of illuminated genital parts.

Underneath, there stood in ecstasy at this bestial ingenuity, Carthusians, Franciscans, Canons of St. Geneviève, Trappists, Dominicans, beardless youths dressed as peasant-girls, Carmelites, begging friars, Sisters of Charity, etc. Titine, as a young Abbé, in a white surplice, pushed back the groups so as to leave the middle of the room free, and chucked the nuns and peasant-girls under the chin, a proceeding which made the hoary satyrs laugh.

Behind Titine followed the procession; choir-boys throwing flowers and chanting erotic couplets, others swinging censers and putting out their tongue at the Benedictines who, as the procession passed by, made indecent gestures.

After them followed the Pope, represented by Bock, who wore his tiara cocked on one side and cast holy water on the crowd with a brush which he dipped into a brimming pisspot.

Then came cardinals in red, arm-in-arm with dancing girls in black tights and white petticoats.

Beneath a canopy embroidered with different obscene figures, Palouff in the cope and stole of an officiating priest, carried a Priapus, inlaid with imitation stones. On either side of him, a churchwarden in a black coat and without breeches, held up a staff which supported the canopy.

After Palouff came the Sisters of the Holy Sacrament, with their petticoats lifted above their hips and leaving one leg free; then young boys dressed only in a *san benito* coming down to their navel, and, to close the procession a big fellow dressed as the Republic, with a Phrygian cap on his head and a tri-coloured dress open behind, revealing a shape too red and too protruding to be natural.

When he was seen, a shout was raised, and everybody, monks and nuns, followed in his wake to kick the most fleshy portions of the representative of the Republic.

When the procession, passing from room to room, had given pleasure enough to the depraved onlookers, the Pope, Bock, having laid aside his paraphernalia as holy-water sprinkler, returned amidst the choir-boys in their cassocks, to a square room which had been selected as the scene of the competition.

The cardinals, priests, dancing-girls,c hurchwardens, nuns, and half-naked little boys mingled among the crowd.

The Pope, Palouff, Feschmann, Prudence, Prince Pompazine and Baron Schling, forming a committee, sat down under a velvet canopy; before them, on a thick carpet, the competitors came to display their elegance.

Strange groups were to be seen there, dancers and nuns, with Benedictines and Cardinals, postures of clowns, embraces of reptiles.

The Pope announced three as the winners, Bethina for strength, Hamberg for elegance, and Clapotis for variety.

It was time. All heads were excited at the sight of the competition and demanded the final scene of the entertainment.

The couples turned round and rolled on the carpet. Bock gave the signal. The gas went out. and their monstrous embraces were veiled in obscurity.......

Bisexuateds.

CHAPTER VI.

GYNÆCOMASTS.

General Considerations upon Bisexuateds.—Gynæcomasts and Hermaphrodites.—Gynæcomasts.—Heredity of Gynæcomastia.—Gynæcomasts are Degenerates.—Observations in support of this Statement.—Accidental Gynæcomastia.—Structure of the Mammæ of Gynæcomasts.—The Gynæcomast J...—Physical Condition of Gynæcomasts.—Genital Aptitude of Gynæcomasts.—Propensity of Gynæcomasts to Inversion.—Gynæcomasts are Weak-minded.

General Considerations on Bisexuateds.

Dr. Legrain's theories on inverteds and the intimate ties which unite them with hermaphrodites, compel us to place the study of bisexuateds after that of inversion properly so called.

Besides, J. Chevalier in his classification places hermaphrodites, as we have seen, among inverteds in Group II., variation of the sexual type, congenital inversion dating from the fœtal existence, (Hypospadiasis, exaggerated size of the Clitoris, Hermaphrodism.)

But Emile Laurent is the author who has studied most deeply these unhappy creatures, the bisexuated, who, having two sexes, end in having none at all. In reality, as Legrain proves, hermaphrodites are degenerates.

Gynæcomasts and Hermaphrodites.

In the preface to his work on the bisexuated, Laurent, who divides them into two very distinct categories, expresses himself thus: "Gynæcomasts and hermaphrodites are not only curious creatures to study for the biologist and the teratological philosopher, but they are also, as creatures called upon to live in society, worthy of attracting the attention of the psychiatrist and the psychologist." (*Gynæcomastes et Hermaphrodites.* Emile Laurent. Paris, Georges Carré, 1894.)

Let us accept Dr. Laurent's division separating Gynæcomasts from Hermaphrodites. It is only just to acknowledge the fact that this author was the first to make a special study of Gynæcomasts.

Gynæcomasts.

"Gynæcomastia is an anomaly which consists in the exaggerated development of the *mammæ* in the man at the time of puberty, together with an arrested development of the testicles." (Laurent.)

A young boy, says Laurent, arrives at the age of puberty without having shown any peculiarity in his physical and moral conformation, with the exception of a little timidity, and slightly feminine ways and tastes. It is believed that, like all his companions, the boy is about to become a man, that his figure will assume a rapid development, that his muscles will stand out under the skin of his limbs, that his features will grow energetic, that his chin will be covered with a beard, that his genital epithelium will develop and that at the same time his testicles and penis will acquire a notable enlargement; it is believed that his tastes will change and that a secret instinct will urge him to seek for the opposite sex. In this boy's case, nothing of the kind will occur. When he reaches puberty, Nature in his case seems to hesitate. His limbs remain slender, his shape rounded, his chin continues smooth and his testicles cease growing; he avoids the noisy society of his companions, without feeling any attraction towards the other sex; then his bosom grows rounder and his breasts develop like those of a girl who has reached puberty. Without being what is commonly called an hermaphrodite, he is but an incomplete man and a spoilt woman: he is what is called a Gynæcomast.

The Gynæcomast therefore is, according to the Doctor, a natural transition between an hermaphrodite and a complete man. This appears to us to be accurate.

The Gynæcomast is not a medical novelty. Aristotle has said already that this anomaly is particularly frequent in two species, men and goats, and he quotes an instance of it. A number of ancient and modern authors have repeatedly pointed out cases of Gynæcomastia which have been of service to Dr. Laurent in his psychological study. Moreover, in what follows, ours will hardly be anything else but a summary.

Heredity of Gynæcomastia.

Gynæcomasts are very often lymphatic or scrofulous. They bequeath their infirmity to their children, just as the aptitude for generation is kept up from father to son. But as it is a physical degenerescence, the family finally becomes naturally extinct, the aptitude for procreation always growing less. Laurent quotes a case where the development of the mammæ kept continually increasing from the great-grandfather to the grandson. The father, D...., had voluminous breasts when he was born; they then kept increasing little by little. He was addicted from childhood to onanistic practices, and was discharged from the army on account of his obesity when he was 21 years old. He attained puberty at the age of 12½, and when he was 24, he married and had three sons, all of whom were Gynaæcomasts. The third: 7 years old, had voluminous breasts at birth; according to his mother, they were as large as walnuts, and in the days which immediately followed his birth, they exuded a lactescent liquid. At the present time, as I have been able to observe personally, the breasts are of the size of a mandarine orange. On palpation, a lobuled mass is felt, which is not at all painful.

D... is a very vigorous man with solid muscles, 1 m. 63 in height, with a broad back, rather large belly, and his face covered with beard. His limbs and chest are also very hairy.

His breasts are the size of an orange. On palpation, one feels a thick layer of fat, and underneath that, a glandular cake as large as a mandarine orange. The mammæ are flaccid and pendant. The nipple is small and more like a man's than a woman's.

The size of the testicles is a little below the normal. The penis in a flaccid condition is only 4 centimètres in length by 8 in circumference. The hairs on the pubis are long but not numerous. In the case of this individual, hereditary Gynæcomastia appeared at birth, as it did in his son. It is nothing less than a mark of degenerescence. The proof of this is the latest child. (Laurent. *op. cit.*)

Gynæcomasts are Degenerates.

But it is much more frequent, among the ancestors of Gynæcomasts, to meet with those nervous taints which are found at the beginning of all degenrescences. An insane, epileptic, hysterical, or alcoholic subject begets degenerates: among the latter, one will be insane, another neurotic or eccentric, another perhaps a criminal, and another lastly with a physical malformation, prognathous, plagiocephalous, suffering from strabismus or hypospadiasis, or a Gynæcomast.

In support of his opinion, Dr. Laurent quotes a case borrowed from Magnan, and another *very interesting* case which came under his own observation. A family in which the father was epileptic and begat nine children, seven of whom were more or less tainted, the eighth, a daughter, aged 26 or 27, was also malformed. She was a vicious creature, debauched and given to drink. Sometimes she dressed as a man, sometimes as a woman, acting indiscriminately as lover or being loved, and running after lustful old women or old libertines alike. At the present time, she lives in close friendship with a woman, and the pair have the means of satisfying one another in a thousand ways.

We also find alcoholism as the origin of Gynæcomastia. Laurent quotes an instance of this. B..., 20 years of age, son of a drunkard who died in a fit of delirium tremens. He looks 16. The subject has an effeminate figure. His face is beardless and his limbs smooth. His pubis is tolerably well furnished, but as in a woman's, the hairs stop suddenly and form a very clearly defined triangle.

The penis is normally shaped, but it is very short and smaller than ordinary. The purses are wide, and the testicles manifestly smaller than in the majority of adolescents of that age. B... declares that he has never had to do with any women. But he has frequent erections, and he confesses that since he was 16 years old, he has masturbated himself about twice every week. He has ejaculations.

His breast is rounded and causes his shirt to project slightly. His mammæ, which are as large as oranges, are developed almost like those of a girl of 15. The skin covering the gland is white, delicate, and shows a few long, stiff hairs. The two mammæ are equal in size.

The nipple is very much developed and rosy in colour; round it are to be seen a few small projections resembling Montgomery's tubercles. The net-work of blue subcutaneous veins is not to be seen, as it is in a woman.

There are yet other causes of degenerescence to be found, entailing Gynæcomastia. Faneau de Lacour in his thesis on *La Feminisme et de l'Infantilisme chez le Tuberculeux*, shows that tuberculous subjects, and particularly the issue of tuberculous subjects, are often effeminated, and that in their case the *mammæ* sometimes acquire an abnormal development. He quotes two instances of this. In the second case especially, the subject was remarkable for an extraordinary exiguity of the genital apparatus which was hardly as large as that of a boy 10 years of age, coincident with an unusual development of the mammæ, (horizontal diameter, 8 centimètres; vertical, about 7 centimètres.) He had no venereal appetite.

Laurent also quotes an instance of a gynæcomast who had a tuberculous father. He refers also to obesity and quotes an instance. I can supply an observation which came under my notice, of a member of my own family.

Louis P... displayed from his very earliest youth a colossal appetite and at the same time remarkable obesity. As broad as he was high, he was 1 m. 60 in height when he was 21, and weighed 117 kilogs. High complexion, beardless face, body quite smooth, a very few fair hairs on the pubis, penis very small, testicles the size of beans. Buttocks enormously developed. His breasts were as large as oranges, slightly pendant and their size increased by the adipose tissue which surrounded them. Of a timid and fearful disposition, Louis P... was the laughing-stock of his cousins and companions. I believe that he never masturbated himself in his life, and he died without ever having any intercourse with women. I doubt if he had erections. When anyone wished to vex him, he told him that he would be obliged to marry and to sleep with a woman.

Louis P... was discharged from the army for obesity. He died when he was 22 years old, suffocated by his fat after a short illness.

"To sum up, all the causes of degenerescence may be causes of Gynæcomastia. In the front rank are madness, hysteria, neuroses and alcoholism, and in the second, tuberculosis, scrofula and obesity. Therefore, by virtue of his heredity, the Gynæcomast is a degenerate, and he bears within the physical and psychical marks of that state." (Laurent. *op. cit.*)

Pathological Origin of Gynæcomastia.

Laurent, together with Gœthe and Geoffroy de Saint Hilaire, attributes the hypertrophy of the mammæ coinciding with the parallel atrophy of the genital organs to the law of compensation, by which one is developed at the expense of the other. His opinion is corroborated by the phenomena which occur in the woman on the extirpation of the ovaries. According to Adelon and Milne Edwards there is in the latter case an advance on the part of the woman towards the virile type, the castrated woman assuming the constitution of the man; the sexual functions are destroyed; the *menses* cease; the breasts wither away, and at the same time the skin loses its whiteness, the shape becomes manlike, the chin is covered with a beard, and the voice grows hoarse and deep.

Accidential Gynæcomastia.

What give weight to this theory are the instances of accidental Gynæcomastia following upon diseases or operations upon the testicles. After a double orchitis, the breasts have been observed to develop slowly and progressively, in proportion as the atrophy of the testicles progresses and the virile appearance and the venereal appetites disappear. These results occur after different kinds of orchites, blennorhagic and traumatic. They are observed also after castration and sometimes also after an accidental mutilation of the genital organs.

Martin, an army surgeon, quotes the following case. A married man and father of a family, was struck, in the course of an engagement, by a piece of an exploded shell which carried away his penis and testicles. The man recovered, but shortly afterwards his beard fell off, his voice changed its note, and his mammæ became hypertrophied.

It is impossible to regard these facts as a mere coincidence and to deny the antagonism which exists between these two organs, the mammæ and the testicles

Structure of the Gynæcomast's Mammæ.

Certain Gynæcomasts have a genuine mammary gland. In others, on the other hand, it is a mere adipose tissue. Gynæcomasts have been observed to have milk like women, and, according to certain ancient authors observations, could have acted as wet-nurses to children. But Laurent remarks that though the liquid secreted by Gynæcomasts may have had the consistency and the colour of milk, yet, as no surgical analysis or microscopical examination was made of it, it is impossible to assert that it was really milk, "although it is logically possible, as, in some cases, a gland has been observed very similar to that of a woman."

Laurent finds that the *mammæ* of Gynæcomasts are slightly different to those of women. "Generally, the gland is almost regularly ovoid: it displays a groove at the point where it unites with the adjacent parts, and is not continuous in spreading out upon a wide base. It may be compared to an orange cut in half and fastened to the thorax.

The nipple usually projects as it does in a young virgin who has reached the age of puberty: it is surrounded by a more or less brown aureola, varying in different subjects. Montgomery's tubercles are frequently found on this aureola. The skin which covers the mammary gland in the Gynæcomast does not usually have that pearly whiteness and fineness which is met with in the woman, and particularly 'that softness to the touch which is found nowhere else.'

Instead of that fine, silky and almost imperceptible down which is to be seen on a woman's *mammæ*, we often find on those of the Gynæcomast a few, scattered, long and stiff hairs.

As for that network of blue veins, that subcutaneous plexus which seen transparently, gives to the skin a marbled and slightly bluish tinge, some observers have come across it; but often it may be absent.

The Gynæcomast J...

Dr. Laurent gives a detailed observation of J... who

has been previously mentioned. We shall quote that portion of his description only which relates to his *mammæ* and genital organs.

"At the present time (he is now 28 years old), J...'s mammæ are about the size of the head of a fœtus. Slightly flaccid, they hang like those of a woman who is giving suck. The length of the breast (from the base to the nipple) is 13 1/2 centimètres, and the circumference at the base is 30 centimètres. The skin which covers the breasts is white, like satin, very soft to the touch, and without any hairs. Through the transparency of the skin, is to be seen a very fine network of blue veins, just as it is in a woman. The nipple, which projects but slightly, is of a rather rosy colour, and becomes erect under the influence of titillation. It is then about 1 centimètre in length. Round the aureola, which also is but slightly coloured, there are some small projecting tubercles. On pressing the breast, a glandular mass of the size of an orange, is very clearly felt.

"The penis is of small size and very short: it measures only 2 centimètres in length and 7 centimètres in circumference; in erection it acquires a length of 5 or 6 centimètres. The gland is of the size of a small nut, well covered with the rudiment of a prepuce which can be raised.

"Under the penis, there exist two small cutaneous folds, about one centimetre and a half in length by half a centimètre in width. These folds resemble an embryo of *labia majora* and the *vulva;* but no *cul-de-sac* exists.

"The testicles are hardly as large as a sparrow's eggs. The one on the left is soft, and smaller than that on the right, and it can be made to ascend into the abdomen.

"The triangle of the pubis is very clearly delineated and well furnished with hair.

"J... began to masturbate himself when he was 7 years old, but ejaculations did not appear until he was 17. Even at the present time, he often masturbates himself without obtaining any result. During his last period of imprisonment, as I was questioning him regarding his habits of onanism and asking him one day to send me a sample of his sperm to examine under the microscope, he confessed to me that he had repeatedly masturbated for long periods together without being able to obtain a single drop of sperm. Nevertheless, he assured me that in the presence of a woman his vigour had never failed him and that ejaculation had always taken place. Since he was 18, he had regularly indulged in coition. Latterly, he had a mistress with whom he had intercourse two or three times every Monday. Only it fatigued him very much, and he was then seized with an almost irresistible desire to sleep. He felt no repugnance at touching the breast of his mistress, and he assured me that she was fond of prefacing the other amorous caresses by touching his breasts or rubbing them against her own, or by titillating his nipples with her tongue.

"J... has never felt any taste for men, nor has he ever wished to dress as a woman. Men have made him generous offers, but he has always refused these proposals. To sum up, he is an incomplete creature, at least physically." (Laurent. *op. cit.*)

Elphan gives an observation similar to the preceding. The subject's breasts, (he was 17 years old), were of the size of an orange cut in halves and fastened to his chest, and absolutely like those of a young girl of the same age. Both his testicles had come down: the right testicle was larger than the left, and the latter was much diminished in size. Pubis well furnished with hair. Penis of ordinary shape, with phimosis. The patient had venereal desires and entered on erection while his genital organs were being examined. He declared that he had never had anything to do with a woman, but confessed to vicious habits.

Physical Condition of Gynæcomasts.

Gynæcomasts are most frequently effeminated. Relatively to the general habitus of the body, they resemble *infantiles* whom we shall consider further on. After puberty their voice remains shrill like that of a woman. This results from the imperfection of the genital organs which are partly atrophied. Generally, with but rare exceptions, the gynæcomast has testicles below the average size, about the size of a small nut. The penis is usually about the size of that of a boy of 13 or 14, who is entering on puberty. Cases are even quoted in which it can hardly be said to exist at all. Bédor declares that he has seen a subject "whose penis was so short that, between the scrotum and the gland, it hardly showed the length of the latter."

Fanaglio also has seen a young soldier who, with an exaggerated development of the *mammæ*, had a rudimentary penis and a bifid scrotum.

Throughout the body, the hair in the case of Gynæcomasts is but little developed: many have no beard and only a fine down upon the upper lip: the chest and limbs are smooth; the pubis is generally well furnished with hair but, just as in a woman, the hairs form a triangle and their limits are clearly defined.

Dentition is generally retarded, sometimes they even retain their first teeth until the ages of 15 and 20. One of the individuals observed by Laurent displayed this phenomenon.

Besides these signs of degenerescence, the Gynæcomast will further display something peculiar in his whole appearance. In him, the adipose panicle is very developed, the skin is white, the hair long and fine, the pelvis is enlarged, and the hips developed; the limbs are round like those of a woman, the muscles do not stand forth vigorously under the skin: to sum all up, the Gynæcomast has rather the appearance of a woman dressed as a man than that of a real man.

Genital Aptitudes of Gynæcomasts.

Given the state of weakness of their genital apparatus, I do not suppose that they are very potent in coition; and I think that as regards quantity and especially as regards quality, they would be far from being able to satisfy a lustful woman. But, in company with Laurent, I do not look upon them as being impotent. They give proof of their virility in their progeny, to whom they transmit their degenerescence most frequently in an aggravated form. There may be some of them who are not fecund, but after all there are some who give proof of it.

Propensity of Gynæcomasts to Inversion.

It is certain that these spoilt men *who are on the road to hermaphrodism*, must be more particularly predisposed to inversion, and that rather of the passive than the active kind.

Laurent has questioned all the Gynæcomasts whom he met as to their genital habits. "In spite of their denials, and without having any certain proofs of it, I strongly suspect two of them of the sin of Sodom." Krafft Ebing states that Gynæcomastia is not rare among inverteds. We find in one of his observations that a doctor affected with inversion of the genital sense observed that, among the 600 inverteds with whom he had relations, the development of the breasts was not an unusual occurrence. He declared that when he was himself between 13 and 15 years of age, he had milk in his mammary glands which his lover sucked.

I will add that in my own practice I have met with in inverted individuals, a considerable development of the adipose panicle and breasts far more developed than in an ordinary man. This *habitus* coincided with a mediocre genital apparatus, with a very enlarged pelvis, and frequently with enormous buttocks.

These persons were not true Gynæcomasts, but they were not far from it. Besides, obesity is a cause of degenerescence. We know the proverb, "a good cock is never fat," and the unfortunate bird is cut in order to make a fat capon. The obese individual is, with rare exceptions, a *natural* capon. Therefore I have not been surprised to meet with many obese individuals among the inverteds who have come under my notice, and the majority of them were *passive* in the act. Those among them who were psychical hermaphrodites were *men when they were with women, and women when they were with men.*

The Gynæcomast, who is at a more accentuated degree of degenerescence than the obese individual, must compare with him and have considerable innate or acquired aptitude for inversion.

This, moreover, is Chevalier's opinion. "Gynæcomasts are persons rather severely affected with degenerescence; they display evident characteristics of feminism, thus are often infecund and sometimes impotent. In any case the sexual impulsion is weak or perverted; they are therefore in every way designed to become pederasts, and observations shows that they frequently are so."

Gynæcomasts are Weak-minded.

If we ask ourselves to what class of degenerates Gynæcomasts belong, we shall with Dr. Laurent, place them among weak-minded. He has no hesitation in thus classing them, creatures as they are of ill-developed intelligence, who possess perhaps some powers of memory but none of assimilation; in whom the impulses often paralyze the will. As children, they have the greatest difficulty in the world to learn to speak; as youths they are the despair of their masters and parents owing to their inaptitude for any work or study, and through their want of memory and inability to fix their attention, and often through their precocious vices and evil instincts.

Dr. Laurent quotes several cases which confirm his statements. He then asks himself whether the Gynæcomast is fit for marriage, and his answer is: "if a Gynæcomast were to come and ask me if he could marry, I should ask to make a microscopical examination of his sperm and my answer would depend upon that examination."

He is of opinion that Gynæcomasts should be freed from military service; for, "placing a young man with *mammæ* and a woman's graces in a barrack-room would be almost an encouragement to pederasty."

Certain doctors, Paul of Ægina among others, propose to extirpate the poor Gynæcomasts' *mammæ*. But this would not have the effect of increasing the size of their testicles and lengthening their penis. On the other hand, Elphan says, "Gynæcomastia ought to be considered as a movement of nature, and therefore to be respected."

We are content, like Villeneuve, with advising Gynæcomasts to wear stays in order to protect their poor breasts from rubbing and the consequent inflammation.

Bisexuateds.

CHAPTER VII.

HERMAPHRODITES.

*Hermaphrodites.—Hermaphrodism of the Human Fœtus.—Classification of Hermaphrodites.—*A. *True Hermaphrodism.—*1. *True Bilateral Hermaphrodism.—*2. *True Unilateral Hermaphrodism.—*3. *True Lateral or External Hermaphrodism.—Different Cases.—*B. *False or Pseudo-Hermaphrodism.—Internal Pseudo-Hermaphrodism, 1st, Masculine, 2nd, Feminine.—The* Valet de Chambre *Guiseppe Marzo.—External Pseudo-Hermaphrodism.—Alexina B..., the Boy-Governess.—Catherine Hohmann, Wife and Husband.—Rosine Gotlieb, Lover and Mistress.—Julie D..., the Inverted Hermaphrodite.—Ernestine G..., Man and Woman.—The Woman changed into a Man by Professor Perro's Bistoury.—Louise R..., the Woman Mechanician.—A Man-Prostitute.—Marie Marius, an Old Man's Sweetheart and a Male Nurse in a Religious House.—Madeleine Lefort, the Bearded Woman.—The Woman who refused to have her Clitoris cut.—The Priest in the Family Way.—The* Tribade *before the Parlement de Paris.—The Girl who was changed into a Boy by jumping over a Ditch.—Sexual Instincts of Hermaphrodites.—Sexual Satisfactions of Hermaphrodites.—Passive Pederast Hermaphrodite.—The Hermaphrodite* Vicomtesse.—*An Hermaphrodite Emperor.—The Debaucheries of Heliogabalus.—The Hymn to Venus and* *the Bloody Sacrifices.—The last Days and the Death of Heliogabalus.—Proofs that Heliogabalus was a Sadistic Hermaphrodite.—His Reign and his Life.—Artificial Hermaphrodism.—Infantilism and Effemination.—External Hermaphrodism of Young Pederasts.—A Little* Jesus.—*Henri de Blondin.*

Hermaphrodites.

Causes of Hermaphrodism.

According to Geoffroy Saint Hilaire, hermaphrodism is the union, real or apparent, complete or incomplete, of *two sexes in the same individual.*

What are the causes of hermaphrodism? According to Laurent, it appears to be almost demonstrated that morbid heredity has an influence upon the production of this anomaly and there is a great risk that an individual who displays some physical or psychical taint, may not in all cases transmit this taint to his descendants, but that he may beget a child displaying some defect or some anomaly. As I have already said with regard to Gynæcomasts, an epileptic may beget an epileptic, it is true; but he may also beget a deformed creature from the physical point of view, suffering from hypospadiasis or strabismus, an hermaphrodite as well as a microcephale. I have frequently observed different forms of hypospadiasis in criminal degenerates.

I have also shown that men with *mammæ* have frequently been the fathers of alcoholics and degenerates. I have even quoted an instance of a family almost exclusively composed of Gynæcomasts and Hermaphrodites.

Hermaphrodism therefore in many cases would not be more or less than a physical sign of degenerescence, as Morel and Magnan have already pointed out. (Laurent. *op. cit.*)

By what mysterious deviations do certain creatures fall back into hermaphrodism which is an inferior form of animality?

Hermaphrodism of the Human Fœtus.

In man, (says the anonymous author of *Elements of Social Science*,) the organs of the male sex have attained their full development and the organs of the female sex have remained in the embryonic state: the opposite to this occurs in the woman: the penis of the man coincides with the clitoris of the woman. In the fœtus the two organs so resemble one another that it is impossible to distinguish them. The development of the one is arrested at an early stage, while that of the other continues its regular progress. The uterus is represented, in the man, by a slight depression of the prostate. It results from this that the separation of the sexes is more apparent than real: in fact, we are all hermaphrodites.

In the early stages of its existence every human fœtus has external genital organs shaped in the same manner, and the conformable type of this apparent conformation is that of the feminine organ.

Two external sexual shapes, female and male, are the two successive phases of a development which spreads from the lateral parts towards the middle line, as has been established by M. Serres' theory of eccentric development. The first phase affords the separation of the two lateral parts, which besides are more developed: thus the feminine external form precedes the masculine external form.

We know that at a more advanced period of development, the female fœtus appears to be a male, by reason of the disproportionate increase of the clitoris. Thus, it is correct to say that, in relation to the apparent conformation of the external genital organs, every man has been a woman in the beginning. It may be understood, after that, how an arrested development of the external genital organs may make an apparent woman out of an effective male, and how, on the other hand, an excess of development, or if it be preferred, an inopportune development of the same organs make an apparent but imperfect female out of an effective female.

It appears to us unnecessary to give any embryogenical details to explain the processus of hermaphrodism which is very well described by G. Hermann. We are content to quote these few words: "To sum up, the young embryo has everything which is necessary to become both *male and female* in its internal genital organs, but only *male or female* in its external genital organs.

"Starting from this very youthful stage, the sexes are seen to differentiate afterwards progressively, according to a perfectly established general plan. Sexual dimorphism does not extend only to the genital organs, but also to the general habitus of the body: carriage, beard, voice, mammæ, conformation of the skeleton, pelvis in particular etc. The physiological differentiation is complete after puberty, when once the secretion of the sperm, on the part of the one, and ovulation and the menses, on the part of the other, regularly appear. At the same time a differentiation occurs in the moral personality of the individuals, which is shown by the general unfolding of ideas, tastes and habits, as well as by the sexual inclinations so called." (G. Hermann. Article on Hermaphrodism, *Dictionnaire Encyclopédique des Sciences Médicales.*)

It is evident that deviations may be produced during the development which may mingle in one individual, in variable proportions, the male and female characteristics. An ovary and a testicle in the deferent canal and a Fallopian tube may develop simultaneously. It may be conceived also that monstrosities are developed externally, as for instance a penis and a vagina.

Classification of Hermaphrodites.

Hæckel and Klebs' (two modern Germans) classification, adopted by Laurent, Chevalier and Hermann, appears to us the most logical.

Thus Klebs admits A., a *True Hermaphrodism*, where testicles and ovaries may be met with simultaneously; B., a *False Hermaphrodism*, in which the subject possesses the genital glands of one sex only.

The latter is divided into masculine and feminine:

and according as the anomaly affects the external organs, or the internal organs, or both at the same time, pseudo-hermaphrodism, in either sex, is divided into *external*, *internal*, or *complete*.

A. **True Hermaphrodism.**

Laurent thinks that "true hermaphrodism or imperfect bisexual hermaphrodism is the form which is nearest to perfect hermaphrodism."

Hermann, after Klebs, distinguishes:

1. *True bilateral hermaphrodism*, in which on each side is a testicle and an ovary.

2. *True unilateral hermaphrodism*, in which there is a testicle and an ovary on one side only the opposite side displaying only one genital gland, or being completely deprived of them.

3. *True lateral or external hermaphrodism*, in which there is a testicle on one side and an ovary on the other.

True hermaphrodism exists and has always existed, and its existence has been recognized by a number of observation of animals from the monkey to the carp.

Cases of true bilateral hermaphrodism are the most rare, according to Laurent, who, however, quotes some instances borrowed from different authors. He also quotes some cases of true unilateral hermaphrodism. Cases of true alternate hermaphrodism are much more numerous. We give some of them.

"In 1767, Mont performed an antopsy, at the Dijon hospital, on the body of Jean Pierre Hubert, who had mammæ, a vulvary aperture, a retracted vagina and a rudimentary matrix with an ovary on the right. The left vulvary *labium* contained a well-formed testicle, the deferent canal of which debouched into a seminal vesicle filled with sperm.

"The same facts were observed by Rudolphi and Berthold.

"Marie Dorothée Berrar had all the sexual instincts of a man, with erections and pollutions. At the autopsy, Mayer found that she had a vagina; a uterus with two Fallopian tubes terminating on the right in a testicle and on the left in an ovary.

"It is unnecessary to say that this deep-seated hermaphrodism is always accompanied by external hermaphrodism." (Laurent, *op. cit.*)

The existence of the neuter hermaphrodite, only displaying external genital organs, the creation of certain authors, is nevertheless perfectly real.

Palaillon quotes an indisputable case of this in his report to the *Société Obstétricale et Gynécologique de Paris*.

The subject who died at la Pitié, had displayed well-marked feminine characteristics all his lifetime, both physically and morally. The autopsy made by Palaillon gave the following indications. "The pelvis is wide and hollowed out like a woman's pelvis. The region of the pubis is prominent, rounded and exactly like a Mons Veneris. From its lower portion proceed two cutaneous folds, thick, exactly representing the *labia majora* of a vulva. When they reunite, the two folds form, on the upper part, a kind of hood; on the lower, a veritable fork. Under the hood there is an appendage which is a penis in miniature. This organ measures scarcely 4 centimètres in length. It is very slender, but perfectly normal, and terminates in a gland which has at its extremity a urinary meatus. The gland is covered with a long prepuce which forms a phimosis. Below the penis, between the two folds which we have compared to *labia majora*, there is a small wrinkled scrotum, containing no testicles. The *labia majora* do not contain any organ which could be taken for testicles. Finally, under the scrotum, there is no depression resembling a vulvary orifice and a vagina.

"It was impossible to find the least trace of a uterus, ovaries, or testicles. To sum up, N... was essentially a neuter hermaphrodite. Through his rudimentary but normally formed penis, traversed by a urethral canal, and through his roughly outlined scrotum, he belonged to the male sex. But he was connected with the female sex by the presence of the *labia majora*, by the conformation of the skeleton, and by all his external habitus." (Laurent, *op. cit.*)

B. **False or Pseudo-hermaphrodism.**

This latter is divided into three classes, as we have said, *internal*, *external* or *complete* pseudo-hermaphrodism, according to the state of the anomaly.

Internal Pseudo-hermaphrodism.

Internal pseudo-hermaphrodism is either masculine or feminine. It is masculine when, in the case of a male, *Müller's conduits are persistent.* Two degrees are to be observed. In the first there may be an anomaly of the deeper organs; the external genital organs not showing any notable anomalies.

Among the few instances which have been collected, let us mention the well-known case, communicated by Petit to the *Académie des Sciences* in 1728. A soldier possessing an ordinary penis, a scrotum and two testicles which had not descended, had in addition to this a vagina followed by a bicornous uterus. But we more frequently meet with a deep malformation of the external genital organs, which constitutes the 2nd degree.

Several cases of this kind have been mentioned by Ackermann, Gunter, Godard, Mayer, Hesselbach, Langer and Arangi. The most remarkable is that of Angelique Courtois. This subject had never had her menses during her life, and had never displayed sexual tendencies of any kind. At the autopsy, Follin, who related the case in the *Gazette des Hôpitaux*, found a uterus and a rudimentary vagina opening into the urethra; on the right a Fallopian tube without an ovary; on the left a Fallopian tube with a testicle, and finally a very small penis with hypospadiasis.

Internal pseudo-hermaphrodism is masculine when, in the case of a woman, *Wolf's conduits are persistent.* In this case, the external genital organs display anomalies to a greater or lesser degree.

A very interesting case is that of Guiseppe Marzo, reported by Luigi di Cucchio.

Guiseppe Marzo, the Valet de Chambre.

Guiseppe Marzo, born at Naples, was declared to be a girl, and brought up and educated as such until he was 4 years old. A surgeon who examined him, declared that he was a cryptorchid male, his testicles having remained in his abdomen. After that he was brought up as a boy, and showed all the tastes and inclinations of one, although at puberty the spermatic secretion did not take place. Neither were there menses.

Marzo went after women and had a number of amorous adventures, after the age of 19, with nurses and chambermaids in his quality of valet de chambre. He had dissolute manners, drank and gambled, and twice contracted blenorrhagia. He had all the external appearance of a man, a beard, a hairy skin, rather narrow pelvis and no breasts. His penis measured 6 centimètres; his gland normal but hypospadic. He had no scrotum, but in place of it he had two cutaneous pads without testicles.

At the autopsy it was discovered that Marzo was a woman, for she was found to have a vagina 6 centimètres long, a normal uterus with Fallopian tubes and ovaries, but also a prostate with ejaculatory canals. The vagina was totally unprovided with a vulvary aperture.

External Pseudo-hermaphrodism.

In all the different cases which occur and which more or less resemble those in the preceding category, it is always the anomaly of the external genital organs which predominates.

The gradation is well marked between the normal individual and the hermaphrodite. It is in the first place hypospadiasis which leads the van, then cryptorchidy. Further on, we find with tne hypospadiasis a commencement of a more or less rudimentary vagina.

Numerous cases have been noticed by many authors. We shall only quote the more interesting.

Alexina B..., the Boy Governess.

This observation made by Goujon is very complete, for the subject who was intelligent and had a diploma as a preceptress, has left memoirs in which she analyzes at length the impressions which were produced in her at different periods of her life. Tardieu has made her the subject of an interesting monograph. It is to be regetted that the limits of this work prevent us from entering into too great detail, and we shall therefore merely sum up the medico-legal report of Dr. Chesnet of La Rochelle.

Alexina B..., stated to be a girl, was brought up and educated as such at a girls' school and afterwards at the Ecole Normale, which she left with a diploma as preceptress, and took a situation as governess in a girls' school. Complaining of pains in her left groin, she was examined by a surgeon, who expressed his surprise and communicated the result of his observations to the mistress of the school. Feeling that there was a mystery surrounding her, and experiencing when she was in the presence of young girls of 15 or 16 emotions which she was unable to repress, Alexina called upon the Bishop of La Rochelle. In consequence of this visit, Dr. Chesnet was charged to carefully examine Alexina and to give his opinion as to her sex.

Alexina, who is in her 22nd year, is dark and her height is 1 m. 59. Her features have nothing characteristic about them and waver between those of a man and a woman. The voice is habitually that of a woman: at times, during conversation and while she is coughing, deep and masculine tones mingle with it. A slight down covers her upper lip; a few hairs of a beard are to be noticed on her chin. The chest is flat and with no appearance of mammæ. Complete absence of the menses. Lower limbs: masculine and virile. Pelvis and hips of a man. The region below the pubis is furnished with abundant black hair. When she parts her thighs, a longitudinal aperture is to be seen extending from the eminence below the pubis to the neighbourhood of the anus. At its upper part there is a peniform body, 4 to 5 centimètres long from its point of insertion to its free extremity, which has the form of a gland; it is imperforated. This small member, as far removed from the normal condition of the clitoris as from that of the penis, is able, according to Alexina's statement, to swell, grow hard and elongate. Erection must however be imperfect, a frenum underneath holding back this species of penis.

On each side of the aperture are the *labia majora*, very prominent, especially the one on the right: in reality they are only the two halves of a scrotum which has remained divided. On palpation, one ovoid body is distinctly felt, mobile and sensible to pressure, which can be nothing else but a testicle. It was its passage retarded with strangulation iuto the inguinal ring which caused the pains which rendered the doctor's visit necessary.

A centimètre below the penis, there is an aperture of a perfectly feminine urethra. Lower down, about 3 centimètres in front of the anus, there is the orifice of a canal into which it is possible to introduce the little finger. This canal, which takes the place of the vagina, is 5 centimètres long and terminates in a *cul de sac*. At the bottom of this infundibulum there is no vestige of a uterus.

Conclusion: Alexina B... was declared to be a man by the decision of the Court of La Rochelle.

Unfortunately for the poor devil, he had to begin a new phase of his double and curious existence, for which he was in no way prepared. Falling into poverty, unable to support himself as a man and still having feminine tendencies, the unhappy creature put an end to painful existence so full of tribulation, by committing suicide in a wretched garret, leaving behind him his memoirs to which he committed his story of despair.

Catherine Hoffmann, a Wife and a Husband.

This really interesting subject underwent examination at the hands of several doctors and her true sex has always remained doubtful.

Born at Millirichstadt (Franconia) in 1824, died in 1881. Masculine habitus. Long hair on her head. No beard. Well developed breasts. Well developed penis with simple hypospadiasis at the root. The right half of the scrotum alone existed and contained one testicle. On the left, behind the pubis, a rounded body could be felt, fastened by a cord to a little organ situated behind the urethra. According to Schultze, the rounded body was an ovary, the cord a Fallopian tube, and the little organ situated behind the urethra a rudimentary uterus.

Catherine had pollutions with secretions of a liquid containing spermatozoides. At 19 the menses were established and continued until she was 40. The subject therefore had both sperm and menses, *and was at the same time a man and a woman.*

As long as the menses lasted, Catherine lived maritally with a man and was his wife. When she was 40, she changed her sex, took the name of Charles, adopted masculine costume, felt a taste for women, and ended by marrying an American woman with whom she took the part of the man in the conjugal duty. An antopsy could not be performed.

Rosine Gotlieb, Lover and Mistress.

The German, Aumon, relates the case of Rosine Gotlieb whose autopsy in a certain fashion showed her to be of the male sex. When questioned about her genital habits, she declared, with effrontery, that she had performed coition both as a man and a woman, but that she preferred the latter way to the former, of which she was ashamed.

Julie D . . ., the Inverted Hermaphrodite.

In 1884, Gerin Rose presented a case almost similar to the preceding to the *Société Médicale des Hôpitaux.*

Julie D..., 26 years of age, was detained in Lariboisière where she had been examined by Gerin Rose. The subject, in the length of her hair and in the delicacy and softness of her features perfectly resembled a woman. The vulva appeared normal, but a clitoris was observed 35 mm. in length, curvilineal and resembling a gland with its preputial crown, but imperforated, with a small linear depression in the place of the urinary meatus. The latter, with a very short urethra in connection, in reality opened underneath this penis-clitoris which became enlarged and curved like a penis in erection. At the vaginal orifice there was no trace to be found of a hymen or of myrtiform caruncles. The vagina, 9 centimètres in length, terminated in a *cul de sac*, behind which the finger, which entered with ease, could not discover the presence of a uterine neck and, on palpation, it was impossible to come across any organ which could be a uterus or ovaries.

Julie D... has never had her menses.

But palpation discovered in the *labia majora* on the lateral parts of the penis-clitoris, two ovoid projections which must have been testicles. This abnormal subject has never felt attracted except by the male sex. She has had sexual relations with men, but she has never felt any sensations, except by coition, in the friction of the vaginal mucous membrane. Her penis-clitoris remains insensible when touched.

Ernestine G..., Man and Woman.

The case was pointed out by Magitot to the *Société de Chirurgie* in 1881.

Ernestine G..., aged 40, has been looked upon as a woman since her birth. When she was 14 years old, she had on three different occasions, each time with an interval of three months, a running of blood from the vulva, but it did not occur again. At the same time her breasts increased sensibly in size. Having an inclination for men, she married when she was 17, but her intercourse was incomplete. She even remarked that she displayed to her husband an erection like his, although smaller, and that she produced a similar ejaculation.

After the death of her husband, Ernestine's ideas were modified and she displayed a very keen propensity for women. She had several mistresses and states that intercourse was effected in a perfectly normal manner. The deprivation of sexual enjoyment owing to the death of her husband, and without her having interrupted her relations with him, was not in any way the cause of this change of part, for she confessed that "while her husband was still alive, and without interrupting her relations with him, she had on several occasions had genuine intercourse with women, but not so regularly nor so frequently as she had since she was a widow."

She is tall, 1m 78; her hair is black as well as her beard which is abundant: voice and ways feminine; hands fleshy and vigorous. Breasts rather voluminous; pelvis has no great width. The size of the penis is that of a child of 12 years' of age; there is hypospadiasis, a bifid scrotum containing a testicle in each of its parts. At the bottom of the scrotal groove there is a small infundibulum not permitting the entrance of the little finger, without any trace of a uterine neck.

The penis is susceptible of erection; it produces an ejaculation giving a apparently normal sperm but in which the microscope does not reveal any spermatazoides.

The Woman changed into a Man by Professor Porro's Bistoury.

On Nov. 15th, 1882, a woman named J. G. F... came to Professor Porro's dispensary in order to find out to which sex she really belonged. She had been brought up as a girl from infancy but had never displayed the tastes of one; on the contrary, everything revealed masculine ideas in her instincts. Her features are manlike with a few black hairs. the thorax is that of a man with a maiden's breasts, but the lower part displays a feminine conformation.

The mons veneris, but slightly prominent, is covered with stiff black hair. The vulva bears a clitoris (or penis) of considerable development, the gland of which projects only $1\,^1/_2$ centimètres beyond the prepuce. From the base of the gland two folds of the vulvary mucous membrane start which resemble the *nymphæ;* on parting them a canal is seen about 4 centimètres long which extends from the base of the gland to an orifice situated on the mesial line, 6 centimètres distant from the anterior margin of the anus. This orifice leads to a fresh canal, which, after a course of $4\,^1/_2$ centimètres, leads into the bladder.

Two cutaneous folds, of larger dimensions than the preceding, develop from either side of the clitoriformed penis, parallel to the *nymphæ:* they are covered with hair and might pass for *labia majora.* At their apex, towards the inguinal region, there are two hard bodies fastened to the ring. When these bodies are pressed, the subject does not complain of any painful sensation, nor of the peculiar feeling when the testicles are rubbed. Are these ovaries or testicles?

The rectal touch proves the non-existence of a prostate or uterus.

With a skilful cut with the bistoury, Porro incised the right cruro-genital fold and discovered a testicle. The patient, cured after 15 days' treatment, left the hospital delighted at being a man.

Louise R. . ., Woman Mechanician.

Péan has given in the *Gazette des Hôpitaux* another case of complex masculine hermaphrodism with arrested development of the genital organs. Louise R. . ., registered at birth as a girl, is a mechanician in a large women's workshop. She possesses a penis 3 centimètres in length, which doubles in size in erection. The gland, which is but slightly developed, has neither meatus nor prepuce. Three centimètres below the base of the penis, there is a meatus which allows the urine and sperm to escape. Below the meatus there is a vulvary orifice: the infundibulum measures 2 centimètres; on either side are rudimentary *nymphæ* and species of *labia majora* containing a tumour of the size of a bean: this is the testicle. No uterus or mammæ. Voice deep. Skin and face hairy: the subject shaves.

Mental condition excitable. Abuse of coition with the young girls in the workroom whom she seduces. The sperm contains spermatozoides.

For this observation we see the hermaphrodite, in reality au incomplete man, inclined to women. The contrary is the case in the following observation, due to Polaillon who commnnicated it to the *Académie de Médicine*, (1891).

The Man-Prostitute.

The subject is a woman who has never had her menses. Her external genital organs (mons veneris, vulva, and clitoris) are of normal conformation, but behind the navicular fosse, the vagina is only represented by a depression the depth of which, when she began her abandoned life, was hardly 2 *centimètres*. On a level with the inguinal canal, there exists on either side, a projection as large as a nut, ovoid, mobile, reducible, painful where it is pressed and without any periodical swelling.

Mammæ of a woman: face and skin smooth. This woman has led an abandoned life, and the attempts at coition on the part of her lovers had effected as much as a surgeon could have done. The vaginal depression measured 5 centimètres in 1888, 7 centimètres in 1889, and in 1890 it was the length of the index finger. The skin forced back had the appearance of a mucous membrane. After her death no female organ wes found *internally*, nor any vestige of a prostate. The tumours of the inguinal canal were atrophied testicles.

Marie Marius, au Old Man's Sweetheart and a Male Nurse in a Religious House

The case of Marie Marius C... was communicated by Benoit and Magnan to the Société de Médicine Légale.

The subject, Marie C..., registered as a girl, was brought up as such, and had the dispositions and tastes of one, retaining her feminine habits until she was 24 years of age. At 13, puberty and the beginning of a beard. Erotic dreams with representations of women. Allowed herself, however, to be taken away by an old man aged 70, and ran away with him to Martinique. As normal intercourse could not take place, *sodomy and reciprocal buccal onanism*. The negresses and mulatto women did not satisfy her. She returned to France, rectified her registration of birth and became Marius instead of Marie. She than entered a religious community after submitting herself to the inspection of the Father Superior who pronounced him to be a man.

He was a masculine hermaphodite with scrotal hypospadiasis and a vulva. The penis measured 4 centimètres; it entered on erection but was confined by a frenum underneath. The imperforated gland carried a prepuce. Below it was a vulva with two species of *labia majora*, which opened into a narrow vagina. The urinary meatus existed between the vulva and the base of the penis. There were never any menses. No testicles could be felt. During the spasm, there was a running of a whitish fluid from the meatus.

Soft voice: breasts rather large. Beard. Prefers the caresses of her lover aged 70, to those of women: is therefore an inverted.

The Bearded Woman: Madeleine Lefort.

Here we are in the presence of a subject displaying the appearances of a feminine hermaphrodite. Marie Madeleine Lefort, examined by Béchard when she was 16 years old. Her menses appeared when she was 8. She displayed a clitoris 37 millimétres in length; the imperforated gland was covered in 3/4 of its circumference with a mobile prepuce. Underneath was a vulvary aperture furnished with two short narrow *labia*. At the upper part of the aperture, under the root of the clitoris, a urethra opened. Mammæ well developed. General habitus of the body that of a youth of the same age. Larynx projecting, voice loud, growing beard, skin on the limbs covered with hair.

Marie Madeleine Lefort felt an inclination for women and declared that she only had relations with them. She died at a great age with a gray beard. The autopsy showed that she was a woman with a clitoris developed to an exaggerated extent and an atrophied vagina. She was therefore an inverted.

The Woman who refused to have her Monstrous Clitoris cut.

We borrow from the old author Jacques Duval a few anecdotes taken from his curious treatise on hermaphrodism. "During the time that I was in the country of Anjou, he says, 45 years ago, a gentleman and his wife came before the Court to plead on his part that the marriage which he had contracted with his wife should be declared null and void, and that he should be allowed to marry again. The cause of the divorce which he claimed, was that this lady had a virile member, as long as twice the breadth of his finger, in the upper part of her woman's oval, where the clitoris ought to be, and that it stood up when her husband wished to have her company and hurt him, so that he had not yet been able to have proper habitation and copulation with her.

"She was inspected and it was found to be true. The husband's offer was judged to be a suitable one, namely, that if she would allow the said part, which is superfluous and useless to a woman to be cut off, he would agree that the marriage should stand, as it had been celebrated: but, as the said lady refused, and declared that she preferred the dissolution of the marriage to the amputation of this part which she wished to keep, as nature had furnished her with it, the marriage was by consent of the two parties declared null and void, and the husband was allowed to take another wife, as seemed him good."

The Priest in the Family-Way.

"It has been told me, says Jacques Duval again, that in the said city of Paris there was a young man, a priest, who was big with child: the fact was known, and he was shut up a prisoner of the Ecclesiastical Court, to wait for the end of his pregnancy and until nature had produced its effects, in order to receive the proper penalty for his offence."

This unfortunate priest was therefore altogether a woman with a large clitoris, like the one in the following tale.

The Tribade before the Parlement de Paris.

"The said Sieur Devisot, an honourable man, related that he had been employed by the Court of the Parlement de Paris in the examination of a woman of the number of the *tribades* and *subigatrices*, in order to find out with what part she had abused many girls and delighted women, by giving them in carnal intercourse, great tickling, and satisfaction. Her clitoris was found to be so large and well equipped that it represented the size and thickness of a virile member stiff and stretched. And after this woman had confessed her fault, and her error had been sufficiently avowed, the said Court opened the doors for this *tribade* and let her go forth and depart whither she thought fit without condemnation, but forbidding her very expressly to return there again, with intimation and threat that should she come back, an exemplary punishment would be inflicted upon her." (Jacques Duval, *Traité des Hermaphrodites*.)

The Girl who was changed into a Boy by jumping over a Ditch.

Let us finish these old-world stories with one that is not wanting in flavour.

"As I was passing through Vitry-le-François, I was able to see a man whom the Bishop of Soissons named Germain at his Confirmation, but whom all the inhabitants of the place had known and looked upon as as girl named Marie, until he was 23 years old. At that time he had a beard and was very manlike. Making, as he said, an effort when he was jumping a ditch, his virile members were produced: and there is a song still sung by the girls of those parts, in which they warn one another not to make long strides for fear that they might become a boy like Marie Germain." (Michel de Montaigne. *Essais.*)

Sexual Instincts of Hermaphrodites.

Chevalier has made a very complete table of them in a few pages from which we borrow:

"What is of more importance here, it the reaction of the physical upon the physiological, that is to say on the sexual instinct considered in its direction as a principal factor, and in its secondary characteristics as an accessory factor. Let us therefore look and see how the malformed may behave in love.

"With regard to the *true* hermaphrodite, who has two sexes, only two ways are conceivable.

"1. He is genesically indifferent: not only does coition with either sex offer him no attractions, but it is repugnant to him: there is sexual anæsthesia; there is therefore no need to concern ourselves with this form of inclination.

"2. The sexual appetite exists, and then there are two alternatives:

"*a.* The amorous tendency is undecided and fluctuating; relations are sought for and take place with either sex.

"*b.* The tendency is precise, clear and fixed for one determined sex; the relations are exclusively unilateral.

We see that in every way, as soon as there is a sexual inclination, there is inversion, since the unhappy individual can do nothing else but love a person of the same sex as his own. But is not this cavilling and casuistry after the fashion of the ancient philosophers? and should we not have an equal right to argue, on the other hand, that such individuals can do nothing else but love a person of the opposite sex to their own?

"As for the apparent hermaphrodite whose sex is only concealed by a deceptive exterior, he may be ranked under one of the two following heads:

"1. The malformed individual has no sexual inclination; the frigidity is complete.

"2. The amorous inclination exists only for individuals of the opposite sex, which is regular.

"I shall have nothing to say about this case, if the great majority of the genitally malformed were only pseudo-hermaphrodites; hypospadics, that is to say individuals whose true sex it is often difficult to discern, which often gives rise to errors of sex.

"An absolute social danger results from this. At birth, the hypospadic generally appears with characteristics of the female sex. The scrotum is bifid in such a way as to have the appearance of a vulva; at this level there often exists a depression or infundibulum which might be taken for a vagina: the two folds which form the edges look like the *labia majora;* they do not usually enclose any tumour or anything that would give grounds for belief in the existence of a testicle: moreover, the atrophied penis gives the illusion of a voluminous clitoris. It follows that in the generality of cases, the hypospadic, that is to say a male, is considered as belonging to the female sex: thence result false declarations and false registrations of sex at birth. This is not all:—the child being taken for a girl, is brought up, clothed and educated as such, and as he grows up, gradually assumes the manners, the habits and the tastes of his false sex. He is sent to a girls' school, to a convent, or to a workroom of young girls. When he reaches puberty and the evolution or migration of the testicles takes place, the unhappy creature, recalled to his natural desires, discovers tendencies and inclinations which he does not understand, which astonish and alarm him at the same time. These desires are sometimes a kind of revelation for the hermaphrodite: he begins to have doubts about his sex and submits himself to an examination which ends in his enlightenment. The man-woman is then restored to his true sex. But if he does not dare to confess his infirmity, or if he follows his inclinations, then, as the old saying goes, the wolf is in the fold. The pseudo-girl will have intimate relations with young girls of her own age, will pervert them almost necessarily and with the more security as facts of this kind are but little known and will not be suspected. It is easy to conceive the disorders which will result from this. Although they are far more uncommon, opposite errors of sex are sometimes to be met with, and account will be taken of the unhealthy appetites aroused by the presence of a gynandre in a school, seminary, or prison.

"However this may be, the only prejudice which the error of sex causes against hermaphrodites, obliges us to concern ourselves with the means of ameliorating the situation in which they are placed at present. Without laying stress upon certain civil rights which are so different in the two sexes, nor on the inconveniences which result in marriage, one of the most serious consequences which may be entailed by an erroneous decision as to the sex, is the anguish, the demoralization, the deep despair which accompany the change of civil condition and social situation. Everything is upset in the individual's feelings, thoughts, and deeds, and it is with the greatest difficulty that, placed in a new sphere, he succeeds in assimilating himself to its tastes, ideas, and duties. Unclassed, undecided, hesitating between instinct and habit, it may happen that the unhappy creature ends by suicide an existence full of vexation. The history of Alexina B... is evidence of this. Can it be said that these facts are rare and exceptional? P. Garnier has collected more than thirty cases of error of sex, and how many cases have escaped his statistics; how many malformed do we elbow in the street who, through ignorance, shame, or weakness of sexual inclination, do not dare to submit themselves to a scientific examination and demand the rectification of their civil rights?

"3. The sexual appetite is equal for the two sexes; there is a double direction of instinct which constitutes a particular form of inversion.

"4. Sexual relations are sought for and practised only with persons belonging to the sex of which the malformed individual himself forms a part: the perversion is therefore very clear." (J. Chevalier. *op. cit.*)

Sexual Satisfactions of Hermaphrodites.

According to Laurent, the majority of hermaphrodites are indifferent to the sexual point of view, which confirms the theories of Chevalier above.

T. Gallard has reported the case of a feminine hermaphrodite who was married twice. Not only did she feel no voluptuous sensation during coition, but every attempt made to accomplish that act was painful, although she willingly lent herself to it. She neither asked for nor desired sexual intercourse; she endured her husband's caresses merely to please him. According to the latter's account, she had never made the least provocative attempt upon him. She had never had the slightest erotic desire, even in a dream.

Hohmann, whose case was observed by Robitanski, was absolutely indifferent sexually.

Some hermaphrodites are not indisposed to commerce with women, and, as in the case observed by Tardieu, may experience desires, excitations and complete enjoyment, as well as a venereal orgasm which may extend to the emission of sperm.

Hermaphrodites are also to be seen who after displaying a very keen taste for commerce with men, are led, through the descent of the testicles, to quite opposite instincts which attract them to women.

But not infrequently also, hermaphrodites are seen who have double tastes and play sometimes the part of the man and sometimes that of the woman.

Laurent thinks that the bringing up may in many cases impel the sexual instinct in an opposite direction to what it ought to take and produce inversion. He quotes in support of this, Magitot's case of Maria Arsano who was married as a woman and found after her death to be a man, also that of Clara Mayer, a hypospadic man who played the part of a woman all her life, and lastly that of Marzo who though a woman, as we have seen above, copulated with women and contracted blennorrhagia.

We prefer Chevalier's more physiological theories. Besides, there are numerous inverted men who have been brought up as men and have normal genital organs, and who nevertheless are inclined towards their own sex. It is the same with regard to inverted women, of the class of viragoes and effeminateds. *A fortiori* will not an hermaphrodite whose genital organs are malformed be capable of the inversion-aberration, either simple or double, with the two sexes?

But if hermaphrodites are often affected with impotence, they are often also very salacious.

Dr. E. Levy, says Laurent, observed at Gripalsheim two sisters, hermaphrodites, who were known throughout the district for their lubricity. They had intercourse both with men and with women.

Are hermaphrodites fecund? Laurent answers in the negative, and I shall not oppose his opinion in spite of the presence of the spermatic secretion in some of them.

To sum up therefore, these unfortunate creatures are for the most part impotent, and always, it may be said, infecund. Nevertheless, when they are potent, they may be very salacious and make use of either the man or the woman, as the case may be. We have seen a remarkably instance of this in the observation of Marie Marius.

An Hermaphrodite Passive Pederast.

A very suggestive instance is due to Tardieu. He saw at St. Lazare a boy aged 16, who had been arrested when in woman's clothes for indulging in clandestine prostitution. He was a male hypospadic who had indulged in the most intemperate habits ever since his childhood, and, above all, had ministered to the pleasures of men of the lowest class. The penis was not more than 3 centimètres in length and as thick as the extremity of the index finger. It was enveloped by folds of skin which fell down in such a way as to imitate the *mymphæ*, and the two halves of the scrotum, which were not joined together, served to complete the appearance of a vulva, and encircled an orifice in the shape of an infundibulum wide enough to admit the virile member, and gave to this false vagina a depth of 7 or 8 centimètres. An easily recognizable testicle could be clearly felt in the left groin. The dilated and sunken anus reproduced exactly behind, the shape of the infundibulum which existed in front. It was evident that this unhappy individual had lent himself to doubly unnatural acts.

We have quoted instances of women hermaphrodites who indulged in tribadism.

"I have moreover been shown, says Laurent, at the aquatic fêtes of the Elysée Montmartre, two women with deep voices and strongly accentuated features who indulged in venereal pleasures with men and women alternately and with the keenest ardour."

In order to divert our readers a little from the monotony of medical observations, we are about to give them as a treat, two literary quotations, one from the naturalist novelist Dubut de Laforest, and the other from the author named Jean Lombard. The former is from a novel, the heroine of which is a feminine hermaphrodite, and the latter refers to the famous Roman Emperor Heliogabalus, who was a male hermaphrodite and an active and passive pederast whose lubricity caused even the Romans to shudder, satiated as they were with things erotic.

The Hermaphrodite Vicomtesse.

Having lost a beloved husband who knew how to show respect for his wife's unnatural formation, the widowed Vicomtesse Germaine de Brandiers left her hôtel in the Avenue de Messine, renounced the world and gave up her travels, her parties and all her distractions, in order to shut herself in an ancient château and there to weep, lament and perhaps to die.

Situated in the western corner of Périgord, in the mountainous and wooded portion which divides Dordogne from Haute Vienne, surrounded by far-stretching moors and wide meadows with their deep pools—on these winter nights the grey, lowering sky seemed to touch its lofty towers, frowning with battlements like a donjon-keep in a Porte Saint Martin melodrama.

Madame de Brandiers rode, employed herself in working tapestry and embroidery, painted in water-colours, or read religious books, visited nobody and lived always alone.

When she dropped her weeds and dressed in violet, many were the suitors who wished to lay siege to her heart, but she dismissed them one and all: many were surprised and a few felt hurt that she still persisted in mourning for him she had lost. Germaine was twenty years old; she was rich and beautiful, but her dark beauty was somewhat too masculine; her figure was that of a Lifeguardsman, and her upper lip was fringed with down. All at once the sleeper awoke; a light shone from her calm blue eyes, and her athletic frame was convulsed with strange, prolonged agitation. Lisa, the young wife of Jacques Michard and daughter of Pincailloux, a tenant on the estate, was installed by Germaine in the post of lady-in-waiting. A pretty girl was Lisa, a village lass but lately married, fair and fresh, with rosy flesh and languorous fondling ways. From the Nuns she had learnt how to read and write, and do arithmetic, and the young widow thought it would be a pleasant task for her to complete the pretty peasant girl's education. Madame de Brandiers taught her to play the piano and the harp and to sing; gave her lessons in painting, tapestry-work and embroidery, instructed her in the secrets of the toilette, and amused herself by taking down and arranging her hair, by washing, soaping and perfuming her with Eastern essences.

Lisa experienced a feeling of comfort mingled with pride from the coaxing touch of these aristocratic fingers and their thousand preparatory cares, and Pincailloux's daughter was already beginning to draw comparisons between the gracious kisses of the Vicomtesse and the rude attacks of her husband. "Michard is a brute: all peasants are brutes," she would say.

She relished the sweet kisses of the Vicomtesse. Every night, in the rose-hung boudoir, reclining with roses in their hair half-naked on the sumptuous couch before a blazing fire, with a round table before them glittering with plate and crested glass and flowers and lights, Germaine and Lisa carried on their orgies. The peasant girl remained a woman, and the hermaphrodite Vicomtesse sometimes took the part of a man.

The servants who guessed what the relations between the Lesbians were, kept silence. As for Lisa's parents, the Pincailloux, they began to appreciate their good fortune: every morning, the Vicomtesse's favourite appeared at her parents' home laden with provisions, and Father François, Mother Catherine. Grandfather Barnabas, Aunt Margoton, and the brothers, sisters, and brothers-in-law, old and young, all gorged and drank to the health of Lesbos. The tenants grew jealous, for the steward, the keepers, and even the lawyers, who were harsh enough to the other tenants, vied with one another in showing attention to the Pincailloux; and the latter trimmed up their cattle and always got what price they asked for them, cut down the trees, paid neither rent nor tithe, and the strong-box grew full with louis-d'or.

François divined the secret of their daughter's amour. What was passing in those stolid uncultivated minds? Lisa grew thin, her cheeks lost their colour, there was a bluish tinge about her temples and dark circles showed round her eyes, her voice became hoarse and her steps unsteady, all the signs of physical and moral degradation appeared as the result of her illicit manœuvres.

Jacques forbade his death-stricken wife to sleep at the Château, and the family rose up in arms against him. They scolded and abused him, they accused him of impotence; for all of them were fat with the exception of the Lesbian, and none wished to grow thin. Indeed! why should this fool who was unable to get a child interfere with Lisa's good fortune?

One evening the husband said:

"I don't want her to go back there."

"She's free to do as she likes," said the Pincailloux.

"Yes! Yes!" clamoured the brothers and the sisters-in-law.

"My wife, my poor wife, the lady is poisoning and killing her! Oh that slut! that slut of a widow!"

And he summed up the situation in a few words: "Lisa was not strong and the other was 'sucking her life's blood.'"

Pincailloux tried to calm his son-in-law.

"Don't be a fool, Jacques. Come, what does it matter to you? We have got money, and we shall get more. Don't meddle in what doesn't concern you. You haven't got a child, have you? Well! our mistress can't make you a cuckold or get a child out of Lisa! Jacques, the lady is not a bad sort, and our Lisa is a good girl. Well! we must let them amuse themselves. They do no harm to anybody. Come, what does it matter to you?"

Jacques yielded to these arguments. Madame de Brandiers, the terrible Vicomtesse, made a present to Lisa of the little farm which her parents titled. Lisa died mad, and the Pincailloux inherited it; they inherited a new Field of Blood, an Aceldama, like that in Holy Writ.

Madame de Brandiers died in erotic madness, and the autopsy revealed "the simultaneous existence of male and female organs in this creature." (Dubut de Laforest. *Pathologie Sociale. op. cit.*)

An Hermaphrodite Emperor.
The Debaucheries of Heliogabalus.

The Brundusinians, forcing their way into the crowd, found themselves face to face with the Pretorians on the threshold of Heliogabalus's apartment: he was reclining in a bed supported on pillars of gold, with yellow cushions at his feet and a yellow garment round his loins, his face was tinged with the yellow reflection which prevailed everything, from the floor which was powdered with gold, to the ceiling which was covered with the same metal. A strong odour of saffron assailed their nostrils. Priests stood motionless in the darkened corners: officers passed to and fro who by their low-born looks might have been thought to have sprung from the quarters of the worst repute in Rome, were it not for their robes of rustling silk and their jewels. The Emperor was almost naked, swinging his legs and exposing his nudity which now and again one of his familiars would devoutly kiss, an act which the others greeted with coarse laughter. Over their shoulders, the Brundusinians saw Heliogabalus place himself in an obscene position and receive the embraces of a young man whom he called his divine husband.

"Horror! Horror!" cried Asprenas, and his dilated eye grew redder still. But the dissolute Pretorians grew angry. With the flat of their swords they beat back the strangers who responded to the blows by louder cries of adoration.

"Joy and peace to the divine Antoninus, whose body is perfection itself!"

"Heliogabalus has taken Herakles for husband. The Emperor is an androgyne like Fate!"

"Rich is he in two sexes, honour to him!"

And they mopped their brow, crying out these abominations with all their might, asking even that they might witness it again and lick the place where the unnatural act had been committed. They seemed enraptured. None complained of having made a long journey, nor of being kept waiting at the gate of the

Emperor who paid no attention to them, nor of knowing when they were present at the marriage of Astaroth with the Black Stone. They were envoys from towns and provinces, tributary Kings of the Empire, or notables of conquered cities, rich landowners, or generals who had abused their powers in order to come to Rome and pay an act of servile homage to Heliogabalus.

Asprenas wished to retire, understanding no better than yesterday the excellence of the Principal of Life. And dominating the strangers with his scornful eye, he took off with him Tulero who brought away Politus, while Mames and Elva, wishing to remain, resisted their efforts.

A path was made through the crowd which was growing more clamorous. An officer in helmet and breastplate was dragging along a child of about twelve years of age with long tresses of black hair, a slave who had been tonded like a delicate plant: the boy was uttering cries of despair, digging his nails in the floor, and twining his legs round those of the strangers who hastily made room.

They recognized Attellius.

Alarmed and not wishing that he should recognize them, they turned away. The crimsoned eye of Asprenas fell upon the face of a Black, who also wore the red paint of the prostitute. However, Attellius lifted up the child and sent him rolling into Heliogabalus's appartment; then he turned back, saluted by all, a little pale and his helmet straight like a consul returning from the fight.

A deep silence, then a thrilling cry. A piteous shriek for aid. A horrible struggle between the boy whom the strangers now saw naked and Heliogabalus who had grown furious, bidding his familiars not to touch the victim before he did so himself. Then the final struggle on the same yellow bed, with the yellow cushions and yellow stuffs and powdered saffron, and the panting child dipped in the golden dust, colouring him with living gold.

At length, Heliogabalus showed himself to the strangers whom the Pretorians had allowed to enter. And, defiling under the gaze of the familiars, they saw him stretched out upon his couch, and, on his robe of purple silk, moist traces of the recent rape; a tiara was on his brow; his eyes, terrible in their look of weariness, had dark circles round them; his features were delicate, his skin polished with pumice-stone, a phallus hung upon his chest, his fingers were covered with rings, on his purple shoes at the instep were large diamonds, and his fine curling hair was powdered with electrum. Negro slaves fanned him with flabellums made of giant peacock's feathers; while in a corner, beneath the icy looks of the priests, the child wept in sinister fashion.

The strangers said no more. They departed in terror, the Pretorians' sword behind them, while Heliogabalus carelessly gave an order for the victim to be removed.

The Hymn to Venus and the Bloody Sacrifices.

They entered the Palace by a low door which was used only by slaves. In the palace too there was a wild trampling of men's feet, a ringing of enormous bells through the endless passages, cries of wild beasts, and the sound of the blows of golden pikes on golden bucklers.

Habarr'att arrayed them in ceremonial robes which glittered with gold and gems; to the loud blast of trumpets, ennuchs led them into the presence of Heliogabalus, no longer the muleteer of a little while ago, the mean muleteer at whom a million asses wondered, but the Emperor, white of skin and with his dazzling tiara, with a robe so covered with gold that it seemed weighted down, and with sandals tied on by straps which wound high round the leg, a sumptuous Oriental figure who shone by his own irradiation.

Men dressed in cloth of gold with golden mitras, in which were set blue, yellow and green stones; Priests who ever maintained a priestly attitude and whose curling beards fell upon their crimson robe; Priests of the Sun who ever made obscene motions with their body; familiars in rustling robes and armour of officers spread out behind them like the tail of some enormous peacock. And all chanted in slow rhythm, interrupted by the shrill sounds of the curved trumpets, a Hymn to Venus, who bewailed the loss of Adonis; lyres, and sistra and flutes died away in unknown strains to the regular pulse of the dance. The Empire was repairing to the Temple of the Sun, there to figure the death of Adonis and the grief of Venus in the full light of day, dangerous though it might be, braving the wrath of the Eternal City, over which the sky, grown still more lurid, seemed like a lake of blood ready to burst forth.

Sæmias and Atillia let themselves be carried on; eunuchs held up their purple palla, œneatores by their side blew discordant strains, and around them, amid the floating clouds of incense, ever rose the mighty chant bewailing Adonis and bewailing Venus. Men and women whom they did not recognise, joined in the procession; chained beasts lashed with their tails their keepers who struck them with iron rods, elephants pushed their way onwards, and everywhere around were the brilliant circles of the golden bucklers, like yellow eyes under the flashes of the golden pikes. They spoke not, they listened not, nor did they think, resigned to a death already felt in the trembling of their flesh, in the loss of their energy, and in the weariness of their frames which outraged nature punished with unconsciousness and the sense of Fate.

They emerged from the Palace; a purple canopy overhead was borne by smooth-faced eunuchs. And Heliogabalus entered his chariot, and they were lifted into a wide litter balanced on the bleeding shoulders of men who yelled in agony under the strokes of the lash, and horsemen in scaly armour, writhing like monstrous reptiles, rode forward on glossy steeds which tossed their manes. Then a sight of Rome unfolded itself before them in its colossal might; through all the quarters, multitudes thronged to the windows, upon the terraces and under the porticoes shout succeeded shout, and they dominated it all from their litter which swung amorously beneath them. The tympana sounded forth, mingling their notes with the laughing music of the flutes and with the shrill sounds of the sistra and the lutes up on high, and there too a freshly severed head was to be seen on the end of a pike, the head of a bearded man, who perhaps had wished to protest against the Imperial frenzy, and whom the Pretorians had cut down in nameless slaughter and left his blood to trickle in the dust.

They climbed up the ascent to the Temple of the Sun with its white pediment shining like snow against the red background of the sky; the tumult died away in the anxiety of the people to see what was passing there. Within, Heliogabalus was seated on on a throne borne on atlantes of massive silver, the feet buried in a litter of enormous palm-leaves, and the back sculptured with symbolical figures of serpents biting their tail and of crowned bull's heads surmounted by torches intercrossed. They sat down on Greek okladias of cloth of gold; around them others too sat down, and others remained standing before the line of crimson priests: half-naked dancing-girls swept round under the vaulted roof lighted by a large round hole, in rhythmic religious dances.

The Emperor ascended a dais strewn with saffron, and, naked, with his sex tied down so as to resemble the Woman more, exhibited his white skin and his white face, while he writhed, and groaned, and bewailed Adonis in the Poem of Venus, by Zopæus, which the Emperor recited, told all: a distracted search through Asia and Africa for the fair Child; mountains overthrown and forests cut down; violet seas which waited yet; all the beasts of the earth which followed; births of Gods and Goddesses in white clouds, apotheosized in the skies ever traversed by mythological birds and by moons born in the bosom of vanished nights. Then the Temple resounded with a mighty chant;

the dancer, now altogether naked, flew round faster, and the priests mechanically turned their curling beard towards Heliogabalus, the familiars displayed their sex, the eunuchs uttered cries of grief; it was like an Olympus of the Gods, a superhuman scene of religious Rome revelling in its glory and triumph, lighted up by the torches which blazed under the lofty columns from which were hung bucklers reflecting the gleam of gold.

And now Herakles, Zoticus, Gordeius, Protogenes and Murissimus appeared upon the dais. Heliogabalus gave himself up to promiscuous male intercourse which the eunuchs looked upon with ardent eyes, the cold priests extolled, and the dancers saluted with the rhythm of their lascivious dance, while others reechoed the sighs of pleasure of their Master, the Emperor.

The priests ascended the dais, from which Heliogabalus came down, followed by his familiars, and then screaming children were dragged forward, children of patrician families, and their throats were cut amid a tempest of cries like those of lambs. A golden knife was quickly buried in the tender victims' throats, and as they still panted, Heliogabalus and the familiars received the blood from the gaping wounds upon their neck and head and naked flesh. And the little corpses grew into a pile before the priests who never ceased their chant, and the crimson of whose robes seemed like unto the blood upon the dais.

The Last Days and Death of Heliogabalus.

The days passed on with their leaden hours in that Rome which had taken a bath of blood, with Heliogabalus always in his Palace and Mammœa always in the Palace of the Cæsars. The male orgies, the voluptuous rites of the Black Stone still went on under that Latin sky from henceforth red, reflecting the blood of the carnage which had occurred. Sorrowful, the Eternal City, now overshadowed by the gigantic shadow of the victorious Black Stone lay groaning and affrighted, listening to its Title which bewailed unceasingly the corpses' stain, looking for a day which might throw a light upon the darkness of its night. From every side the face of Heliogabalus rose in its living beauty resplendent with the gems of his tiara and the jewels round his neck; and from his long purple robe, his feet shod in gold and silk treading the powdered saffron, the enormity of his sex, the nudity of his body rose everywhere with apotheoses of dancing girls, of familiars who violated him, of priests of the Sun with indecent movements of their hips. Herakles, Zoticus, Murissimus, Gordeius, Protogenes, all his familiars, proud as with the Aves of a Triumph, exhibiting themselves in his ways and not yet tiring of the Black Stone, had abominable intercourse with Heliogabalus before the very eyes of the Romans who dared not show their anger, and to whose wounded feelings it was now but an ignominious accumulation of men's thighs, men's buttocks with their sex ever brandished forth.

But once again Rome was convulsed with revolt, one morning in March: the Title recovered from its yellow outbreak, the monuments became white, the country regained its serenity. And the City again saw the Pretorians descending from their camp, with their bristling pikes and javelins, their rattling swords, their gleaming helmets and breastplates, and it saw too the wild escape of the Beasts which the soldiers shot down with arrows, and the cavalry pouring forth in wild squadrons, leaping into the air while the earth shook with fresh cries of death. But Rome itself was unmoved and took no part in it, absolutely broken by these two seditions, and it was but a combat between the parties of Heliogabalus and Mammœa.

. . . .

Madel distractedly carried off Atillia whom the Pretorians had struck down as she rushed forward to save Sæmias slain with Heliogabalus, discovered in the privies of his sumptuous Palace. They had thrust his head, his golden head of Emperor with his tiara of gold and precious stones, into the excrement, then they had killed Herakles, gouged out the eyes of Aristomachus and Antiochanes, empaled Zoticus and Murissimus, beheaded Gordius and Protogenes, sown afresh the Gardens with quivering corpses, cut off and thrown into the lake the privy parts of the familiars, and sacked the Palace in which nothing remained standing, neither the candelabra with atlantes for feet, nor vases, nor statues, nor triclinias, nor thrones of gold and ivory and bronze, on which were sculptured the symbols of obscenity, nor cathedræ, nor sigmas, nor tables of thyas, nor anything of all which formed its glory. Then, dragging the Black Stone out of the Temple of the Sun, they had covered it with filth and broken it into pieces which the people carried away, so that this symbol of Life might never return, raised as it had been in such a terrible way over Rome, like a shadowy obelisk with the appearance of a gigantic phallus.

At the time of the insurrection, Habarr'at had called Gheet and Amon to carry off Atillia from the revolted Pretorians and, feeble though he was still, Madel followed them. They penetrated into the Palace, where they were soon dispersed. Scarcely could Madel step into a corner of the room swimming with blood to reach Attilia now violated, her belly naked, her breasts cut off, her neck swollen and her face pounded by kicks from iron heels. He took her and had only just time to avoid an arrow shot from a private passage; it struck Habarr'at who fell there, dead, without a cry, his black body forming a spot in the pool of blood which flowed everywhere. (Jean Lombard. *L'Agonie.* Paris, Albert Savine.)

Proofs that Heliogabalus was a Sadist Hermaphrodite. His Reign.

Fault perhaps will be found with us for introducing into a medico-scientific work a literary element which always requires more or less caution. Our reply is that Jean Lombard has revived the Rome of the time of Heliogabalus, just as G. Flaubert has revived the

Carthage of the time of Salammbo, and that these two authors draw their constant inspiration from ancient authors. Besides this, it is easy to give proofs that Heliogabalus was an hermaphrodite, which serves to explain his taste for both active and passive pederasty. His history has been written by the Latin authors, Lampridus, Herodian and Xyphilinus, as well as by the Greek Dion Cassius, whose writings serve to complete one another. This Emperor was the worthy son of Caracalla and the courtesan Semiramis, one of the most shameless women of the period. When quite young, he was taken away to Emesa, in the East, and there became a priest of the Sun which was adored in this Syrian city under the form of a conical black stone (believed to be an aeorolite), a rude representation of a phallus, the virile organ. His youth, his beauty, and above all his hermaphrodism soon made him an inverted, and he quickly learnt all the turpitudes of pederasty. Named Emperor after the defeat of the troops of Macrinus who was massacred, he came to Rome to be crowned as Emperor. The City of the Cæsars one day witnessed the arrival of her Syrian Emperor, a strange personage of two sexes, dressed as a woman in a trailing robe of silk and gold in the Phenician fashion, with blackened eyebrows and painted and vermilioned cheeks, with bracelets on his arms and wearing a tiara-shaped crown enriched with pearls and precious stones. Immorality and immodesty had long been seated on the throne of the Roman Emperors. Sanguinary lust showed itself there in the person of Heliogabalus, who was fifteen years old at the time of his accession. Besides political murders, the sacrifices of human victims to the God of the Sun, chosen from among the first families in Italy, must also be noted. Every extravagant act of which a frenzied imagination could dream, was realized by Heliogabalus: this insensate child gave a spectacle to the world of every kind of excess, abomination, and infamy, and his reign was but a Saturnalia of which we vainly seek a second instance in history. His shameless conduct casts in the shade that of Tiberius, Nero, and even Commodus himself.

His habits inspired even the most debauched Romans with horror. Who in fact, says Herodian, could approve of a Prince who received pleasure through every orifice of his body, when there is nobody who could endure a beast which indulged in the same acts. Heliogabalus did not reach this excess of sensual depravity through the excess of power; the Empire found him as corrupted and degraded in the sanctuary of his Phœnician God. It may be said therefore that in becoming Emperor he did not become more perverse and more infamous than he was before, even if he became more cruel. What could be expected of a miserable wretch, mad with lust, who made the principal advantage of his sexual conformation to consist in his being able to satisfy the passion of several persons at the same time (*cum fructum vitæ proecipus rem existimans si dignus atque aptus libidine plurimorum videretur.*) He boasted publicly that he was able to give pleasure to five persons at a time. The luxury of his table was on a par with the orgies of his lust, and in his banquets for 22 guests, at the price of a hundred thousand sesterces (19,875 francs in present money) appeared every day all the products of creation.

During the winter which he passed in Nicomedia before taking up his quarters at Rome, Heliogabalus gave free rein to his infamous tastes; so that the soldiers who had chosen him blushed for their act when they saw then their chief in the company of his vile favourites.

He continued this kind of life at Rome. His whole occupation, says Lampridus, was confined to selecting emissaries whom he entrusted with the task of searching for everywhere and bringing to his Court, men who were most endowed with beauty, and especially with regard to the proportions of their genital parts. Those who were adjudged worthy of being presented to the Emperor figured in the indecent pantomimes which he put upon the stage, and in which he always took the part of a Goddess. Xyphilinus is very explicit on this point. He was especially fond of representing the loves of Venus and, in order to take this part, he painted his face and rubbed all his body with unguents. Often, in the disguise of Venus, he reenacted the principal scene of the judgment of Paris: all at once, his garments fell down to his feet and he was seen naked, one hand before his breast, and the other before his sexual parts from which the hair had been plucked and which he hid entirely, while he made the rotundity of his posterior project as much a possible, and applied the latter part against his fellow actor.

Heliogabalus selected the companions of his debaucheries from among the strongest athletes and best-made gladiators in the theatre and the circus. It was there that he marked out the charioteers, Protogenes, Gordius and Hierocles, who took part in all his infamies. He had such a passion for this Hierocles that he kissed his natural parts in public. *(Hieroclem vero sic amavit ut eidem oscularitur inguina coram populo.)*

In order to do all this at his ease and to choose his lovers for the qualities which he sought for, he had public baths constructed in his Palace, in which he bathed with all the populace of Rome. It was with the same object that he visited every day the houses of ill-fame, the banks of the Tiber, and the cross-roads. And he raised to the highest dignities of the Empire those who possessed the most enormous virile attributes *(commendatos sibi pudibillum enormitate membrorum.)*

One day he met a slave of gigantic height and athietic form. He carried him off, all covered as he was with sweat and dust, and installed him in his bed-chamber. And, the next day, he solemnly espoused him. Dion Cassius gives the following account of the union. "He made his husband ill-treat him, abuse him and beat him so violently that he sometimes had on his face the marks of the blows which he had received. It was no unstable and transient affection that he felt for him, but a strong and constant passion, so that, instead of being offended at the ill-treatment which he received from him, he loved him the more dearly for it. He would have declared him Cæsar, had not his mother and grandmother opposed this act of insane immodesty."

This slave was not the only favoured lover of Heliogabalus. He had as rival the cook Aurelius Zoticus, whom Heliogabalus made his Chamberlain without knowing him, but merely on hearing the account of his priapic advantages. "As soon as Heliogabalus saw him enter, says Dion Cassius, he ran to meet him with a blush upon his cheek, and when Zoticus, saluting him, called him Lord and Emperor, as was the custom, he answered, turning away his head with an air of affected modesty, and casting upon him a lascivious look, 'Call me not Lord for I am a lady.'" He took him to the bath at the same time as himself, and finding him to be such as he was represented, he supped lying in his arms as his mistress."

Heliogabalus had a weakness for public prostitutes whom he greatly resembled in the infamy of his manners, and felt the greatest sympathy and kindness towards them. One day he summoned to a temple all the prostitutes inscribed on the registers of the Ædile police, and himself presided over this strange assemblage, to which he also admitted the *souteneurs*, old debauchees and pederasts. He showed himself at first in the costume of a priest of the Sun to have more effect upon this infammous crew and he delivered a speech prepared for the occasion, beginning with the word, Comrades (Commilitiones). He opened a discussion upon several abstract questions of pleasure and libertinism, treating upon all the various possible ways of procuring luxurious enjoyment. His immodest audience clapped their hands and uttered tokens of approval, every time that he enunciated some particularly horrible idea of depravity. Intoxicated with his success, he disappeared for a moment and returned dressed as a woman, wearing the toga and fair wig of a prostitute and false breasts, showing his bare legs, and displaying all the arts, the gestures, the provoking ways and words of a common street-whore. In this costume he pleased the harlots whose costume his caprice had led him to adopt, and proved to them that he was as skilled an adept in their profession as themselves. Then casting aside his false bosom (popillâ ejectâ) he assumed the ways and dress of youths who indulge in pederasty, and turned towards his minions to let them see that he was no less expert than themselves in their calling. Lastly, he brought the meeting to an end by delivering a fresh harangue more monstrous than the first, promising to everybody present a gift of three pieces of gold and commending himself to their prayers that the Gods might grant him the health, vigour, and pleasure which he required until his death.

When he went on a journey, he was followed by 600 chariots filled with favourites, procuresses, prostitutes, active minions and passive *cinedes* with ample members.

He always had women with him in the Baths, and he would pluck out their hairs himself. In order to prevent his beard from growing, he used an epilatory paste, which he adopted in preference to the mode which he used in the epilation of women. He also used for shaving the same razor with which he had cut off the hair from the *pudenda* of his minions. It is impossible, says Xephilinus, for anybody to endure the recital of the filthy abominations which he practised or allowed others to practice upon his body. This author shrinks from entering into those details which Dion Cassius has so carefully collected and which the Greek language covers with a kind of veil which renders them more tolerable.

In the translation of Dion Cassius we find the following passage: "Heliogabalus used to go to the brothels, drive out the courtisans and take their place with visitors, thus indulging in the most vile pleasures. Finally, he set apart for the satisfaction of his lust, an apartment of his Palace itself; he stood at the door of his room, entirely naked after the manner of a courtesan, and called the passers-by in a soft and effeminate tone of voice; satisfied to draw over those who entered in, a curtain which blew to and fro in the breeze and was hung on golden rings. He had near his person other individuals addicted to the same vices as himself: their mission was to offer themselves to the lewd persons of the City, and when they found any of sufficiently depraved tastes who shrank from no act of immodesty, to bring them to the Emperor. He took money from the accomplices of his debauchery, and gloried in this infamous gain.

If the sensual appetites of Heliogabus were immoderate, his depraved imagination was even yet more powerful and active. In this way, he sought unceasingly and with restless curiosity for fresh means of defiling his eyes, his ears and his mind, by defiling also the modesty of another.

In the lavish feasts which he gave to his minions and gladiators, he placed in their hands cups of obscene form, and passed round amphoræ and vases of silver engraved with erotic scenes. It must be remembered also that his God, the Black Stone, before which he made his entrance into Rome, walking backwards before the idol which was placed in a chariot, represented an enormous virile member. All this obscene plate shone upon the table especially when he gave his formal suppers at Vintage-time, and at which he delighted in bringing dishonour on the most worthy citizens, and the old men of the noblest positions. Those who attempted the least resistance were immediately put to death.

This Emperor, the hermaphrodite and advocate of polygamy carried to the highest degree, wished to have several *legitimate* husbands and wives. He penetrated by force into the temple of Vesta, where he was with the greatest difficulty restrained from extinguishing the sacred fire which it was the duty of the Vestals to keep burning under penalty of death, and he *deflowered* some of them. Finally he carried off one of them (Aquila Severa) and married her with great pomp.

Heliogabalus, as a woman, married several husbands: we have mentioned the slave Hierocles and the cook Aurelius Zoticus, who was of extraordinairy genital vigour. But Hierocles, who was jealous, gave an anaphrodisiac potion to Zoticus which completely took away his powers. Heliogabalus was furious and wished to cast the unfortunate Zoticus, who had become impotent, to the wild beasts.

This extraordinary Emperor celebrated with great pomp the marriage of the statue of the Goddess Pallas to his God of the Sun, Heliogabalus, from whom he had taken the ancestral name by which he is identified. While he paid him the deepest homage, he joined himself also with the eunuch priests of Cybele and celebrated impure rites with them. He also associated himself with the curious and obscene rites of Isis, Priapus, Flora and Cotytho.

The feasts which he gave were extraordinary and nothing can give any idea of them: he gathered together in them everything which luxury, prodigality and gluttony could suggest, in order to satisfy his passions, his senses and his perverse instincts. He only lived, so to speak, that he might discover new pleasures. Lampridus has enumerated some of the marvellous extravagances of these repasts which lasted for whole nights and days, with no other interruption than the intervals devoted to lust, accorded as periods of repose for the stomach which did not grow weary any more than the genesic ardour.

The description of these fantastic repasts must be read in *L'Agonie* of Jean Lombard; this French author has drawn his inspiration from the Latin authors quoted above, a task in which he has been perfectly successful.

This monster with a human face dishonoured the Empire during a reign of three years in which he heaped up every extravagance, every atrocity and every imaginable idea which could outrage nature. In his table he gloried in imitating Apicius, and boasted of surpassing Nero and Commodus in his lust. He caused a lofty tower to be constructed within his Palace;

the walls of this tower were incrusted with gold and at its foot was a kind of wide pavement formed of precious stones. He also had poisons compounded, into the formation of which entered pearls of the highest price. In case of a revolution he intended to break his neck by throwing himself from the top of the tower, or to take poison. But when the revolution took place, he did not think of his tower or his poisons. He took refuge in the privies of the Palace, where he was killed by his buffoons. He was 18 years of age.

The revolted soldiers who drove him from the throne, multilated his favourites by tearing out their genital parts from some and impaling others, so that they might die even as they had lived. When they found the Emperor's body in the privies, they cut off his head, and, as his body would not pass into the sewer, they threw it into the Tiber.

Such was the end of this greatest monster that ever existed, this Cæsar who seated the quintessence of Sadism upon the throne of the Cæsars. We have drawn up this biography of the hermaphrodite Heliogabalus by making a summary of the text of Leo Taxil, (*Prostitution Contemporaine*. Paris, Libraire Populaire,) who himself has abridged Dufour's life of Heliogabalus. (*La Prostitution chez tous les peuples du monde*.)

Artificial Hermaphrodism.

We shall not bring this chapter on Hermaphrodites to a conclusion without saying a few words about what Dr. Laurent calls *artificial hermaphrodism*. He classes under this heading Infantilism and Effemination which are, in his opinion, almost the same as hermaphrodism, "if we regard the individual from the point of view of his general shape, which is thin and spare; the beardless face, the smooth pubis, the penis and testicles like those of a child, and the shrill voice."

Infantilism and Effemination.

I observed formerly in the prison of La Santé, a

little Savoyard, aged 25, who looked hardly 15, with his diminutive stature (1 m. 49), his absolutely beardless face and his voluminous ears, wide and projecting. He was a very inferior creature from the genital point of view, and as yet had no knowledge of women.

I have seen two or three others who, at the age of 20, had a penis and testicles like those of a child of 10. Others again are still more feminine-looking, with their fine hair, their shrill voice, their long eye-lashes and their developed hips.

I have also been shown, in the prison of La Santé, a small thief aged 16½ years. He had a pretty face, fresh and beardless, a smooth penis, an enlarged pelvis, fine hair, blue eyes shaded with long lashes, and a soft and fluted voice. He was like a pretty little girl of 11 or 12.

"You are all, says Brouardel, acquainted with the type of the little urchin, that essentially Parisian type, the child who passes as a prodigy in his classes until he is 12 or 13 years old, and whom in the street we sometimes hear making those astonishing rejoinders which make us turn our head and smile. I had an opportunity of observing several of them at Ste. Barbe.

"When they were 12 or 13 years old, they came to consult me for an inflammation of their breasts, and I remarked that their genital organs were not developing, that these boys grew plump, and often remained small and smooth. At the same time their intelligence diminished considerably, and they went from the top of their class to the bottom.

"When one of these individuals is dissected, we find a very small bladder, a rudimentary prostate, no ischio-cavernous muscles, a very small penis, and an extremely narrow pelvis.

"A young man took first place in the entrance examination in one of the large Government Schools, and was one of the first also in the final examination. His father called upon me one day to communicate his fears respecting his son who, though he was 24 years old, was as innocent as a young girl. He added that he could not manage to ride, and he fell off every time that he tried. I had the young man brought to me and I observed that the adductor muscles were completely atrophied. This young man sat down as though he were on hinges, like a German doll. I applied electricity, and he is now able to ride gently. On the other hand, we have succeeded in overcoming his obstinacy and fears upon the subject of his impotence; he is now married and the father of two children. He performs some genital acts, but so rarely that in spite of all he may be considered as impotent."

External Hermaphrodism of Young Pederasts.

The individuals whom I have just sketched are hardly men physically. From the psychical point of view they are almost women, and it is among them that the professional pederasts are recruited; the *passives*, those who are called "little Jesuses."

Their form and their ways are already feminine, and become more and more so through their bringing-up. Their mind also becomes feminine, I could quote innumerable instances of these accidental hermaphrodites.

A little Jesus.

One day, a young rascal of 17 was brought to the Infirmary of La Santé, who tooked hardly 14 or 15. He was immediately the object of numerous proposals, and assignations were already made for the night in the water-closets. For fear lest there might be some sanguinary combat, I had him sent back to his cell. As I tried to explain to him that it was his interest to leave the Infirmary, he replied to me with rare cynicism.

"Oh! it's a long while ago since I did it for the first time. When I go to the Central Prison, I shan't die of hunger: I shall choose my sweetheart."

I have observed another whose history is very curious and deserves to be related at greater length. (Laurent. *op. cit.*)

Henri le Blondin.

I slightly abridge Dr. Laurent's narrative.

When he was 13 years old, Henri was brought to Paris by his mother: he was then a regular street-urchin. At 14, he entered the service of a so-called Countess, a lady of light repulation, as page-boy; a situation in which he did not exactly receive lessons of virtue. He ran away from her to associate with his former companions and to play pranks with them.

These consisted of a band of a dozen young fellows from 14 to 20 years of age, all of them living by pederasty, under the protection of sinister scoundrels who were for the most part twice their age: they lived together in pairs, the husband being a man and the wife a youth. The former made his profit out of the latter whom he looked upon as his property and called his "worker."

After a couple of days, Henri le Blondin, as he was called, was linked with one of these Don Juans of the urinal who rapidly made a proficient of him and undertook his education. The pupil made rapid progress. He quickly learned to walk in a lascivious manner, to make provocative gestures and to give languishing looks. He haunted the Place du Châtelet, the water-closets in the Halles and the omnibus stations, places where he was most likely to meet with "amateurs," and satisfying his clients most frequently on the spot, or in some low hotel in the neigbourhood.

Henri did not remain a very long time with these individuals. His juvenile graces marked him out for specialities even more elegant and for a higher rank in vice. He found himself one day comfortably installed in furnished apartments in the Faubourg Montmartre. Then he only frequented the Cafés on the Boulevard, or walked about in the passage Jouffroy, the Galérie Vivienne near the Palais Royal, or in the Tuileries Gardens when the band was playing.

One day Henri received an injury to his anus in a violent and disproportionate coition. Enormous vegetations began to develop round that orifice. It might have appeared as if the development of these excrescenses would put a stop to his commerce with his body. It did nothing of the kind. It was, on the contrary, an additional attraction in him and, strange as it may appear, young debauchees and old libertines sought him out for this cause.

But as it was a source of acute pain for him, he renounced pederasty and set up as a dealer in contraband matches, for which offence he was sent to prison.

I was able to observe him in the prison of La Santé, where I operated on him for these vegetations. He was very short, with a gentle expression, blue eyes, and fair silky hair; he had long eye-lashes, a smooth and feminine-looking face, and slender figure. The arch of his eye-brows displayed a most harmonious curve. His ears were a trifle wide and far apart, but the outer edge was well marked. His limbs were rounded, smooth, and almost destitute of muscular projections. His genital organs were those of a child. Henri le Blondin was a real little woman, almost a little girl.

A prisoner, who occupied a bed near him in the infirmary, thus depicted him in a letter which I succeeded in intercepting. "He is as fair as ripe wheat, with two azure eyes which are almost innocent, and sometimes immersed in a mysterious reverie. To see him in repose, when no passion agitates him and his cherubic head is resting on the pillow, one dreams involuntarily of the ravishing creations of Murillo or of the lovely figures which fill the frescoes of Lebrun." And his admirer adds with sorrow: "This flower is without any perfume; these eyes have never opened but on filthy sights; and this mutinous and laughing mouth has spoken no other language than the vile idiom of the mob." (Laurent. *op. cit.*)

Asexuateds.

CHAPTER VIII.

Eunuchs and Skoptzys.

Definition of Asexuateds.—Two Classes: A. *Involuntary Asexuateds.* B. *Voluntary Asexuateds.—* A. *Involuntary Asexuateds or Eunuchs.—Causes of Eunuchism.—Castrati or Spadones.—Thlibias.—Lewd Employment of Spadones by the Roman Women.—Castration as a Punishment for Adulterers.—Employment of Castrated Women as Eunuchs.—Eunuchism predisposes to Inversion.—Genital Aptitude of Eunuchs.—Employment of Eunuchs for purposes of Masculine Prostitution.—The Castrati of the Sixtine Chapel.—Lasciviousness of Eunuchs.—An English Lady's Action against a Castratus.—Eunuchs in the East and how they are employed.—Paul de Regla's opinion on Eunuchs from a Physical and Physiological point of view.—* B. *Voluntary Asexuateds.—The Skoptzys.—Why do the Skoptzys castrate themselves?—Processes of the Operation of Castration.—Amputation and Bistournage.—Transfixion of the Deferent Cords.—Ligature of the Penis.—Places and Circumstances of Castration.—Material Proofs of the Operation.—Consequences of Castration.—Salacity of Skoptzys of the Little Seal.—Modification of the Organism in the Skoptzy.—Women Skoptzys.—How the Date of Castration may be known.—Two Men who Castrated themselves, one through*

Jealousy, the other through Love.—The Eunuch Priests of Cybele and their Infamous Habits.

Definition of Asexuateds.

We include under this heading the individuals who have lost their sex as the result of an operation of a more or less surgical nature, or through a traumatic accident.

These are, naturally, Eunuchs and Skoptzys.

In the Physiology of the First Volume we have described the different surgical methods of removing the genital organs. It is unnecessary therefore for us to repeat them here, and in the following portion we shall study the asexuated from a wider point of view.

And, in the first place, let us distinguish between two large classes of the asexuated.

A. Those who have lost their virility in spite of themselves and from a cause independent of their own will.

B. Those who have lost it voluntarily.

A. **Involuntary Asexuateds.**

The causes are numerous: 1st, a criminal attempt upon the child for the sake of gain, in order that he may be sold at a high price as a guardian of the Seraglio; 2nd, vengeance or hatred on the part of a woman or a male lover. We have given several instances of this in another Volume. 3rd, By the fortune of war. We know that before the time of Menelek, the Abyssinians were in the habit of castrating their prisoners. Besides, there are cases in which brave soldiers have been deprived in battle wholly or partially of their genital organs through the bursting of a shell. 4th, By a traumatic accident, by the teeth of an animal (or even of a human being), through gangrene, etc.

B. **Voluntary Asexuateds.**

These lose their virility voluntarily, 1st, through a disappointment in love or through insanity, and usually perform the operation themselves; 2nd, through religious fanaticism, like the priests of Cybele and the famous Russian Skoptzys, on whom the operation is performed by appointed co-religionists.

Whatever be the cause of mutilation, we shall study the first asexuateds under the general heading of Eunuchs. We shall then make a special study of those who are eunuchs voluntarily through religious fanaticism, *i. e.* the Skoptzys.

A. Involuntary Asexuateds or Eunuchs.

The employment of eunuchs dates back to the highest antiquity. They existed in China as guards for the Chinese Emperors' Seraglios, thousands of years before the Christian era. The ancient Hebrews had them, as the passage of Isaiah informs us.

Causes of Eunuchism.

It is certain that the use of eunuchs originally came from Asia. They existed in China, they existed and still exist in India, Persia, Turkey and Egypt. The Romans imported them into Europe after their Asiatic conquests.

The causes of eunuchism are twofold. Men were first castrated and then children, in order to make them the faithful guardians of feminine fragility. Afterwards, debauched persons of both sexes made use of these unhappy mutilated creatures for the satisfaction of their passions.

Castrati.

There are thus three categories of eunuchs, according to the use for which they are intended. The first is that of the *castrati*, the whole of whose organ of generation has been entirely taken away. These were faithful guardians, as can be understood.

Spadones.

It was not the same with the Spadones. From these latter only the testicles were removed.

Lewd Employment of Spadones by the Roman Women.

When the operation was performed before puberty, the penis remained atrophied like that of a child; but when it was performed after puberty, the penis naturally retained its dimensions, and could have connection without ejaculation, which increased the duration of the carnal act to the great pleasure of a voluptuous woman who into the bargain had no pregnancy to fear. Therefore many Roman ladies did not have their slaves castrated until their virility was well accentuated. The Satire of Juvenal is witness to this.

"There are (women) who delight in the soft caresses of eunuchs; there is no beard to fear, nor any need of abortive drugs. The ingenious search for pleasure does not hand over the youth to the surgeon until his virile member is shaded with black hair. Until then, they wait, they let the testicles grow and when they begin to weigh two pounds, Heliodorus amputates them."

And Martial: "You ask Gellia why she has so many eunuchs. Gellia wishes to be *futuata*, but not to grow big with child."

"But before thee, oh law, the very eunuch was an adulterer." The Edicts of Domitian forbade the castration of males.

The Thlibias.

The *Castrati* and Spadones were operated upon by barbers, *tonsores*, or by those who dealt in slaves. The 3rd category, that of Thlibias, required more care. The operation performed to obtain them resembled that which is practised in veterinary surgery and known under the name of *bistournage*. Hippocrates describes the manœuvre which was performed in order to obtain this kind of eunuchs.

"The child being placed in a bath, his testicles were steadily rubbed between the fingers for a sufficient time to bruise the substance and destroy the organisation; or the cords of the spermatic vessels were twisted to such an extent as to intercept the course of the liquids destined for the nutrition of the parts, and the testicle soon degenerated into scirrhus or sarcocele." A less barbarous process was also adopted to arrive at the same result: the scrotum was covered with the thickened juice of the hemlock, which produced the same effect.

Castration as a Punishment for Adulterers.

The Romans sometimes employed castration as a punishment for adulterers. This was the sad lot which Carbo Atticus underwent, surprised in the very act by Bibienus, and Marcus Pontius whom P. Cervius also surprised. Martial makes allusions in two places to this penalty for adultery. "Thou dost indulge, young Hylas, in lewd acts with the wife of a military tribune, because thou fearest from the husband only the punishment which is inflicted on little boys of thine age; but take care, thou shalt be castrated."

"It is no longer permitted, dost thou say? but what thou doest, is that then permitted?" and further on, to a husband: "Who then has advised thee to cut off the nose of thy wife's lover? That is not the organ which has done thee wrong, poor fool!"

Horace also speaks of an adulterer who was punished with complete castration. "His testicles and salacious penis were cut off with the knife."

Employment of Castrated Women as Eunuchs.

We find but a single notice of women being employed as eunuchs, but without any details regarding the castration of which they were the object. Was it the ablation of the ovaries, or more simply the amputation of the too developed clitoris or of the hypertrophied *labia majora?* We have spoken of these two operations.

However this may be, one historian alone, Xanthus, mentions the fact of the employment of women as eunuchs. As his text is lost we know about it only through two quotations borrowed from other authors; they are as follows:

"Xanthus says that Gyges, King of Lydia, was the first to castrate women to make use of them by preserving their youth and beauty for a longer time," quoted by Suidas and Hesychius.

"Xanthus relates that Adranitus, King of Lydia was the first to castrate women, and that he made use of them in the place of eunuchs," quoted by Athenæus.

Employment of Eunuchs for purposes of Male Prostitution.

Spadones did not alone serve for the pleasures of the Roman Matrons. *Castrati* served also for purposes of male prostitution and became passive pederasts, not being able to do anything else. Spadones and Thlibias were able, on the other hand. to be both active or passive, according to the choice of the client. They were called *cinædi* and *pathici*, according as they were used.

The Castrati of the Sixtine Chapel.

Christian Rome did not preserve the manners and customs of ancient Rome, with exception of the habit of making *castrati;* not, let us hasten to say, for the service of the noble Matrons, but for that of the Sixtine Chapel. I suppose that the *soprani castrati* served only for this latter use.

"It appears that this tradition has been perpetuated in Rome even to our own times. A composer who held at the same time a most distinguished position in the medical world, relates that, in his childhood, his fine voice caused his genital organs to undergo the gravest dangers. He owed his safety to the energetic intervention of Rossini alone, to whom he has vowed on this account eternal gratitude."

Eunuchism predisposes to Inversion.

As regards the Anparishtaka of India, *id est* buccal coition, we have seen that eunuchs were generally employed for that operation in India and that there was a whole theory of the movements to be performed for the final accomplishment of that act.

In Persia, Turkey and Egypt, eunuchs are still used in the service of the Seraglio. They are usually blacks from the Soudan, completely castrated. Mussulmans however, still have Spadones and Thlibias whom they sometimes compel to minister to their unnatural vice which is still very widely spread among the sectaries of Mahomet.

It is certain that the amputation of the testicles effeminates the subject and predisposes him to passive inversion, particularly the *castratus* who has lost everything. Nevertheless the Spadones and the Thlibias may also be the first potent and the second fecund.

Genital Aptitude of Eunuchs.

In fact the poor complete *castratus* has lost everything. He becomes less than a woman in character, *habitus*, and energy. He is an unhappy being who deserves pity, and should be commiserated with for being obliged to seek in passive anal coition, a vain shadow of the venereal pleasure.

"Eunuchs and *castrati*, says Ambroise Paré, degenerate into the feminine nature; as a sign of which they have no beard, their voice changes, and their courage is lacking; they grow timid and ashamed; in short they are useless for many good human actions, and their life is miserable."

Eunuchs often become Gynæcomasts, and there is nothing in this which ought to surprise us. Bédor saw at the Cathedral of Cadiz a Gynæcomast eunuch. "I have myself, he says, often looked upon with compassion but heard with delight, a young *castratus* from Italy who was attached to the Cathedral of Cadiz. His voice could be compared to that of the most brilliant *prima donna*. He went about the city, giving music lessons to young ladies. Through the tight and supple tissue of the long and narrow cassock which he wore, he was as remarkable for the volume and roundness of his mammary regions as he was for the different excrescences with long scattered hairs which appeared on his pale fat face, entirely without beard and rendered still more strange by his enormous hat."

Salacity of Eunuchs.

We have said that Spadones are potent, as is proved by the annals of ancient Rome. It may be added that they are very salacious, for they can have connection for an almost indefinite period: their erection, not being followed by ejaculation, producing only a slight nervous fatigue.

Brantôme, in his crude naturalism, relates some amusing anecdotes which leave no doubt on this point. And Franck declares that in a town, the name of which he does not give, four *castrati* so perverted the morals of the sex that the police were obliged to interpose their authority to put a stop to these scandalous excesses.

Action brought by an English Lady against a Castratus.

We find in that curious work, "*Les Dessous de la Pudibonderie Anglaise*," (Paris, Charles Carrington, Editeur) the story of a strange action brought by an English lady against a *castratus*.

Dorothy Kingsman (1784).

Miss Kingsman when scarcely yet of marriageable aid, ran away with a *castratus* named Penduci. She lived with him for seven years without bringing any complaint against him on the ground of his impotence, behaviour which argues a rare amount of patience on the part of an Irish woman who is as warm and as physically inclined to love as any woman upon the Continent.

After this long silence, she wrote to her father as follows: (1)

(1) Copied literally from the letter read before Doctor's Commons.

"My very honored Father,

"I am greatly troubled by what has taken place between me and Penduci. My misfortunes in this are due to my youth and *want of experience.* I have only been *infatuated* for some years by his beautiful voice; *but it has pleased God* to send me a bitter judgment, and the conviction that what has taken place in the matrimonial way between me and a eunuch, is not a sacred bond in the sight of Heaven.

"Naples, 1784."

The kind father immediately sent her two hundred guineas to rescue her from the hands of this impotent monster.

The Englishwoman's statement is a very curious document: "Penduci, she says, was born at Sienna forty years ago. (Observe what a wrong this was in the eyes of a woman who was not get 22.) When he was about nine years old, he was deprived of his virility; he underwent entire castration, in the Italian way. By this operation both his testicles were removed, rendering him a eunuch (1); incapable therefore of the act of generation, (2) and consequently of consummating the marriage.

"Penduci, being in Dublin eight years ago, introduced himself to my father's family, who is a lawyer and squire, under the pretext of teaching me singing. It was not difficult for him to take advantage of my inexperience. We were secretly married, by an old Catholic priest. We went away with the same secrecy. When we arrived in Italy, Penduci gave out that I was a pupil entrusted to him by her parents: he gave me the name of Signora Dorothea. He carefully refrained from speaking about the alleged marriage, as there is a law in Italy condemning a castratus who

(1) The English jurisconsults and physicians give to the castratus the name of eunuch. They ignorantly confound the two.

(2) Yes; but not of copulation. According to Buffon, the castratus exceeds other men in the vigour and duration of the act.

marries to be hung." Miss Kingsman prayed that the marriage should be declared null and void, and Penduci condemned in costs.

The Irishwoman lied before Doctors' Commons, in accusing Penduci of impotence. We have known this celebrated singer in Paris; those fair ladies who are fond of a *castratus* with a flat nose, were desirous of according him meetings. A *castratus* is indefatigable; he does not engender children, a precious gift for a prude who wishes to taste the pleasures of vice with the honours of virtue.

This digression is not useless, if it serves to enlighten an Ecclesiastical Court which is acquainted with all the mysteries of love, with the exception of this.

The Court heard a crowd of witnesses who, at the public exhibition, recalled the scenes of the ancient ordeal which President Lamoignon abolished after reading four verses from Boileau. The first was an Irish officer: he had displayed some curiosity about Penduci. The singer did not let himself be asked twice; he shewed him tho mark of the cruel wound. (1) This officer was present one day while Penduci was dressing and saw him draw out from his fob a red velvet purse; he asked him if it contained some holy relic brought from Rome. "No, no," replied Penduci, "these are my t....s. I have kept them in this purse ever since my castration."

At this last proof, the Court declared the marriage null and void, with the more pleasure because it had been celebrated by a Catholic priest, whom English clergyman look upon as heretics.

Eunuchs in the East and their Employment.

In the East, among Mussulmans, the eunuch has always been retained. We merely give a couple of quotations from the writings of two travellers. The first is one from Madame Louise Collet who went to Egypt for the opening of the Suez Canal,

(1) On the left side of the groin, a little above the scrotum.

"The youngest, the best looking and the richest drive in landaus or open carriages into which as many as six crowd together. Their dresses, instead of being black, are of brilliant colours; rose is the shade most in favour among the smart ladies of the harems. They are to be met at sunset in the drives of the *Choubrat*, the fashionable promenade of Cairo; they make play with their eyes and fan like the fast women of Paris when driving round the Lake. Proud eunuchs, seated on the box on either side of the *arbadji* (coachman), and two others standing up behind the carriage like the footmen on an aristocratic turn-out, keep guard lest these ladies' coquetry should have any effective result. It sometimes happens that they are led by their eager desire for the diamonds which the richer ladies wear, and of which the eunuchs are passionately fond, to deviate from their usual watchful behaviour.

"These guardians of the enforced chastity of women are uniformly dressed in trousers and frock-coats of black cloth which make them look like our priests dressed in mufti; they all carry a large gold chain from which hang trinkets, and one of those large gold or silver watches called warming-pans. On the black hands of the negro or half-breed shine jewels of more or less value, according to the wealth of the harems to which they are attached. Formerly the eunuchs exercised a formidable authority in the harems. Invested by their masters with the rigorous supervision of the women slaves, they had the right to beat them, if necessary, to restrain their passions and caprices. Instruments of a barbarous tyranny, the unnatural condition to which this same tyranny had reduced them, rendered them cruel and malignant; unable to practise their reprisals upon men, they avenged themselves on the unfortunate women dependent like themselves upon the good pleasure of their masters. No sympathetic feeling could mitigate the severity of their guardianship, and they exhibited in it a kind of bestial pride; slaves themselves, they imagined themselves to be masters when they tortured other slaves. Denunciation, were it even false, gave them the continual power of life and death over the women entrusted to their care, who were compelled to purchase their silence by presents and cajoling familiarities, so there grew up between the two an exchange of meanesses, venality and turpitude, which made the harems the most corrupt places in the world.

"But now a purifying breath is borne into these Oriental cloisters on the current of European thought.

"Thus the French Revolution, penetrating into the Convents, diffused there a moral wholesomeness. The majority of our customs do not authorize the harems at the present day. Poor lions whose claws have been cut at the same time as something else, they are now but peevish cats of sorry appearance. These poor mutilated wretches are now reduced to the position of servants of a great house, a kind of barbaric luxury for the rich Mahometans, just as there is in Europe the ridiculous luxury of powdered footmen in ancient families aud among haughty parvenus. There is nothing more repulsive than to see these sexless creatures in their semi-ecclesiastical garb; their great black eyes have but a spiritless flame, and their originally energetic features are sunken and withered before their time, When they stretch out their hand or bent wrist to assist you to get out of the carriage, one shrinks as from that of a corpse in which decomposition has begun. It might be supposed that when that which constitutes life was taken, death obtained a foothold in their living bodies. When I describe my visits to the harems, I shall speak of the insurmountable impression of disgust and almost of dread which these poor creatures always caused me. Some of them I have known to be excellent, gentle, humble, sad, resigned, having for their mistress the limitless devotion of watch-dogs, and extending their eager services even to their European friends. In spite of my pity and my philosophic reasoning, I have never succeeded in overcoming the repulsion which they cause me." (Louise Collet. *Les Pays Lumineux.*)

Opinion of Paul de Régla upon Eunuchs.

The second quotation is from Dr. Paul de Régla's work "El Ktab," which has been already several times quoted. This author analyzes in a remarkable manner the physical and physiological condition of eunuchs.

As you know, oh men! there exist three varieties of white and black eunuchs.

These varieties consist of the perfect or complete eunuch, the incomplete eunuch, and the eunuch of the third category.

The complete eunuch is he whose complete organ of generation, that is to say the *Dkeur*, the scrotum and the testicles, was removed while he was a child; the incomplete eunuch is he whose testicles have been removed after puberty; the eunuchs of the third category are those whose testicles have been atrophied by rubbing in infancy.

The first is the only one which, from the point of view of coition, offers an absolute guarantee.

As for the two others, they can copulate up to a certain age and are the more dangerous to morality, inasmuch as they are generally able to satisfy women without exposing them to the danger of engendering.

The first resemble the female sex in their physical constitution and their intellectual and moral faculties; they have no beard, their larynx retains the small dimensions of childhood, and their voice is at the same time infantine and shrill. Their life is shortest, especially when they belong to the black race. (1)

The others have more or less beard, according as they belong to the second or the third category; but it may be said generally that it is very thin. Their voice is deep; their venereal desires are sometimes rather keen; their intellectual faculties resemble those of the complete man, but they weaken at an early age, and their person soon displays the stamp of premature old age.

(1) Many black eunuchs succumb to pulmonary and mesenteric tuberculosis when they are between 25 and 30 years old.

Although the case is rare, eunuchs of the third category have been known to make the woman pregnant who by using their *Dkeur* imagined that she would satisfy her desires without any disagreeable result.... Strange as the fact may appear, its possibility may easily be understood, by supposing that some of the seminal vesicles have escaped the atrophy which results from the rubbing of the testicles in infancy, as has been already mentioned. (1)

The Turks, the Persians and the Mussulmans who are ignorant of the laws of the Koran and the principles of our holy religion, have sinned the more in introducing the eunuch into our society, inasmuch as they have, by this fact, singularly contributed to the lax tone which has penetrated into the morals of our great personages. By his woman's and feminine tastes, the complete eunuch has promoted the evil instinct of pederasty in men, and developed it to a singular degree. Having no manly energy in his organism, he has ceased to be a true Mussulman and become a weak, malleable creature, ready to agree to every evil suggestion. He has grown to be a worthy rival of the Jews who, as everybody knows, make money from their own body and from the bodies of their own family.

The habit which this category of eunuchs have of cultivating *perverse* love, makes them the greatest enemies of the woman, and the most vigilant, ferocious and jealous guardians of the harems which are entrusted to their keeping. Jealous of women, they are equally so of one another. Their passions, though less keen than in men, are no less deep. When they want to avenge an insult, or even a mere want of respect, they know how to wait for the time of vengeance with astonishing patience, even though the opportunity may not occur till after several years. This

(1) I saw a similar case during my last stay at Constantinople. A woman of C... Pacha's harem, a slave, gave birth to a still-born child, owing to her intimate relations with one of the Pacha's white eunuchs. (P. DE R.)

tenacity is met with particularly among the black eunuchs; whence the saying: "When a black has taken it into his head to kill anybody, he must either kill him or be killed."

If the white eunuchs are less to be feared in their spirit of revenge, they are, on the other hand, more spiteful and cunning, and more inclined to onanism, which they practise if necessary with the mouth, although this method is rather rare, even among the Turks. It is these eunuchs who generally take the part of women in certain *hammams* frequented more particularly by Greeks and Armenians.

It is very rare,—as you are aware, oh Believers!—for even the most perverse women to fall in love with complete eunuchs; but it is the contrary with those of the second and third category. Numerous are the scandals produced by these amours contrary to the faith of Islam, which can only be excused on the part of the woman by the too pronounced desertion of the husband.

Generally speaking, eunuchs are melancholy, sad, and somewhat inclined to the sciences of observation; but they have no courage and energy to avenge themselves on an enemy, except when he is a eunuch like themselves. In the presence of complete men, they are weak and like women.

In truth God is pitiful! pitiful by reason of his Almighty power; but the women who seek for ithyphallic pleasures, who forget their duties in order to abandon themselves to an unfertile barren coition, ought to be severely reprimanded, for, by sinning grievously, they risk their salvation for ages and ages, and expose themselves here below to the risk of taking that road which, owing to the unproductive over-excitement of their senses, leads them to the disorganizing practices of Saphism and of all the works which result from the temptations of Satan.

And not only do women who thus yield themselves to eunuchs see their salvation compromised, and their health transformed into nervosism, but, what is still more serious, they destroy within themselves every principle of fecundation and maternity, that is to say that they become *failures* useless for the working of the individual and universal life.

Reprimand then, oh men, those of your wives who indulge in copulation with one or more of your eunuchs. Reprimand her, beat her, and if your corrections do not bring her back to the right way, send her away if she is a lawful wife, and sell her if she is a slave.

B. Voluntary Asexuateds.

The Skoptzys.

This is the name of a Russian sect who mutilate themselves through religious fanaticism. This is not the place to treat this important question—the influence of Religion upon Love. Neither shall we say anything about the origin of the Skoptzys, their beliefs, their manners, their way of making proselytes, or of their social and numerical importance in Holy Russia. We shall examine them in these different lights in the "Philosophy of Love." For the present, let us be satisfied with studying the Skoptzy from the twofold point of view—the physiological and the psychopathical.

Why do the Skoptzys Castrate Themselves?

It is because they condemn sexual intercourse as a sin, and because the organs of generation are an object of abomination to them, that the Skoptzys amputate them either wholly or in part, for in this brotherhood also there are degrees of holiness. The most perfect, those who are worthy to "ride the white horse," the bearers of the "imperial seal," are deprived of penis, testicles and scrotum; the operation is performed with a single cut, or, that there may be less danger, at two different times; it leaves, as the case may be, a common cicatrice, or two cicatrices separated by a strip of sound skin. Sometimes a small stump of the penis remains. Those are more numerous who have been submitted only to the first purification, which confers upon them, together with the "little seal," the right to ride upon the piebald horse, and have only their scrotum and testicles amputated. They have lost the "Keys of hell," but the "Keys of the abyss" remain to them, (the woman's genital parts are *the abyss* in the language of the sect.) Others who are less fervent remove only one testicle; the case is rare, as also is that of the amputation of the penis alone: it is still rarer to see the penis bound up with twine or with gold thread so as to prevent coition.

Processes of Performing Castration.

When it is a matter of the great or the little seal, the process of operation is most simple. It consists in seizing with one hand the parts to be removed, and in cutting them off with the other with a red-hot iron, as in the early days of the sect (whence the expression, "baptism of fire"), or with a more or less sharp instrument. The case where the testicles are removed by a lateral aperture, without any loss of the substance of the scrotum, is exceedingly rare; only two or three of them are known. Therefore the scrotal cicatrice is almost always mesial, and its position is infallible witness to affiliation with the sect, the lateral cicatrices leaving this in doubt. The shape of the cicatrice is always elongated, and the more linear in proportion as the process of healing has been simpler. Sometimes it is longitudinal, that is to say parallel to the raphe, sometimes transversal, according to the manner in which the scrotum has been seized. When it has been grasped downwards, between the thumb and the fingers directed transversely to the perineum, the cicatrice is always perpendicular to the raphe; when, on the other hand, it has been grasped laterally by the hand parellel to the perineum, the cicatrice is in the same direction as the raphe. The transversal cicatrice usually assumes the shape of a horse-shoe, because its extremities are raised by the contraction of the cremasters, while its middle is brought down by that of the sphincter, of the anus. This double muscular action does not, as may be understood, exercice any influence on the longitudinal cicatrice; at the most it tends to lengthen it a little. These are the simple cases, but different circumstances may produce variations in the cicatrice. If, for instance, the two cords are not cut at the same level, the inequality of the retraction of the cremasters may render the transversal or longitudinal cicatrice oblique to the raphe. In the same way, the irregular dressing of the skin of the scrotum, producing a wound with an irregular outline, may give to the cicatrice a more or less jagged appearance. Lastly, accidents in the course of cicatrization, prolonged suppuration, phlegma, erysipelas, diphtheria, result in variable contractions for the cicatrice. In the case of the Skoptzys of the Great Seal, a distinction must be drawn between those whose penis, scrotum and testicles were removed at one time, and those whose penis was amputated separately. In the former case, there is but a single oval wound of large diameter, parallel to the raphe and consequently but a single cicatrice elongated in the same direction. In the latter case, there are two distinct cicatrices, one on the scrotum, generally transversal; the other round or polygonal, at the root of the penis, separated by an interval of sound skin. The situation of the second wound which exposes it to frequent contact with the urine, and the slightest movement of the skin leaving it completely uncovered, cause it to close up less quickly and less regularly than that of the scrotum. This peculiarity does not authorize the declaration, when the two cicatrices differ in their solidity and colouration, that the penis has not been removed at the same time as the scrotum. The existence of two cicatrices, whatever their differences may be, merely shows that the operation may have been performed on two occasions; a single cicatrice is the proof that the amputation was at one time. The date of the amputation may be known approximately by the appearance of the cicatrice which, in the absence of complications, takes from four to six weeks to form. When it is recent, it is granulous, projecting, and the subjacent capillaries may be seen through it; when it is ancient, it is smooth, not very transparent, level with the skin, and greyish or yellowish; when of still longer standing, it is discoloured, of a pure white which stands out clearly against the dead background of the scrotum; very old cicatrices sometimes can hardly be distinguished from the adjacent skin by a lighter colouration. In Skoptzys who were operated upon in infancy, the cicatrice does not follow the general development; on the contrary, it gradually shrinks up, without however becoming ever completely obliterated; it remains an indelible sign preventing castration from being confused with congenital anorchia. Sometimes the castration affects only one testicle, either because the other has escaped the instrument owing to the awkwardness of the operator, or through the victim's resistance, or again because the operation was performed upon a very youthful subject before the descent of the second testicle. The cicatrice is then either linear, oblique to the raphe, or irregularly polygonal with starred prolongations. The testicle may be felt on the side which is intact; on the other side, there is only to be found the end of the cord thickened and attached to the cicatrice by a loose, connective tissue.

Bistournage.

Some authors speak of other methods of castration more uncommon than amputation, the reality of which has not been demonstrated. Nadeschdin points out in the governments of the interior, and particularly in that of Tambow, a variety of Skoptzys, called *Bistourneurs* (Pevewezliscki). Instead of amputating, they twist the spermatic cords, probably in infancy; the vascular communications being broken and the sperm not being secreted, the Skoptzys attain their object in this way without leaving any trace of the operation. In theory this is not inadmissible. The Greeks, as we know, had eunuchs (thlasias, thlibios, thladias) operated upon by an analogous process. But it is doubtful whether in fact the Skoptzys have recourse to this means.

Accused of propaganda in the government of Orloff, the peasant Matreï Nartjuchion, who was declared by public report to belong to the *Bistourneurs*, (Wywertiscki, Keutscheniki), did not display any lesion of the genital organs indicating that he had been castrated in any way. The supposed *Bistournés* examined by the Commission of 1843, had their testicles atrophied, "dried up" according to the expression of the experts, and the scrotum very elongated (26 ct. in length) and thin; they attributed their condition to a hernia and wore a kind of bandage. The physicians appointed to examine them were inclined to took upon them as Skoptzys. The umpires declared that the proofs were wanting. In 1868, in the government of Tauris, where the Skoptzys were known under the name of "Sckaloputi," a man named Kinon Jarkin was suspected of endeavouring to castrate children by violently pushing the testicle into the abdominal cavity through the inguinal canal. A child, aged 9, accused him of having performed this operation upon him, and two other cases were also alleged. The medico-legal enquiry was unable to establish the truth of this accusation. In short, there is no definite proof of the existence of a sect employing *bistournage*. No verified case of this operation is known; still less is it known how the operation is performed. In his experiments on dogs, Dr. Pelikan never succeeded in breaking the cords by twisting them, and his manœuvres never produced atrophy of the testicles. He holds with Nesson that with lambs it is easy to twist and break the cords, but that with bulls it is much less easy; as to the pushing back of the testicle into the inguinal canal, he always killed the lambs in doing so. Dr. Pelikan concludes that it is impossible to perform successfully any of these manœuvres upon man. He remarks besides that in the doctrines of the Skoptzy, amputation, the bloody operation with loss of substance, is the essential part of the ceremony of initiation, as is also indicated by the expressions employed to designate it.

Transfixion of the Deferent Cords.

Mention has also been made of the transfixion of the cords which Skoptzys say was proposed in 1819 by a surgeon of St. Petersburgh in order to conceal the castration. The scrotum was tightly bound underneath the penis and bathed several times in very hot milk; it was then, in order to damage the cords, transfixed with a thin needle in parts with which the surgeon was acquainted; the operation was very painful and often occasioned death. Legrand quotes two cases in which men were accused of this; the two subjects had the scrotum retracted and shortened; the testicles were very small and indolent to pressure. In the government of Morschansk, four peasants were arrested in 1863 on suspicion of having been emasculated by this method: the experts found that the testicles were in an abnormal position and that there were lateral cicatrices a quarter of an inch in length; they believed that there had been some operation which they could not state precisely. The accused were acquitted and Dr. Pelikan who saw them afterwards with Inspector Lederholm was unable to discover any anomaly, or to find the trace of any cicatrice. The existence of the transfixory Prokolischi is therefore very doubtful.

Ligature of the Penis.

Nor is it any more certain that certain cases of ligature of the penis with consequent fistula, observed in 1890 in the Hospital of Moscow in young boys, ought to be regarded as a practise of the Skoptzys. Two of these children maintained that they were ignorant of the cause of their fistula, which dated from as far back as they could remember. A third in the first place accused a peasant of having tied up his penis with a hair, and then, when confronted with him, he withdrew the charge and said that he had done it himself by way of boasting. A fourth, whose penis was almost detached at the root, after attributing his condition to sexual relations with a woman unknown, confessed that he had tied his penis in order to avoid military service. Nothing in all this showed the hand of the Skoptzys; their intervention could only be suspected in the case of another child. He related that an individual had tied up his penis with a ribbon, saying: "Christ is risen," to which he had replied: "He is risen indeed." These are in fact phrases in use among the Skoptzys during the castration. But the same child said afterwards that he had done it himself in order to remedy an incontinence of urine, and slight importance must be attached to these contradictory statements.

Places and Circumstances of Castration.

We have scarcely any information of a positive nature regarding the places where the mutilations are performed, or the circumstances of the operation. No credence can be given to the statements of the accused sectaries, and the only means of discovering the truth is to surprise them in the act. Unfortunately this is very rarely done. It has sometimes happened that an individual who has just been operated upon has been seized on the spot, but the operator had disappeared together with his instruments, and it was then necessary to apply for information to the castrated man, whose sincerity it was impossible to guarantee. It may however be asserted that the place chosen for the operation is always some retired spot in an isolated building. Skoptzys have declared that the operation has been performed upon them in a bathing-house, in a barn, in a cellar, in a subterranean dwelling, on a foot-path, in a water-closet, on the bank of a river, under a bridge, in a cemetery, in a smithy, on the sea-shore; more frequently in woods, on the high roads and in the fields. In these latter cases the account varies to some degree; a simple peasant meets an unknown individual, usually an old man, who at first enters into conversation with him and induces him to take a soporific drink; when he wakes up, the peasant finds his testicles gone and forthwith sets out to catch the old man! But one Skoptzy says that the operation is never performed on a high road.

With regard also to the ceremonies which accompany castration, the statements of the Skoptzys are unworthy of credit: one states that he was made to cross his hands while those present sang a hymn, of which he remembered only these words: "Ah! Spirit! what mercy, what joy, what Spirit!" Another says that during the operation, the formula which we have previously mentioned is uttered. The castrator would collect the parts which had been cut off, show them to the victim, and say: "Lo! the serpent is crushed."

Material Proofs of the Operation.

It is very rare for the expert to find material proofs of the operation immediately after it is performed; the enquiry reveals only stains of dried blood or matter upon the linen, bed, garments and other objects. Sometimes, the amputated parts are found in the neighbourhood of the Skoptzy's abode or elsewhere. Terrible in their simplicity, the instruments used by the Skoptzy in the operation are extremely primitive: a razor with its blade inserted in a piece of wood, or knives of various sizes; a pocket-knife, pruning-knife, or kitchen knife, or a piece of a blade wrapped in a linen rag, an axe, a pair of scissors or a sculptor's tool. For some well-authenticated cases they have used fragments of glass, pieces of steel or sheet-iron, or bits of beef-bone well sharpened. There have also been seized bloodstained bands and strings intended for the subsequent dressings, iron wire and lint, sponges, various ointments made of fat, of olive oil, etc., different salts, blue copperas or alum, herbs and medicaments, saltpetre, aqua regia and other medicinal substances. The bandages employed after the operation are suspensory or T-shaped bandages, with which have been found tin or lead nails, used to preserve the permeability of the canal.

In spite of the rude nature of the instruments, the brutality of the operation, and the ignorance of the operator, the castration of the Skoptzy rarely entails death. There are only nine cases of death known; the statistics are certainly incomplete, but these results are none the less surprising.

Consequences of Castration.

The consequences of castration which can observed during life are better known, as there are more frequent opportunities of meeting with them. They vary, be it understood, with the nature of the mutilations, and are more pronounced in the completer forms of operation. They are local and general. With the Skoptzys of the Imperial Seal, and with those who only have their penis amputated, the local consequences, independently of the date at which the operation was performed, affect micturition above all. They carry in the urethral canal, like the Egyptian eunuchs observed by Godard, a zinc or lead nail which they regard as a cork, to prevent the involumtary excretion of the urine. In Dr. Pelikan's opinion, the chief utility of this nail must be to form an obstacle to the contraction of the canal and to guard against any symptoms of retention which may result from the inflammation, retraction, or stoppage of the canal. Upon this latter point, a reservation appears to us to be required. Without going so far as to deny with Malgaigne the contraction of the canal, even admitting that combined with inflammation, it renders the spontaneous evacuation of the urine impossible and the introduction of a *sonde* difficult, we cannot see how the introduction of the nail, necessarily introduced after the operation, can take the place of the india-rubber *sonde* which Barthélemy advised should be introduced into the penis after the amputation of that member. Dr. Pelikan says nothing as to how micturition is performed by the Skoptzys who are deprived of their penis; it may be supposed that they squat down like the eunuchs in the East.

Salacity of Skoptzy of the Little Seal.

In the case of the Skoptzys of the little seal, when

the operation has taken place before puberty, the penis undergoes an arrest of development, and is then only capable of imperfect erections which are difficult to produce even mechanically. Those who were operated upon when they were adults, keep for a considerable period, though it is continually growing weaker, the possibility of entering upon erection by mechanical or even by psychological means. This is a fact which has always been a matter of knowledge, and which is frequently to be observed among domestic animals which have been castrated. The Roman ladies knew how to profit by this, nor are some of the Skoptzys at all backward, despite their doctrines, in using and abusing the powers they have retained. Liprandi knew a wealthy Skoptzy at St. Petersburg who was in the habit of keeping women, especially Germans who were sent to him from Kœnigsberg; very few could stay with him longer than a year: they retired with a handsome reward for their services, but irretrievably injured in health.

Modifications of the Organism in the Skoptzys.

The usual modifications of the organism as the result of castration are to be found in the Skoptzys. The best known is that affecting the voice which, in the Skoptzys who have been operated upon where they were young, remains like that of a child, in consequence of the arrested development of the larynx; it grows stronger only by reason of the enlargement of the thoracic, buccal and nasal cavities. It is said that castrati experience a difficulty, just as children do in pronouncing the letter R; the Skoptzys do not display this pecularity, and Dr. Pelikan makes the remark that Italian castrati would not have been so highly valued as singers if they were unable to clearly articulate such an important letter in the Italian language. In our opinion, the contradiction is not complete: all children, particularly at a certain age, have not this defect of pronunciation; castration does not give rise to it, it only perpetuates it in those who have it already. After puberty, castration does not modify the voice in any degree; generally speaking, it is only weakened, and sometimes grows hoarser; when it retains its natural purity it is never to be compared to that of a youthful castratus. The growth of hair in the Škoptzys does not display any peculiarity. As is always the case, when they have been castrated in infancy, there is no hair upon their face, armpits or genital parts, or, if there is any, it is scattered, short, thin and downy. When castration has been performed upon them as adults, it acts in the same way upon their growth of hair, but with less energy; when it has been performed at a more advanced age, it has no effect. With regard to the effects of castration upon the general habitus, the Skoptzys form no exception to the rule; the shape of the body grows like that of a woman, the shoulders become contracted, the pelvis is enlarged, the skin grows pale, the subcutaneous tissue and the muscles become flaccid, the face is withered, yellowish, expressionless or aged. At an advanced age, the stomach is large, the legs massive, the feet œdematous and the gait difficult and heavy. The digestion is less active, the urine is acid and deficient in urea and in other azotic products. The excessive elongation of the lower limbs, observed by Godard to occur in eunuchs at the time when puberty would normally begin, has also been noticed by Dr. Merschajevski to take place in Skoptzys who were castrated when young. Godard has stated that the eunuchs of Cairo always look as if they were frozen and are always thin. Dr. Pelikan does not point out anything similar in the Skoptzys. The modifications produced by castration are not confined to the exterior only, they apply also to the mind and intelligence. Among eunuchs there have never been any men of really superior attainments, nor are any such to be discovered among the Skoptzys. But if the Oriental eunuchs are attached to their masters, love them and watch over them with devotion, these good qualities are wanting in the Skoptzys; they are incompatible with their doctrines. The Skoptzys are capable of a certain attachment, which may extend to adoration, but only for the Superiors of their sect. They are egotistical, cunning, untruthful, sly and covetous; but it is difficult to say if this is the effect of castration, or the result of their doctrines and of the persecutions of which they are the object. Dr. Pelikan seems to attribute to castration the rarity of insanity among the Skoptzys. We could not undertake to prove that this is false, although it may be opposed to the influence which is attached to affections of the genito-urinary organs and to the loss of the testicles in particular upon the development of the melancholy forms of mental alienation. But we may dispute this explanation and look for it rather in the peculiar intellectual condition which leads to adhesion to the beliefs of the Skoptzys. These beliefs prevent them at least from grieving over a situation which would be to others a cause of profound vexation.

The Skoptzy Women.

The mutilations undergone by the women have, in the intention of the Skoptzys, the same object as those which are suffered by the men. But it is necessary to divert the word from its usual meaning where speaking of the castration of the women of the sect: there is no instance known of the extirpation of the ovaries. The operations performed upon the women are, 1st, the ablation by the knife, fire or caustic, of one of the nipples, or much more frequently of both; 2nd, the amputation of the whole or a part of one or both breasts; there is nothing particular about the cicatrice; 3rd, various gashes, principally upon the breasts and generally symmetrical in form; 4th, amputation of the nymphæ only, or of the nymphæ and clitoris; 5th, amputation of the nymphæ, clitoris and upper portion of the labia majora, resulting in an irregularly shaped cicatrice which diminishes the size of the vulva to a considerable extent. All these operations tend only to lessen the sensibility and perhaps the inclination for coition, and to interpose, to a greater or less degree, mechanical obstacles to sexual intercourse and to parturition. There are instances of women whose vulva had been considerably contracted by the 5th operation, and yet who have successfully given birth to children without any great difficulties. As to the general effects upon the constitution, they are very disputable. Nadeschdin, sharing the Skoptzys' opinion, declares that owing to the close sympathy which exists between the breasts and the uterus, their ablation is almost equivalent to an absolute castration, that it diminishes the aptitude for conception and the pleasure in coition; the complexion of women who are thus mutilated grows pale and fades. He also says that all the women of the sect, even those who do not display any sign of mutilation, always recognize one another by their yellow and faded skin and by their small and flaccid breasts. This appearance, according to him, is also to be found in those women who abandon themselves to the Skoptzys of the little seal and are exhausted by this imperfect intercourse. His statements are inconsistent with the real facts: many women who belong to the sect and are even mutilated, are fresh-looking and handsome; as for the others, it is more reasonable to adopt Dr. Pelikan's explanation of their fatigued and debilitated appearance and attribute it to their prolonged continence, to their food which is insufficient in quality and quantity, to their wild dances (radenige), and to other circumstances which have nothing to do with mutilations.

How the Date of Castration may be known.

Can the date of castration be determined even in an approximate degree? In the case of the men the answer is usually easy. The more extensive the scrotal cicatrice, the more wrinkled, projecting and transparent, the more visible the adjacent capillary ramifications, the more recent is the operation. On the other hand, old cicatrices are flat, smooth, less transparent, of a dirty yellowish-grey colour, or yellow through the deposit of pigment in their tissues. Very old cicatrices are contracted in all their dimensions and are scarcely to be distinguished by their roughness from the neighbouring skin; the pigment has completely disappeared from them and they are only to be recognized by the white colouration of their outlines which stand out clearly against the delicate brown of the scrotum. The local and general modifications undergone by the Skoptzys after castration furnish the means of deciding, if not the year, at least the age at which the castration look place.

When it has been performed before puberty, the general habitus always becomes effeminated, the face is soft, bloated, sometimes wrinkled, and has an aged appearance; the voice is shrill and hoarse, and there is an absence of hair on the face and on the genital parts; the virile member, if it has not been removed, is extraordinarily small and slightly developed. It will be known that the castration has taken place in youth, from 14 to 20 years of age, or at the beginning of the evolution of puberty, by the feminine appearance being less pronounced; the voice is higher and softer than ordinarily, and does not sometimes have the same note as that of individuals castrated in infancy; slender, short, soft, and in one word downy hair, is to be found on the face and on the genital parts; the dimensions of the virile member are inconsiderable, but it is more developed than in the preceding case. Finally, if the subject was already of ripe age when the operation took place, the general and local symptoms are still less pronounced, and in a slighter degree as the age was more advanced; hair is growing everywhere, the voice is not altered, and the consequences of the operation are confined to the pallor and inertia of the face.

But in the case of women, the same problem is almost insoluble. Most frequently there is a shrinking of what remains of the nymphæ, but the labia majora are not diminished in size if they have not themselves been amputated; the breasts are usually withered; the face also is faded, swollen and pale. Nevertheless Skoptzy women have been met with, who have lost their nipples and breasts and have been mutilated in their genital parts, and yet who have displayed no general characteristic modification, and were even pretty; it is impossible therefore to reckon upon these general modifications in order to decide the period of the operation, and we are reduced to the meagre information supplied by the appearance of the cicatrices.

We have found the greater part of the preceding information in a very interesting little work: *Les Skoptzy*, by E. Teinturier; Paris, Adrien Delagrave, 1877. Publication du Progrès Medical.

We cannot bring this chapter to an end without mentioning two anecdotes which are to be found in Montaigne.

Two Men who castrated Themselves, one through Jealousy and the other through Love.

"About seven or eight years ago, a villager who lived about two leagues from here and who is still alive, having long been distracted by the jealousy of his wife, came home one day from his work; and she welcoming him with her usual wranglings, he fell into such a passion that on the spot he cut off with his pruning-hook the parts which threw her into the fever, and cast them in her face.

"And it is said that a young gentleman of our times, an amorous rogue, having by his perseverance at length softened the heart of a fair mistress, was in despair because at the critical moment he was soft and lost his vigour.

.....non viriliter
Iners senile penis exculerat caput.

"He went home in haste and cut it off and sent it to her as a cruel and bleeding victim for the purgation of his offence. Had he done this for religion's sake, like the priests of Cybele, what should we not have said of so noble and pious an undertaking?" (Michel de Montaigne. *Essais.*)

The Eunuch Priests of Cybele and their Infamous Customs.

Since we are in company with Michel de Montaigne on the subject of the priests of Cybele, sacred eunuchs who were nothing else but sacred pederasts of the passive kind, we will quote a couple of pages from Apuleius stigmatizing their depraved manners.

The Golden Ass is purchased by an old priest to bear the statue of the Goddess.

He took possession of me immediately and led me by the bridle to his home, crying out upon the threshold: "Young girls! I bring you a pretty slave which I have just bought for you."

And what young girls they were! A troop of vile eunuchs who bounded forth with pleasure and delight, raising the discordant notes of their broken, hoarse and effeminate voices, imagining that the slave was really some young man who would be of service to them in their secret and shameful orgies. But when they saw, not a bitch instead of a virgin, but an ass instead of a man, they pulled a wry face and hurled a thousand scoffs against their chief, saying: "It is not a servant but a husband that he has bought for himself." Then apostrophizing him: "Ah! Master, don't eat up such a nice chicken all by yourself, but pass him on to us sometimes, your doves." Sneering in this way they tied me up to the manger.

Among them there was a young man, well-fed, who played excellently on the horn and whom they had bought with the money which they begged for their food; when he was out he sounded the horn before those who carried the goddess, and at home he lent himself like the rest to their monstrous pleasures. He had scarcely seen me before he gave me a bountiful meal: "At last," he said with pleasure, "you are come to aid me in my painful labours; may you live long, please your masters, and give rest to my poor loins!" At these words I already saw my misfortunes which were to come.

The next day they went out, dressed in various colours and ridiculously attired. Their face plastered with dirt, their eyelids painted, with a mitre on their head, clad in robes of linen or silk, of a saffron yellow, sometimes white with small purple stripes, held in by a girdle and wearing yellow sandals, they laded me with the goddess veiled in silk: and with their arms bared to the shoulder, they brandished threateningly hatchets and swords in the air, setting forth to the sound of the flute, leaping and shouting like wild Bacchantes.

. . . .

One day when they were in a country-house, joyful at having made a more abundant collection than usual, they wanted to regale themselves; for a few words of pretended fortune-telling, they asked of a farmer a fat sheep, to sacrifice to the Syrian Goddess, who was, as they declared, very hungry; and when they had finished their preparations for the repast they went to the baths. On their return, they brought a stalwart peasant to supper with them, a suitable fellow to withstand their assaults; and they had scarce tasted a few vegetables before they began at table the monstrous scene of their obscenities, and, holding the young man laid on his belly, they assailed him on all sides, pressing him to yield to their abominable desires." (Apuleius. *The Golden Ass*, Paris, CARRINGTON, 1904. *In-extenso* edition, with twenty-one illustrations.)

Saphism.

CHAPTER IX

Lesbians, Tribades, Fricarelles and Saphists.

Examination of Saphism in General.—Classification of the Inversion-Perversity given by Chevalier.—General Causes of Saphism.—Saphism through Lust.—Professional Saphism.—Saphism from Necessity and through Fear.—Origin of the Name of Saphism.—Women Tribades, Fricarelles, and Saphists properly so-called.—Injurious Influence of Modern Literature.—"Les Femmes Damnées," by Baudelaire.—Special Causes of Saphism.—Bashful or Occasional Saphists and Averred or Habitual Saphists of High Life.—Brothels and Houses of Call for Lesbos.—Employment of the Lap-dog as a means of Saphism.—Saphism among Prostitutes.—The Brothels are Haunts of Tribadism.—Secret Alliances of Saphists.—Intermittent Tribades.—Saphism among Children.—Influence exerted by Men upon the Development of Saphism.—History of Two Alliances of Saphists.—Woman carried off by a Saphist.—The Pantomime of Saphism.—Tribadism in Nuns' Convents.—Special Hospitals, Prisons and Scholastic Establishments are Centres of Saphism.—Psychical

Love of Saphists.—Undeniable Progress of Saphism.—Saphist Practices and accompanying Vulvary Deformations.—Local Lesions due to Clitoridian Manuelization.—Clitoridian Deformations due to Lingual Friction and Suction.—Dangers of Saphism to the General Health.—Differentiation of the Signs of Saphism from Physiological Clitoridian Symptoms.—Tribades and Fricarelles of the Court of France by Brantôme.—Do Lesbians make their Husbands Cuckolds?—The Noble Lady Fricarelle.

Examination of Saphism in General.

Saphism is the taste of the woman for the woman, just as pederasty is the love of the man for the man. Here we quit the medical domain of inversion to enter that of vicious love. We leave the Temple of Æsculapius to enter that of the Venus of Gomorrha while waiting to enter that of the Eros of Sodom.

It is an artificial inversion acquired through perversity.

Classification of the Inversion-Perversity given by J. Chevalier.

Just as we have studied in the inversion-malady the parallel march of the degrees of this inversion in the man and in the woman, so it would be logical to study side by side the different degrees of the inversion-perversity.

This has been done by Chevalier who recognizes four very different cases in pederasty and saphism and simultaneously.

We, on the contrary, consider it useful to separate the study of saphism from that of pederasty, while still holding in high esteem the classification of Chevalier which we append below, as it gives the general causes of Saphism.

Perversity-Pederasty and Saphism properly so-called.

Acquired Artificial Inversion.	1. Pederasty or Saphism through Lust. 2. Professional Pederasty or Saphism. 3. Pederasty or Saphism from necessity. 4. Pederasty or Saphism through Fear.	Sociological Factors. Surroudings.

Origin of the Name of Saphism.—Women Tribades, Fricarelles and Saphists properly so-called.

The name of this vice comes from Sapho the poetess-courtesan who was addicted to it and celebrates its charms in verse. Saphism is the general term, but there are other appellations which are based upon the processes employed by the subjects.

Thus the name of *Lesbian* comes from the town of Lesbos, the women of which had the reputation of being addicted to Saphism, not only in kisses, caresses and various palpations, but also in satisfying themselves principally by mutual onanism either with the hand, or by means of a phallus tied with strings round the stomach of a woman who thus played the part of the cavalier in the game—on condition, no doubt, that she received the same in return. As a matter of fact, this is nothing more than a more refined kind of onanism, and we can understand that this has brought about a class of reciprocal onanism. It is no less true that the mental perversion exists, whether it is innate or acquired.

The *Tribades* or Fricarelles are the perverted women who employ for their accoupling a simple contact, accompanied by a rubbing together of the external genital organs, as is indicated by the etymology (from the Greek τριβαω and the Latin *fricare*, to rub.)

Clitorism is the same process but a step further, consisting in the intromission of a clitoris sufficiently long to take the place of the penis. But the latter is a very rare case and belongs to the province of hermaphrodism, for the women who are so favoured as to have a clitoris of the size of a little boy's penis, are very uncommon.

Lastly under the name of *Saphists* are designated more particularly those women who practise buccal coition.

It cannot be denied that during the last quarter of a century Saphism has attained a formidable development and that the evil is still increasing.

At first it was studied more especially by physicians. In the first rank of these we may quote the names of Parent-Duchatelet and after him Béraud, Jeannel, Pouillet, Rey, Lacour, Mireur, Petrus Borel; the writer, Maxime du Camp, Macé, the ex-head of the Police, then Coffignon, Humbert, Drs. Fiaux, Martineau, Chevalier, etc., to whose works we shall have recourse.

But literature was not slow to adopt this ticklish subject as the groundwork of novels.

Injurious Influence of Modern Literature.

J. Chevalier has no hesitation in referring to the injurious influence of literature, to which he attributes the really formidable development of Saphism.

"In a purely scientific work like this, it is proper to speak of purely literary works, because their influence has been and is still injurious, and because we ought to have the courage to say aloud that the contemporary novel is the most active among the agents of contaminination and of the propagation of the evil. Therefore I might well add to the list of the different forms which I have passed in review a 5th heading, that of *Saphism through literature*. Strange as this proposition may appear, it is only too well demonstrated that the Lesbian through the influence of literature is no paradox. Besides, it should not be uninteresting to know the opinion of writers and novelists upon this point which is almost entirely in the domain of Psychiatria.

The writers who have been attracted by the study of Lesbian love are principally novelists, psycholgists and poets."

Chevalier then quotes in chronological order: Diderot's *La Religieuse*, for which the Abbesse de Chelles, one of the daughters of the Regent, it is said served him as a model. Balzac, that powerful psychologist, has described the torments of *Lesbicus Amor* in the *Fille aux Yeux d'Or*. In his opinion, "the most powerful feeling known is a woman's love for a woman." *La Regine* of Lamartine has some points in common with Balzac's work. The *dénouement* of these novels strongly marks the savagery and tragedy of these loves: in one the heroine commits suicide, in the other she dies by the hand of her female lover. Besides this, Balzac has made a study of bestiality, *Une Passion au Desert*, and another upon the passion of a woman for a castratus, *Sarrazine*. He gives as a pendant to the *Fille aux Yeux d'Or*, a study of the lateral passion. In the *Illusions perdues* and the *Dernière Incarnation de Vautrin*, De Rubempré and the Spanish Abbé, Carlos Herrera, are two typical antiphysical heroes. Theophile Gautier in *Mademoiselle de Maupin* treats the matter as an artist and a poet; he shows the actual androgyne and has a glimpse of the inverted-born.

Ernest Feydeau timidly alludes to the subject in his novel, *La Comtesse de Chalis*.

The *Mademoiselle Giraud, ma Femme* of Adolphe Belot constitutes the classical literary treatise on the question. The success of this work, which moreover is written in a decorous style, must be acknowledged to have drawn the attention of authors to this class of studies, and he has been followed in this path by a large number of others. We will merely give the names of the principal masters, the Goncourts, Zola, Daudet, Catulle Mendès, Peladan and Verlaine.

Baudelaire has sung the sterile delights of Lesbos in *Les Fleurs du Mal*, *Femmes damnées*, and *Delphine et Hippolyte*.

In German literature, Krafft Ebing quotes the following novels as touching upon Saphism: *Secret Love*, by Wildebrand; *Light in the Shade*, by Emerick Stadion, *Venus in Furs*, (1) and the *Damnation of Cain*, by Sacher-Masoch.

In *Ame d'enfant*, the powerful Russian writer Dostoiewsky gives us to know to what a degree of transport the still chaste love of two little girls may extend.

"Les Femmes Damnées," by Baudelaire.

We cannot resist giving here Baudelaire's poem, *Les Femmes Damnées*.

Comme un bétail pensif sur le sable couche,
Et leurs pieds se cherchant et leurs mains rapprochés
Elles tournent leurs yeux vers l'horizon des mers,
Ont de douces langueurs et des frissons amers.

Les unes, cœurs épris des longues confidences
Dans le fond des bosquets où jasent les ruisseaux,
Vont epelant l'amour des craintives enfances,
Et creusent le bois vert des jeunes arbrisseaux.

D'autres, comme des sœurs, marchent lentes et graves
A travers les rochers pleins d'apparitions,
Où Saint Antoine a vu surgir comme des laves
Les seins nus et pourprés de ses tentations.

Il en est, aux lueurs des résines croulantes,
Qui dans les creux muets des vieux antres paiens
L'appellent au secours de leurs fièvres hurlantes
O Bacchus, endormeur des remords anciens.

Et d'autres, dont la gorge aime les scapulaires,
Qui recélent un fouet sous leurs longs vêtements,
Mêlant, dans le bois sombre et les nuits solitaires
L'écume du plaisir aux larmes de tourment.

O vierges, ô demons, ô monstres, ô martyres
De la réalité, grands esprits contempleurs,
Chercheuses d'infini, dévotes et satyres
Tantôt pleines de cris, tantôt pleines de pleurs.

---

(1) Paris, Carrington.

Vous que dans votre enfer mon âme a poursuivies,
Pauvres sœurs, je vous aime autant que je vous plains,
Pour vos mornes douleurs, vos soifs inassouvies,
Et les urnes d'amour dont vos grands cœurs sont pleines.

(Baudelaire. *Fleurs du Mal.* Callman Lévy, Editeur, Paris.)

Translation.

"Like pensive cattle stretched upon the sand,
They turn their gaze towards th'expanse of sea,
The lingering pressure of their feet and hands
Makes languorous shivers thrill throughout their frame.

And some within the groves where streamlets fall
Unfold their mind and long confession pour,
Recall the pure delights of love's young dream
And carve upon the bark the well-loved name.

And some, like sisters, walk with stately step
Beside the rocks where visions haunt the mind,
Like those in which the saint of old beheld
The tempting whiteness of a woman's breast

And some by light of dripping torch descend
Within the dumb recess of ancient pagan cave,
And call to quench the furies of desire
Bacchus who dulls the edge of old remorse.

And some who tell their beads at wonted hours
And hide a scourge beneath their trailing robe
Yet love within their lonely cell to mix
The foam of pleasure with the tears of woe.

Oh maidens, demons, monsters that ye are,
And yet poor martyrs for the truths ye hold,
Ye seek to find th'unknown, satyrs yet saints,
Oft full of laughter and oft full of tears

You whom my soul has followed to your hell,
Poor sisters, love and pity stir my heart
For all your griefs and all your deep desires
Which fill your overflowing hearts for aye.

Special Causes of Saphism.

There are numerous special causes of Saphism besides the great divisions admitted by Chevalier.

Among domestic servants the promiscuity in which they sleep in the garrets produces a considerable amount of licentiousness, not to speak of the corruption of young maid-servants by a dissolute mistress.

Among work-girls the enervated condition arising from too prolonged work in a sitting posture, produces those rollings of the hips, of which doctors are well aware: the disastrous affects, comparable to those which are produced in many horse-women by the motions of the steed. Shall I also mention the physiological inconveniences of the sewing-machine? I have already alluded to them in my chapter on onanism. The women who work at it are predisposed to reciprocal manual onanism and thus become Lesbians.

In the middle classes the boarding-school develops Pederasty among boys. In the upper classes, the domestic servants are the danger; the habit of leaving very young girls to the care of chambermaids is deplorable. Parisian life does not seem to leave some women the time to be mothers. This is what may result, says Coffignon, from a young girl being placed in contact with servants such as are described in an account cut out of a newspaper.

"Among her attendants, the Duchess of X . . . had a chambermaid, of Italian origin, named Justine C . . ., 24 years of age, a tall girl with dark eyes and very pretty. Four months previously, rumours happened to reach the Duchess's ears from the servants' hall about this girl's strange habits. There was a vague report of clandestine debauchery, in which the cook, a woman named Rose R . . ., aged 30, was said to take part. In support of their talk, the servants called attention to the fact that the latter had for some time deserted her husband, a *valet de chambre* in a Hôtel of the Boulevard Saint-Germain. Let us add that Rose R . . . is the mother of two children.

"Madame de X . . . refused to credit these scandalous reports.

"After being away for four days, the Duchess returned home yesterday morning. What was her astonishment, to find her apartment, in utter confusion. Indignation succeeded surprise when, on entering her bedroom, she saw lying side by side in her own bed, the two women whom we have mentioned.

"After her departure, Rose R... and Justine C... had installed themselves in her apartment, wearing her best clothes and decking themselves out in her finest jewels. The other servants, not daring to go and inform the police of this conduct and wishing to avoid a scandal had determined to await the return of their mistress.

"Madame de X... immediately sent for the police; the two women were arrested and conveyed to the Police Infirmary where they were found to be suffering from hysterical mania.

"This, as far as I recollect, occurred in June 1888; a few days afterwards I happened to go into the Tenth Correctional Chamber, at the Palais de Justice. There was a woman in the dock, Marcelle P..., about 40 years of age, accused by her mistress of having stolen a ring.

"The case is of no importance. The actors alone are interesting. The prosecutrix especially, an ethereal blonde, Madame de S..., a self-styled Baroness. The President was interrogating this lady of easy virtue.

"Q. What situation did Marcelle P... hold in your establishment?

"A. She was not one of my servants. She used to come in every day. I was tired of her.

"Q. Why then did you not send her away?

"A. She told me that she loved me too much.

"Q. What do you mean?

"A. Oh, you understand me, gentlemen!... One day she wanted to scratch me, because I would not let her do it to me.

"Much was forgiven Marcelle P... because she had loved much!

"The Judges of the Tenth Chamber pronounced an acquittal."

(A. Coffignon. *La Corruption de Paris*, *op. cit.*)

Bashful or Occasional Saphists, and Avowed or Habitual Saphists.

Saphism is to be met with particularly among two categories of women, those belonging to good society, and prostitutes. The first category may be divided into bashful or occasional Saphists, and into avowed or habitual Saphists.

Occasional Saphists satisfy their vice only by accident, as the result of an unexpected meeting or of a violently excited desire. Not being on terms of peculiar intimacy with any woman, they repair of their own accord to a brothel like a man.

Brothels and Houses of Call for Lesbos

" The brothels, says Martineau, facilitate the practice of Saphism through their opening their doors, which hitherto have been reserved to men, to those women who wish to be saphised, or to saphise the women of the house. I could thus mention several houses in Paris, where Saphism is practised upon a large scale. Every day women come in, generally one after the other, *demi-mondaines*, kept women, but rarely married women, to saphise or to be saphised by the women of the house. The women pay their entrance like men clients. The price varies between 5, 10 and 20 francs

" According to the information which I have received, there are numerous clients from abroad. Several times a year women come from England, Russia and Germany to pay a visit to these houses. Often they take away one of the women of the house to spend a few days with them: they pay to the house a sum which is left to their generosity, and then bring her back. It is an interesting fact that in those houses where the Saphism of the man by the woman was formerly most frequent it is now almost abandoned, the women preferring to devote themselves to this new kind of prostitution."

(Martineau. *Deformations vulvaires et anales, op. cit.*)

But on certain days, owing either to a passing caprice or a momentary requirement, the fashionable lady must have intercourse with a stranger. At these times she has recourse to the good-will and hospitality of those excellent individuals, the proprietors of "Furnished Apartments for Ladies." In Paris there are about forty of these establishments in existence devoted to the cult of Lesbos, which open their doors to ladies of the fashionable world only. They are situated for the most part in the neighbourhood of the Madeleine or of the Chaussée d'Antin.

The model establishment of the class is situated near the church previously mentioned. It is of respectable appearance and possesses two perfectly distinct entrances; it has two different sets of clients, and frequently carriages may be seen drawing up in front of it, one conveying Monsieur and the other Madame, who each enter at their separate door.

Madame comes to meet her amiable "friends"; Monsieur comes to have a little conversation with some agreeable ladies. Neither of them feels at all uneasy at their being separated by so slight a distance; do they even know they have very nearly met in this place by chance? Perhaps they do, if the report is true which attributes this remark by the holder of one of the noblest names in France to the proprietress of this house:

"Well! have you not seen my wife this week?"

The reputation of the house is carefully maintained; no rowdy behaviour is permitted to disturb the equanimity of the visitors. Madame never replies to any indiscreet questions, and the respectable ladies and gentlemen who honour her by a visit, hold her therefore in high esteem.

This house is of a peculiar class, in that, being bi-humanitarian, it unites Lesbos and Cythera without compromising the claims of either nor commingling them profanely; owing to this it has but few rivals, and is distinctly separate from similar establishments. It most frequently happens that each has its peculiar speciality, from which it hardly ever departs. (Pierre Delcourt. *Le Vice à Paris*. Felix Brossier, Paris 1889.)

Employment of the Lap-dog as a means of Saphism.

Some of these occasional or bashful Saphists, who are subject to veritable hysterical crises, fear the risks which they run in visiting brothels or have a feeling of repulsion for persons of their own sex. How can they satisfy their passion? I leave the description to Dr. Martineau from his lecture to his pupils in the Clinical Hospital of Lourcine.

"In spite of my wish, says the worthy Professor, to confine myself to the limits of science, I cannot however neglect to notice certain circumstances under which Saphism is practised, and I am compelled to tell you that these women do not shrink from having recourse to animals, and to point out to you the use for which they intend those magnificent poodles which they take for walks and tend with such passionate care. A patient education has trained these animals to afford their mistresses those caresses, which an equal disgust for one and the other sex leads them to seek, I repeat, in the society of animals. To overcome the repugnance which these sometimes indocile instruments display for their pleasures, these women employ certain rather primitive processes, which consist not in *gilding*, but in *sugaring* the pill."

Saphism among Prostitutes.

We find in the work of Dr. Louis Fiaux a very interesting monograph on Saphism among prostitutes.

Brothels are the Haunts of Tribadism.

From the depths of this medullo-cerebral filth which the prostitute has become, how should there not arise, almost instinctively, the vicious curiosity to know what sensations can be afforded by a contact other than that of the natural contact of the man.

Some of them come to it through hate of the *souteneur* who has made a martyr of them, or through disgust for the long procession of males whom they are condemned to satisfy; they are satiated, they are sick of them; they recall but confusedly the masculine rout, and that no longer as individuals but as physical types; they know it all so well, and they must know and feel something fresh. Others, without experiencing this misanthropical disgust, come to inversion merely by the life which they lead together in common: such a cohabitation of persons of the same sex can have no other consequence. How can ten, twenty, thirty women, possessed of such morals, live for purposes of venereal exploitation under the same roof, eat at the same table, sleeping nearly always two and sometimes three in the same bed, without inevitably falling into interfeminine practices?

Since the time that the brothel has become the pivot of official prostitution, the heads of the Police have struck against this rock. Their rules have been of no good. The women are doubled or sleep together, there is nowhere a bed apiece. Everybody acknowledges this, even the police-officers. The Head of the Department, A. Tribuchat, admitted after reading the Inspectors' reports relating to their night visits, that few of the women were exempt from the vice of tribadism.

"If these infamous connections exist, it is the fault of the proprietors," Parent-Duchatelet and Jeannel have written: after Macé, and Lerouge, Moll, Carlier, Ruess and Coffignon do not contest thist statement: they even quote the slang term given to tribades, *gougnottes*, or more properly *inséparables*, or "little sisters."

We cannot omit to state that one of the most ordinary and innocent occupations of these unhappy creatures is to hold a beauty show among themselves and to mutually exhibit before their comrades who form the jury, not only their bosom, but also their most secret charms, and after successive examination to award the prize for which the three Goddesses disputed in the old story.

Thence comes the *frictrix*, the *cunnilingua.*

Thence too come those symptoms of proteiform nervosism, those unisexual loves, those alliances of women, which are almost the rule in the tolerated houses.

Dr. Martineau has made a remarkable study of Saphism in his works which we have already quoted. *(Prostitution et Déformations vulvaires et anales.)* He puts the problem in these terms, and he replies as follows:

What part do the tolerated houses play in the practise of Saphism? A letter addressed by a woman at St. Lazare to one of her friends will edify you on this point. This letter shows the ascendancy which one tribade can gain over another.

After a scene of jealousy which had occurred on account of a third woman and which is alluded to in the first lines, the suspected woman invites her friend to get herself inscribed together with her upon the police registers and to enter a tolerated house together, so that they might not be parted again but always live together. In this way, she adds, no suspicion of jealousy can arise between us and we shall live happily. The answer,—it is hardly credible—contained in a most erotic letter, shows that the consent was not delayed.

The tolerated houses, open to the inspection of the police, serve, in fact for the establishment and formation of *alliances between women.* I will say more: these connections are favoured and encouraged by the masters or mistresses of these establishments for the following reason. It is they who speak; I, Gentlemen, only transcribe the information which has been given to me.

When they see the women have a lover, they leave the house on the days when they are permitted to go out, and spend outside the house the money which they have amassed during the week. The tribades, on the contrary, do not take advantage of the day when they can go out; they remain shut up in their room, where they pay for one another for dainties and liqueurs bought in the house which thus benefits by their expenditure. This is, as you see, a powerful agent emanating from the proprietors of the establishments in favour of tribadism, for, from motives of self-interest, they prefer a tribade couple in their house to a solitary woman. Therefore you see them eagerly seeking for them and coming to gather their harvest even in our Hospitals, where, alas! the preliminaries of these unions are often arranged.

Private Alliances of Women Saphists.

There is no doubt that alliances of Saphists are to be met with in the brothels. Martineau points to their existence also in private life.

In private life, unions of this nature are frequently to be met with. The taverns supply opportunities for the formation of the alliances, and therefore two women are often to be seen together in these places. They manage almost to support themselves by the presents they receive from those who come to drink there; they refuse as far as possible any sexual intercourse with men. When they are compelled by penury to accept a man's embraces, they hide it one from the other. Tribades often prefer to pawn their clothes or ornaments to committing an infidelity. They are generally to be recognized by a distinctive sign; their dress is usually exactly alike; they wear the same ornaments and call themselves sisters. Therefore the expression "little sisters" has become a synonym for tribades at the public dancing-places, in the taverns and on the Boulevards.

Most frequently tribades energetically deny their vice. Some however are fond of publishing abroad their vicious habits, by their language and by their demeanour, in order to attract the attention of other tribades; they do so in order to rise, so to say, in their profession, and they boast of their feminine conquests which they love to display in public.

The alliances of these women sometimes become

complicated; the arrival of a man imports a third element, whether the women see one another without the knowledge of their lover or husband, or whether the tribade imposes upon the lover or husband the presence of a woman friend for whom she retains a passionate affection.

The intermittent tribades form a separate and very distinct class. Thus in their letters it may be noticed that the style or orthography generally denotes a more rudimentary education and coarser feelings, than in the letters of those who have continuous relations. It is to be remarked, in fact, that the women who form these unions, that is to say those who observe a certain kind of fidelity one towards another, have usually received a better education and possess greater delicacy of mind.

The intermittent tribade is more brutal. There is none of that sentimentality which binds the former together and makes them love each other passionately. One day when her nerves are out of order, she feels a desire to satisfy her sensual appetites, and then. for a present of money, she has recourse to the modern Lesbians who make a trade of Saphist prostitution.

Some intermittent tribades, more rarely to be met with it is true, in no wise conceal their vicious habits. A notable instance of this is a woman no longer young, fifty years old at the least, the proprietress of a tavern, who only keeps in her establishment women who will consent to her lustful caprices. Sometimes she even takes her seat in the first row at the *café concerts* and publicly throws bouquets on the stage to the female singers for whom she feels an inclination.

Saphism in the Child.

Childhood itself, unfortunately, is not exempt from the degrading practices which are here in question. There are little girls from ten to fifteen years of age who frequent the women's taverns under pretext of selling flowers, and who are well known for their Saphic manœuvres which they perform for a more or less high price. These unfortunate children who are most frequently pretty, with their dark-circled eyes, have a precocious assurance in their ways and a language full of audacious repartee, giving them a cynical air of self-possession which contrasts painfully with their age, and which characterizes them. These young and unfortunate agents of the prostitution of Saphism are to be seen of an evening going about the cafés, the Boulevards, and the public dancing-rooms, offering little nosegays. They generally have behind them individuals a little older than themselves who watch and warn them of the approach of the police, while they are making their offers of service to women as well as to men.

Influence exercised by Men upon Saphism. Before terminating this study on the etiological conditions and on all the circumstances favourable to the prostitution of Saphism, I must add a few words on the continual extension and progress of this libidinous act. It must be confessed that the action of men is the most manifest and often the most active. Instead of restraining this sensual passion which, I repeat, is affecting woman more and more, they favour it. I have the most conclusive evidence of this in the observations which I have gathered in my practice among my patients. In alluding to the facts which I have just pointed out, I have not in view the *souteneurs* who, living at the woman's expense, compel her to practice Saphism on the man or the woman, in order to obtain a larger payment. I am speaking of married men, of men living in concubinage or having only an ephemeral *liaison*. These men, whose genesic ardours are more or less extinct, try to excite them by awakening strong voluptuous sensations in the woman. To obtain this result, they do not hesitate to have recourse to paid agents. Therefore we see them after a joyous supper, conducting their companion to special houses, to submit her to Saphism, and this to develop in her, most frequently ignorant of the act, a genesic passion which she will be the more inclined to satisfy, in proportion to the amount of the pleasure which she has obtained from it. But, from this moment, the woman seeks for Saphism with ardour, only yields herself to the man with repugnance, and soon takes rank among intermittent or professional tribades. Such is the confession of many of my patients. I do not exaggerate. It is a duty I owe to truth not to be silent upon the part played by men in this circumstance. (Martineau, *op. cit.*)

History of Two Saphist Unions, by Martineau.

It would be an easy matter, says Martineau, to give you numerous proofs of the existence of these unions but I will confine myself to the two following instances.

The first refers to a young woman, aged 17, who became a patient of mine in 1888 for non-infecting chancres of the vulva and other chancrous accidents.

In this woman's case the clitoridian region immediately attracted attention. The clitoris is so prominent and voluminous that it forms a projection of the size of an adult man's thumb; it points directly forward. The hood, smooth above, is in folds at its lower extremity. The free edge of it is thickened and hypertrophied as well as the frena of the clitoridian gland. It does not completely cover the clitoridian gland which is voluminons, elongated, flattened transversely and projecting at its mesial portion.

These lesions, as I have just remarked, are typical of Saphism; they prove, moreover, that that act is of frequent and even daily performance. On questioning the patient I found that the data furnished by the observation were confirmed.

The young girl informed me that she had been an orphan for several years and had lived unhappily with some relatives who had brought her up. Two years before, she had been deflowered by an individual unknown who took her one evening into an hotel, as she was returning from her work-room.

Since that date she had from time to time indulged in clandestine prostitution. It was under these circumstances that she met a few months ago another prostitute, aged 19, who offered her her apartment. From this day, or rather from this evening, these two women, deeply in love with one another, lived together in intense misery, and practised Saphism reciprocally upon one another, two, three, four, and even five times in the course of the twenty-four hours. When money was lacking and hunger made its presence felt, one of them went out, indulged in clandestine prostitution, and thus gained a sufficient sum to keep them going for a few days. As long as the pair had any money, neither of them indulged in prostitution; they lived together, for, as she said, they did not like men. It was during one of these acts of prostitution that the patient contracted the complaint for which she entered the hospital.

The second instance is that of two women who together came under my care for a syphilitic affection. One was aged 20, and the other 18. Both of them display in the most marked degree the clinical characteristics of Saphism and manuelization; elongation of the clitoris, hood smooth, folded and wrinkled, projecting forwards, completely detached from the clitoridian gland which is voluminous and augmented in its transversal diameter; it is also flattened, and at the same time arched and projecting on the mesial line. It is of a violet colour; the frena are hypertrophied.

These two women have lived together for a year. They love one another passionately and, in order that they may not be parted, they entered the hospital on the same day and contrived to be placed in the same ward. They sleep together in their apartment and indulge in erotic practices upon one another. They practice both Saphism and masturbation. They daily repeat these manœuvres, as often as six and seven times in the course of the twenty-four hours. They are extremely jealous of one another. During the past year they have had numerous scenes of jealousy, passing from invective to blows, especially when one of them has practised Saphism with another woman. They follow one another about therefore everywhere, and never leave one another; they say that they love one another like "lover and mistress."

In the ward these two women do not leave one another; they pass the whole day seated side by side, they work together, eat out of the same plate and drink out of the same glass.

They detest coition; "men are generally disagreeable to them." When a man wishes to perform Saphism upon them, they accept it, but without pleasure, rather with disgust. Besides they prefer to indulge in manuelization than in sexual intercourse.

When the want of money makes itself felt, one sacrifices herself to indulge in prostitution. In this case the other is sad and sullen, and can only endure this infidelity because they must obtain something to live on.

These two instances will furnish you with complete information as to the reality of these unions, the intimate bond which unites the Saphists and the profound disgust which they feel for men and for sexual intercourse. With regard to this, there is no doubt. Besides, the answer is always the same; question hundreds of women who live together in this way, and you will find the same intimacy, the same jealousy, the same repugnance for men and the same self-sacrifice in prostituting themselves in order to keep themselves in food.

A Young Woman carried off by a Saphist.

We find in Coffignon an anecdote relating to a young woman being carried off by a Saphist.

Contrary to the practise of Pederasts, Saphists are almost all active as well as passive. In a union of two Saphists, there is always one who exercises her influence over the other in an indisputable fashion, sometimes with a really hypnotic power.

One day a personage of very high rank,—something like a Minister or Under Secretary of State—came to the Préfecture of Police. He was very agitated, and asked the Préfet to be good enough to seek with the utmost speed for a young woman who had just disappeared. This disappearance had taken place under inexplicable circumstances. The young woman was on the eve of being married to this personage of very exalted position. She was apparently happy in thus repairing the error she had made in agreeing to be the mistress of the gentleman who was about to marry her.

In spite of the most active search, it was impossible for the Préfecture of Police to find any trace of the fugitive. They despaired of finding her again, when, about a fortnight afterwards, she presented herself at her mother's residence.

But, alas! in what a condition! She who had been so fresh, seemed to have suddenly faded, and could scarcely drag her languid limbs along. Is it necessary to say how she was pressed with questions on the subject of her disappearance? For a long time they entreated her in vain to speak; at length they succeeded in drawing from her the key of the enigma.

The unfortunate girl, while on a round of shopping for her wedding presents, had gone into a shop to make a purchase. The assistant who served her displayed peculiar amability, disturbing the young woman by the strange look which she fixed upon her. She refused to allow the purchaser to carry away the article, declaring that she would be only too happy to come and deliver it herself.

The next morning the assistant came and insisted upon seeing Madame. The young woman came down to see her in a dressing-gown and the Saphist immediately threw herself upon her and covered her with kisses and caresses. The disappearance of the young woman took place the same day; the *two friends* went and shut themselves up in a village in the neighbourhood of Paris, from which only the want of money recalled them at the end of a fortnight.

The marriage did not take place; the assistant was dismissed from the shop where she was employed, but it was useless to try and break the unhappy young woman of the vice which she had contracted and which was ruining her existence. Nothing could do so, not even the fear of death. (Coffignon. *La Corruption à Paris. op. cit.*)

The Pantomime of Saphism. The Working Fleas.

What satiated individuals of either sex come especially to see in the brothels, are the pantomimes of Saphism, a kind of *tableau vivant* in action which is called *the working fleas.* Dr. Fiaux gives the following description of it:

A young reservist, in barracks at the Ecole Militaire, relates the following fact. Six young soldiers went to a tolerated house on the left bank of the Seine and asked to see some Saphic scenes. The proprietor replied that he was ready to satisfy their curiosity, but that they must previously guarantee him the ordinary profit for the night (300 francs); drinks were served, the blinds were drawn and the doors shut; no interruption was to be feared. The bargain is made. A woman is pointed out by the proprietor as being the principal tribade of the troop. The choice is left to her of a partner from among her companions. Great disappointment of the spectators! The proprietor then interposes and points out himself the tribade's mistress, declaring to the clients that if they do not wish to be robbed or duped, it is she and not the other whom they must make take part in the drama of passion. This time the six soldiers had something for their 300 francs.

Tribadism in Nuns' Convents.

In the chapter relating to masturbation among women, we have seen that it is very rife in large educational establishments, both in those managed by the State and those in private hands, and that from this point of view they are in no way inferior to the similar establishments for boys.

From solitary onanism to mutual onanism and to tribadism, there is but a step which it is easy to take. A work of the anti-clerical library states that the convents are haunts of tribadism, just as much as the brothels. We leave to the anonymous author of the work the responsibility for his assertion, and we only mention it in order that we may not be accused of incompleteness in our task. We simply draw upon a document of human interest without giving any guarantee for its sincerity.

The cult of Lesbos was held in honour in the convents of women and in almost all the monasteries; the nuns burned with impure fires, loved one another and abandoned themselves to every kind of immodesty. Let us discreetly cast a veil over all the practices of the nuns, over such turpitudes as these.

Have the nuns in the women's convents changed for the better since the Middle Ages?

We reply as follows: If the actual state of civilisation does not permit the scandals and dissoluteness of the good old times, it is none the less true that the same causes produce the same effects. Now, in many women's convents in Catholic countries, in France, Spain, Italy, Belgium, Austria and elsewhere, the Abbess still exercises sacerdotal functions, she blesses and hears the confessions of her nuns, she punishes or rewards at her pleasure, she receives them in her oratory or in her cell by day or night, she remains shut up with them there, and no indiscreet eye or curious ear can see or hear what is done by these pretty sinners and the Mother Abbess.

But we, who have received the confessions and confidences of nuns at the tribunal of penitence, are able to affirm that no women's convent exists, or hardly any, where there are not doves of Lesbos, Abbes-Confessors who are in love with nuns, tribades and Mœnades, Nymphs, Bacchantes and Hamadryads.

All the nuns, even those who have no ideas of wrong, play and sport among themselves. We have received singular confidences in confession with regard to these innocent games. The nuns, condemned to an idle and contemplative life, seek for distraction; it is natural for them to do so. Two or three pretty young nuns get together, out of sight of Abbess, and admire one another's charms, and measure them with their rosaries.

"Good Heavens," says Sophie, "who would have thought, darling, that you had a larger one than mine, just a pair with Maria's?"

(*Manuel des Confesseurs*. Translated by Frenquin. *Librairie du Progrès*. Marick Lebrun. San Remo.)

We do not think. that these bitter criticisms are applicable to our convents and female monastic orders in France. We are not acquainted with any in which the Abbess has retained the right of confession. And it seems to us that our admirable Sisters of St. Vincent de Paul, the Petites Sœurs des Pauvres, Garde-Malades, etc., lead a far from idle and contemplative life. Besides, the author of the *Manuel des Confesseurs* is an unfrocked priest, and there is no brood worse than that.

The Special Hospitals, Prisons, Scholastic Establishments, etc., are Centres of Saphism.

If there is no certainty regarding the existence of Lesbian love in the Convents of Nuns, it is, on the other hand, undeniable that it is fatally prevalent in all places where women are brought together, (Hospitals, Penitentiaries, Boarding-schools, etc.) The special hospitals for the care of women affected with venereal complaints, such as Lourcine, Saint Lazare, L'Antiquaille, are infected with it to such a degree that Bourneville declares that 75 out of a 100 of the inmates are Lesbians. According to certain writers, Ratier, Lande, Garcin, these hospitals are really schools of depravity, and the women leave them more corrupted than when they enter. Acquaintances are made there and unions are effected, and the only result is a recruiting for this association of women, "of women for women," which they designate by the name of the "Society of the Little Medal," and which is carried on upon an extensive scale (Joly). Woman have been known to make themselves ill and to inflict wounds on their genital organs, in order to rejoin a friend who is under treatment at the hospital. Saphism is sometimes to be observed in the non-special hospitals: M. Lacassagne has made several observations of this kind, which have given place to a report. The same depravity is to be met with in women's prisons, gynecœa, harems, etc. Dr. Fischer, Physician to the House of Correction of St. Georges, reports that "it is not uncommon to see young girls accustomed to sexual pleasures forming relations in the House itself and satisfying their passion as soon as an opportunity presents itself. Their passion is of a surprisingly exalted nature, and they experience all the torments of love and jealousy, just as happens among persons of opposite sexes." Krausold, quoted by Krafft Ebing, "has observed in these establishments the same forbidden friendships," and he says that "if the friend of a prisoner receives merely a smile from another the most violent scenes of jealousy and even blows ensue. If it happens that by the rules of the establishment, the one who inflicts the blow is put into irons, she says that her friend "got a child by her."

Dr. Gaston Nicomède, a naval surgeon who resided in New Caledonia for a long time, reveals *(Un Coin de Civilisation penale—Bourrail in N. C.)* the manners of the convict-women. "The Convent of Bourrail, he says, is a strange and monstrous prison. Here are sent the worst characters, the pick of the basket from the central prisons... While waiting for the time when they will regain their freedom for licentiousness, through the marriage which is promised them, they indulge in an abandoned way in the most cynical

Tribadism and Saphism." An eye-witness has declared to us that the *pétroleuses* of the Commune, when prisoners and penned all together under the guard of sentries, seeing that their provocative offers to the latter were of no avail, indulged publicly among themselves in the most utter lewdness.

Vice at school is perhaps still more to be feared among young girls than among boys, considering the peculiar amative sensibility of the woman. Young girls are generally loving, unconstrained, and are always lavishing caresses upon one another; nor are mysticism and curiosity wanting among them. Let us recognize the fact that in the great majority of cases, the tender and demonstrative embraces which schoolgirls bestow upon their friends are void of all sensuality, and without being guilty of any excessive simplicity we may poetize them as Lamartine has done in *Regina;* but let us also say that we must not show an over-amount of confidence. In many instances these connections have been known to last long after school has been left; more than one suitor for a young girl's hand has been rejected, after others have been so also, and has never been able, any more than they, to discover the cause for his rejection. (J. Chevalier. *op. cit.*)

It was upon such a groundwork as this that the novelist, Belot, wrote *Mademoiselle Giraud, Ma Femme.* It appears unnecessary to give any quotations from such a well-known work.

Psychical Love of Saphists.

Parent-Duchatelet, who was one of the first to contribute to the study of Saphism and to point out the *female unions* among prostitutes, draws a lively picture of the passion which Saphists import into their love and of the unbridled jealousy which they display in it. In the first place, Parent-Duchatelet (whose works are already half a century behind the times) does not believe that the evil is as deep as it actually is. The terribly propagation of Saphism outside the brothels, contradicts his opinion.

I cannot avoid treating, says Parent Duchatelet, a very important subject in a history of the manners of prostitutes. I am about to speak of those lovers whom a depraved taste induces the women of the house to select among persons of their own sex.

These disgusting and monstrous "marriages" which are so common in houses of detention that hardly any prisoners can escape from them, are they as common among prostitutes as many persons seem to believe? The information which I have gathered from the lips of those who, through their position, were able to make observations, is as follows:

With regard to the number of public women who are addicted to this vice, I have found a great divergence of opinion: some persons declare that all or nearly all indulge in it in an immoderate manner; others have assured me that the number is very limited. This contradictory opinion, both in one and the other, is based only upon a vague feeling and some elusive information, acquired by chance, and not upon a study made with the object of throwing a light upon this question, and after collecting a certain number of observations.

This contradiction arises principally from the fact that not one of these girls is willing to own that she is addicted to the vice in question; for, where they are asked, they reply impatiently: "I only go in for men, and have never done so for women." Everybody who has been able to study them at all periods of their life, and particularly in the hospitals and prisons has assured me that they preserve the most absolute silence upon this point; that they are equally ashamed of the vice on their own account and on account of those of their companions who are in the habit of indulging in it; the guilty ones are those who, when in prison, do not fear to show themselves to be what they are.

It is deserving of remark, continues Parent-Duchatelet, that there is very often a considerable disproportion of age and accomplishments between two women who unite together after this fashion; and it is also surprising that when once the intimacy is established, it is usually the one who has the advantage in age and accomplishments who displays towards the other the greatest attachment and the most passionate love.

Whence comes this attachment and how are these unions formed?

I have managed to gain access to the correspondence of tribades when in prison; I have always found it to be romantic, containing expressions which are familiar to lovers, and in every way indicating the greatest exaltation of the imagination. The most curious fact in this way which has come under my observation is a set of letters written by the same person to another prisoner; the first of these letters contained a declaration of love, but of a veiled, covered and most reserved kind; the second was more unreserved; the last letters expressed in burning terms the most violent and unbridled passion.

Usually, the lack of education does not afford the means of coming together which are supplied by a cultivated mind; it is by caresses, care, attention and kindness of every kind, that superannuated and sometimes aged woman seduce young girls and succeed in attaching them to themselves in a truly extraordinary way. The older women may be seen working with extreme industry, in order to increase their earnings and to make liberal presents to those whom they wish to seduce; they offer to complete their task in the prisoners' work-rooms; in a word, they employ every means which the art of seduction can suggest in order to make up by peculiar and artificial qualities, for what is lacking in them and which may tend to keep them apart.

When these unions are once established, they display some peculiar and curious features to which I will draw your attention.

In the case of prostitutes, there is no giving up a lover of the same sex as they give up a lover of the opposite sex. In the latter case, they are easily consoled and soon find a means of forgetting him upon whom they have lavished the liveliest protestations of affection. What a difference with regard to the others! In this case their attachment resembles frenzy rather than love. They are devoured by jealousy; the fear of being supplanted and thus losing the object of their affection, causes them never to leave them, to follow them step by step, to be arrested for the same offences, and always to find the means of leaving the House of Detention at the same time.

When they enter the prison and are designedly placed in two separate dormitories, they make endless complaints and give way to their vexation like children, crying and yelling; they indulge in numberless devices in order to rejoin those from whom they do not wish to be separated; they pretend to be ill in order to be sent to the infirmary: they have been know to inflict upon themselves with this intention the most serious wounds. Some of them, more cunning than the rest, and consummate mistresses in the knowledge of all the resources of their profession, have applied small pieces of caustic potash to their genital parts, by the aid of which they obtain ulcerations so exactly similar to venereal chancres, that the most skilful individual could not tell the difference. Most of them have a marvellous talent for shamming the itch, which they do by pricking with a red-hot needle those parts of the body where this complaint appears.

The desertion of a tribade by the woman whom she loves becomes in the prison a matter deserving the particular care of the warders: the deserted woman feels that she must inflict a terrible vengeance upon the one who has abandoned her, and upon the one who has supplanted her. Veritable duels arise from this, in which they fight with dishes used for their meals, and sometimes even with knives; but the instrument which is most frequently used in these combats, is the hair-pin. Very serious, sometimes even mortal wounds are the result. These duels used formerly to often occur in the prison of La Force; the Governor. therefore. M. Chefdeville, wrote to the Prefect of Police, every time that he knew of any infidelity, to obtain authority to put the woman who had become the object of another's hatred into a separate place.

This hatred and fury among creatures so changeable as prostitutes does not last long; when she has satisfied her vengeance, the deserted woman tries to lure back her faithless friend, a task in which she often succeeds; or, if she is unable to do so, she tries for new conquests and brings her pernicious talents again into use.

There is one case however which is unpardonable, and which demands undying vengeance: when one woman leaves another to attach herself to a man and make him her lover, it is an unforgiveable crime which can never be forgotten. It is an unhappy thing for the woman who is guilty of it, for, if she is not the stronger of the two, she is sure to be beaten each time she meets the woman who thinks that the most bitter insult which a tribade can receive has been inflicted on her.

The vengeance of a deserted tribade, under the circumstances in question, offers a remarkable peculiarity: in this case the other prostitutes are never to be seen interposing their good offices and endeavouring to separate the combatants, as they never fail to do when disputes arise about ordinary matters. But in this case they look at it all with indifference, and coolly leave the quarrel to come to a natural end.

I am told by several Inspectors and by some ex-warders of gaols that pregnancies are to be observed much less frequently among tribades than among those prostitutes who have not contracted this dissolute taste; this may be understood and can be explained up to a certain point. The same persons have remarked that pregnancy, under this circumstance, is known to and becomes the object of the derision of all the prisoners, who never display for the object of their mirth that care and attention which prostitutes in prison are always most ready to afford to those of their companions who happen to be in this condition.

Tribades therefore may be looked upon as having reached the lowest stage of vice which a humain being can come to, and, owing to that very fact, demand particular watchfulness on the part of those who are entrusted with the care of public women, and more especially of those persons to whom is confided the management of the prison devoted to these women.

To sum up the details which we have given: when we consider the circumstances which favour the development of these infamous inclinations in prostitutes, when we examine the age at which this vice is most usually developed in them, and lastly, when we see the manner in which tribades are looked upon and treated by those who have not yet imitated them, we think we may conclude that the number of women who have reached this last stage of vice is more limited than some persons have maintained, and that, if is impossible to say what is the exact proportion in which they are, we are not far from the truth in saying that they do not form a quarter of the whole number of prostitutes now plying their trade in the city of Paris.

In my opinion this estimate is below the truth and at the present day is considerably exceeded especially among prostitutes.

Undeniable Progress of Saphism.

On the other hand, it must be taken into consideration that Saphism has made undeniable progress since the time of Parent Duchatelet. Maxime du Camp expresses himself as follows in 1872, more than a quarter of a century ago.

The different political phases through which France has passed dnring the last sixty years, have been singularly favourable to the corruption of morals. The instability of our institutions, the inconsistency of our social condition have necessarily brought about a mad whirl of existence, and people have been in a hurry to enjoy it, because they were not sure of possessing it for any length of time. More than ever, Paris has been a city of pleasure, a kind of Venice of the seventeenth century. Amusement has become the most important, if not the only preoccupation of the greater number. There has been a brutalizing influence at work before which the higher faculties have been swept away, and the most precious instincts of our race have been blasted. Mind having repudiated its rights, matter has naturally abused those which it possesses.

The licence of manners seems to have endeavonred to equal that which was a cause of reproach against the Regency and the Directory. We are to-day in the presence of Augean stables into which people of every category and every condition have hastened to cast their filth. What Hercules will have the courage and the strength to endeavour to cleanse the sewer? Never has the gangrene been so deep: it has attacked the limbs and, if we do not watch, it will soon destroy the whole body.

Louis Fiaux and Martineau in particular have informed us that Saphism, starting from the brothel, has overflowed into modern society and that it is now to be found in some degree in every class, but principally in the upper and lower extremities of the social scale.

Some Stories regarding Tribades.

In the same way as Pederasts, Tribades and Saphists combine together to form associations—veritable seminaries of Lesbian vice—in which they practise the arts of unbridled debauchery. Each of these associations or clubs usually has for its head an adventuress of foreign extraction. We were on one occasion enabled by chance to gain some knowledge of one of these seminaries, presided over by a woman whose birthplace was in the United States. Under the pretext of studying the art of painting, she possessed a sumptuously furnished studio in a street adjoining the Avenue Friedland. There she used to give afternoon tea-parties to which ladies only were invited. Her circle consisted principally of foreigners resident in Paris, female students, grass-widows, wives divorced from their husbands, and single women of uncertain age.

The older members of these associations contend fiercely for the possession of those who are newly recruited for the vice, and scenes of terrible jealousy and hatred frequently occur. Nor do they hesitate to have recourse to forcible abduction. We will give an instance.

One day—not so many years ago—a gentleman of about forty years of age, of large private means, came to the Prefecture of Police and made the following statement:

"My marriage with Mdlle Lucienne X . . . was fixed to take place three days from now. She is twenty-two years of age, and of a quiet and modest disposition. I did her a wrong in seducing her, and after due reflection, determined to make amends to her for my misdeed. My fiancée resides with an old relative; she was delighted at my proposal to marry her, as were also the other members of her family, who live in a neighbouring department. For the past few days she has been engaged in making purchases for her *trousseau*, and for this purpose I placed in her hands a considerable sum of money. Yesterday afternoon she went out again, no doubt to buy other articles that she required; but she has not returned home. Her aunt is distracted. We have telegraphed to her parents, but they have seen nothing of her. I do not know what to think, and I fear lest a crime has been committed."

The matter was placed in the hands of detectives, who made numerous enquiries, but without any result.

About a mouth after the date fixed for her marriage, the young girl quietly returned home, and declared, without giving any reason for her decision, that she refused to marry the man to whom she was engaged.

He, as well as the aunt, was struck with the altered appearance of Mdlle Lucienne X . . . . on her return from her inexplicable escapade: the young girl's features were drawn, her face had grown thin, and a sombre light shone in her sunken eyes; moreover, she coughed incessantly.

It was impossible to draw the slightest explanation from her. Her mother came to Paris, but was unable to induce her to see again the man she had promised to marry; she summarily dismissed him, and handed back to him all the money that he had given her up to the date of the publication of the banns. Moreover, she displayed her purse which was well filled, and cynically declared that henceforth she needed neither husband nor protector.

What could this mystery be? What had occurred? Eventually it was discovered.

Lucienne, while making her purchases in a shop, had met an elegantly dressed lady, who suddenly appeared to take a lively interest in her, an interest which was shared by the woman who served behind the counter. The latter, who had taken down her address, came in person at an early hour the next morning to deliver the articles she had purchased, obtained access to her apartment, and there succeeded in corrupting her by Sapphic embraces, to which the young girl had been unable to oppose any resistance. In the afternoon of the same day, Lucienne, who had made an appointment with her seductress, was taken by her to the house of the elegantly-dressed lady whom she had seen on the previous day, a woman of fashion and a member of one of those Lesbian seminaries to which I have made previous allusion.

The unfortunate Lucienne was captured without hope of release. For the space of four weeks she was the prey of the numerous adepts of the Friedland gang; astounded at the experience of sensations with which hitherto she had been unacquainted, she in turn practised in a species of frenzy the refinements of the vice which had been revealed to her, and was delighted to accept the presents, the jewellery, and the bank-notes that were heaped upon her. At the present moment, no doubt, she is still a member of the gang, in the capacity of passive subject, and will remain so until consumption hurries her to the grave.

Such cases as this are by no means rare. We have already cited on the authority of Coffignon an analogous instance of abduction.

Distinctive Signs of Tribadism.

A few words relating to the distinctive signs of Tribadism will not be uninteresting.

Tribades are everywhere to be met with at the present day. We come across them in taverns--young girls in pairs, dressed exactly alike, and surnamed by students "little sisters." We see them at the theatre, sitting together in the same box and never leaving one another for a moment. We find them in the upper circles of society—the married woman of about forty years of age with her young friend, her inseparable companion, who for some unexplained reason refuses every eligible offer of marriage.

The tribade, in quest of a companion of similar tastes, has a distinguishing mark—a magnificent poodle, closely clipped, with its tufts of hair frizzed and tied up sometimes with ribbon, which always accompanies her when she is walking or driving.

In the Champs Elysées, the careful observer will have no difficulty in picking out the elegantly-attired Lesbians who are searching for a companion of similar vicious tastes. Look at that smart turn-out; in it reclines a woman by herself, more or less gorgeously apparelled, with the inevitable poodle seated beside her. The carriage stops at the Place de l'Etoile, and she gets out. How attentively she regards the women who are strolling along between the cross-roads and the Place de la Concorde! One of them catches sight of the woman with the poodle, and as their eyes meet each performs a rapid motion of the tongue and lips; this is the conventional sign, adopted by tribades to signify, "I am on the look-out for a woman." In a few moments the carriage will be driven back again along the Avenue; the lady with the poodle will order her coachman to stop, and, inviting her newly-found acquaintance to enter, will drive off with her to dinner.

But this is not all. Sapphism, as well as Sadism, has its special training, and, to close this chapter, I will reveal a fact which constitutes the most horrible scandal of the present day. Yes, after all that I have said, there remains something in the backgronnd more terrible than anything that I have brought to the knowledge of my readers.

There was a picturesque word coined and brought in to use some fifteen years ago to describe members of the class of courtesans in general; they were called from their social position "horizontals."

At the present day, at the dawn of this corrupt century, we have something else besides the enormous class of "horizontals." In order to pander to the insatiable desires of the male and female frequenters of the public brothels, degraded mothers—there

Note. The tribades who walk about the streets and who are at the service of ladies of position and the swell courtesans, are usually from twenty-five to thirty years of age, and dressed quietly, but with a certain style; they have their hair cut short, wear clothes of masculine cut, and have a boyish look. They might be taken for foreigners of an eccentric type, but nevertheless of a respectable position, by anyone ignorant of their peculiar calling; they look like women students from Russia belonging to the higher classes. These prostitutes of the Sapphic school practise both the active and the passive art. One of them, at the time of the Exhibition of 1889, was greatly sought after; she used to look charming in male attire, and in the privacy of her rooms, used to put on a false beard of a light shade and pointed shape which made her resemble General Boulanger; she went by the name of "Handsome Ernest."

Candidates for Lesbian honours are in the habit of plying their trade in the Allée des Poteaux, in the Bois de Boulogne, from ten to twelve o'clock of a morning. They are to be found in the Champs Elysées in the afternoon from four o'clock to nightfall, that is to say when the carriages return from the drive in the Bois. The night restaurant mostly frequented by tribades is situated near the Halles Centrales.

are hardened prostitutes who have reached even this depth of infamy—degraded mothers, I say, have trained their young daughters up to the most habitual practises of Sadism and Sapphism. They are usually about eight or ten years old; and they sell flowers in the streets of an evening.

Saphists' Practices and accompanying Vulvary Deformations.

The vulvary deformations, in fact, due to Saphism are characterized by an elongation of the whole clitoridian organ, and by a wrinkled and flaccid appearance of the sheath and hood which is partly detached from the gland. The latter is partly uncovered, and is voluminous and turgescent. These characteristics belong to clitoridian friction. Through suction, some of them are more accentuated; and others, which did not exist in the former case, are developed. Thus, the prominence of the clitoris is more marked, forming a projection between the *labia majora.*

The hood especially is voluminous; it is completely detached from the clitoridian gland which, for the greater part of the time, it leaves uncovered. It is slightly elevated in an upward direction, forming in this way, above the gland, a projecting fold which may be compared to a helmet. At the same time its free edge is thickened and is of a firmer consistency. The frena of the clitoris, folds formed by the division into two of the anterior extremity of the nymphæ, are more accentuated, more projecting and thicker; they also have more consistency. These modifications of appearance and structure are sometimes observed to a distance of two or three millimètres beneath, on the free edge of the nymphæ. The gland is very developed and very projecting, and, while it is elongated, its extremity also is swollen. Its transversal diameter is increased; it is slightly flattened at the edges, projecting and a little arched at its medial portion; in a word it is club-shaped; its appearance resembles the deformation which it undergoes in masturbation through the rubbing of the thighs; but it differs from it though the arched projection of the mesial portion which is much accentuated by the fact of suction.

Its coloration is an intense red, sometimes violet; there is an almost constant turgescence, especially when Saphism is of daily performance and practised several times in the course of the twenty-four hours, as you may observe in the case of tribades living together, and also in the case of some women who are married or living in concubinage. Upon this subject, I could quote numerous observations which I have collected in my hospital and private practice; I shall be satisfied with giving you a few instances.

In No. 29 of the Nathalie Guillot ward there is a young girl, aged 21, a saleswoman in the Markets, who entered the Hospital for a syphilitic affection. You will observe in her case characteristic signs of Saphism carried to an exaggerated degree owing to the frequency and duration of the act. This woman in fact states that for several years past, she has been saphised by her lover almost every night, and often two or three times in the night. The clitoris is remarkable for its size, which is that of the little finger of an adult man. It is almost normal on a level with its upper portion, but at the root is suddenly swells towards its lower third, so as to form a hard, rounded mass, projecting and raised at its free extremity. Exact account may be taken of the action of suction upon this portion of the clitoris which is brought forward and upward. The gland is voluminous, of the size of a large pea, and violet in colour; the frena are considerably hypertrophied.

In No. 18 of the same ward there is a young woman, 24 years of age, a cook, who displays the most characteristic signs of Saphism. The clitoris is so voluminous that it resembles the penis of a child about four years of age. Its length is 3 centimètres. The gland is enormous, flattened and club-shaped; it is detached from the hood with the greatest facility. For about the last two years Saphism has been performed daily and sometimes even three or four times in a night. In this woman you will also find the physical signs which characterize masturbation when it is practised from childhood. Thus the nymphæ are so elongated that they are hanging down between the thighs. They are of a black colour, like shagreen, velvety upon their internal surface, which is sprinkled with a large number of hypertrophied follicles.

In the following observation the subject is a married woman, aged about 30, the mother of several children, who, either through fear of having more children, or because coition no longer procures her any sensual satisfaction, compels her husband to perform Saphism two or three times in the course of the twenty-four hours.

In this woman's case the clitoris has acquired a considerable development. Its length is four centimètres and a half. The hood is raised like a helmet, leaving the clitoridian gland bare. Its free extremity is thickened, as well as the clitoridian frena. The clitoridian gland is of a violet colour, voluminous, turgescent, and projecting between the nymphæ. Its mesial portion is arched.

In another observation which treats of a young woman who, some years before her marriage, indulged in reciprocal Saphism with one of her girl-friends, and who, unable to resist the love which she bore her friend, imposed, so to say, the obligation upon her husband of living with her, and thus forming a household of three, the third member of which was in this case a woman and not a man, as usually happens under these circumstances; in this case, the characteristics of Saphism are most marked. I have observed an exaggerated development of the clitoris, an extreme laxity of the hood, a thickening of its free edge, an hypertrophy of the clitoridian frena, a considerable volume of the clitoridian gland which is continually turgescent, of a violet colour and displaying a very pronounced mesial projection,

In a third observation collected in the course of my

hospital practice, the subject is a woman aged 27, a lace-maker, who had been saphised every day for two years by her lover. Each operation lasted about half-an-hour. In the case of this patient whose nervosism is very extreme, I have made you observe the characteristics of Saphism carried to their highest degree of development. Those of you who were not present at this examination have only to glance at the perfectly executed drawing which is due to the talent of M. Puech, a pupil of mine. You will find a very hard clitoris forming a considerable projection between the nymphæ beyond which it juts out. It is seven centimètres in length, and of the size of the index finger of an adult. The hood is thickened; the edges of it are hard and raised up. The clitoridian organ points directly forward. The gland is large, of the size of the extremity of the little finger; it is of a violet colour and constantly turgescent; the mesial projection is very pronounced; the frena are very elongated and hypertrophied.

Differentiation of Vulvary Signs of Deformation due to Saphism, from physiological Clitoridian Conditions.

Before bringing this clinical study to an end, I will sum up in a few lines the signs which will enable you to differentiate the clitoridian deformations due to the manœuvres with which we are acquainted, from physiological clitoridian conditions. I have told you, in fact, that some women have a clitoris of exaggerated size, and that this size is normal; it is, accordingly, necessary to establish a differential diagnosis between the pathological condition and the physiological condition, so as not to accuse the patient unduly of illicit manœuvres. This diagnosis is very necessary, when it is a question of a medico-legal enquiry. Gentlemen, it is most easy.

When the clitoridian deformation results from masturbation or saphism, you base your diagnosis on the elongation, the wrinkled, flaccid and brown appearance of the clitoridian prepuce; on the gland, which is easily uncovered and which, besides, is large, violet-coloured, flattened, projecting and even prominent; and on the clitoridian frena. At the same time the nymphæ are long, flaccid, withered, wrinkled and hypertrophied. These characteristics are especially to be observed when masturbation dates back to the time of infancy.

In the case of physiological malformation, however long and hypertrophied a clitoris may be, if there is neither masturbation nor Saphism, the prepuce is smooth, even, white and not withered or brownish. Finally (and this a pathognomical characteristic), under this voluminous clitoris a small, rosy gland is to be found, without any deformation and the smallness of which offers a contrast to the size of the rest of the organ. The frena are not hypertrophied, the nymphæ are normal, smooth, rosy, and the prepuce does not rise up like a helmet at its free extremity, as is frequently to be seen in cases of Saphism.

Therefore, the level appearance of the prepuce, the smallness of the gland in comparison with the size of the organ, the very slight development of the frena and nymphæ, are the principal elements which enable us to make a positive diagnosis and to say with certainty in the presence of two hypertrophied clitores: "here the hypertrophy is due to masturbation and Saphism; there it is owing to a physiological malformation." (Martineau.)

Here we bring to a stop our quotations from Martineau, the eninent gynæcologist, carried off by premature death from the world of French Medical Science.

The Tribades and Fricarelles of the Court of France, by Brantôme.

In company with other writers, we have pointed out in this chapter the development of Saphism in the upper classes. Now, in this, they do but follow the example given by the ladies of the Court of France from the time of Henri II. to that of Henri IV. It is enough to refer to Brantôme.

CHAPTER X

Masculine Prostitution and Blackmail.

Various Definitions of Pederasty.—Sodomy and Anal Coition, by Raffalovich.—Acquired and Non-Morbid Pederasty.—Active and Passive Pederasts.—Moll's Opinion of Pederasts.—Pederasts and Inverteds, by Dimitri Stefanowski.—Various Causes of Pederasty.— I. *Pederasty from Lust or from Taste.—The Origin of Pederasty from Lust, by Krafft Ebing and Moll.—Pederasty from Taste belongs to all Classes of Society.—The Pederast Lord.*—II. *Professional Pederasty.—Professional Pederasts, by Coffignon.*—Rivettes, *Little Jesuses, Filles Galantes and Pierreuses.—The Aunts.—A Bal Masqué at the Opera.—The Portrait of the Duchess.—The Marriage of Pederasts.—Pederasts, by Canler.—Pederasty at the Brothel.—Masculine Prostitution in the Streets.—The Street-walking of the little Jesus.—Pederast Prostitution and Blackmail.—Pederast Prostitution and Murder.—The Blackmail of Pederasty in the Year of Grace 1898.*

Various Definitions of Pederasty.

If we hold to the strict definition of Tardieu and Littré, the Pederast is the man who loves children, independently of the sexual satisfaction which he seeks to obtain from them. He is therefore an inverted of a particular species. We have seen that Martineau gave the name of *Sodomy* to anal coition. Now custom has applied the name of *Sodomists* to the men who practice anal coition with women, and that of *Pederasts* to those who seek for the same anal coition with men. We have accepted these definitions.

The name of *active pederast* is given to those who themselves perform anal coition, and that of *passive pederast* to those who lend themselves to the operation and take the part of the woman.

It will thus be observed that the word *pederast* has been diverted from its original signification.

But an agreement upon this question has not been arrived at by the leaders of Medical Science.

Tardieu and the representatives of his school have made the capital distinction between Inverteds and Pederasts. On the other hand, Laupts and Raffalovich in all cases see only *innate or occasional Inverteds.* Raffalovich calls Oscar Wilde a paidophile inverted. These authors therefore have retained for the word *Sodomist* its strict definition, and apply it only to the follower of anal coition in the man as well as in the woman.

Sodomy and Anal Coition by Raffalovich.

Raffalovich's argument in fact is as follows: "This kind of coition (anal), we are told in books which treat on the subject of lunacy, is rare among the inverteds of Europe. We have already seen that it is a deviation of the habitual physical desires of the Uranist. If we still feel surprise that this kind of coition is not the natural object of the Uranist, we have but to remember that in the natural and uninstructed condition, vaginal coition is not the natural and indispensable object of the desire of the young boy or the young girl. Let us remember the story of Daphnis and Chloe. And among civilized, and highly civilized men in Asia and Europe, this is not always what they ask of the woman they love, nor is it above all the object of their dreams regarding her. Moreover, anal coition being contrary to the point of view of the European, from the fact that he is a European, it can naturally be understood that it does not appear to the inverted as the object of his love and his desire, unless he is very young, very ignorant, and very much in love with him who is the male, and believing that he will in this way compete with the woman's sex.

I do not deny that the Uranists in Europe who revolt at the idea of Sodomy, and who on this accout think themselves very superior to Sodomists, would not thus revolt if they had been born in China, Africa, Turkey, Persia or Afghanistan—I do not say in Italy.

It remains an undeniable truth that the inverteds of Europe, (perhaps because Sodomy has been treated so severely, because it has been the excuse for certain punishments, because it is generally and commonly considered as the object of inverteds, because it is often painful to perform both for the active and passive participator, and because gross, ignorant, uneducated individuals do not hesitate to indulge in it), do not commit the act of anal intromission, or do not suffer it except from lewdness, gross brutality, or ignorance, because they believe that it is the Greek love, because they imagine that it is complete unisexual love, not knowing that it is a deviation of heterosexual love.

As for the effeminated or passive pederasts who, for one cause or another, do not like to perform the suction of the penis, or who, in consequence of their physical conformation, (extreme thinness, painful or over sensitive penis, etc.) are not suited for anterior perineal coition, Sodomy represents to them the physical ideal. And even these individuals would be content with the usual coition between the buttocks, if their vanity and passivity did not place them in the power of debauchees who are intent on trying everything, and who take advantage of their docility.

We have here reached the confines of madness and crime: passive Sodomy touches on madness, and active Sodomy on crime. Ignorance, vanity and grossness impel men to it who are neither lunatics nor criminals, as well as local morals. It may be objected that debauchees having no reason to tell the truth on this subject, and Sodomy without violence leaving no indelible traces which have been enumerated, the question is and will remain obscure.

The essential fact is that all inverteds would be agreed to urge that the law should be set in action against Sodomists exclusively among unisexuals, and that they themselves should not be regarded as offenders in their pleasures, their rights or their loves. This fact is certain and of great practical importance. (Raffalovich, *op. cit.*)

Acquired and Non-Morbid Pederasty.

Krafft Ebing, and Chevalier after him, appear to us to be more correct in their views than Raffalovich. Let us quote their opinion.

Pederasty represents one of the most frightful pages in the history of human debauchery.

The motives which lead to pederasty in a man who *originally* is of normal sexual sentiments and healthy mind, are various. It may serve temporarily as a means of sexual satisfaction in default of normal means, just as, in rare cases, bestiality occurs in consequence of forced abstinence from normal sexual enjoyments.

It takes place on board ships on a long voyage, in prisons, convict establishments, etc. It is highly probable that, when a number of individuals are brought together, there are some who have a very low standard of morality and very strong sensuality, or that there are veritable Uranists who become the seducers of others. Pleasure, the imitative instinct, and rapacity do the rest.

However, it is a very characteristic proof of the genital instinct, that these motives are sufficient to overcome the horror of this unnatural act.

Another category of Pederasts is represented by those old *roués* who are satiated with normal sexual enjoyments and who find in Pederasty the means of rekindling their voluptuous feelings, the act having for them the charm of novelty. They stimulate temporarily by this means their diminished psychical and somatic powers. This new situation renders them, so to say, relatively potent, and gives them enjoyments which sexual intercourse with women cannot offer them. In course of time, the power for the pederastic act also disappears. Then these individuals may come to passive Pederasty as a passing stimulant to render them capable of performing active Pederasty, just as occasionally they have recourse to flagellation and to the contemplation of lascivious scenes. (Case of Bestiality quoted by Maschka.)

The end of the sexual activity in individuals affected with such moral degradation, consists in acts of immorality of all kinds with children, *cunnilungus*, *fellare*, and other horrors.

This kind of Pederasty is the most dangerous, for individuals of this sort pursue young boys above all in the majority of cases, and corrupt them body and soul.

The observations which Tarnowsky has collected on this subject in Society at Saint Petersburg are horrible. There are schools which are the theatre and foci of Pederasty. Old *roués* and Uranists play the part of seducers. At the beginning it is a painful matter for the person seduced to perform this disgusting act. At first he has recourse to his imagination and evokes the image of a woman. Little by little he grows habituated to this abomination. Finally, like the man who is sexually led astray by masturbation, he becomes relatively impotent in the presence of a woman and at the same time lustful enough to take pleasure in this perverse act. According to circumstances, this individual becomes a venal male prostitute.

That these facts are not uncommon in large towns has been shown us by the observations collected by Tardieu, Liman and Taylor. It is evident from numerous communications which I have received from Uranists, that there is a professional prostitution in existence, and that there are veritable houses of prostitution for intercourse with male individuals.

It is also a noteworthy fact that artifices of coquetry are employed by these male harlots, under the form of toilette luxuries, perfumes and feminine apparel, in order to attract Pederasts and Uranists. This intentional imitation of the pecularities of the woman is also to be found spontaneously among the congenitally inverted and sometimes in (morbid) sexual inversion.

Active and Passive Pederasts.

The theory held by Raffalovich appears to us ingenious, but it fails to agree with certain facts and cannot explain them all. It makes Pederasts a mere subdivision of the inverteds, while we have seen Tardieu, on the other hands, grouping together all inverteds under the general heading of Pederasts.

Krafft Ebing, for his part, has sought for the explanation of this division of pederasts into active and passive, in the nature of the anal act. "As regards the form of the sexual satisfaction, we may in short characterize the different categories of men who love men by this feature, that the congenital Uranist only becomes a Pederast exceptionally, and that he is brought to it eventually after having tried and exhausted all the other acts of immodesty which are possible between individuals of the male sex.

"Passive Pederasty is ideally and practically the form which corresponds to the sexual act. The Uranist performs active Pederasty out of complaisance. The essential fact is his congenital and unalterable inversion. It is not the same with the Pederast who has become so by training. He has behaved sexually in a normal manner or at least he has felt so; and episodically in his hours of freedom, he has still had relations with the other sex.

"His sexual perversity is not original or unalterable. He begins with Pederasty and finishes eventually with other sexual practices which are still possible, in spite of the weakness of the centre of erection or of the centre of ejaculation. His sexual desire, when he is at the apogee of his powers, is not for passive but for active Pederasty. However, he agrees out of complaisance or from the greed of the male harlot to lend himself to passive pederasty; sometimes also it is his means of stimulating his powers which are on the way to extinction, in order to be still able from time to time to perform active Pederasty."

Krafft Ebing therefore clearly distinguishes the fundmental difference which separates the Inverted from the Pederast. But while severely stigmatizing the latter, he mitigates in some measure the over-severity of the judgment of Tardieu and his school.

"We leave aside the question of knowing in what degree Pederasts by breeding may be considered physically and morally normal. It is probable that the majority of them suffer from congenital neuroses. In all cases *we find transitions which almost blend with acquired congenital inversion*. Nevertheless, speaking generally, we cannot have any doubt regarding the responsibility of those individuals who are far beneath the female prostitute."

Kraft Ebing therefore disagrees to a very considerable extent with Raffalovich, or rather it is the latter who disagrees with Kraft Ebing, Moll, Chevalier and Laupts. The opinion of these latter seems to us to be the correct one.

Opinion of Moll upon Pederasty.

"As we have already said, the immission of the virile member into the anus of an individual of the male sex, is generally designated in Germany by the name of Pederasty. In this act, one is active, namely he who introduces it, and one is passive, namely he who receives it into his anus. The majority separate very clearly active from passive Pederasty, by admitting that when relations of this kind occur between two individuals, one is always active and the other passive. Coffignon, who has made a valuable study of this question in Paris, shares this opinion and believes that, in homo-sexual love, this separation is much clearer and more decided among men than among women. I believe however, that it is quite as much decided, if not more so, among women as it is among men. The one who takes the passive part is often designated by the term *Cynede;* but this word is more especially applied to designate those passive Pederasts who take money for their services. However, Mantegazza uses the word *Cinedi* to designative active Pederasts, and reserves the word *Patici* for passive Pederasts. I knew of several cases in which this separation between active and passive Pederasts is not very rigorous, and these cases are the more important for us to know as Pederasty is in short *rather uncommon.*"

The origin of pederastic lewdness is therefore perfectly indicated by the representatives of the German School and by those of the Modern French School. We shall, in consequence, reserve the generic term of Pederast for application to the individual who indulges in anal coition with another male, and, with Tardieu and Chevalier, retain the difference between the passive and the active Pederast, while drawing attention to the fact that a considerable number of Pederasts are at the same time active and passive.

Pederasty and Its Agents.

These disputes about words might easily have been avoided if physicians had been willing to make use of the terminology employed by the German *savant*, Forberg: "This is all that we have to say concerning *fututíon.* Let us now allude to another kind of pleasure; that which the *mentula* takes by means of the anus. Whoever performs the act, the mentula when introduced into the anus *pedicates;* and he is called the *pedicator*, the *drauque,*' (active from δράω, I operate, I perform), and the one who is pedicated, *patient*, *cinede*, *catamite*, (from corruption of the word Ganymede), *aignon*, *effeminated;* the adult or emerited patient takes the name of *exolite.* The masculine pleasure (it is thus designated because women allowing themselves to be pedicated much more rarely than men, the more frequent usage of the word has determined the appellation), the masculine pleasure is tasted, either in the active part, which is that of the pedicator, or in the passive part, which is that of the patient." (Ch. Forberg. *Manual of Classical Erotology*, Latin text and literal English version. 2 vols., 8vo., Manchester, (Paris?)

But as this terminology has not been accepted, let us keep to the term *pederast* for pedication with the man, and *sodomist* for pedication with the woman.

The Russian professor, Dimitri Stefanowski, traces in a very clear manner the fundamental differences which separate the Pederast from the Inverted, and ranges himself on the side of the French School.

Pederasts and Inverteds, by Dimitri Stefanowski.

Active Pederasts, only true Pederasts, feel themselves attracted towards beardless youths of a feminine appearance. These Pederasts behave as real men: their way of feeling and acting always remains virile, for they have very often maintained relations with women, while as regards the Uranists these relations are absolutely impossible, since they feel towards women a "rivality of profession," which sometimes attains the highest degree of *horror feminæ*.

The preference of Pederasts for anal coition may easily be explained by a pathological association of a similar enjoyment and voluptuous sensation.

Lastly, I wish to show in a systematic table the differences between the two principal forms of Sexual Inversion, that is to say between Pederasty and Uranism.

Sexual Inversion.

Pederasty.	Uranism.
1. Pederasty seems to be acquired rather than innate: often appears at a rather late period, sometimes even only in old age.	1. It is absolutely innate and manifests itself in youth.

2. The manner of feeling and acting has remained masculine, the inclination for women sometimes continues.

3. The external appearance always remains masculine; the tastes and habits have continued virile.

4. The Pederast is attracted to boys of a feminine appearance (gitons.)

5. The Inclination is purely material and gross, and consists in the satisfaction of a brutal passion by anal coition.

6. Pederasty is often accompanied by Sadism as we see in the instances of Nero, Gilles de Rays, the Marquis de Sade, and so many others.

7. Pederasty is sometimes a vice, sometimes a disease: it frequently accompanies another psychical disorder, as epilepsy, senile dementia, or general progressive paralysis, of which it appears as a symptom.

2. The manner of feeling and acting is completely feminine; it is accompanied by envy and hatred towards women.

3. The external appearance sometimes becomes altogether feminine; the tastes, habits and occupations have become those of a woman.

4. The Uranist adores robust men, tall, bearded and hairy (drauci), the strong men, acrobats, and clowns at fairs, etc.

5. The Inclination is sometimes purely platonic, ideal, pure and disinterested. Anal coition is rarely practised. It is replaced by Onanism, and by buccal Onanism in particular.

6. Uranism is almost always accompanied by a state of more or less pronounced passivism.

N.B. This point is, in my opinion, of capital importance.

7. Uranism is always a disease, that is to say a congenital perversity; it is sometimes one of the symptoms of degenerescence, an episodical syndrome of Magnan. Perhaps it is caused by disorders during the embryonnic inter-uterine existence.

8. Pederasty may sometimes be restrained and repressed by an energetic effort of the will. It remains to be discovered if it can be cured by a rational treatment, appropriate to the circumstances, through hypnotic suggestion (Krafft Ebing), by the use of bromides (Hammond.)	8. The Uranic passion is absolutely beyond the government of the will. Its cure appears to be impossible, unless it is by a complete annihilation of all erotic passion by the prolonged use of anaphrodisiacs.
9. Pederasty as a vice or profession ought to be repressed and forbidden by the law; masculine prostitution ought to be severely prohibited.	9. Uranism, as an innate moral deformity, can never be punished or prosecuted by the law; nevertheless its manifestations ought necessarily to be repressed in the name of public morality, but its manifestations ought to be judged as an expression of a morbid condition, and as a kind of partial alienation.

(Dimitri Stefanowski. Laupts, *op. cit.*)

Various Causes of Pederasty.

In our study of Pederasty we will adopt the classification put forth by J. Chevalier. This author admits the existence of four principal causes of Pederasty: 1st, Pederasty from lust; 2nd, Professional Pederasty; 3rd, Pederasty through necessity; 4th, Pederasty through fear. To these four principal divisions, we will add two others: 5th, Pederasty through peculiar predisposition of the anus; 6th, Pederasty through disgust or hatred of the woman.

Let us study each of these principal causes or classes of Pederasty in succession, summing up the often contrary opinions of the different authors who have treated the subject.

I. **Pederasty from Lust or Taste.**

This is the most common form, and it has for its co-partner Professional Pederasty which lives upon it.

Those, and those only, are contained in this class, who display this contradictory feature that during a longer or shorter period of their life, have been in possession of normal sexual aptitudes, have had regular relations with the opposite sex, have sought after and performed coition, have even had children, and afterwards, when they have reached a certain age and exhausted the whole series of pleasures between the two sexes, have become addicted through satiated sensuality almost exclusively to unnatural relations: the vice has gradually installed itself by degrees.

There are some for whom the satisfaction of the sexual instinct is the sole aim, the sole preoccupation of life; they make everything subordinate to it, and to it they make all their activities contribute, and sacrifice everything. A period of genital maturity is passed in commerce with women; but after use comes abuse, and after abuse, satiety. At first, lawful pleasures are eagerly pursued; this however, is a daily fare, the monotony and insipidity of which soon makes itself felt. Under the influence of repeated shock the nervous system is unhealthily exacerbated and requires stronger and stronger excitations. Thus it happens that at a not very advanced age, individuals find that they have run through the whole scale of lust and performed every kind of sexual debauchery: one excess calls for another. Nevertheless, the mind is not satisfied and the pursuit of a never-attained ideal is soon complicated by the weakening of the genesic powers which gradually become refractory to natural excitants. The image of the woman loses its brilliancy; her form, her grace and her style of beauty can no longer be appreciated. At this period, by rest and by a wise direction of the genesic activity, everything will return to order; but, in the great majority of cases, this is not what occurs; the will still speaks when the senses are silent;

the desires continue with their former power, while the sexual vitality diminishes from day to day; in a word, there is no longer an agreement between the spinal and cerebral nervous centres. It is the head "which is corrupted," or wills without the power of carrying into effect. The imagination indulges in dreams; works, seeks, finds or invents. Fresh excitants and refinements hitherto unknown must be found at any cost, in order to re-awaken an energy which has disappeared. Obscure and unavowed desires take precise form; the individual seeks in the woman for the features, the general shape, the flat breast, the narrow pelvis and the short hair of the man, and perhaps will recover momentarily his vigour of former times. This is stepping back in order to take a better leap; women leave him decidedly impotent and finally inspire him only with disgust; on the other hand, unnatural actions no longer appear with that repugnant character under which they have hitherto been viewed. It is then that old debauchees have recourse in despair to the only means which remains to satisfy their desires, to pederasty.

But there are degrees even in this abject condition. Active pederasty is at first practised exclusively; it is sufficient to produce the excitation, and the sensation of these individuals restores to them their powers and renders enjoyments possible to them which they no longer find anywhere else.

At length, the aptitude for active pederasty becoming paralyzed in its turn, they indulge in passive pederasty which may cause them to recover momentarily their active powers; or forms a compensation, and finally they have recourse to buccal onanism, the last stage of depravity, the end of all genesic power.

Use and abuse of sexual pleasures, consecutive satiety and neurasthenia, impotence in presence of the woman, disgust of natural relations, pederasty. Such is the path ordinarily pursued by those individuals whom Casper and Tardieu looked upon as old libertines at the end of their resources. Let us add to this, as frequently concomitant conditions of origin, the spirit of imitation, that mark of the absence of personality in individuals, morbid curiosity for the unknown, love of the extraordinary, a wish to astonish, a certain parade of vice, weakness of the moderating powers, and absence of moral sense, when solitary onanism dating from early manhood has not brought on sexual neurasthenia and diminished the inclination for the woman. (J. Chevalier, *op. cit.*)

The Influence of Dissoluteness upon Pederasty, by Moll.

Moll is not altogether of the same opinion as Krafft Ebing, Chevalier and Laupts with regard to the origin of Pederasty proceeding from dissoluteness.

A certain number of authors attribute to a dissolute life and to the abuse of normal coition, the same etiological part as is played by masturbation. Coffignon, who upholds this opinion, particularly states that these cases occur principally among persons who are in easy circumstances. I do not believe that this is true, nor do I admit that men of dissolute life become addicted to Pederasty with the sole object of discovering new pleasures, as often as it is stated.

Even from the theoretical point of view, it is not impossible to find a relation between excess of coition with women and the development of the inclination for the man. How, in fact, can a man who feels sexual aversion for another man, find himself attracted to him one day, for the sole reason that he has made au excessive use of women? It is as impossible as to see a man who is satiated with pastry and cakes, seized one day with a passion for the mud and filth that is thrown into the street.

If the abuse of women really conduces to Pederasty, it should be admitted, on the same grounds, that homo-sexual love, long indulged in, ought also to to lead, through disgust, to the return of the inclination for women. Unfortunately it is not so and I am not acquainted with a single case of this kind.

Moll's theory is ingenious and constitutes a true sophism. It disagrees with the medical observation of the three authors whom he contradicts, and who consider inveterate dissolute life to be a powerful cause of Pederasty.

Prderasty from Taste belongs to all Classes of Society.

The Pederast from taste belongs to all classes of Society. This fact, pointed out by Tardieu, is confirmed by a number of authors, and by Chevalier in particular.

Frequently they are learned, distinguished, and even refined men. occupying a conspicuous position in the world and good situations, in the full enjoyment of all their faculties and reasoning powers; they sometimes have an illustrious name, a large fortune, a wife, children, and everything which ordinarily contributes to happiness. They perform all their duties with ability, and apparently lead a regular life; nothing allows the aberration to transpire, when a fine day comes which compromises their name, their family, their position and their fortune, and shatters all their honourable and laborious past. The passion masters them to such a degree that they do not shrink from being compromised in any way, nor from incurring any danger in order to satisfy it; they deliberately expose themselves to swindling and blackmail, to robbery and even murder.

Pederasts from taste are the true pederasts: these are the men who keep alive and maintain pederastic prostitution, the favours of which they purchase.

In short, pederasty in this case appears rather as a means of excitation than as an object; and it is the active part which, for the greater part of the time, is its tangible manifestation.

The name of amateurs or *Rivettes* is given to these Pederasts from inclination.

We give below the history of one of these amateurs, who are much more common than is supposed.

A Pederast Peer.

Lord Malwitch had resided for three years in Paris, and the old gentleman's false air of brilliant youth fully justified the saying attributed to a witty writer: "Take away from him all that does not belong to him and he will be as dead as a door-nail." He was to be seen in the Bois in an open carriage painted yellow, drawn by two magnificent steppers and driven by an Indian dressed in a kind of yellow livery; he was to be seen at all the first nights enthroned in a box and always accompanied by his groom in brilliant livery.

Except for his visits to the theatre and his drives, Malwitch hardly left his villa in the Avenue Saint James.

The old man surrounded himself with impenetrable mystery. In the opinion of some he was an exiled sovereign of a vast Empire spending in Paris the money for which he had sold the Crown diamonds; others thought that he was a high official of the East India Company; others again, that he was a spy in the pay of Germany. The reporters questioned the men-servants who, by their master's orders, replied only: "My lord is an Englishman; he has a title, he is exceedingly rich; my Lord requests that you will not call again." The police suspected the stranger of being concerned in an indecent assault committed in the Valois Gallery of the Palais Royal; enquiries were made, but the matter was hushed up.

He whom Madame Lemercier—an illustrious matron—called her best client, suffered from and yet enjoyed a peculiar monomania, and the pleasure and the pain of this exceptional case had a curious origin.

When he left the military academy, Lord Arthur, a younger son, went out to India with the rank of Lieutenant of Lancers in Her Britannic Majesty's Service, and amidst the enervating solitude of a small town in Bengal, in a fiery climate deadly to the European, the young man braved the chance of sun-stroke, and after the manœuvres of his regiment and the parades of the Sikhs and Gourkhas, he rode or took long walks in the country in order that he might obtain a thorough knowledge of it. Profiting by his leave of absence, he traversed the immense forests in which rose giant edifices and ancient pagodas; he studied archeology, and investigated the ancient remains ever living in their casings of stone. A man of high courage, he visited the temples with hardly any escort, studied the languages and penetrated the inner life of the various castes, from the Brahmin who sees men bow and lick the dust before his yellow robe, the juggling, snake-charming fakirs, and the voluptuous dancing-girls, to the miserable pariah, the beast of burden, hiding in the verdant depths his indolence, his misery and the ignominies of Sodom and Gomorrah.

Shortly the officer began to write the history of this people; he had it printed in the metropolis and soon received news of his election as a member of the Archeological and Anthropological Societies; he also sent home specimens of the Indian fauna and flora, and his learning received recognition at the hands of the Zoological Society as well.

Lord Arthur identified himself with the manners and customs of the country; he was unable to resist their attractive influences. An animation hitherto unknown displayed itself in this officer but lately so correct, so haughty, so glacial in his red tunic with white facings, with his gold epaulets and crossed shoulder-belts, wearing a white helmet with a green veil which sheltered his face from the terrible heat of the sun. There were a few unimportant drills of an evening, sometimes a military expedition or some rapid skirmishes, the few distractions of garrison life, the leisure occupations of an army of more than three hundred thousand men including the natives. During the day, Lord Arthur lay upon his mat of rice-straw with a cigarette between his lips, and around him the nautch girls, hired from the neighbouring temple, performed lascivious dances, or cooled him with their fans of peacocks' feathers. By night the dancers pirouetted by the flare of torches, and by night and day the gallant officer gave lustful tokens of his susceptibility to their personal charms.

When he gained the rank of Captain, he was suddenly driven from his terrestrial paradise by news coming from London of a double loss which had befallen him; his elder brother had died from the results of an accident while riding, and his father had succumbed to his grief at the death of his son. Arthur Malwitch sent in his resignation, and found himself all at once in possession of an immense fortune and of a seat in the Upper House. Tall and distinguished-looking, his face framed in a red beard with the reflection of Eastern lights in his eyes, he initiated the English ladies into the maddening scenes of Oriental lust. Then, fleeing from the fogs of the Thames and the dull routine of political talk, he took a journey round the world, visiting Russia, Siberia, the Caucasus, Sweden, Norway, Lapland, America, from the icy Polar regions to the burning prairies and the Brazilian deserts. He explored Central Asia, Corea, Japan, China, Africa and Oceania; from every people of the earth he enquired the secret of their passion, and when he returned to London worn out and wrinkled, his nocturnal meetings were talked about in whispers.

Almost an old man, he rebelled against the inevitable advance of age; he wished to remain young, and he first dyed his beard and then shaved it off; his wrinkles he covered over with cosmetics. His hair began to fall off, and enraged at the absurd results of infallible hair-restorers, he took to wearing a wig. He tried to overcome the feeling of despair which crept over him; he applied himself with faith and ardour to fresh archeological researches, but the reports which he sent to the learned societies were but caricatures of their predecessors. Then his monomania began. In its first evolution, Malwitch imagined himself to have been born and to be living in the different countries through which he had travelled; at length the monomania cast aside the variety of phenomena and established itself on one central point: when he was at his Hotel in Piccadilly in London, the traveller imagined himself at Constantinople; his dining-room became a mosque, his drawing-room a harem; he went into Westminster Abbey as though it had been the basilica of Saint Sophia, and the smoky Thames assumed to his eyes the enchanting aspect of the Golden Horn.

Unfortunateiy his diseased mind was not satisfied with changing old London into Stamboul, and his body also adapted the customs of the Holy City. His friends and colleagues were concerned at his proceedings, and the "Pall-Mall Gazette" revealed the sodomist orgies of Lord Malwitch; the newspaper gave names and addresses, and had it not been for his title as an English peer and his renown as a *savant*, he would have been charged at the Old Bailey. (Dubut de Laforest, *op. cit.*)

Professional Pederasty.

We now come to pederastic prostitution, a far more ignoble trade than female prostitution. It is inseparable from Pederasty by inclination, and it is impossible to study one without the other. Tardieu has the particular merit of bringing it to our knowledge: we shall not however tie ourselves down to giving his opinion *in extenso*, as we shall also have recourse to other authors (Caspar, Brouardel, Carlier, Canler and Coffignon), who have completed the studies of Tardieu.

Professional Pederasts. *Rivettes, Little Jesuses, Filles Galantes and Pierreuses. Aunts. A Pederast at the Opera Masked Ball. The Portraits of the Opera Masked Ball. The Portraits of the Duchess. The Marriage of Pederasts. The Renifleurs.*

Coffignon admits a division of active and passive Pederasts into two classes.

The first consists of amateurs, *entreteneurs* and *souteneurs;* the second is subdivided into *little Jesuses, Jesuses* and *Aunts.*

Pederasty is not like Saphism; in the former the parts taken are clearly divided.

The amateurs or *rivettes* are the Pederasts who are ashamed of their vice. Belonging to families of honourable position, occupying a high rank in society, having a position in the world, they are compelled to use discretion and to take great precautions in satisfying their vice. Houses of assignation, even the tolerated houses and the lodgings of swell women who are all connected in some way or other with passive Pederasts, offer them a secure rebreat.

Some of these amateurs prefer to go and seek for adventures in solitary places, in the Champs Elysées, or at the landing stages on the Seine. In order to avoid the remote risk of blackmail, they incur the imminent danger of being arrested; but it must be admitted that in the case of Pederasty, fear is a sentiment which doubles the power of the sensation.

The *entreteneurs* are hardened Pederasts, who are perfectly aware of the dangers to which they expose themselves, but, as I have said before, finding in them a spice which makes them brave everything. Generally, these *entreteneurs*, although they are perfectly well acquainted, flee from one another and endeavour to be alone. It is rarely that they group themselves in bands of five or six individuals, and sometimes more. We shall meet with them by and bye.

The *souteneur* is the Pederast who has been previously convicted, and lives with a *jesus;* he sends him out as a decoy, looks after him and blackmails his clients. He also waylays his victims by night. He lives with others very often in a band; from time to time the band is increased by another member, always either an active or a passive Pederast, to whom is given a *man* or a *woman* according to his tastes.

This is called making up a marriage. One of these ruffians who was captured three years ago, used to celebrate these kinds of marriages in a chapel which he had set up near the Halles. The chief of the band, clad in priestly robes, united the filthy couple. Afterwards there was a banquet. In the evening, all the affiliated members were bound to come and "see the newly-married couple into their new abode." The nuptial chamber was furnished at the expense of the community.

It was on leaving one of these strange wedding-parties that the associates took it into their heads to garrotte a passer-by in the middle of the Rue Rochechouart. The result was unfortunate for them, for they bungled the affair, and, being somewhat unsteady on their legs, were unable to get away when the police came up.

It is the active *souteneurs* who train the passive agents of Pederasty. The *little Jesuses* are originally children of a vicious turn of mind, who, impelled by their evil instincts, have begun to prowl about in solitary places of an evening, unaware themselves what evil spirit is prompting them. Just like female prostitutes, they commence with chance lapses from the path of virtue, until the day when they find a *souteneur* Pederast on their track.

Then a complete transformation takes place in them; they become what a fresh hand is among prostitutes. The *souteneur* teaches the young boy how to paint his face, how to soften his voice and give it a high note, to stick out his hinder parts in a short jacket, to put on an affected manner and to feminize his whole person.

The *little Jesus* begins by leaving his work, and soon after runs away from home. From that time forth he is irredeemably given over to anti-sexual prostitution. Experience coming to him little by little, he tries to break off his relations with his *souteneur*. The latter is never jealous of the lucrative infidelities committed by the *little Jesus*, but it is not the same if he shows a desire to abandon him.

To rid himself therefore of his companion, the little Jesus often has recourse to informing against him. Besides, the anonymous letter is the principal weapon in use among all Pederasts; these individuals are always the incarnation of cowardice allied to ferocity.

The *little Jesus* is usually between 15 and 20 years

of age when he undergoes his second transformation. He then becomes a *kept woman* and is in partnership with one or with several individuals. We shall return again to this subject: let us first finish with the various stages of passive Pederasty.

By plucking out the hair on his face, by care of his person, by retaining his childish ways and by painting his face, the *little Jesus* succeeds in retarding the period of adolescence until he is 25 years old, which is the extreme limit. He then becomes a *Jesus*.

Many *Jesuses* however have never played the part of a *kept woman*. They have been nothing else than obliging *valets de chambre*, or have acted as hair-dressers, *café*-waiters, etc.

The *Jesuses* are divided into three classes: *filles galantes*, *pierreuses*, and *domestics*. The *filles galantes* are *Jesuses* who have fallen again into the power of the *souteneur*, carrying on operations in the same way as prostitutes who keep a man on their earnings. The *pierreuses* correspond to the old and worn-out female prostitutes who infest the quays, the benches in the Champs Elysées, or the thickets in the Bois de Boulogne.

Lastly, the *domestics* are Jesuses looking for employment as *valets de chambre* with a Pederast, to satisfy the latter's passions in their own person, or to serve as pimp for him among the *little Jesuses*. Other *Jesuses* take situations as *femmes de chambre* with *Jesuses* who are being kept; but all this comes to the same thing in the end; they spend in the one situation or the other the time necessary to collect the evidence which will enable them to obtain an honourable livelihood by blackmail in their old age.

The last variety of passive Pederasts is that of *aunts*. All the former categories are usually wrongly grouped under this generic name. The *aunt* is the *souteneur* of a female prostitute, seeking for commerce with women against the interests of other Pederasts, and only indulging in pederasty for the purpose of gain or blackmail.

In spite of this distinction, the aunt partakes for the most part of all the other generic traits of his congeners, and notably in their ferocity. This ferocity is so characteristic, that when a large number of wounds are found to have been uselessly inflicted upon the corpse of an individual who has been murdered by some person unknown, the first enquiries about it are made in pederastic circles.

The pederast murderer indulges in unreasoning passion upon the corpse of his victim; he "sees red" more than anyone else. He frequently attacks the genital parts, when the body is already but a corpse.

This account has sufficed to clear the ground for us. The various personages who play a part in Pederasty are brought upon the field. We shall now see the puppets work.

It is midnight; we are at the entrance of the Opera on the night of a masked ball. There is a general agreement that it is tiresome and unfashionable, and yet everybody crowds there in search of the least intrigue and of the slightest scandal. Ah! if all the bored and wearied individuals had but eyes to see and ears to hear, they would not regret beforehand the empty night which they are going to spend.

Here is a young woman who is just entering, leaning on the arm of a perfectly correct gentleman. She leaves behind her a perfume of ylang-ylang. The women turn round to take in the details of her trailing gown, the work of a fashionable dressmaker; the men try to catch a glimpse of her face and opine that she is pretty under the mantilla and mask which hide her features.

Let us follow her to the box which she has opened for her and where she finds herself admidst a joyous party. Let us listen, if you like, to the chatter which goes on among these women amidst the rustling of fans.

"How are you, my dear? Take off your domino. It is really too hot in this box."

"I compliment you, dearest, you are looking your best to-night."

"Has Valentine told you if La Roussotte will be in our party to-night?"

"No, I have not seen him ... Oh, dear me, I have forgotten my powder box!"

"I will lend you mine, dear."

"Where are you going to have supper to-night?"

"Gaston is going to take me to X ... 's."

And the conversation continues full of these nothings in which fast women nevertheless find so much to interest them; if one among the attendant cavaliers wishes to take liberties of a too indecent nature, a rap with a fan recalls him to order.

At one of these balls, I was much interested and puzzled by one of these boxes, which seemed to contain a large and merry party. At one period, the door was closed, and it seemed to me as if one of the boxkeepers was specially posted in the neighbourhood to prevent any disagreeable interruption while an amorous interview was in progress.

The rest of the party were scattered about in the corridor, and I more particularly remarked a young woman who was carrying on an outrageous flirtation with a middle-aged man. I was not the only observer, for, a few paces off, a very high functionary who has since become Prefect of Police, was attentively watching the behaviour of this couple.

I passed close by him and bowed, thinking that I might ask him the young woman's name. Before I could open my mouth, he appeared to divine my question, for he said to me, at the same time turning away:

"Come and see me to-morrow, or the day after to-morrow ... I shall be very pleased to see you ... We can then have a talk ..."

I did not stop, but went to see him a few days after at the Prefecture of Police, where he did not as yet occupy the chief post. After a short preamble, this amiable functionary opened a drawer and took out of it a photograph which he placed before me.

"But that is the young woman who was at the Opera!" I cried out directly.

The photograph represented a young woman leaning on her elbows at a window, with her head covered with a mantilla, and resting upon her nervous and slender hands; the eyebrows were well marked, the nose delicate, and the lips smiling so as to give a sight of the superbly regular teeth.

"What is her name?" I cried, expecting to hear a story by the manner in which the photograph had been presented to me.

He mentioned an old historical name which during latter years has been mixed up with interminable law-suits, brought to an end by the death of another duchess, also named De C...

"The Duchess de C...," I repeated, nonplussed... "Then it is the name of some celebrity of the half-world."

"You are very near the truth. But give me back that photograph and take a look at this."

The second photograph represented a young man of 16 or 18 years of age, with a bold expression, who looked like a precocious *souteneur*. The second photograph was, like the first, impressed with the stamp of the Prefecture of Police.

"Well?"

I expressed my opinion, and I must confess that it was not such as to give the future Prefect of Police a high idea of my perspicacity.

"Look at it again."

And placing the two photographs side by side, my interlocutor handed them to me concealing the upper and lower portions of each, so as only to let me see the faces. The resemblance appeared striking to me immediately.

"Brother and sister?"

"Closer than that... one and the same individual."

I then learned that the young woman who with such coquetry was attracting attention in the Opera lobbies was nothing else but a celebrity in pederastic circles.

This individual had been arrrested on numerous occasions. He had been sentenced to imprisonment, but as soon as he was set at liberty, he repeated the offence; at the present time he was profiting by the license of Carnival time to attend the masked ball in his woman's dress, which he could pass off as a disguise.

The Opera, during the nights of the masked balls, is perhaps the only place where Pederasty holds its meetings, openly for the initiated, but invisibly for all other individuals.

Pederasts who unite in bands generally display a greater amount of reserve, fearing that a scandal may arise which may react upon them and oblige them to disperse. Ordinarily, their meetings take place at the house of a *little Jesus* who is kept by somebody; the *little Jesuses* visit one another in turn; they have their 'at-home' days; they receive, and it is during these receptions that they deserve their name of *tapettes*, the slang term for a chatter-box.

It sometimes happens that a *little Jesus*, after having been closely shut up by a jealous protector for several years—during the flower of his youth, as he sorrowfully describes it—finds himself all at once abandoned without resources, through the death of his protector, or from some other cause: he swears that he will never again belong to a single master. In order to collect clients, he seeks for a place as page-boy in a hotel, or gets hold of rich foreigners. It is very unusual at the end of a few months for him not to possess a cosmopolitan circle of clients, the members of which forward him very regularly larger or smaller sums every month, and make a journey at fixed periods to Paris to visit him.

The bands of rich Pederasts celebrate their *unions*, just like the bands of ex-convicts. These celebrations consist of a banquet, followed by a nameless orgy; the men are in dress clothes, the *women* in evening dress. The principal Master of the Ceremonies is an old *Jesus*-Pederast; for the rest, only Pederasts are engaged as waiters and as musicians, when there is a dance.

I think I ought not to expatiate too long upon this category of *little Jesuses*, and I pass on to the *filles galantes*. These usually retain the masculine dress, but they give it an effeminate appearance by means of varnished shoes, neckties of soft stuffs, and long hair. In case they happen to be arrested in the public street, the feminine costume is in fact for them the occasion of unheard-of annoyances, the least of which are the amorous advances of drunken men shut up with them in the look-up, who mistake their sex, and irritated at the resistance they meet with, tear their dress to rags and leave them in a pitiable condition. These Pederasts practise solicitation in three different ways; by looks, provocation and touch.

The look is addressed to averred Pederasts whom they recognize as such; provocation is practised either verbally or by means of an indecent attitude; the touch is frequent in crowds, especially in the Palais de Justice, in that portion of the Courts reserved for the public. It appears at first as though it had taken place through inadvertence; if the individual solicited makes a movement of surprise, the *Jesus* retreats a short distance, leaving him to suppose that the gesture was as involuntary as it was unfortunate; if the subject, on the contrary does not stir, the *Jesus* grows emboldened and repeats his provocation.

When the *landing* has once been effected, whither do the Pederasts repair to perform their acts? In the first place to special hotels scattered almost everywhere about Paris, or to certain vapour-baths, or to shops which are kept by procuresses.

The Public Morals Department of the Prefecture of Police had been informed that one of these baths, situated in the middle of Paris, was, on certain days in the week, the theatre of absolute outrages upon public decency. In order to make sure of this, it was necessary to organize a systematic watch. It was arranged that the officers should go two by two in turn to take a vapour-bath. The first squads were unable to detect any acts of indecency. Finally, a whole brigade of officers was sent, and waited until the steam was turned off, about 10 p.m., before entering the sweating-room. They found out the secret, but as the principal actors were in bathing-drawers, it was impossible to arrest them as having been caught in the very act. The most comical part of the affair was that one of the two officers, a sturdy, well-built fellow, positively aroused the enthusiasm of one of the frequenters of the place who made profuse advances to him of the least equivocal nature. This was another reason to prevent the officers from taking any action, lest they should afterwards be accused of instigating to crime. As for the proprietor of the establishment, when severely called to task he affected surprise: "I don't know what you mean!" He knows still less about it to-day, if we may believe what we are told.

The shops which receive Pederasts are placid-looking curiosity shops or something of that kind. The amateur enters by the door leading into the street; the *fille galante* arrives by a door entering upon an inner court; the couple meet in a room behind the shop.

The *Jesuses* find invaluable allies in prostitutes; in return they warn the latter of the dangers which they may incur when they have seen anything unusual in the public street. Sometimes they associate themselves with them, giving them half their gains on condition that they harbour them and facilitate their relations.

During the daytime, solicitation is hardly practised except at the Hôtel Drouot, the Palais de Justice and the Bourse, under the peristyle, where the outside market is held, or in the public gardens when a military concert is going on. I have already remarked that Pederasts are very often devoted to music. Besides that, music attracts nurses and around them there are always soldiers fluttering about; now, the presence of soldiers is an attraction for *rivettes;* lastly, wherever there are active amateurs, there also passive Pederasts are always to be found. Need we recount under what circumstances a certain Pederast, a pianist as well as as Captain, was arrested in the neighbourhood of the Fort de Vincennes?

The *Pierreuse-Jesus* wanders about at random and

carries on his operations in the open air. He is to be recognized by certain very characteristic labial deformations.

Pederasts, according to Canler's Account.

Coffignon gives us a description of Pederasts at the present time. Canler, formerly Chief of the Police de Sureté under Louis Philippe and Napoleon III., has left us a faithful picture of the Pederasts of his time. It is curious to compare it with that of Coffignon. Canler gives to Pederasts the name of *antiphysitics*.

The *antiphysitics* who are ordinarily called *aunts*, are divided into four categories entirely distinct one from the other, by their habits, dress, and character. They are:

1st. The *Persilleuses*,

2nd. The *Honteuses*.

3rd. The *Travailleuses*.

4th. The *Rivettes*.

The first category is entirely composed of young men belonging for the most part to the working classes, who have been brought to this abject condition by a desire for luxury and pleasure, by greediness and laziness, the principal cause of the depravity of the larger number. Being of an apathetic temperament, they have left the laborious occupations of the workshop and asked from debauchery the means of an often precarious and always miserable existence. Known by the name of *persilleuses*, through their likeness to those women who in the public street incite the passers-by to improper acts, these young fellows are entirely different to other men in face, speech, dress, manners, and general appearance, They may easily be recognized by their likeness to the following type: the beard is completely and very closely shaved, the hair is worn long, greased and almost always curled at the ends; the drawling, weak, woman-like voice also adds to the illusion. The dress, without exactly being of a peculiar kind, displays in its various parts an exceptional appearance. The *persilleuse* always wears a neck-tie *à la Colin*; on his head there is a cap, the varnished leather peak of which falls over his eyes and serves in some sort as a veil; he wears a short frockcoat, or a vest buttoned so as to freely display his waist which is already held together by a corset; the trousers, of unmistakable English cut, have no buckle and are perfectly fitted over the loins; finally the dress is completed by varnished shoes or pumps. Noticeable by their face and dress, the *persilleuses* are also to be recognized by the way in which they endeavour to imitate as far as possible the gait of a woman, whose tastes and caprices these individuals affect in addition. They habitually frequent the Passage des Panoramas, the Passage de l'Opéra, and the Galerie d'Orléans at the Palais Royal, where they walk about in pairs. When their presence in these places causes too much scandal, when the inhabitants complain and the police are at length compelled to take measures against these individuals who offend against public morality, a dozen officers make a raid and carry off an equal number to the police-station, whence they are sent the next day to the Préfecture de Police. There they are kept administratively in prison for a few days; after that time they are released, and a month or two afterwards they have to be driven away again. This means is therefore insufficient to repress a permanent scandal, but it is hardly possible to take any other action against men who are not amenable to the penal law by this fact alone. Unless they are caught in the very act, and withont the application of simple regulations of police, which is often a difficult matter, what can be done? Perhaps there is a gap in our Code which requires to be filled up, or perhaps the spirit of the legislator has recoiled before the delicacy of such a task.

The *honteuses* form the second class. They are so called because the individuals who compose it, hide with the greatest care from every eye the vice which dominates them. Just as the *persilleuses* try to attract attention. so the *honteuses* endeavour to avoid it;

the former make it a profession, the latter only a matter of taste; and while the first-named wish to satisfy their brutal inclinations and draw from them a living which they are unwilling to extract from honest toil, the latter seek only to satisfy their own desires and to quench the impure flame which consumes them. The *honteuses* put aside and discard with the greatest care everything which may enable them to be recognized. Besides, as they dress like everybody else, there is nothing to betray them, if it be not their feminine voice. This category is composed of persons belonging to all classes of society, without any exception.

The third class is entirely formed of individuals belonging to the great family of labour and living only by the produce of their toil. From this comes their name of *travailleuses.* Dressed in a clean blouse and in a cloth cap with a peak descending over the forehead, they are perfectly recognizable by their languorous, drawling voice, and by their gait, which resembles that of the *persilleuses.* With them as with the *honteuses*, it is a matter of taste; only, in this case, there is less feeling of shame.

The fourth category is composed of *rivettes.* There is nothing about the latter to distinguish them from other men, and, to recognize them, the observer requires the greatest amouut of attention and knowledge. They are to be met with in all degrees of the social scale. To satisfy their inclinations, these individuals address themselves in preference to the young. Blackmailers therefore pay attention more particularly to *rivettes*, whom they almost always exploit with success. Nevertheless some of them are able to evade the toils of the blackmailer by taking into their own pay a *persilleuse*, a *travailleuse*, or a *honteuse*. I will mention, among others, a rich foreigner, an old man aged 70, related to one of the greatest families in the North of Europe, who came and took up his quarters in a sumptuous hotel in order to live there apart from the exigencies of society and to have complete freedom of action. He brought with him a young neophyte of the *honteuse* class, a boy of eighteen, with silky moustaches, a *retroussé* nose, and feminine voice and ways, whom he passed off as his nephew. He followed him like his shadow, and, like Henri III. and his boy-darlings, he passed his days shut up in his apartment, where his young man, dressed as a woman, employed himself in needlework, and in tapestry and embroidery. At dinner time, the pretended nephew resumed his masculine costume, and, when they finished their repast, the two inseparables took their carriage to go to the café to have a glass and read the newspapers; then, at ten o'clock, they drove back again to their villa. Such was their existence every day, and so the blackmailers never found an opportunity of putting his lordship under contribution.

The four categories which I have just sketched out, although very similar at bottom, hardly know one another. The *persilleuses* and *travailleuses* outwardly affect an extraordinary propriety, a kind of feminine coquetry, while inwardly they are repulsively filthy. It is impossible to imagine how they neglect the simplest attentions demanded by ordinary cleanliness. The body hidden beneath their clothes is never washed; their hands, which appear so white, soft and carefully tended, contrast with arms more dirty than those of a chimney-sweep. These creatures can only be compared to whited sepulchres which, perfectly clean outside, are full of nothing but rottenness. The *persilleuses* are fond of taking the names of courtesans celebrated in history; some call themselves, *Marion Delorme*, *Dubarry*, *Ninon de l'Enclos:* others join on to their own name a feminine epithet, and call themselves *pretty Adolphe*, or *pretty Alexander;* and others again have made themselves celebrated among all under the names of *La Palissandre*, *Le Rasoir*, *La Négresse*, *La Marinière*, etc. All or nearly all of them live by robbery and plunder. As for the *honteuses* and *travailleuses*, in default of morality, they possess a certain probity which, with some exceptions, they never lay aside.

To sum up, like the chameleon which changes, not its shape, but its colour, the *aunt* is sometimes called *tapette* and sometimes *serinette;* by sailors she (he) is designated *corvette*, but she (he) always remains an object of opprobrium.

Pederasty at the Brothel.

Coffignon has pointed out the assistance which public prostitutes, for money's sake, afford to Pederasts ot all kinds. Louis Fiaux, in his turn, denounces in indignant terms the pederastic practices which are the ordinary rule in brothels.

But in view of the number of pederastic clients who beset the tolerated houses, and are in continuous relation with the mistresses, there is room only for anger and prosecution by the authorities.

Simple as this avowal may appear, we will confess that even while writing this portion of the present work, it was our wish to obstinately doubt the accusations vaguely brought by this Chief against the tolerated houses. It seemed incredible to us that the vice of Pederasty could find public hospitality and protection in establishments said to be under the supervision of the police. It is nevertheless but pure simplicity to exempt from these unlawful practices the clients of these houses, and to make them the attribute only of the debauchees of high and low degree who freely carry on their operations elsewhere, in assignation houses, in our public gardens, on the seats in our avenues, and are to be met with in cabs and on the landing-stages and bridges of the Seine.

The tolerated houses are, on the contrary, thanks to the keepers of them, active centres of Pederasty.

The regulations prescribe very uselessly that no client shall be received who is under age, that no young child over six years of age shall be kept in the house, even though the proprietress herself is the mother: these prohibitions are evaded every day in the most open fashion (we shall return to the subject of minors further on), and on the other hand, Pederasts have no more devoted procuresses than the mistresses of these establishments. Tardieu, who was in no way opposed to the *police des mœurs*, has denounced the keepers of the houses in the following terms as favouring inversion. "One of them, he writes, was obliged to confess in the course of the course of a law-suit that two-thirds of the men who came to her house did so only to ask for little boys." The same medico-legist pointing out, with Casper, the taste of Pederasts for indecent pictures, extraordinary dresses and masquerading attire to be put on in the quarter of an hour of sexual aberration, mentions a house in the outskirts of Paris, in the back part of which were erected small rooms hung with obscene engravings with descriptions which left no doubt as to the vices which were concealed by the walls; in some of these rooms were found muslin chemises, veils of gold-net, garlands and crowns of artificial flowers which were used as attire in these strange moments.

Tardieu did but touch the fringe of the question as regards the tolerated houses.

We should like to place before our readers' eyes the precise information which has been given us, together with the names of the proprietresses, the addresses of the houses, and the hours at which this kind of commerce reaches it height at five or six of the large tolerated houses in the central quarters: they would see stationed in the cafés and wine-shops of the vicinity a number of young fellows of very dubious appearance; they would see coming and going under pretence of delivering various articles and of doing business within, boy-hairdressers, café-waiters, and lads from the taverns (looking as if they did no work); little pleasure-merchants who are nothing else but *Jesuses*, or *little Jesuses*, kept or sent for at the express invitation of the mistress of the house. The proprietress had recourse to the most shameful devices in order to procure these small boys, for "we have everything that is wanted." [1] One woman who keeps such a house, in order to evade the notice of the neighbouring shopkeepers before whose doors children and youths are obliged to pass, sometimes dresses them up as women, and makes them look older by fastening false beards on to them. Three years ago, a brothel in Paris of the second class was described to us as receiving several times a week a poor little boy 11 years of age, "utterly ruined," as our informant told us. The fashionable amateurs *(rivettes)*, finding in the tolerated house a security and discretion not afforded them in hired apartments, the door of which is not so well guarded, and where warning is not so casily given in case of a serious alarm, make use also of the services of the proprietress to procure them young fellows.

Under pretext of having a party of four, two men will enter together (a proceeding which gives no cause for suspicion), each select a woman and ask for the double-bedded room, of which we have already spoken; after indulging in improprieties of a natural kind, they send the women away and remain alone. This dodge is of frequent occurrence in tolerated houses, and nobody is surprised at it. The proprietress merely receives an extra payment, as may naturally be supposed. In the suburban tolerated houses, the proprietress always has a knowledge of some small apprentice, some vicious stable-boy, or of some young *souteneur* who has grown up under the shadow of the tolerated house, in the neighbouring workshops, livery-stables or wine-shops: immediately a request is made, she sends to look for "the young boy."

The presence of the Pederast in the tolerated house and the procuring of boys or young adults by the proprietresses, can be the better explained by the fact that the Pederast is not absolutely a misogynist. It is an opinion generally held, it is true, that the individual who is a prey to the vice of love of men never

[1] Notes collected by an Inspector of the *police des mœurs.*

seeks in any way for the possession of women, but it is a manifest error. Besides the facts which prove every day the falsity of this widely-spread assertion, there is a decisive reason, which is that the foundation of Pederasty is merely Sodomy, and almost every woman in the tolerated houses is addicted, and or more properly speaking is compelled to become addicted to sodomitical practices. The classifications of writers and police bureaucrats, forming as many chapters or paragraphs in their treatises and reports as the so-called distinct and separate vices which they pretend to find, are the absolutely arbitrary views of a mind which upsets the brutal reality of facts. The truth is that all these vices overlap and work into one another, and that the instinctive Pederast, who is absolutely a Pederast and anthropophile, such as has been studied in many cases by Tardieu and Casper, and recently by Charcot, Magnan, Ball, Krafft Ebing, Moll and Westphal, has a morbid ideal, we were about to say a pathological entity. His genesic aberration in any case is incontestably the principal episode of the hereditary degenerescence of his nervous system, a monomania as the old alienists called it, a partial delirium, as it is named by the contemporary school.

The ordinary Pederast, he who has been pursued by the Prefecture of Police with its sub-brigade of Inspectors since 1873, has arrived at this condition as the result of abuses of every kind which he has himself committed, or which another has committed upon his sexual organism, and in the immense majority of cases it is the premature use of women—a taste for whom he never absolutely loses—which first led him into this path. Acquired Pederasty is therefore quite the rule; it is the abuse of women, vicious feminine habits and alcoholism, the considerable part played by which in leading to it, must not be omitted.

Congenital Pederasty is the extremely rare exception. (Louis Fiaux. *op. cit.*)

We see by this quotation that Dr. Fiaux clearly

belongs to the old school of Tardieu. We may be permitted not to be of the same opinion as he, and we shall refer the reader to the preceding chapters in which we have studied sexual inversion in all its forms and contributed in a small degree to its study.

Masculine Prostitution in the Street.

The little *Jesuses* solicit in a public manner. The open air concerts in the evenings, the public promenades, the Boulevards, certain covered passages, the neighbourhood of the Opéra and the Palais Royal are their favourite hunting-grounds: eccentric manner of dressing, leers, affected ways, alluring looks, smiles, all is brought into play in order to ensnare the client. There is a well-known description by Tardieu of the appearance of Pederasts. "The curling hair, the painted complexion, the bare neck, the waist squeezed in, so as to display the shape; the fingers, ears and chest laden with jewellery; the whole person exhaling odours of the most penetrating perfumes; a handkerchief in the hand, as well as flowers or some kind of needlework: such is the strange, repulsive and suspicious appearance which betrays the Pederast. A no less characteristic trait which I have observed a hundred times, is the contrast between this assumed elegance and cultivated exterior with the sordid unclean linen which of itself would be sufficient to cause a distaste for these wretches." Tardieu confirms what Canler had previously remarked.

Chevalier observes that is a curious thing how this portrait reproduces almost feature for feature that which has been left by Latin authors: the same eccentric way of dressing, the same listless gait and lewd gestures, the same languor of look, the same profusion of perfumes and, apart from the *immodest finger*, the same general appearance of obscenity. Let us note, *en passant*, another coincidence; the *cynedes* at Rome had a preference for garments of a green colour. Now, a few years ago in Paris, a band of Pederasts was arrested who, as a conventional sign, had adopted a green neck-tie, (the Gilles and Abadie affair).

Must we see in these facts the mere effect of chance, or a very tenacious tradition in such matters? However this may be, they go to and fro in this get-up, giving vent to little bursts of shrill laughter, alone or in pairs, walking affectedly and swaying themselves on their hips, sticking out their chest and posteriors; with their mouth screwed up and a languishing look, they smile at every man they meet. Sometimes placing themselves in a crowd round a street-juggler, or before a shop-window where engravings are exhibited, they provoke and excite those standing behind them by "making lace," that is to say by moving to and fro their fingers crossed behind their back, or those who are in front of them by means of the *poussette*, that is by letting them feel a hard body, often a long cork, excite the senses of those who they think are likely to respond to their invitation; sometimes this behaviour results in their receiving a sound thrashing, but if they are successful, then there is a cab, a low-class hotel or restaurant close at hand, and well known to them to offer a shelter for the amours of the lewd pair.

We borrow from the works of the novelist D'Argis the picturesque account of solicitation by a little Jesus.

Solicitation by a little Jesus.

Cautious as regards his own temptations, Soran was but rarely alone, well knowing how harmful solitude might be to him. One night he chanced to be crossing the Champs Elysées as he was slowly making his way home.

It was hardly ten o'clock and the place displayed a peculiar appearance. Here and there, gleams of light and sounds of music were issuing from a few *café-concerts*, while all around them was plunged in silence and obscurity. Jacques walked on without looking about him and perhaps scarcely thinking, when a passer-by lightly brushed against him. He paid no attention, thinking it had been done through carelessness, when, a little further on, he again came across the same individual whom he had looked at mechanically a short time before. Soran was struck by his appearance. He had curly hair, his face was painted, his neck bare, and his waist squeezed in; he had projecting hips and he cast at Jaques an effeminate look which struck him as being strange. His hand was working to and fro in a disgusting way, while he protruded a portion of his nether garment in a provocative manner which could not escape Jacques' attention, and like some filthy nightmare he was clearly offering his girl-like body for a monstrous satisfaction. Jacques Soran shuddered at this strange obstinacy of fate. The enormous temptation of this protean Sodomy which had shown itself to him in such numerous shapes was again before his eyes.

He thought of Giraud whose ripe yet childish ways had perhaps sown in him the germs of a disease which he felt growing within. And now, in this retreat where he had thought to find shelter, had appeared...... Jacques had force enough to drive this image from his mind; he still thought of his first fall, the foretaste of delights now fully and completely offered to him. His feelings of curiosity held him to the spot, when he ought to have fled away. The individual of dubious appearance saw in this attitude a tacit encouragement, the only language which these creatures of strange sex address to one another. He came nearer to Soran and made some casual remark, as if he wanted to strike up an acquaintance; Jacques replied in monosyllables, but a reply was more than enough. He had a wish to learn about the matter, and so he talked, and the male prostitute's conversation agitated him strangely.

The fellow saw clearly that he had to do with a timid young beginner, and skilfully replied in advance to any objections which he might raise, confining himself, in view of eventualities, to generalities and to vague phrases which could be understood by the initiated alone; Jacques knew what he meant.

He grew more explicit. There would be no danger; there, on a seat behind the Café des Ambassadeurs it was very quiet. Even the policeman on his beat went a little out of his way so as not to disturb the people of good position who were in the habit of going there; and, with interested civility, he pointed out to Jacques an old gentleman who was hiding and waiting.

"He is an officer of the Legion of Honour," he said, "but he takes off his ribbon when he comes here."

Jacques listened with unwholesome pleasure.

"And do you only come here?" he said in a careless way.

"This is the place I prefer; but I sometimes go to the neighbourhood of the Grand Hotel; that's a good part because of the rich foreigners; or to the Palais Royal, or to the Tuileries."

"And," persisted Jacques, "have you many regular customers?"

"Oh yes!" he replied; and as though to prove it and tired of carrying on a useless conversation, he turned to go away. Jacques then felt himself seized with an insurmountable desire.

"Do you know of any less dangerous place?" he said.

The fellow smiled in a satisfied way; he had gained his ends. They both passed along through quiet streets. Jacques blushed as though he were ashamed of being seen in such company. Not far from the Rue de la Boétie, they stopped before a house of respectable appearance.

"This is the place," said his companion. He knocked at the door and gave a slight cough ... a stout woman received them very amiably and after a few words in slang which Jacques could not understand, they entered a luxuriously furnished apartment. Jacques would now have liked to go away, but he did not dare.

Thick red curtains hung before the windows, through which no sound could penetrate, and all round the room there were divans covered with cushions.

In a heap on the table, Jacques observed nuns'

dresses, women's corsets and drawers, peacock's feathers, pieces of wood shaped like phalli; in one corner, there was a lav-figure; a large dog of savage appearance leapt from an arm-chair and came and fondled him; on the walls were engravings in which a filthy imagination had depicted men in strange postures and contorsions satisfying their lust in monstrous fashion.

Jacques was ill at ease, and when his disgusting companion laid himself out on the sofa for an act of shameless passivity, Jacques Soran felt overcome with horror and loathing, and this filthy creature, unmentionable in any language, shocked him.

At this supreme moment, the past came up before him, and that past which had failed to ruin him, saved him from an ignoble stain. In a moment he thought of the days of his childhood, so good and pure, of his noble aspirations which once had raised him above the level of man, and, blushing at having fallen so low, he fled... (Henri d'Argis, *Sodome.*)

Pederastic Prostitution and Blackmail.

Pederastic prostitution inevitably entails blackmail which, though it is punished by our laws, still finds its victims among the *rivettes* who dread the revelations of the blackmailer. All the writers who have written on prostitution, feminine as well as masculine, have alluded to the prevalence of blackmail. Canler has devoted long pages to this subject and gives most circumstantial details, which we regret that space does not allow us to reproduce in this chapter. It will be sufficient for us to quote Tardieu and Coffignon.

It was under the form of masculine prostitution that the monstrosities of Greek or Socratic love, a worthy brother of the Lesbian love which threatens at the present day to be reproduced in the corruptions of certain circles, displayed themselves in ancient society in almost the full light of day. It was under this form that Zacchias observed it in Rome during the 17th century; that it is still met with in Italy where the stranger is followed by vile proxenetes who offer for his selection either a *bella ragazza* or a *bello ragazzo*; and that it is to be observed to some degree in French Africa, where the young Moors offer themselves, so to say, publicly, and where the shameful sore of Pederasty has increased to such an extent as to invade the Metropolis. Lastly, in Paris, pederastic prostitution has grown secretly to an almost incredible degree, and has admitted of a secret organization especially intended to foster that culpable industry known by the name of *blackmail*, the infamous details of which we have learned by the revelations of more than one well-known case, from the affair known as that of the Rue du Rempart, in 1845, in which forty-seven prisoners figured, down to those numerous prosecutions, which for several years, brought before the Correctional Tribunals bands of fifteen and twenty Pederasts at a time, and which, not so frequent now, seem to have wearied Justice without discouraging the culprits.

I have said that I should not recoil before the ignominy of the picture; it is thus that we must depict its most hideous features, and even borrow the language of the degraded beings, whose repulsive likeness we wish to try and sketch.

The men who practise that kind of knavery called *blackmailing*; and who, to use their own expression, *occupy themselves in politics*, are, generally, only thieves of a particular class, who, without being always themselves addicted to Pederasty, speculate upon the vicious habits of certain individuals, in order to attract them, by the bait of their secret passions, into the traps which they lay for them. Among them are to be found men who have grown rich by robbery and dressed with a certain refinement, and young boys whom they have corrupted and ruined, who are in their pay, whom they enlist and domineer over, and whom in their frightful cynism they designate as their instruments which they make use of to attract their dupes and seize their victims. These miserable children, sometimes led away from the honest toil of the work-shop, more often picked up in the streets or found when leading an idle life in places of ill-fame, are sent out each evening to quiet and well-known places where they may easily ensnare their wretched prey. When they have succeeded in finding someone to accost them, the individuals with whom they are in league present themselves at once, assuming the manner and the language of police-officers charged with the duty of maintaining the respect due to outraged morality, exact a heavy toll for their leniency, and only restore their dupes to liberty when they have received an often considerable sum as ransom.

Some play the double part of pander and blackmailer. After inciting the person who has accosted them to acts of impropriety, they change their tone all at once, *turn a somersault* as they say, and, giving themselves out as detectives, threaten an arrest unless their discretion in this respect is generously recompensed.

It is impossible to conceive to what an extent this criminal industry of theft in connection with Pederasty has been carried. The blackmailer does not extract all that he requires from his victim at the chance meeting in a public place. Accompanying to his domicile the wretched man who has not been able to pay for his silence on the spot, the pretended officer, who has succeeded in getting hold of a name and an address, assures himself in this way of a rich capture which he will exploit to a degree which exceeds anything which can be imagined. Blackmailers therefore take the greatest precaution to keep the secret of the discoveries which they make in this way, and to hide from the young fellows whom a moderate payment associates in their infamous manœuvres the precious mine which they wish to retain in their own possession. They thus form a circle of clients whom they pass on and dispose of to one another. A deplorable instance of this kind may still be remembered of a well-known scientific man whose name was published through the indiscretion of the judicial press, an indiscretion which we shall not imitate. The blackmailers had succeeded in inspiring him with such terror, that he never hesitated to submit to their demands, and some of them reckoned upon his purse as upon their own. For many years he allowed himself to be pillaged by several generations of swindlers, who bequeathed him as an assured income, and who on several occasions disputed at his door who should be the first to levy the almost daily tax guaranteed them by his shameful weakness. "It was not fifty thousand francs," one of these informants who had been the most active participator in these depredations, declared in Court, "it was more than a hundred thousand francs that he gave; it has gone on for the last thirty years; we ground him down; he has given to individuals who are dead and to others who have retired from business." Besides this monstruous case, I will quote another which gives, from a double point of view, a singular idea of the ways of Pederasts. In the affair of the Rue du Rempart, an old Englishman confessed that having already been the victim of the same kind of knavery, he took the precaution when he frequented the streets to satisfy his shameful passions, to put on mean attire and only to give away small sums, so as not to awaken the cupidity of those with whom his immorality brought him into relation. But his calculations were falsified by the cunning of two young rogues, who followed him to the fine hotel where he resided, and gaining admittance to his apartment, avenged themselves upon his assumed poverty by robbing him completely.

But, in the criminal practice of blackmail, pederastic prostitution occupies, so to say, but secondary rank. It is carried on also under other conditions, in which its true character and its analogy to feminine prostitution are more exactly revealed. Like the latter, it has its own special staff, its places devoted to meetings and its peculiar habits.

Pederastic Prostitution and Murder:
Blackmail is not the greatest danger which may be

incurred by a *rivette* who has been carried off by a *little Jesus.* Behind blackmail, in the case of Pederasts, lurks crime. Long is the list of all the victims of this ignoble vice, longer even than may at first appear, for many names do not figure in it for very different reasons.

How many nocturnal assaults, for instance, are only attempts at blackmail on the high road, transformed into assaults in consequence of victim's resistance to robbery? Tardieu has indicated this danger which the amateur Pederast incurs.

"There is one last point upon which we must insist as a terrible consequence of pederastic prostitution; namely the danger to which it exposes those who seek after its ignominious pleasures, and who have too often paid with their life for shameful relations which they have contracted with criminals. Instances of the murder of Pederasts are not uncommon; and the circumstances under which they have occurred have the characteristic that the victim has, in a way, gone of his own accord to meet the murderer. To quote those crimes only which have disturbed Paris, the murder of Tessié in 1838, of Ward in 1844, of Benoît and Bérard in 1856, of Bivél and Letellier in 1857, to which must be added that of the child Saurel, by Castex and Ternon in 1866, have revealed the cruel end for which those persons may be reserved who can only find among the vilest scum of the world those unavowed connexions from which they demand the satisfaction of their monstrous desires.

"A more recent case has shown that a violent death may overtake Pederasts under accidental circumstances, or in struggles provoked by their culpable relations. In 1861, the corpse of a well-known Pederast was found in the vestibule of a house in Paris, who had fallen or been thrown over the banisters of the staircase in the middle of the night."

END OF VOLUME.

www.ingramcontent.com/pod-product-compliance
Lightning Source LLC
Chambersburg PA
CBHW011220290326
41931CB00043B/3447
* 9 7 8 1 5 8 9 6 3 7 3 7 5 *